John Stuart Mill and the Meaning of Life

JOHN STUART MILL AND THE MEANING OF LIFE

Elijah Millgram

OXFORD
UNIVERSITY PRESS

Oxford University Press is a department of the University of Oxford. It furthers
the University's objective of excellence in research, scholarship, and education
by publishing worldwide. Oxford is a registered trade mark of Oxford University
Press in the UK and certain other countries.

Published in the United States of America by Oxford University Press
198 Madison Avenue, New York, NY 10016, United States of America.

© Oxford University Press 2019

First issued as an Oxford University Press paperback, 2021

CIP data is on file at the Library of Congress
ISBN 978–0–19–087324–0 (hardback)
ISBN 978–0–19–761781–6 (paperback)

Contents

vi   Acknowledgments

viii   Note on the Text

1   1   Introduction

18   2   From Principle to Project

33   3   Mill's Epiphany

50   4   Mill's Postdoc

63   5   How to Write a Letter of Recommendation

80   6   Logic and the Problem of Necessity

91   7   Mill's Incubus

105   8 Justice, Freedom of Speech, and Other Higher Pleasures

119   9 Taking Liberties with Utilitarianism

136   10 Mill's Aftermath

147   11 A Very Quiet Tragedy

173   12 Concluding Remarks

180   Appendix: Mill's Metaphysical Paradox

183   Notes

235   Bibliography

243   Index

Acknowledgments

I've been very fortunate to have had the help of many people over the course of this project. Buket Korkut-Raptis, Huei-chun Su, and three anonymous reviewers gave me comments on a draft of the entire manuscript, and parts, sometimes large parts, were improved by comments from Chrisoula Andreou, Carla Bagnoli, Alyssa Bernstein, Michael Bratman, Steve Buckle, Sarah Buss, Janice Carlisle, Phoebe Chan, Pepe Chang, Alice Crary, Ben Crowe, Ben Eggleston, Leslie Francis, Harry Frankfurt, Jennifer Johnson, Bruce Kinzer, Chandran Kukathas, Alasdair MacIntyre, Cei Maslen, Dale Miller, Dana Nelkin, Lex Newman, C. Thi Nguyen, Lee Overton, Vicki Robbins, John Robertson, David Schmidtz, John Skorupski, Aubrey Spivey, Mariam Thalos, Valerie Tiberius, Michael-John Turp, Candace Vogler, David Weinstein, and Laura Wharton.

In addition, various people helped me talk through the material, including Lori Alward, Irene Appelbaum, Margaret Bowman, Ed Brody, Alice Clapman, Gerald Cohen, Catherine Elgin, Melinda Fagan, Alisa Garcia, Don Garrett, Ken Gemes, Svantje Guinebert, Brooke Hopkins, Amy Johnson, Kim Johnston, Gabriele Juvan, Clif McIntosh, Maria Merritt, Yael Millgram, Maneesh Modi, Ram Neta, Gloria Park, Jerry Ravetz, Henry Richardson, Sherri Roush, Jan Schiller, Philip Schofield, Jonah Schupbach, Bill Talbott, William Twining, Nancy Wecker, and Nick White.

Freestanding pieces of the book-in-progress were presented at the International Society for the History of Philosophy of Science (HOPOS) 2006 conference, the University of Constance, the University of London, the University of Alberta, Brigham Young University, the Institute of Advanced Study at Hebrew University, the University of Utah—among other venues at its Tanner Humanities Center—Oxford University, Utah State University, Vanderbilt University, Friday Harbor Laboratories, the University of Miami, the University of Southampton, the University of Sheffield, Bowling Green State University, and the University of Parma. The University of Amsterdam kindly hosted a workshop on the manuscript; Thomas Nys and Susan Wolf generously served as commentators. The University of Bremen and the University of Canterbury allowed me to try out the complete story in their classrooms; I'm grateful to the International Office of the University of Bremen for support. And students at the University of Utah, in many iterations of courses on the meaning of life and on John Stuart Mill, helped me debug the narrative and the arguments.

Along the way, I was supported by an Erskine Fellowship at the University of Canterbury, and fellowships from the John Simon Guggenheim Memorial Foundation, the National Endowment for the Humanities, and the Center for Advanced Study in the Behavioral Sciences; I am grateful for the financial support provided through CASBS by the Andrew W. Mellon Foundation. In addition, I benefited from the opportunity to be in residence at All Souls College, at the University of Arizona's Freedom Center, at Keble College, and at the Helen Riaboff Whiteley Center. The University of Utah's College of Humanities provided sabbatical year, research, and travel support, as well as a Sterling M. McMurrin Esteemed Faculty Award, through its Philosophy Department. I'm also grateful to Margaret Bowman for research assistance.

Some material in this book previously appeared in:

Mill's Incubus. In B. Eggleston, D. Miller and D. Weinstein, *John Stuart Mill and the Art of Life* (New York: Oxford University Press, 2011): 169–191.

John Stuart Mill, Determinism, and the Problem of Induction. *Australasian Journal of Philosophy* 87(2): 183–199. June 2009. Copyright © Australasian Association of Philosophy, reprinted by permission of Taylor & Francis Ltd, http://www.tandfonline.com on behalf of Australasian Association of Philosophy.

Liberty, the Higher Pleasures, and Mill's Missing Science of Ethnic Jokes. *Social Philosophy and Policy* 26(1): 326–353. Winter 2009.

On Being Bored Out of Your Mind. *Proceedings of the Aristotelian Society* 104(2): 163–184. 2004.

Mill's Epiphanies. In C. Macleod and D. Miller, *Companion to Mill* (Oxford: Wiley-Blackwell, 2017): 12–29.

I'm grateful to the respective publishers for permission to upcycle these essays.

I would like to dedicate this book to Parsnippa, who wasn't a project.

Note on the Text

John Stuart Mill's *Collected Works* (1967–1991), cited by volume and page number, are available online at oll.libertyfund.org. Because several of Mill's shorter writings are widely distributed in many different editions, I will provide chapter and paragraph for some of these, abbreviated as follows:

    U : *Utilitarianism*

    OL : *On Liberty*

    SW : *On the Subjection of Women*

    A : *Autobiography*

    RG : *Essay on Representative Government*

Thus, X:234/U 4:2–3 refers to volume X, page 234 of the *Collected Works*, *Utilitarianism*, ch. 4, paragraphs 2–3.

Many of the individuals we will be discussing are related, and they share confusingly many names; I'll follow these conventions for referring to key characters. "Mill" will always mean John Stuart Mill, and his father, James Mill, will be given his full name. Mill's long-time companion and, eventually, wife was born Harriet Hardy, became Harriet Taylor on her first marriage, and Harriet Mill after her second; she will be referred to as "Harriet Taylor" or just "Taylor." Her daughter Helen will go by "Helen Taylor." Harriet Taylor's first husband, John Taylor, will be referred to by his full name. "Harriet Mill" will name John Stuart Mill's mother, born Harriet Burrow.

1 Introduction

The intelligent layperson thinks of the meaning of life as one of philosophy's central and perennial problems, and one of the reasons that the enterprise has a claim on our most serious attention. For nearly a century, however, the analytic school has dominated the English-speaking philosophical world, and our layperson might well be surprised to learn not just how little attention analytic philosophers have allotted to the meaning of life, but how dismissive they have generally been of the very notion. There is probably more than one explanation, and before we start in on laying out our own agenda, let's mark what has gotten in the way of thinking about it.

1.1

The dismissiveness is likely a legacy of analytic philosophy's origins in logical positivism, a research program that made exposing concealed nonsense into a philosophical method. To a positivist, 'the meaning of life' would have sounded like a demo-quality target: "What do you *mean*, 'the *meaning* of life'? Do you think that lives have meanings, in the way that words have meanings?"[1] The positivist would have concluded that when you talk about the meaning of life, you don't actually mean anything at all.[2] And, as we'll see in a moment, even when philosophers are not predisposed to dismissiveness, interest in the meaning of life is likely to get rechannelled into work on the metaphysics of value, practical rationality, and old-fashioned moral theory; once a philosopher has become immersed in one or another of these problem areas, it is all too easy to let work on the well-structured positions and debates displace the original but hard-to-articulate concern. Somehow, you just never get back to the reason you were interested in value theory in the first place.

While the meaning of life may not have been the official business of most analytic philosophers, the topic has nevertheless come in for occasional but thoughtful consideration. It even has a state of play, defined by two reasonably widely read pieces, and my discussion is going to treat one of them as a launch pad. During the 1970s, a densely and delicately argued paper by David Wiggins described Richard Taylor's subjectivist view as "ha[ving] a strong claim to be [the] secret doctrine of the meaning of life" of the philosophers who were Taylor's contemporaries.[3] Briefly, as noncognitivists about value (translation: values aren't real, but are at most projections of our desires and emotions),[4] they took a life to be meaningful if, roughly, it *feels* meaningful—and tended to construe the feeling as that of awareness of and pleasure in the satisfaction of one's preferences, whatever they happened to be. Wiggins went on to criticize noncognitivism and related positions to which one could fall back from it; he spelled out a way in which values could be understood to be real (anyway, as real as required for these philosophical purposes); finally, he went on to propose—but not actually argue for—an alternative account of what it takes for a life to be meaningful.[5] I will return shortly to Wiggins's proposal, as well as to what to make of the relations between the two notions of a meaningful life, and the meaning of life.

A good deal of water has passed under the bridge in the meantime, and, in metaethics (that is, the theory of what a moment ago I called the metaphysics of value), noncognitivism or subjectivism is no longer the consensus of the sensible, but one position among several.[6] Thus a new idea has come to have a strong claim to be analytic philosophers' implicit doctrine of the meaning of life: that what makes one's life meaningful, when it is meaningful, are the projects one pursues, and that if one of these projects is large enough and central enough, identifying it will be as close as we can come to finding the meaning of one's life.[7] This idea is not just the property of a school of philosophers: a great many people talk and act as though a career was the meaning of their life, and a career, we will see, is something of a paradigm case of a life project. Perhaps it is not the way everyone is inclined to see things: we should acknowledge that this sort of attachment to careers is largely a middle-class phenomenon. The poor have jobs, not careers; the wealthy for the most part have neither.[8] Since, in today's world, philosophers are almost without exception college teachers, and college teachers are middle-class, we should keep in mind the possibility that the philosophers' affinity for the project view is an expression of class prejudice—not as an argument against the proposal, but rather as a reason for being willing to entertain second thoughts about it.

I need first to explain what 'project' means in this discussion (after which I'll connect the view with Wiggins's treatment), and the most straightforward way to introduce the concept is to describe the problem it was meant to solve. Suppose your life were organized around the goal of, say, building a temple, and that what gave your life meaning was the means-end structure the goal imparted.[9] If the goal were unachievable, then your life would be merely quixotic; but if it *were* achievable, then once it was achieved, you would be *done*: it is no accident that another word for 'goal' is 'end,' because that is where your action stops.[10] After you have finished building your temple, you will spend the rest of your life sitting on your thumbs; the meaning of your life will be in the past, and the remainder of your life will be empty.

Projects are meant to solve this problem by having no termination point—no *end*. Like end-directed activity, a project has means-end or instrumental structure, and, crucially, as far as justification and reasons go, it has *solely* instrumental structure: within a project, every subtask or subproject is justified by showing that it advances the project, moving it on to its next stage. (The justifications are, each and every one of them, *in order to, for the sake of, to bring about....*) But a project never runs out, in the way that goals or ends do. In a medical career, for instance, the aspiring high school student works hard to get into a college with a good premed program; in college, he works hard to get into a good medical school; he goes to medical school to get a good internship; gets the internship to get a good residency; goes through the residency in hopes of setting up a successful practice ... but while every step is preparation for the following step, there is no finish line: when, finally, the physician has to retire, that is not the payoff that justifies all that hard work, and if retirement can be deferred, there will, for practical purposes anyway, always be more career stages onto which to move. Perhaps this is not the only way to solve the problem Taylor noticed with end-directed lives: perhaps you could find goals that are sized just right for a life, and perhaps you could do that even if you never really know how long you have to live. Or perhaps there is nothing wrong with spending your golden years basking in your achievements. But it is *a* way, and a way that seems to have especially attracted philosophers over the past few decades.

One of the reasons that projects have become the philosophical default is that it often escapes notice that there are alternatives to them. Some terminology: practical rationality, as contrasted with theoretical rationality, means the rationality of decision and choice, as opposed to the rationality of views about matters of fact. Likewise, practical reasoning is reasoning about what to do, as opposed to reasoning about what the facts are. (Sometimes a great deal is made out of distinguishing rationality from reasoning, but I'll be able to use these notions almost interchangeably.) Now, the standard philosophical view about practical rationality is instrumentalism, the idea that all reasoning about what to do, and so all justification of choice, is means-end. If the only way you can imagine justifying a choice is to show it to be a way of achieving a goal, it is hard to see how a life could be organized around anything that *wasn't* a goal—or, allowing for the open-endedness of some means-end structures, a project. Accordingly, Bernard Williams, who was responsible for much of the currency that projects have come to have within the discipline, accepted a softened-out version of instrumentalism (which he called 'internalism'), and this committed him to treating anything one could possibly care about as a project. (We find Williams taking marriage as an uncontroversial example of a project, even though we ordinarily think that people who treat their relationship or marriage as a *project* are adopting a distinctive, optional, and probably suboptimal approach to their personal lives.)[11] But, as we will see in a moment, there are contrasting alternatives, and we will want to keep them in mind. Perhaps the second-most popular, both among philosophers and the bohemian set, is to treat one's life as a work of art.

Projects that serve as the organizing principle of a life are a special case of the proposal with which Wiggins wrapped up his discussion, and let us turn to that now. His suggestion, put more formally than he put it himself, was that a life is meaningful when, for anything that matters within the life, the explanation of *why* it matters will draw in—at one or several or perhaps many removes—all of the other things that matter within the life. To spin out an example Wiggins mentions, suppose that digging a ditch with someone is an important afternoon to me. If I am required to explain why, I will tell you that the ditch is meant to direct the water away from our tent, and is needed to make the camping trip a success; I will also (if I have the flavor of Wiggins's example right) mention the intimacy that can arise between two people digging silently in the hot sun. When I am asked why I care about going camping, or about such intimacy, I will tell you that the other person is a longtime friend, and I will start to talk about the ways nature can be sublime. When I am asked why my friend is important to me, I will explain that our friendship formed around our shared interests in theory of computation; when I am asked to explain why I am so interested in theory of computation, I will explain that today fluency in certain areas of computer science ought to count as basic literacy for a philosopher ... and eventually, my explanation will adduce every one of my significant concerns; moreover, such explanations will fill out to the entire set of concerns no matter where they start.[12]

Recall that Wiggins had been arguing against philosophers who took it that nothing was *really* valuable, and had established to his own satisfaction (and let's just allow, for the sake of the argument, to our satisfaction as well) that there are many genuinely valuable items that might become part of a life—in fact, *too* many to be encompassed by any one life or even any one culture. In a vivid metaphor, Wiggins compared the way one lives one's life to moving a spotlight, and thereby illuminating some values, while letting the remainder recede into the darkness. The problem, he thought, is to light up a suitably cohesive set of values; the worry that one might be leading a meaningless life was thus an expression of the difficulty of getting the valuable elements of a life to hang together. Wiggins's way of putting his very strong coherence condition is that the valuable things within a life must *add up* to a life, and although his suggestion is now over forty years old, it remains the best idea about meaning in life on offer in analytic philosophy, and it is the one I intend to investigate here.

Wiggins's proposal is not just an isolated, if promising, bit of brainstorming; it is so much in the spirit of recent analytic ethical theory as to have been almost inevitable. Much of the strongest and most interesting work in moral philosophy, over the last half century, has consisted in attempts to explain what it is to be a unified agent, and to show that morality (or practical rationality, or . . .) is somehow part of, or a consequence of, or presupposed by being, for practical purposes (that is, purposes of decision and action), a single, cohesive personality. Throughout, it has been assumed—treated as too obvious to require much argument—that we are, almost all of us, more or less unified agents, and furthermore, that unified agency is a *good* thing: the more unity, the better.[13] So in thinking through Wiggins's suggestion, we will be asking a new question of mainstream moral theory: how can it understand its ideal agent to have a meaningful life? If we find that such attempts are bound to backfire, that will be a reason to reconsider this strand of contemporary moral philosophy.

1.2

Proposals about how life is to be lived, and what it is to live life meaningfully, are best thought about concretely.[14] Now, what Wiggins's very abstractly characterized proposal comes down to in practice depends on what sorts of explanations are available to link together the values found within or introduced into a life. That is, it depends on what formal possibilities there are for justifying your evaluative commitments: for taking something to be important or to matter to you; and of course it depends on which of the available formal possibilities are actually being applied within a particular life. That is, it depends on what the correct theory of practical rationality turns out to be, and on what theory of practical reasoning a life implicitly presupposes. Let's consider an illustration or three.

One can imagine a life in which the justifications are solely conventional, and at bottom have the force of: if it's Thanksgiving, it must be turkey. A life whose valuable elements make up a cohesive package of the Wiggins variety, but where all of the explanations and justifications are of this sort, will amount to an extreme version of a familiar personality type, caricatured in fiction by Evan Connell's Mr. and Mrs. Bridge.[15] This kind of life is not the one I propose to explore here, because almost no one (or almost no philosopher) believes that this is the only form of practical justification we have available, and whether or not a life that confined itself to solely conventional justifications would be unsuccessful, it would at any rate be theoretically artificial.

Next, one can imagine a life in which the justifying relations between its valuable bits and pieces are aesthetic (perhaps a bit like color harmonies and contrasts in a painting). When we develop the formal structure which Wiggins suggests, using *this* sort of justification, we have the ambition I mentioned a few paragraphs earlier, that of a life as a work of art. One natural way such an ambition can be tightened up is by adding in the notion that life is a *narrative* medium (rather like fiction, drama, and so on, but for real). In that case, the justifying aesthetic relations have to do with narrative structure and coherence of character, which gives us something on the order of the view that Alexander Nehamas attributes to Nietzsche: lives are to be tightly constructed narratives, modelled on the protagonist of the classic nineteenth-century novel.[16] Oscar Wilde is a disturbing but well-known and instructive example of someone who lived out his life this way. Convinced that he wanted his life to be a work of art, convinced that it would have to take narrative and specifically dramatic form, and convinced that the highest type of drama was tragedy, he determined to live his life out as a tragedy, and coerced both its broad sweep and its details to fit. Armed with a theory of tragedy, on which the qualities responsible for the rise of the tragic hero inevitably bring about his downfall, at the height of his career as a playwright he sued his boyfriend's father (for libel, apropos an easily documented accusation of sodomy), and so managed to get himself sentenced to two years at hard labor. Wilde emerged from the ordeal a broken man, and one obvious moral to draw is that what is good aesthetically isn't necessarily good for *you*.[17]

As intriguing as this variation on Wiggins's proposal is, I don't propose to focus the discussion on it. One problem is that aesthetic justification, and narrative structure in particular, isn't sufficiently well understood. Without a fairly confident grasp of the formal machinery with which we are working, our arguments are too likely to fizzle out. Aesthetic reasons tend to slide all over the place, in the first place because they are particularist: that is, what counts as a reason in one set of circumstances may not be a reason at all in another set of circumstances—or may even be a reason for the very opposite.[18] A second concern is that our stake in such formal structures isn't at all clear. For example, narrative shares with our first instantiation of Wiggins's requirement a great deal of reliance on convention: the fairy has to grant three (not two, not six) wishes; the detective will be hard-boiled; the heroine will be saved at the last minute. Why and how should any of this matter for someone's *life*?[19] Finally and relatedly, such lives tend to strike onlookers as precious and self-indulgent; that tends to get in the way of taking the idea that they are meaningful (presumably, in whatever ways works of art are meaningful) seriously.

A couple of turns back, I introduced the theory that the only reason one can have for doing something is to attain one's goals or ends, or, equivalently, to satisfy one's desires. Instrumentalism has a number of advantages for us. First, despite a certain amount of debate, it is still the default view among philosophers: they pretty much all agree that means-end inferences are fine, and disagree among themselves about whether there are any further forms of practical justification or reasoning, and if so, what they are. (Disclosure: I'm one of the philosophers who has taken the stand that there's more to practical rationality than instrumental rationality.[20]) Second, the formal nuts and bolts are taken to be relatively well understood: we know what we're talking about when we talk about taking the means to our ends.[21] Third, it's not just the philosophers: that all there is to think about, when you're making up your mind what to do, is how to get what you are after; that arguing you out of going after one or another goal involves appealing to further goals; that, consequently, there is no such thing as argument for or against ultimate ends; and that someone who is trying to give you reasons to reject your ultimate, bottom-line ends is wasting his time or (as the idiom has it) messing with your mind—all of that strikes many people as just hard-headed commonsense.

Now, if only instrumental rationality is available to link the valuable elements of a life into a highly cohesive whole, we get the project life: a life that is coextensive (or as close to coextensive as possible) with a single project. That is to say, the project life is not just formally the most tractable version of Wiggins's proposal, but the most popular, both among contemporary philosophers, and in the general culture.

Let me preempt a possible confusion. Not every project life will be fully—or even very—coherent in the way we are starting to think about: imagine a loosely characterized project that someone advances by engaging in a number of mutually unconnected enterprises. But because activities compete for scarce resources, and because an open-ended project tends to grow ever more elaborate, projects also tend toward ever tighter strategic integration; subprojects are soon enough selected in view of one another, and subsequently folded together so as to make each support the rest. And these are the sorts of life project in which we are now interested.[22]

I mean to assess Wiggins's proposal by assessing what—for now, anyway—looks like its best case, namely, life projects. And since proposals about the meaning of life are, to reiterate, best thought about concretely, I intend to do that by taking a long, close look at a best-case project life. That, I want to suggest, would be John Stuart Mill's.

1.3

Most of those who know Mill by more than vague reputation think of him as the author of one or another short volume of beautifully written Victorian prose, encountered on the reading list of some introductory class in college, and assigned as the standard presentation of some standard view. If the class was called Introduction to Moral Philosophy, one probably read his *Utilitarianism*, the standard presentation of utilitarian moral theory; if the class was called

Introduction to Feminism, one probably read *The Subjection of Women*, usually used as an instance of liberal (as opposed to radical) feminism. If the class was called Introduction to Political Philosophy, one is likely to have read *On Liberty*, the classic argument for the state keeping its nose out of your business, and for the American constitution's First Amendment; if the class was called Introduction to Political Theory, perhaps one read Mill's *Essay on Representative Government*, a recognizable blueprint for the modern democratic state. But the handful of writings that—because they are so very teachable—have become so very familiar misrepresent what Mill did with his life, and in fact, in his own time, he was known (and was famous) not just for other and rather different writings, but for a career of political activism. Over the remainder of this Introduction, in the course of explaining how the pieces of the argument I'm about to start in on fit together, I'm going to give an on-and-off thumbnail preview of what Mill wrote and how he spent his time, starting with a bit of context that, nowadays, tends to go missing. However, I'm going to be just a bit selective; some of Mill's undertakings will make more sense once we know what problems motivated them, and I'll hold off on those until the appropriate background has been put in place.

"Utilitarianism" is, today, the name of a slightly stodgy moral theory, but, at the beginning of the nineteenth century, it was a radical political movement with a handful of adherents and utopian plans to remake the world. So I'll follow this convention: when I'm talking about the moral theory, it will be "utilitarianism," in lower-case, and for the political movement, I'll use the capitalized "Utilitarianism."[23] The Utilitarians were astonishingly successful: almost everything at the core of their platform is now reality, and, unlike other equally ambitious radical nineteenth-century reformers, such as the Marxists, no one, in the West at least, is so much as contemplating rolling back these reforms. As the movement matured, its planks came to include a universal franchise, with voting rights for women; universal primary and secondary education, subsidized by the state; cost-benefit analyses applied to policy initiatives as a matter of course; complete freedom of speech and of the press; freedom of religion (in Britain at that time, this meant the freedom to be an atheist without incurring legal disabilities); the right of women to be employed in the same occupations as men … to start off a long list of what were then lunatic-fringe objectives. All of these initiatives were in the service of their guiding ideal, rendered by the slogan, *the Greatest Good of the Greatest Number*. We will presently explain how the ideal was understood, but already we can see that when John Stuart Mill took the Utilitarian political program on as his own, he thereby came to have a project, rather than an end with a termination point or finish line: there is obviously always more to be done in the name of advancing the greatest good, or, as they also called it, the general utility.

It's hard to retain the sense, today, of how unrealistic this agenda sounded, and how small the band of radical revolutionaries was.[24] There was so much to be done, and so little to do it with; the tiny group of activists centered around

Jeremy Bentham must have wished that they had on their side a figure capable of the immense amounts of work the task required: someone who was, as it were, *made* to be the intellectual flagbearer of their revolution.

Just after the turn of the nineteenth century, James Mill became one of the activists. Now remembered primarily for his political writings, and for being John Stuart Mill's father, he was, among many other things, a psychologist in the associationist tradition. We will get a much closer look at associationism in due course; for now, think of it as the intellectual ancestor of both Skinnerian behaviorism and connectionism: a theory of how training-by-repetition could, by building up associative connections between ideas, give shape to a mind.[25] And so James Mill, following the imperatives of his party's needs and the dictates of his psychological theory, conditioned his oldest child into the radical revolutionary leader they needed. Later in his life, John Stuart Mill worried about the public impression that he was a "manufactured man," and that impression was not at all mistaken.[26]

Most people come to their projects later on in life. This means that the earlier parts of a life are not normally integrated into one's project. Moreover, because one normally finds one's way into a number of different and relatively independent activities, and because projects usually take time to crystallize and grow, most people—if they adopt any projects at all—end up not with one, but several of them. The upshot is that there is rarely a single project that ties the whole life together. Mill was an exception to the rule: he was *born* into his project.

John Stuart Mill (1806–1873) was raised and educated at home, entirely by his father. The curriculum was fast-forward. He started reading Greek at three, Latin at seven, and by eleven was his father's research assistant, working on a history of India. As of his late teens Mill had acquired, by today's lights, a very good college education, followed by the equivalent of doctoral training in philosophy, law, economics, and political science. He never studied at a university; at the time these were religious institutions, and he would have had in various ways to affirm his religious faith, something he and his father regarded as a violation of principle. At around eighteen, he was put to work rewriting a number of Bentham's half-finished manuscripts, partly laying out the Utilitarian movement's agenda for legal reform, and putting them into publishable form; this apprenticeship, which we can think of as Mill's postdoc, marks his transition from precocious student to highly productive intellectual, and we'll take a close look at it in chapter 4. Many sacrifices were made for the sake of his high-powered training: he was reputed to have never learned to tie his shoes; until a trip to France, in his early teens, he did not socialize with children other than his siblings;[27] the year he turned twenty, he had his first nervous breakdown, at which we'll also take a close look.

There is (more or less by definition) always more to be done on a project, but this one was invested with great political and moral urgency; it had enormous scope, and living up to its demands meant working enormously hard, which

Mill did his whole life long. Bentham and James Mill had probably not thought that what they needed was the party theoretician; wouldn't Bentham have done most of what needed doing on that front? But the role ended up consuming the preponderance of John Stuart Mill's efforts. His *Collected Works* runs to thirty-three volumes, any of which would make an effective doorstop; it includes writing on almost every philosophical subject, and, in particular, the most prominent nineteenth-century volume in English on logic, metaphysics and epistemology; it includes an economics textbook that not only became the standard, but was so popular that it went into an inexpensive edition, to make it possible for working-class people to afford it; it includes all those short and still-assigned textbooks I mentioned a few pages back. The list goes on and on, and as our argument proceeds we will also get an overview of how its different parts fit together.

Most of Mill's work on behalf of the Utilitarian movement consisted in writing.[28] But the writing took many different forms, and it served many different near-term goals. I have already mentioned the longer and shorter book-length treatments of logic, political economy, moral theory, political philosophy, and the like, but these were not by any means the only sort of assignment that Mill took on. For some time, he edited the *Westminster Review*, a periodical meant to represent the views of the Radical party.[29] (*The Nation* might be a contemporary American analog.) Because the movement was so small, there simply were not enough contributors to fill the pages, and Mill produced many essays and much political commentary. He wrote for other and more popular magazines; during America's Civil War, when British sympathies lay preponderantly with the South, he argued, in *Fraser's*, that Englishmen should take a principled anti-slavery stand. He corresponded voluminously with, among others, such still-notable figures as Thomas Carlyle, Alexis de Tocqueville and Auguste Comte (whom we will encounter in due course). He wrote letters to newspaper editors, on behalf of freedom of the press, land reform in Ireland, and a great many other topics. And, late in life, he edited a second edition of his father's psychology textbook, adding lengthy footnotes—sometimes twenty pages long—and working in extensive critical supplements by three other contributors.

Certainly, however, not all of his work was writing. As a child, he was required to teach his younger siblings what his father had taught him, and I suspect that Mill's in-family TAship was not just a labor-saving shortcut on James Mill's part. The "monitorial system," which sidestepped the shortage of trained teachers by having older students teach younger ones, was part of the Utilitarian platform of educational reform. Had the trial run worked (it didn't), Bentham and James Mill would have been able to point to it as a proof-of-possibility. As a youth, Mill helped run debating clubs (he describes these under the heading of "propagandism") and reading groups, the first of which he called the "Utilitarian Society."[30] As an adult, he testified before government commissions on the regulation of prostitution, lobbied on behalf of Lord Durham's proposed reform of Canadian colonial administration—this indirectly laid the groundwork for the Commonwealth system—and campaigned to have a Jamaican colonial governor who had brutally suppressed an insurrection put on trial. As an MP, he took the precedent-setting step of introducing an amendment to a bill that would have granted women the vote, and seems to have taken an interest in women's higher education; he personally intervened to prevent a Tiananmen Square–like confrontation between the government and working-class protestors; he proposed a London County Council; he filibustered an attempt to prevent demonstrations in Hyde Park; and he managed to get the death sentences of important Irish revolutionaries commuted.[31]

Finally for now, it is worth noting in passing that although Mill scheduled himself ruthlessly, the extent to which the Utilitarian project organized his life had its limits. First, Mill went for long walks in the countryside, and as far as I can tell, the great outdoors lay beyond the reach of Utilitarian objectives.[32] Second, India was at the time a colonial possession of the British Crown, run until 1858 on behalf of the government by the East India Company. Mill held down a day job at the East India Company for most of his adult life, and while the Utilitarians did manage to influence its policies in important ways, my own sense is that—although he seems to have spent a great deal of his time at the office on writing and correspondence that was not at all related to his job description—it would be overreading Mill's job to construe it as a component of the Utilitarian project.[33] It *was* subservient to (and thus a component of) Mill's own life project in the obvious way: like any expedient for paying the bills, it enabled Mill to engage in his other pursuits. Moreover, the political experience he acquired as a high-level long-distance administrator for a very large country no doubt improved his political judgment. Political philosophers with such experience are quite rare, and I take Mill's work in political philosophy much more seriously than I do most philosophers', just because he had it. But when he was not using his time for his own purposes, he seems to have been thinking about how to get the business of the East India Company done, and not about how to improve the world as a whole.

Now, if Mill had been the sort of person who was so obsessively involved in his dominating project that his attention was fixed on it all of his waking hours, he might come to seem scarcely human, and for that very reason not the sort of person from whom the rest of us can learn life lessons. The sometimes sizable pieces of his day that were not devoted to thinking about how to make the world safe for a better tomorrow thus allow us to see him as a plausible testing ground for exploring the ups and downs of project lives.

However, there is something of a case to be made that one side of Mill's life, a side which we normally contrast with work, business, and career, was, in Mill's own case, fully integrated into his dominant project. As we will see in chapter 5, his romantic involvement with and ultimately marriage to Harriet Taylor was in the first place a political and intellectual collaboration on a series of tasks generated by the Utilitarian enterprise, and Taylor seems to have had a strong awareness of and stake in them specifically as her husband's life project. And more generally, recall that I remarked, a few turns back, that not all life projects will satisfy the coherence condition we found in Wiggins; as we will see, Mill's own project exhibited a high degree of just this sort of integration (with important exceptions that I will take up in section 9.7 and chapter 10).

Recall that Wiggins was concerned to defuse problems having to do with the metaphysics of value: in the first place, that nothing in your life could be valuable, because *nothing* is valuable. But the threats to a meaningful life are not only metaethical. In Kazuo Ishiguro's novel *The Remains of the Day*, its narrator and protagonist looks back on a life identified with the project of being a perfect butler, and comes to realize that he has wasted his life, because the project was not worthwhile.[34] A servant, Ishiguro shows us, surrenders his autonomy to his master; as it happens, the butler's master is a Nazi fellow-traveler, and thus the butler becomes complicit in a morally bankrupt enterprise. The lesson is that a project life can fail to be meaningful—or at least be fatally flawed, in a way that makes it harder to see if it is meaningful—if the projects in it are badly chosen. But Mill's project is one that just about anyone in today's political and moral mainstream will endorse as eminently worthwhile: who could object to freedom of speech, education, personal liberty, the right to vote, transparent government, equal opportunity employment, and so on, all undertaken in the name of making people generally happier overall?

Even the most worthwhile and intrinsically important projects can fail, and lives built around such failures may thereby be meaningless, or in any case problematic. I am of several minds about the matter myself, but this was in any case not a problem for Mill. All that hard work paid off, and in the end, as I have already remarked, the Benthamite Radicals won. The impossibly ambitious list of objectives has become an astounding series of accomplishments. Almost everything the Utilitarians fought for has come to pass, and the revolution was so dramatically successful as to have made itself invisible.[35]

His was not just a life built around an ambitious, worthwhile, and spectacularly successful project. As a well-known and influential public figure—so well known, that he was able to run for Parliament, and get elected, even though he refused to campaign!—his life and times are extensively documented from the outside. And as a thoughtful and prolific writer, his life is extremely well documented from the inside as well: to anticipate, a large part of the large body of writing that Mill left us is devoted, directly or indirectly, to figuring out what had gone so terribly wrong with his life. If we want to think through analytic philosophy's current doctrine of the meaning of life, we cannot do better than to take a careful but hard look at John Stuart Mill.

I propose to tell the story of Mill's life and thought as a reductio ad absurdum, first, of the view that a project ought to be the meaning of your life, and second, of the more abstract and general proposal, that justifications for your concerns should unify the valuable and important elements of your life into a highly cohesive and unified pattern, one that ideally has no loose ends at all. That is, as by this point the reader is no doubt expecting, my conclusion is going to be that neither project lives nor the sort of evaluative over-organization recommended by Wiggins are a particularly good idea: if this is what it is to have a meaningful life, nobody should want one. To restate that conclusion—since people who think seriously about meaning in life do not assume that a meaningful life is necessarily a happy one—the conclusion I am after is that, *even* if you think that an unhappy life might be worth choosing, meaningful lives of this sort are not choiceworthy, because, as it will turn out, they aren't what they're cracked up to be.[36]

Now, there are already biographies of Mill, and there are a great many discussions of Mill's philosophy, but while I am going to be engaging both Mill's life and thought, because I will be doing so in the service of an argument, my objective here is not to add one more of either to the pile. I am about to explain what I propose to do instead—and if you don't feel like you need to read the itinerary before getting on the tour bus, come the end of this section, it would be a good time to skip ahead to the next chapter.[37] However, before you make that choice, let me pause to say something about how I am going to be writing.

First, in the interests of full disclosure, I'm *ethnically* an analytic philosopher, meaning that while I don't believe many of the articles of faith, that is the intellectual idiom in which I was raised to speak and think. So, on the one hand, I mean to respect the obligations that are central to that tradition: among others, to explain myself clearly; to provide careful arguments for the claims I make; when appropriate, to be scholarly about history. On the other hand, the topic of this book is, again, the meaning of life, and I expect that most readers who are interested in it do not come either from professional philosophy or from Mill scholarship. Accordingly, I will be writing both for the general reader and the professionals, but prioritizing the needs of the former. That means in turn that I will often enough take time out to explain—as, you will have noticed, I have already started to—how analytic philosophers see matters, or how they do things. If you are an analytic philosopher yourself, please don't take those explanations, or the critical appraisals that will occasionally accompany them, as dismissive gestures; although I do have changes to suggest to philosophy as we now practice it, those criticisms are coming from one of the tribe.

In the practice of analytic history of philosophy, one normally advances theses by attributing them to the figure one is studying. So if you are a Mill scholar, please bear in mind that I will be proceeding differently here. The present exercise is to assess a view about the meaning of life by considering a life that instantiates it, but as I will explain in due course, people who live out project lives cannot normally accept the ideas about coherence that we are using to motivate the enterprise. And here is perhaps a more delicate cautionary remark: scholars tend to identify with the figure on whom they work, and I've found that maintaining the critical distance required for treating a life as an object lesson is liable to be interpreted as dislike, and a personal attack on one's hero. In order to see what life in the projects looks like, we will need to develop a balanced view of our case study, one that does not take sides, either with him or against him, but proceeds, as Mill said in the course of his own discussion of Bentham, "in a spirit neither of apology or censure, but of calm appreciation."[38]

Finally for now, if you are neither a professional philosopher nor a Mill scholar, even having been assured that the book is written for you—not just *also*, but in the first place—you may be wondering why it is a good idea, in a matter so very first-personal as the meaning of life, to be preparing to pass judgment on the meaningfulness of someone *else's* life. So let me further assure you that the point is not to be judgmental, but to rather learn lessons that I hope will be useful when the time comes to think about meaningfulness in one's own life, and both whether and how to pursue it.

1.5

Turning now to the itinerary, if we are going to treat Mill's life as materials for an argument, we will first need a terse but substantive account of the enterprise to which he devoted it. So in chapter 2, I will start by explaining the organizing ideas of the Utilitarian program. Then, in the course of describing how the Philosophic Radicals proposed to translate their very abstract conception of their ultimate aim into policy, I will spell out the relevant parts of Mill's curriculum vitae; again, the point will not be to give a standard biographical sketch, but to exhibit how Mill's life was nearly coextensive with a single, tightly integrated project. And because the reader may at this point be simply impressed with Mill's many and spectacular accomplishments, and starting to think that such a life is positively enviable, I will also introduce the first sign that all was not well; not (as readers already familiar with Mill might expect) the descent into clinical depression that marked his early adulthood, but a disturbing pattern that seems to pervade the life: to anticipate the problem in a word, that Mill lived *perversely*.

The biographical peculiarity on which I earlier remarked, that John Stuart Mill was literally made for his project, is bound to raise the worry that whatever went wrong with his life is unlikely to have been an effect of the philosophical theory it happened to instantiate, but rather of the way his life's agenda was determined not *by* but *for* him. I will address this issue in chapter 3, which will trace out the sources of Mill's commitment to the Utilitarian project. First, I will talk my way through an epiphany, the moment in which Mill seems to have made the Utilitarian program his own. In doing so, I'll introduce associationism, the psychological theory that Mill grew up with, that he eventually emended, and that served as the intellectual lens through which he understood his own inner life. Then I'll construct an explanation of his epiphany in the terms of that theory, which will allow me to argue that the epiphany makes him an especially good fit for the concerns about unity of agency that motivated Wiggins's proposal. I'll also register what seem to me to be limitations of the intellectual tools that Mill had at his disposal, limitations that are shared by philosophers today who worry about what it takes for your attitudes and enterprises really to be fully your own: the aesthetic dimension of Mill's experience, I'll suggest, isn't captured by his philosophical psychology, nor by ours. Finally, I will briefly consider his famous but very puzzling argument for the Principle of Utility.

Although Mill did take on the life project he had been bequeathed, he didn't simply execute a plan he had been given. When I turn to the capstone of Mill's early education, in chapter 4, I will be trying to explain what motivated him to rewrite a great deal of the Utilitarian project, by recounting how he came to be disillusioned by the very enterprise he had found so emotionally gripping just a few years before. In doing so, I will also be diagnosing Mill's very famous "Mental Crisis," the depressive episode that he experienced as a twenty year old; in chapter 5, I'll take up what I think is the best reading of it out there, and how the problem that reading identifies for project lives generally was actually solved, in Mill's own life, by three authority figures, namely, his father, his wife, and his stepdaughter. Over and above exhibiting a disturbing and almost inevitable feature of project lives, having a clear picture of Mill's closest personal relations, and the way in which they turned out to be a side-effect of the theoretical constraints which we used to introduce our investigation, will confirm chapter 3's reading of his epiphany, by showing Mill to have been as deeply and thoroughly committed to the project on which he was embarked as anyone can reasonably expect to be.

Mill was a philosopher by training and predilection, and his preoccupation with the sense of constraint that pervaded his life expressed itself in the remarkable quantities of attention and intellectual energy that he devoted to freedom of the will. Chapters 6 and 7 will reconstruct his treatment of the subject, in a way that incidentally exhibits how the often far-flung components of Mill's systematic philosophizing fit together in ways that revealingly served his need to think through a very personal set of problems. Mill understood his Mental Crisis to have resulted from living inside the Benthamite version of his life project, which had had the effect of making his will unfree. In a life organized, Wiggins-style, around a single project, the patterns of choice and the activities of which they are part will become locked in, and one will end up unable to abandon the project, even if one wants to. But by the lights of Mill's psychology, it is almost inevitable that one *will* want to abandon one's project. That is, the theoretical machinery that Mill used to make sense of his life told him that project lives like his own turn into lives that one neither controls nor cares about, but merely *occupies*. He resolved the problem both by redesigning his life project and by working up an account of how a project could be looser and less constraining than the early Benthamite form his had taken.

To see how this played out, in chapters 8 and 9, we'll take a look at Mill's defense of liberty, which was both a theoretical contribution to the political enterprise he shared with other Utilitarians, and a large part of his own revised life project. As we show why Mill thought Utilitarians had to be committed to both freedom of speech and freedom of action more generally, we will encounter his very personal motivations for insisting on them, and introduce his notion of 'genius' (or, a near-equivalent, 'originality'): the character trait of figuring things out for oneself. Our reconstruction of Mill's argument for the Principle of Liberty will elicit his reasons for thinking originality or genius to be enormously important—and although I will register second thoughts about those reasons, the more minimal conclusion we will need to carry forward to chapter 11 is just that Mill *did* think that originality was enormously important.

But before we get there, we'll turn to a puzzle we find set by his *Autobiography* which, although composed toward the end of his life, was weighted almost entirely toward the personal and intellectual problems we've been previewing, and which take us up to about Mill's mid-twenties. Mill came to see almost all of his adult life, and so almost everything that made him famous in his own day, as *aftermath*. By this point in our narrative, that will seem very peculiar indeed. As we will see, if Mill's resolution of his adolescent nervous breakdown was to build enough flexibility into his life project to allow him to reshape it as his personality evolved, and if the reason for insisting on that flexibility was that healthy personalities *do* evolve, then Mill's life project should have taken one swerve after another over the course of the subsequent four decades. If the version of the project that Mill settled on at age twenty-two or so was in fact the end of the story, then Mill must have failed to get to the bottom of what were evidently deep structural problems in his project life.

Finally, in chapter 11, I will offer my own diagnosis. On the one hand, a life that is constrained to be globally coherent in the way Wiggins proposes turns out to presuppose an overwhelming demand for originality or genius in the person who leads it. On the other, it simultaneously requires that one quash one's originality whenever it strays past the defining boundaries of the project life. A life in which both of these imperatives are enforced is almost inevitably tragic, and although, when we took it up, it was envisioned as being unified and fully coherent, on closer inspection, such a life proves to be almost inevitably disunified and systematically incoherent.

At this point, we will have sorted out which of the various commitments under consideration are responsible for what disturbing features of Mill's life, and our reductio will be complete. I will wrap up, in chapter 12, by drawing the obvious practical conclusion, and taking a retrospective glance back at the shape of the argument; in doing so I'll be contrasting it with the way that arguments generically get run within analytic moral philosophy. Finally, I will make a suggestion or two as to how we should proceed in thinking further about what it would be to live a meaningful life.

2 From Principle to Project

The heart of Utilitarianism is the Principle of Utility, and the first item on our agenda is to get that out on the table so we can see how the Utilitarian program was put in place around it, and Mill's own life around the program. In doing so, we will want to keep careful track of the differences between what Mill's Benthamite predecessors (including of course Bentham himself) made of it, and Mill's own more sophisticated reconfiguration and extension of Bentham's enterprise. To do that, I'll start off with the components of the project that make sense within the Benthamite theoretical framework. Most of Mill's work was in his capacity as party ideologist and propagandist, and as we proceed, we will see both how Mill reframed some of those components, and took on new tasks that were motivated by his modifications to the inherited framework.

2.1

Here is Mill's canonical statement of the Principle:

The creed which accepts as the foundations of morals, Utility, or the Greatest Happiness Principle, holds that actions are right in proportion as they tend to promote happiness, wrong as they tend to produce the reverse of happiness. By happiness is intended pleasure, and the absence of pain; by unhappiness, pain, and the privation of pleasure. (X:210/U 2:2)

Ingredients:

> Possible actions
>
> Outcomes of actions
>
> Utilities of outcomes
>
> Probabilities of outcomes, given that a particular action is performed

Procedure:

1. Identify the outcomes of your actions.
2. For each outcome, assess the amount of utility it involves (making sure to treat everybody's utility equally).
3. If the outcomes are certain, choose the action whose outcome has the highest utility. You're done.
4. If the outcomes are *uncertain*, then: for each action, and for each of its possible outcomes, determine the probability of the outcome, given that you perform the action.
5. Multiply the utility of each outcome by its probability; for each action, add these products together to get the action's *expected utility*.
6. Choose the action with the highest expected utility.

> Serves the greatest number.

The discriminating chef may worry that the prepared dish will in fact be raw. Many philosophers deal with the problem by first cooking the numbers.

FIGURE 2.1 Meat-and-potatoes utilitarian choice.

Perhaps at the prompting of that mention of the "foundations of morals," contemporary ethics classes present the Principle of Utility as a guideline to be invoked in making moral choices, where that in turn is assumed to mean that the primary application of the Principle is to choices with ethical or moral content that one faces personally. But remember that Utilitarianism was in the first place a political movement; when Bentham introduced the Principle of Utility, it was meant as a political tool. The Utilitarians' radical innovation was to have, and consistently apply, a model of cost-benefit analysis.[1] (See Figure 2.1 for a quick-and-dirty recipe.)

Cost-benefit analysis is no longer an alien idea to any of us. If government agencies are considering building a dam, we expect that they will do a study (or hire a consulting firm to do a study), and we expect them to proceed, more or less, by adding up the benefits from the dam, such as hydroelectric power and flood prevention, and subtracting the costs, such as of losing the salmon population, the inconvenience suffered by the displaced families, and the enormous costs of the dam rupturing, this last discounted to the small probability that it will actually happen. Their mandate will be to recommend construction only if the total utility (benefits minus costs) is higher than the utility of any of the other feasible alternatives.[2]

The early Utilitarians (in the first place, Jeremy Bentham) thought of this model of decision not only as what it is to make a *rational* choice, but as closely following the actual psychology of choice. We'll return to the psychology in due course, and for now only note a proviso, that people normally choose what maximizes their *own* utility, rather than fair-mindedly trying to maximize the utility of all. Benthamites were obsessed with the systematic application of the model to decisions throughout public and private life, and here are some illustrations of the cast of mind that typified that early period of the movement.

Since they thought that individuals could be counted on to make choices that serve their own interests, a democratic form of government, in which policies are determined by the demands of majorities, would be bound to serve the interests of the largest majorities, and thus to maximize the utility of a population generally. (Mill himself later came to appreciate complications his predecessors had overlooked, especially regarding what happens to the leftover minorities.) Britain at the time had an elected parliament but, by our standards, the franchise was narrowly restrictive; with the utility-driven argument we have just sketched firmly in mind, the Utilitarians put extending the franchise to all adult males at the top of their policy agenda—and the far-seeing young guard, Mill in particular, understood the argument to require voting rights for women.

Voters could of course be counted upon to defend their interests only if they were properly informed, and thus Mill tells us his father believed that, with universal suffrage in place, "all would be gained if the whole population were taught to read" (I:109/A 4:10). Not just literacy, but educational policy generally became a Utilitarian priority, and Bentham took the time to design a model curriculum—one that amusingly exhibits the almost automatic way he would embark upon a systematic taxonomy of anything that came his way.[3]

Bentham's equally taxonomy-oriented program of legal reform was driven, first, by the idea that legal structures had to be given a cost-benefit justification; second, by his conviction that people were psychologically constructed so as to pursue their selfish interests; and finally, by his conclusion that the utility-maximizing objective of a legal system must be to distribute incentives (schedules of punishment, for the most part) that would bring self-interest into line with the interests of all.

The early Utilitarians tended to dismiss any practice or institution for which they could not see such a cost-benefit justification as an effect of vested interests and—champions of the Enlightenment that they were—mere superstition, and Bentham's "auto-icon" is a bizarre example of what it meant to act on such views (see Figure 2.2). On his death, Jeremy Bentham had his skeleton put in one of his best suits, which was then stuffed with straw, and eventually put on display in the secular university for which his writings had so influentially paved the way.

FIGURE 2.2 Jeremy Bentham's Auto-Icon.
Image courtesy of UCL Culture © UCL Digital Media

The techniques used to preserve his head worked out badly, and so the auto-icon is topped off by a wax likeness; the head, no longer on public view, wears the sort of expression you'd expect to see in a horror movie. Bentham supported his recommendation that having yourself stuffed and mounted become the general practice by touting what to us are the merits of snapshots; could there be a better way to remember the dear departed than to have him sitting around your living room? Visitors to University College London can still see Bentham on display, in a wood-and-glass case on the ground floor of Senate House.[4]

2.2

Utility is the concept used in assessing costs and benefits, so what the Principle of Utility really amounts to depends on what utility is. In his statement of the Principle, Mill tells us that utility is happiness, and that happiness is pleasure, but while that much was the party line, we will see that Mill often took significant liberties in interpreting the views and aims that had been handed down to him. His education had left him sharper and philosophically more sophisticated than his movement's founders, but also entirely loyal to them, and he dealt with the ensuing tensions not by disagreeing verbally with his fellow Philosophic Radicals, but by finding interpretations of the party line with which he could live. Bentham had stated that utility was pleasure, and Mill repeated the claim, but managed to make it mean something else. Because his willingness to engage in this sort of reinterpretation is going to be important when the time comes to assess how free his life project left him, I want to take the time now to sort out both the different meanings "utility" has taken over the course of the last three hundred years, and what Mill did with the concept he had inherited.

Prior to Bentham, "utility" was used by philosophers like David Hume and Adam Smith in a sense very close to "usefulness." This older sense of the word is out of place in cost-benefit calculations, and is to be kept in mind in reading Mill only because it sometimes confused later audiences.[5] When we get to Bentham, the meaning of the word has changed: now, utility is a sensation. (More accurately, it is used to characterize the mix or balance of two sensations, pleasure and pain; the more pleasure, the more utility; the more pain, the less utility.) This turn to feeling had two main theoretical motivations: First, cost-benefit analysis of the sort we've just seen requires a fungible currency of decision: utility has to come in quantities that can be added up, multiplied, and compared. Second, by insisting that what was ultimately valuable was the subjective payoff, Utilitarians were giving themselves a way of short-circuiting traditionalist insistence on the objective value of one or another old-fashioned institution; utility maximization was definitely meant to be the new broom that sweeps clean. That is, often one chooses between items that look very different indeed; this faced the early Utilitarians with the question of how there can be a correct choice when the items are as qualitatively various as you like. They answered that the objects of choice are valuable only through their payoffs in the currency of pleasure and pain: pleasure is just pleasure, no matter how produced; pain is just pain, no matter how produced. Albeit with a little fuzz around the edges, the difficult comparison becomes simply one of *amounts*, and opponents who interposed the special, inviolable value of family estates, or aristocratic privilege, or private property, between the Utilitarians and their reforms, or (to modernize the examples) endangered species, the sanctity of fetal life, national rights to an independent state and a nuclear arsenal, or what have you, could be dismissed as obscurantists pleading on behalf of special interests.[6]

Mill's education left him with what is now a standard accomplishment in a decent graduate education in philosophy, but was in nineteenth-century England practically unknown, namely, command of the mechanics of philosophical argumentation. As a matter of fact, Mill's graceful mastery of the argumentative nuts and bolts puts him at the very high end even of today's scale. Consequently, the most reliable method of figuring out what Mill is using a term to mean is to examine how it functions in his arguments, and "utility" is a case in point. While his argument for the Principle of Utility is in general hard to make out (and in chapter 3, this very fact about it will turn out to be important for us), the part of it in which Mill argues that people desire only happiness (or utility) is quite clear.[7] Distinguish between desiring something solely as a means—a way of getting something else—and desiring something on its own account. Suppose for the sake of the argument that something other than happiness, say, music or virtue or money, is desired for itself. If so, then it counts as *part* of happiness, and thus is not after all a counterexample to the claim that people desire only happiness on its own account. At second glance, there can't be any counterexamples, and so it follows that people desire only happiness on its own account. Now, for this argument to make sense, one's utility or happiness has to consist (to a first approximation, anyway) in the agglomeration of all the things that one wants, rather than a distinct end, such as Benthamite pleasure.

A bit of compare-and-contrast, to make sure that Mill's usage isn't confused with the contemporary meaning of the word. Nowadays, when an economist talks about utility, he has in mind a mathematically sophisticated way of representing preference satisfaction: thus, like Mill, of how much you're getting of what you want.[8] Sensation plays no role in the current concept: being satisfied means that you have gotten what you preferred, and has nothing to do with a feeling of any sort. Mill buys into one component of the contemporary preference-satisfaction concept, namely, that what your utility consists in is determined by what your preferences are (equivalently, for Mill, by what your desires are); happiness is getting what you want, or having your preferences satisfied. However, on Mill's psychological theory, which we'll be looking at as we go, pleasure has an important role in the psychological machinery that *implements* desire and its satisfaction: having a preference or desire satisfied produces the feeling of pleasure, and the idea of pleasure is actually a functionally important element of one's desire. This is why Mill feels that he can stick with the inherited slogan that identified happiness with pleasure, and he deemphasizes the substantive shift in the content of Utilitarian terminology by frequently referring to objects of desire as pleasures (as when a work of great literature is described as a higher pleasure). But Mill has dramatically departed from the understanding of utility shared by Bentham and his father, James Mill.[9]

Mill's philosophical motivations for this departure were complex, and we're not yet in a position to explain the most important of them. Right now let's register just one of his reasons. The Benthamites had turned to pleasure as a qualitatively homogenous currency for measuring value, one in which cost-benefit analyses could be conducted. But if you think carefully about sensations, and more specifically about sensual pleasures, you will notice that pleasure and pain are not qualitatively homogenous: when you look at actual pleasures, it's as though things are priced in *different* currencies. Consider a short list of real-life pleasures: kvetching (whinging, if you're English); running your fingertip against the wall as you walk downstairs; laughter, in the course of a bout of extended silliness; finding a message on your voicemail from a friend who's been out of touch; getting a good grade on schoolwork, or a positive annual review; being scared out of your wits at a horror movie; tormenting your younger sibling.... The Benthamites had thought that pleasure is pleasure is pleasure is pleasure, but once we have decided to treat sensations as the currency of decision, we find there to be many different such currencies, and no principled way of setting the exchange rate. Mill noticed that, as far as this problem went, there was nothing to be gained by the turn to sensation. "Neither pains nor pleasures are homogeneous," he observed, "and pain is always heterogeneous with pleasure," and so he reconstrued utility in terms of baskets of goods, retaining the Benthamite thought that what matters to us about getting those goods is that we want them and are pleased when we get them.[10]

That leaves us no longer having a way to compare quantities of utility, and so back with the problem of how to conduct cost-benefit analyses. Mill's alternative proposal will occupy us in chapter 8.

2.3

"The Greatest Good for the Greatest Number" is not yet a platform. Even once you have decided that the Good consists in the total amount of pleasure experienced by everyone, minus the total amount of pain, before taking steps, you still need to determine what would best advance that objective.[11] Now there are really two questions here, and we will ultimately want the answers to both of them: first, how did Mill's mentors translate their Principle into a large-scale political project, and second, how did Mill's own translation diverge from theirs?

Our crude Utilitarian recipe is a decent representation of the Benthamites' officially endorsed procedure, but, once we have complemented that with their understanding of utility, applying the procedure directly would involve measuring the sensations, which obviously no one knew how to do. Moral philosophers of a few decades back used to talk about imaginary gadgets they called "hedonometers," calibrated in imaginary units called "utiles," but you're not going to find any such devices down at your local medical supply headquarters.[12] So instead, what drove the policy recommendations were more or less intuitive arguments about what would make more people better off, where a good faith attempt was made to understand being better off in terms of subjective payoffs. We've already seen a handful of examples of such arguments: for extending the franchise, for public education, for legal reform, and for changing the rituals having to do with corpse disposal. While we're at it, let's add one more for good measure. The Benthamites were impressed by Malthus's observations of the dangers of an exponentially expanding population; over and above the threat of starvation, when population expansion was coupled with the economic law of supply and demand, it was seen to entail subsistence wages for workers. A rising standard of living, the Utilitarians concluded, required restraining population growth, and the young Mill took this seriously enough to get arrested for distributing birth control literature.[13] As we'll see, Mill put some but not all of these causes on his own agenda—although, as we'll also see, he added to his mentors' reasons further arguments that were distinctively his own, and which changed the shapes of the subprojects he adopted.[14]

From the point of view of the procedure we provided as an interpretation of the Principle of Utility, policy decisions were being made on the basis of arguments that had to be acknowledged as unprincipled stopgaps. Maturing political movements experience growing pressure to replace temporary theoretical expedients of this sort with the tight, systematic analyses and justifications to which their ideology commits them. Although we can see the task as having always been on the Utilitarian agenda, it had never been pursued full force by Mill's companions in arms. Mill took it on, and it became one of the largest components of the Utilitarian life project to which he found his way. So we need to bring that theoretical task into somewhat tighter focus.

2.4

It's important to keep in mind that all that highly theoretical philosophizing had a political point, or rather, several of them. When philosophers today read Mill's philosophical writing, for the most part they behave as though its intellectual interest, from our present disciplinary perspective, is a sufficient explanation for its existence. That is a mistake: the disciplinary background the philosophers are taking for granted postdates Mill, who was in any case never the employee of an academic institution.

The earlier Benthamites had generally responded to philosophical disagreement with dismissive and not very well thought out invective; Mill recalls their willingness to label whatever views they did not like "vague generalities" (I:113/A 4:13). But, whatever the merits of this posture, the intellectual trends of nineteenth-century England were rapidly making it ineffective. Mill seems to have eventually understood the problem as arising out of—though this is our way of putting it, not his—the reception of Kantian philosophy.[15]

That needs a bit of explanation. Immanuel Kant's *Critiques* are now classics, the well-understood intellectual common property of all philosophers (and not just philosophers); it is hard to put oneself into the frame of mind of the time, in which Kantian philosophy was not well understood at all. Partly because they were obscure, foreign, and exotic, and partly because they were nonetheless obviously important, Kantian ideas, mostly half-digested, made dramatic headway in English-speaking circles. If you like, Kant and his followers occupied something like the cultural position that Foucault, Derrida, Bourdieu, Latour, and other recent French philosophers have had very recently in Britain and the United States.

Those followers and fellow-travelers of Kant may not have understood exactly what his theses were, but they took away this much: Kant had defended synthetic a priori knowledge.[16] Not that Kant's British followers could in general explain what that meant, but they realized that a deep German thinker had made respectable once again the idea that there were important and contentful truths one could know without empirical evidence.[17] The Utilitarians dismissed—as radical reformers, they *had* to dismiss—the appeal to what "everyone just knows" as a basis for morals, policy, or anything else. Their opponents now had a response: they could treat Kant as license for whatever elements of a conservative outlook they needed. If you had no argument for some traditional moral or political position, you could just insist that it was self-evident, and self-evident because it was a synthetic a priori truth.[18]

Kant had in fact given arguments to back up his theses about just what the synthetic a priori knowledge was, but because control of those arguments only came much later, let's leave them to one side.[19] Let's consider instead how arguing about what is and isn't self-evident can turn into a trap, in a way that's brought out by a couple of philosophical urban legends.

In one anecdote, a professor of philosophy has just given an example of a claim which (he thinks) is immediately intuitive, undeniable, and self-evident: that, in a plane, you can't draw a line from a point inside a closed curve to a point outside it, without cutting the curve. (See Figure 2.3.) A student raises his hand, and announces that it is not self-evident to *him*, whereupon the professor draws a circle in chalk on the floor at the front of the class, and has the student stand in the circle. The professor then beckons to the student: "Now, come over here, but without crossing the circle." The student, so goes the story, edges back and forth inside the chalk line, and then gives up, announcing, "I'm sorry, Sir. It won't work with *this* one."[20]

In a second story, a mathematics or perhaps philosophy professor writes a claim on the blackboard, of which he says, "Now, *that's* obvious." A worried expression appears on his face, and he paces back and forth abstractedly. He scribbles formulae on the blackboard. Visibly distraught, he rushes out of the classroom. Eventually he returns, a look of relief on his face. "I was right," he announces to the class. "It *is* obvious."[21]

There was a tactical choice to be made here. Where the Utilitarians' opponents appealed to the intuitiveness and self-evidence of one or another religious or

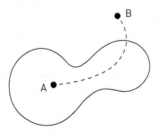

FIGURE 2.3 How obvious is Jordan's Theorem?

moral proposition, the Utilitarians could have decided to argue about whether that particular proposition really was self-evident or a priori or necessary.[22] But as our stories remind us, such arguments easily run aground on irresolvable disagreements over what is and isn't obvious or self-evident. So Mill decided to show that there *was* no such special status: there were no a priori or necessary truths, not even in logic or mathematics, which had always been treated as their uncontroversial home. Mill had thus embarked on a systematic rethinking of philosophy of logic and philosophy of mathematics—for, in the first place, political reasons. (But, and to anticipate, not only for political reasons; in chapter 6 we will trace out his further and personal motivations for the subproject.) His *System of Logic* is largely devoted to it, and so is his almost-forgotten *Examination of Sir William Hamilton's Philosophy*, a frontal attack on someone who at the time was one of the better-known representatives of Kant-influenced apriorism in Britain.[23]

Put more generally, the very large task Mill had taken on, one apparently quite removed from the political battlefield, was that of showing how philosophy—*all* of philosophy, because Mill was a very systematic philosopher—could be done without appealing to intuition (and I'll introduce that word properly in just a moment). In my own view, that subproject is still worth careful consideration today. For most of the last hundred years, English-speaking philosophy has proceeded as the following sort of exercise: The typical philosopher would invite one to imagine, perhaps a moral dilemma, perhaps a metaphysically tricky set of circumstances. (If you have the opportunity to save five people, by letting a trolley run over one, should you? If I can somehow be surgically split into two people, are either or both of them *me*?) The circumstances imagined, one would then be invited to have a response to them. (E.g., "yes, pull the switch and divert the trolley," or "no, neither is *me*.") That response was called an *intuition*. The correct theory was believed to be the one that reproduced all (or as many as possible) of the intuitions, and philosophizing thus consisted in systematizing intuitions.[24] In chapter 12, I will return to questions of methodology, and briefly discuss attempts to approach the problem of the meaning of life as this sort of exercise in conceptual analysis.

Recently, some philosophers have started to wonder about where those intuitions come from—what accounts for them, and what, as a matter of psychological fact, they are—and the preliminary results in so-called experimental philosophy suggest that no one should take them very seriously at all.[25] That conclusion has not been embraced, mostly, I think, because many of the professionals don't see *how* to do philosophy without relying on intuitions: after all, doesn't any argument have to get back, sooner or later, to things you just think? Mill's attempt at intuition-free philosophizing is thus a test case, and, if he was successful, a proof of possibility of great interest to us now.

Mill's second very-large-scale theoretical subproject was to bridge the Principle of Utility with the substantive claims that made up the Utilitarians' political platform. Since the Principle of Utility tells you to do what will produce the most happiness, that meant showing that a policy being defended *would* produce happiness, and more than competing policies. It should be obvious enough, to any thoughtful person, that it is not always obvious what makes people happy.[26] And it is equally obvious that, when it comes to public policy, there is normally a great deal of disagreement about what the results—leaving happiness to one side—of implementing any particular policy will be. The Utilitarians evidently needed a social science or two that would allow them to demonstrate what policies and institutions were utility promoting and maximizing.

In section 10.3, we will turn to the question of just what science Mill had it in mind to construct. But before getting down to work on it, there was a good deal of preliminary groundwork to be put in place. The very idea of social science was, at the time, relatively new, and so Mill was concerned with the possibility that methodological obstacles might prevent it from ever getting off the ground: for one thing, controlled and reproducible experiments, at the scale of public policy, are scarcely ever possible. Mill thus took it upon himself to lay the methodological foundations for social science generally: to show that there *could* be such sciences, and how they would work. In the *System of Logic*, Mill wrote his way through the theory of (what he, confusingly to us, called) "Deductive" sciences, but did not leave it at that. He then proceeded to author an economics textbook, *Principles of Political Economy*, and while one reason for that subproject was to lay out the economic theory that (for instance) supported Utilitarian tariff reforms, another was to show that social sciences really were possible, methodological obstacles notwithstanding. If economics could be made to look like a viable science, why not the science that would explain what happiness consists in, and what conduces to it?

Since Utilitarian policies were to be utility promoting, what was good for the movement was good for everyone. Thus, subsidiary projects intended to make the movement more visible and respectable were warranted, and under the heading of propaganda we have already mentioned the *Westminster Review*, which Mill both wrote for and edited. Under this heading we also find, perhaps surprisingly, Mill's *Autobiography*. His unusual upbringing had not escaped public attention; he was widely regarded as a bookish version of a Frankenstein's monster, and James Mill, as a cruel and unsympathetic father.[27] Their public image was not an asset to their movement, and Mill's account of his own life was meant in the first place to humanize him, and to defuse the outrageous stories circulating about his childhood.

The *Autobiography* is instructive for our present purposes, in that it also exhibits how Mill's personal concerns inflected the project he took over from his mentors; in chapter 8, we will also give some consideration to how deep that transformation went. Although it is in the first place spin doctoring, it contains a number of very revealing moments, and we will make frequent (but cautious) use of it in the sequel.

2.6

I have been suggesting that Mill's life was, as gets said colloquially, a train wreck, and have proposed to use that fact to show what is wrong with a life that is for all practical purposes identical with a single project. But, by this point, the reader may have been noticing only a string of ever-more-impressive accomplishments, and so may be wondering if anything really has gone wrong. We have mentioned Mill's Mental Crisis in passing, but a period of depression, especially around the time when someone is emerging from adolescence, does not condemn a life plan, and in any case, we are concerned here with meaningful lives, which are not necessarily happy ones. So I am going to sketch a pattern in Mill's life, not quite as an argument, but as a preliminary suggestion that something is amiss.

Mill has provided us with what is still, a century and a half later, the most sophisticated and influential rendition of utilitarian moral theory. Its central thesis is that what matters is happiness (or "utility," and we saw that utilitarians of the time identified utility with pleasure); they drew the conclusion that decision-making should be aimed at everyone's overall happiness. As we proceed, it will become striking how unhappy Mill was himself; in fact, toward the end of his life, he told his friend and biographer, Alexander Bain, "that with himself the difficulty was not so much to realize pleasure as to keep off pain."[28] And it will also become striking how very little he did to make his life more pleasant. He imposed on himself a work schedule that produced the thirty-three volumes of his *Collected Works* ... in his spare time, because, recall, for most of his life he held down a day job as an administrator for the East India Company. Except on some of his vacations, he seems to have eaten the same inedible breakfast every day for most of his life.[29] I don't want to enter into the question of whether Mill had a sex life (and later on I'll explain why not), but for present purposes it's to the point that many of the people who knew him found it very plausible that he didn't: he gave one the impression of someone who didn't indulge his sensual side at all. Although he seems to have been a very social person, for a long stretch of his life he dropped just about all of his friends. Overall, he gives the impression of someone who was miserable, who didn't do anything about it, and who didn't even when it wouldn't have meant sacrificing anyone else's happiness.

Mill, the author of *On Liberty*, held the view that both censorship and restrictions on action more generally produce weak, cramped characters. Such people would be unoriginal and uninventive, because they would fail to have the strong motivations necessary to make them strike out in novel directions.

Moreover, it was not merely *legal* restrictions on speech and action that produced these deadening effects; the pressures to conform to others' views and mode of collective life which Mill thought were the hallmarks of British society of his day sufficed. As we are starting to see, and will see at much greater length, Mill was himself an individualist, both intellectually, and in his unusual, rule-breaking life: he was himself what he famously called an "experiment in living."[30] As we will also see, in chapter 5, he was closely supervised, almost his whole life long, first by his father, then by his wife, and finally by his stepdaughter. Briefly for now: Mill was not only home-schooled by his father, but reported to him at work; he associated for the most part with other Utilitarians, collectively as dogmatic and narrow minded a group as the members of most radical movements; both James Mill and Harriet Taylor monitored his every action, and exercised tight control over Mill's published work. Mill is, and I will return to this point in chapter 9, a counterexample to the passionately presented central claim of one of his two most widely read and intellectually important works.

Mill is the author of *The Subjection of Women*, which puts him in the odd position of being the father of liberal feminism. Now, there had certainly been earlier discussion of the so-called Woman Question, but it had generally been about just that: the (capitalized, singular) abstraction, "Woman."[31] Mill introduced a breath of fresh air into that debate by his insistence on keeping the discussion in the lower-case plural; women are real people, just like anyone else, and if we can't justify our policies on the basis of what we see, when we look to see who's there, then we can't have those policies. That is, the book's argument, or one of them, turns on the demand that women are not to be mythologized or put on pedestals; instead, we are to pay attention to who the women, here and now, are. In his own life, however, it will turn out that he put the women who figured most importantly in it on pedestals that were, variously, so low and so high that Mill didn't have the slightest notion who his mother, stepdaughter, and wife were.

Mill was the staunch advocate of universal public education, and (here one of the architects of the modern democratic state deviates from ground rules we take for granted) someone who thought that the more advanced degrees you have, the more votes you should get. Although he proposed that the state certify educational achievement, however produced, and pay for it on the basis of need and test results, he seems to have conceived of it in practice as a matter of getting pupils into properly run schools. However, as someone who was entirely home-schooled, he is the best argument against public education that one could have. When one reads about Mill's childhood, it's very natural to have the reaction: all those years one spent in school were just *wasted*.

Mill was the theoretician of representative democracy ... who made his living governing a faraway country whose inhabitants had never voted for him, and didn't so much as know of his existence. (True, he had an explanation of why democracy wasn't for everybody.) When the government was deciding to nationalize the East India Company, and run India directly, Mill was assigned to write up the Company's defense. He argued that the Company would do a better job of running India because company employees were hired on the basis of impartially assessed merit, and were not tied to politicians or political parties, unlike government employees, whose jobs were often granted through political connections or outright nepotism.[32] And he made a great deal of the way that company employees spent most of their working lives in India; because they were well acquainted with the circumstances on the ground, they would be equipped to make intelligent decisions, unlike government employees—and especially the minister of Indian affairs whose creation was then being contemplated—who would just rotate out every few years.[33] Of course, Mill himself had been hired, not on the basis of a standard employment interview or competitive entrance exam, but by his father, the radical Utilitarian activist. And it was a matter of public knowledge, which must have added a significant amount of awkwardness to Mill's testimony before Parliament, that neither of them had ever been to India.[34]

Mill was the theoretician of representative democracy who argued against the secret ballot. Even though having to vote in public presents obvious opportunities for coercion, retribution, and corruption, he thought the benefits to your character of having to stand up in public for what you believe are so great that they outweigh the costs (XIX:488–491/RG 10:1–7). In his own life, Mill let Taylor's views appear under his own name, and, even though he once remarked to John Cairnes that "anonymous journalism can dare anything with impunity" (XV:836), didn't worry too much about the effects on her character. Mill was the philosopher who ridiculed Comte for literally worshipping his wife (and for designing a religion in which every husband would do so)—and who, though not adopting the bizarre rituals that Comte had concocted, for all practical purposes worshipped his own wife. And he was the philosopher whose whole metaphysics and logic were meant to show that there was no need to rely on intuition—that is, on ungrounded opinions not empirically tested—but who took Harriet Taylor's intuitions as fixed points in his own philosophizing.

Mill was the philosopher who argued, in the *System of Logic*, that logic is an empirical science: that the right way to do logic is to investigate how successful scientists solve their problems, and then generalize from that. But Mill didn't do it this way. The first draft of the *System* had no examples: *after* he'd finished working up his view of logic, he had Bain rummage around and dig those out.[35]

Mill was the philosopher who argued against the nineteenth-century version of coherentism and inference to the best explanation—and who, as we'll see in chapter 3, seems to have adopted the Principle of Utility because it cohered so beautifully with everything else.

I could go on; there's much, much more of the same. But there's a pattern emerging. Mill lived as though to spite his official views, and seems to have done so systematically. In Mill's case, I am going to claim, an upshot of leading a project life was living perversely, and I am going to suggest that the reason he did so was that a life of this kind is unlivable. Now, of course not everyone who lives a project life will exhibit precisely Mill's symptoms, and on its own, it is hard to know what is responsible for the disturbing pattern. Let's treat it as grounds for wondering whether a project life is after all backfiring, and turn to the question of Mill's investment in the enterprise that shaped his life.

3 Mill's Epiphany

I proposed assessing the idea that a project ought to be the meaning of one's life by examining a test case. Project lives, I suggested, were the upshot of imposing two distinct but interlocking philosophical commitments: to a life that is unified, ideally in that every component of it is part of the justification for every other component; and to instrumentalism, which here entails that the practical justifications that might serve in unifying a life are all and only means-end.

If a project unifies an entire life, and if childhood is part of anyone's life, such a project ought to reach back into the early stages of a personality's development. The thought here isn't that, if you're coming to a unifying project later than Mill did, it's already too late for a project to be what makes your life meaningful; surely we want to allow that a project may anchor a life, even if it does not tie every last bit of it together, and so even if it does not integrate the life's initial segments. Nonetheless, if we want to see what the fully realized aspiration amounts to, we need to look at a case in which the life *is* entirely integrated into the project, or as close to that as we can get.

But now, if the person whose project it is has been inducted into it while still a child, there is an obvious worry to have when pointing to problematic aspects of the life: they may well be the result of the child's parents and teachers having chosen the life for him. Indeed, this is typically the reaction to Mill's biography; all that education and political activism being forced down his throat meant that

John Stuart Mill's project was his father's, and his father's friend's, rather than his own. The problem here isn't Mill's unhappy childhood: we already knew that a meaningful life isn't necessarily a happy one. (Maybe unhappiness is just the price you pay for a meaningful life.) But how could it be reasonable to use someone with *this* sort of childhood—one in which you have no opportunity to find your way to a project that is really your own—as Exhibit A in the examination of a theory of the meaning of life? And suppose it was inevitable, or on the way to inevitable, that you did have to use such a case study: wouldn't it be a decisive objection to this understanding of meaningfulness if the closer your project was to being the meaning of your life, the more likely it was to turn out to be the meaning of someone *else's* life, rather than yours?

So, in the first place in order to field the objection, I'm going to tell you about a moment in the life of, as the popular song has it, "a real live emotional teenager," the occasion on which Mill enthusiastically and wholeheartedly claimed the life project he had inherited for his own.[1] Then I'll turn to a discussion of the intellectual resources that he had available to make sense of that event—much of which will be stagesetting, but the topics I'll take up I am hoping are of stand-alone interest as well.

3.1

In his *Autobiography*, Mill describes "an epoch in my life; one of the turning points in my mental history" (I:67/A 3:2). Mill had spent some time in France with Jeremy Bentham's brother Samuel and his family, and by his mid-teens spoke and read French fluently. A good deal earlier than that, Bentham (once again, the father of utilitarianism and his mentor) had shipped off a very large pile of manuscripts to Étienne Dumont, who translated, edited, abridged, and rewrote them into the *Traités de législation civile et pénale*, since retranslated into English under the title *Theory of Legislation*.[2] Mill is about to describe what it was like to read Dumont's French rendering of Bentham, and although the paragraph is lengthy, I am going to quote it nearly in full.

My previous education had been, in a certain sense, already a course of Benthamism. The Benthamic standard of "the greatest happiness" was that which I had always been taught to apply ... Yet in the first pages of Bentham it burst upon me with all the force of novelty. What thus impressed me was the chapter in which Bentham passed judgment on the common modes of reasoning in morals and legislation, deduced from phrases like "law of nature," "right reason," "the moral sense," "natural rectitude," and the like, and characterized them as dogmatism in disguise imposing its sentiments upon others under cover of sounding expressions which convey no reason for the sentiment, but set up the sentiment as its own reason. It had not struck me before, that Bentham's principle put an end to all this. The feeling rushed upon me, that all previous moralists were superseded, and that here indeed was the commencement of a new era in thought. This impression was strengthened ... when I found scientific classification applied to the great subject of Punishable Acts, under the guidance of the ethical principle of Pleasurable and Painful Consequences ... I felt taken up to an eminence from which I could survey a vast mental domain, and see stretching out into the distance intellectual results beyond all computation. As I proceeded farther, there seemed to be added to this intellectual clearness, the most inspiring prospects of practical improvement in human affairs. ... [A]t every page he seemed to open a clearer and broader conception of what human opinions and institutions ought to be, how they might be made what they ought to be, and how far removed from it they now are. When I laid down the last volume of the *Traité* I had become a different being. The "principle of utility," understood as Bentham understood it ... fell exactly into its place as the keystone which held together the detached and fragmentary component parts of my knowledge and beliefs. It gave unity to my conceptions of things. I now had opinions; a creed, a doctrine, a philosophy; in one among the best senses of the word, a religion; the inculcation and diffusion of which could be made the principal outward purpose of a life. And I had a grand conception laid before me of changes to be effected in the condition of mankind through that doctrine ... the vista of improvement which he did open was sufficiently large and brilliant to light up my life, as well as to give a definite shape to my aspirations. (I:67–71/A 3:3)

This is John Stuart Mill's epiphany, the day when the Utilitarianism which the (not-quite-)sixteen-year-old had inherited became *his* project, when the Utilitarian project became "the principal outward purpose of [his] life"—as we would say it now, when he realized what the meaning of his life was. It is important for our argument that there *is* such a moment, because it shows us that the objection we were considering can be sidestepped. True, the project was foisted on him by others, when he was too young to have a say in it, but at almost the earliest possible opportunity, he signed onto it for himself. And unlike most such "realizations," Mill lived up to this one; as we know, Mill stayed a Utilitarian until the day of his death.

3.2

Judith Shklar once remarked that "John Stuart Mill's *Autobiography* does not really enrich our understanding. We would know all there is to be known about his philosophical outlook without it, and we do not learn much about his inner being. It is not at all certain that we would really gain anything by deeper revelations. It is interesting, but not an essential part of an intellectual and artistic edifice."[3] While the *Autobiography* does sometimes seem like a dry document, that assessment of it was mistaken. In particular, just right now there are a few observations we will want to register about the epiphany we've just seen, and I'm going to be by turns anachronistic and antiquarian as I talk through them: the former, so that we can see Mill as speaking to our present-day concerns; and the latter, so that we can see Mill's inner world as he saw it himself. And there is a point I'll be using them to make. The first question likely to occur to a philosophically inclined reader is whether Mill's new-found commitment was well-grounded: did he have reasons—*good* reasons—for it? Or not? One point that will emerge from pressing on the lengthy passage under consideration is that this way of framing the alternatives is Procrustean; neither option is a good fit for what we have in front of us. And since both in Mill's out-of-date way of thinking, and in ours today, those *are* the alternatives, something has gone wrong with how both we and he ask such questions.

Our observations will take up the remainder of the chapter, and let's turn to the first of them.

Readers who are not professional philosophers will feel like they are having all of their worst suspicions about the field confirmed when they hear about a debate that, over the last half century, has occupied center stage in analytic moral philosophy: one devoted to explaining the difference between wanting something, and *really* wanting something; between merely thinking something, and *really* thinking it; and, by extension, between what you *really* did, and what just kind of happened. (If you are a philosopher by trade, you're probably so familiar with this debate that you have a hard time remembering how strange it is.) To have a short way of talking about it, I'll say that philosophers have been attempting to analyze the *superlative attribution* of attitudes and actions to their owners or producers, and intuitively, that means they're trying to explain what it was you were saying, the morning after the party, when you protested that you don't know what came over you, that you didn't really mean it, and that it wasn't that you'd made up your mind to join in those end-of-the-night activities, but things just got completely out of control. (Alright, you did all that, but you didn't *superlatively* do it.) That distinction between *merely* and *really* tracks being alienated from your action or attitude, as opposed to being identified with it and prone to endorse it retroactively; just to give the nonphilosophers the flavor of this sort of theorizing (and to remind the professionals quickly what I'm talking about), possibly the earliest entry in the long list of ever more complicated treatments of the topic had it that desire is really—rather than merely—your own when you have a further desire: you want that first desire to get you to actually take steps to attain its object.[4]

In the way of talking I've just introduced, Mill's epiphany is the occasion on which his life project becomes superlatively attributable to him: whatever that distinction plausibly comes to, he has clearly taken on the Utilitarian program as his own. The objection we were responding to takes it for granted that for a project to count as the meaning of your life, it has to be full-fledgedly yours, in this present-day philosophers' sense. We haven't asked why it's so natural to think so, or whether it's so much as true, but the objection has in any case been met.

And notice that Mill's coming to own his life project was driven by—as far as we can see, just *was*—the response to Dumont's Bentham, a response which was of the general sort that normally gets discussed when the topic is the appreciation of art. When he tells us that he "felt taken up to an eminence from which [he] could survey a vast mental domain, and see stretching out into the distance intellectual results beyond all computation," that is someone experiencing the sublime, more or less as Kant understood it. Mill is responding to the vastness of the terrain he is able to survey, and indirectly, to the far-reachingness of the project mapped out by those intellectual results: in part, that is to say, to the very open-endedness that made his Utilitarianism a project rather than merely an end. Mill seems to have adopted the Utilitarian project as his own in large part because he found it *aesthetically compelling.*

This is not the place for a review of the literature on superlative attribution, so for now just take my word for it: the treatments have no room for identification which consists, even on some occasions, in a mode of aesthetic uptake. Our philosophical mainstream reconstructs superlative ownership of an attitude or action in terms of such things as attitudes taken toward your own attitudes, or deliberative procedures, construed as the personal analogs of the constitution of a political state, or action on the basis of a desire that one understand what one is doing as one does it, or evaluations of the merits and demerits of a course of action one is contemplating; more generally, theorists look for *structural* features of a psychology that can support the distinction. But the mobilization of one's sensibilities by beauty or by the sublime isn't something we're likely to understand by blueprinting mental architecture, and none of these reconstructions are a very good fit for the contrast as we are seeing it in the young John Stuart Mill's life. His preferences as to what desires to have and act on did not change; his judgment as to the substantive merits of the Benthamite political program did not change, either. His deliberative procedures remained the same throughout, and his understanding of what he was doing, and why, persisted. We can draw a quick conclusion: Mill's sudden identification with his inherited project was an aesthetic response; the theoretical apparatus available to us has no room for having a heart's desire consist in aesthetic uptake; so we should not rely on our present-day theories of superlative attribution to understand Mill. And in fact, we can send those theorists back to their respective drawing boards; Mill is just one counterexample, but this philosophical debate has evidently been pointed in very much the wrong direction.

The most likely diagnosis is that we analytic philosophers don't appeal to aesthetic theory to address problems in other parts of philosophy because our treatments of topics in aesthetics don't provide enough in the way of usable intellectual equipment; thus our tradition does not make it easy to think through the almost-sixteen-year-old Mill's experience. But we can nevertheless say this. In a philosopher's ordinary practice, a reason is something you could unpack into an argument; "give me your reasons for such and such," and "argue me into accepting such and such" are stylistic variants.[5] And in that practice, arguments are supposed to be compelling: they are able to *force* you to accept their conclusions.[6] When we're considering what I'm for convenience calling aesthetic responses, that equivalence breaks down: you can't argue someone into getting a joke, even though you can often talk through what makes a joke funny, and likewise, while there is often a good deal to say about what makes this but not that sublime, you can't force the issue with an entailment to that stunned-but-elated feeling.[7]

When Mill comes to his commitment in this way, it's not for no reason (in something like the way that when you laugh at a well-crafted joke, it's not for no reason), but his commitment is not anchored by anything like a traditional argument (and I'll try to convince you of that over the remainder of the chapter). And as we'll see in the next chapter, much of the discussion of Mill's Mental Crisis has also been framed by the supposition that either he had reasons for his life project, or he didn't; but neither of these alternatives is quite right.

3.3

John Stuart Mill was raised to have not only a life project but a psychological theory; that psychological theory provided Mill with the vocabulary in which he later on tried to explain to himself what had gone wrong. So it's surprising that he seems never to have discussed directly how his epiphany would be accounted for within the psychology of British Empiricism. I think it will be instructive to consider how he could have done so, and I will begin by introducing the bare bones of associationism.

A mind contains or is composed of two types of mental states, sensations and ideas; to have either type of mental state is to be conscious of it. Ideas were thought of as being, or as made up of, copies of sensations; for instance, if you think of an old friend, the idea that comes to mind reproduces what he looks like, that is, the visual sensations which you had when he was present, or some recombination of them, perhaps also the sound of his voice, and no doubt various other memories. Mental states can be associated with each other, which means in the first place one sensation or idea tending to bring a further idea to mind; associative links control the flow of thought. Sensations, however, are direct effects of experience, and can't be produced by association of ideas.

Now, those associations can come in different strengths: the stronger the association between ideas A and B, the stronger the tendency to think of B, once you've thought of A. Such associations are produced by repetition or training, namely, thinking first A and then B a number of times; the strength of such an association is a matter of how much repetition there has been, and the strength of accompanying feelings of pleasure or pain. If the training is done with sensations rather than ideas, the strength of an association is also a matter of the vividness of the sensations, which are generally thought of as more vivid or intense than ideas. Since sensations are the products of experience, training through experience is generally faster than training through, say, written instruction. Finally for the moment, if you don't reinforce an association, it fades away.[8]

Let's pause for a trivial example or two of the core of the theory at work. Every day, I pass a soda machine on my way into work, and when I do, most of the time I see people buying and drinking sodas. After a while, seeing the machine brings the thought of drinking a soda to mind, even when there's no one actually using it. And even when I'm not seeing it, merely thinking of the soda machine brings the thought of buying and drinking a soda to mind. In this case, the ideas are connected because their objects out in the world are causally related; I think of sodas after I think of soda machines because the machines dispense sodas. But this sort of causal connectedness isn't necessary. An advertising campaign for a brand of automobile will show the car being driven by gorgeous models on a beautiful country road. Although I understand very well that purchasing a car will neither make the scenery on my commute any nicer, nor the people in my car any prettier, enough repetition will make me think of beautiful people and places in connection with the brand. Associationism may no longer be respectable in psychology departments, but it remains the theory implicit in most advertising even today.

There's more to those associative links than one mental state evoking another. Pleasure and pain, which the associationists thought of as sensations, traverse associative connections. If the idea of A is already associated with the idea of B, and thinking of A is pleasant, then thinking of B will come to be pleasant, too.[9] In James Mill's psychology, to desire something is analyzed as finding the idea of it pleasant.[10] A crude but clear explanation of action drops out of that analysis: an object of desire would be associated with its causes, those causes in turn with their causes, and so on back to the idea of a muscular movement. Pleasure associated with the object of desire, cascading down the chain of associated ideas, enlivens the idea at the terminus of the chain, and the muscle contracts, resulting in an action: I find myself reaching into my pocket for coins to put in the soda machine.[11]

Pleasure and pain also traverse associative links that do not track causal structure; when the pleasure associated with beautiful scenery and people travels over links constructed by advertising campaigns, people buy cars. As before, although driving a car will neither make me into a model nor put a model in the passenger seat, and although it will not improve the view through the windshield, associating pleasure with the idea of the brand is equivalent, in Millian psychology, to wanting the car. A friend recounts that her high school art teacher used to hold up her drawings of ducks as examples of what to do if you wanted to fail art class;

the result was that she came to dislike ducks. Because one brings ducks to mind when one is trying to draw a duck, eventually thinking about drawing a duck makes you think of ducks; and because pleasure and pain travel over these associative links, the displeasure of the classroom experience became associated, not just with the activity of drawing ducks, but with the ducks themselves.[12]

Mill was brought up not only as a Utilitarian, but in the philosophical tradition of British Empiricism, whose most famous members were John Locke, George Berkeley, and David Hume.[13] We are only now once again getting used to the notion that a philosophical research program might be built around what looks to be an empirical psychological theory.[14] But British Empiricism had the theory we have just quickly surveyed at its center, and John Stuart Mill's father, James Mill, was a convinced adherent who wrote a two-volume textbook of associationist theory, the *Analysis of the Phenomena of the Human Mind*. Later in life, John Stuart Mill edited a second edition, to which he added extensive critical footnotes; these are more than occasionally the length of short journal articles, and there are, for our purposes, two upshots. First, if you want to know what Mill thinks about psychology, this is where you go: to James Mill's text, if there are no corrections in the footnotes, or to those lengthy footnotes, if there are.[15]

Second, Mill was home-schooled by his father, and as we've just seen, his father was an enthusiastic proponent of a theory that is a mentalistic predecessor of B. F. Skinner's behaviorism. Growing up the oldest son in the Mill household must have been very much like growing up in Skinner's household: it was the next best thing to being raised in a Skinner Box. We can treat his father's psychology as a retroactive child-rearing manual; if we want to understand the theory that informed James Mill's parenting, this is where we go.[16] We will in due course revisit the scene of the young Mill's education and take up the question of just what effect the regimen of conditioning would have had.

3.4

Modeling Mill's epiphany in associationist terms seems initially straightforward. We'll have to do a good deal more of this sort of antique psychological theorizing, and so this is a good occasion to get our feet wet.

Mill was being brought up by an ideologically fervent Utilitarian. Imagine a mind containing a great many unconnected ideas that it has already been conditioned to find pleasant; bringing the model to bear on the case we are using it to analyze, suppose they are "the detached and fragmentary component parts" of "a course of Benthamism" (I:67f/A 3:3): a lively interest in reform, in representative government, and in mass education; impatience with obstructionist appeals to one or another "law of nature" as a reason for blocking reforms; a predilection for neat and accurate classification—and so on.[17]

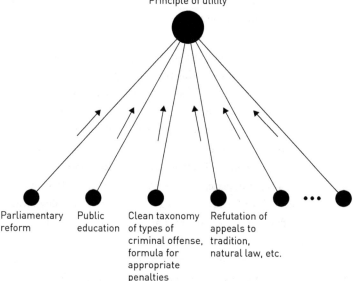

Principle of utility

Parliamentary reform

Public education

Clean taxonomy of types of criminal offense, formula for appropriate penalties

Refutation of appeals to tradition, natural law, etc.

FIGURE 3.1 An associationist model for Mill's epiphany.

Now, the Principle of Utility—that "Benthamic standard of 'the greatest happiness'"—is itself an idea. Imagine that the disparate ideas are suddenly connected to that further idea, which now serves as a "keystone." Reading the *Traité* had brought it about that the various ideas of political activism and so forth on which Mill had been raised, along with their associated feelings of pleasure, were suddenly far more strongly associated with the idea of the Principle of Utility. Accordingly, all those feelings of pleasure infusing those various ideas could flow up the associative links, and accumulate at the keystone to which they were all connected. (See Figure 3.1.)

Because to find an idea pleasant is, in this theory, to desire it, once the Principle of Utility has become associated with a very great deal of pleasure, the general utility is very much desired: if there are enough of those connections to already-pleasurable ideas, wanting to bring about the greatest happiness for the greatest number becomes what is now desired most.[18] That concentrated idea of pleasure associated with the keystone idea will in turn be transferred down the associative links to those original ideas (versions of political activism and so forth), and make them more pleasant to think of than they had been at the outset, and so more desired. The mind in which this occurs is now motivated by all of the various components of what is now its life project. As the sensations of pleasure travel round and round the network, they are amplified, and the coherent project, reflected in a highly connected network of ideas, makes one feel happy and alive.

We can briefly verify the fit between the proposal we are testing and our Millian psychological reconstruction of Mill's epiphany. Recall that a project has no termination or closure point (even when it has a statable description, such as "the Greatest Good of the Greatest Number"), and that the justification for any component of the project is that it advances the project: either it is itself one more building block of the statable objective, or, more typically, a stepping stone toward yet another stage of the project.[19] Mill is proposing to bridge the gap between "what human opinions and institutions ought to be" and "how removed from it they are now"; since the young Mill suddenly had "a clearer and broader conception of ... how they might be made what they ought to be," that is, of the steps to be taken, his enterprise is instrumentally structured—unsuprisingly, since the mode of justification that Mill found in Bentham was uncritically instrumentalist. Once the organizing idea is put in place, it can be connected to new ideas (in particular and especially, ideas about further ways to advance the general utility); when it is, pleasure will flow down the associative links, and those subsidiary tasks will become desired, and accordingly part of the project: there is always more to do. While Mill does not describe the "unity" which the principle of utility gave "to [his] conceptions of things" in exactly Wiggins's vocabulary, it evidently is very close in spirit: Mill adopts the Principle of Utility, along with the project that it launched, because it "fell exactly into its place as the keystone which held together the detached and fragmentary component parts of [his] knowledge and beliefs." So the Utilitarianism of Mill's epiphany is a project in our present sense; Mill's investment in his life project mirrors our own interest in it.

3.5

Although the fit is good, there are a number of tensions, ironies, and blind spots already visible in the enterprise.

Important elements of the mature project are foreshadowed in his epiphany. The teenage Mill sees as central to the version of the project he will pursue the importance of displacing disguised appeals to what people happen to think (or rather, feel) with transparent Benthamite cost-benefit analysis. The notion that you have knowledge that comes built in at the factory is just "dogmatism in disguise imposing its sentiments upon others under cover of sounding expressions which convey no reason for the sentiment, but set up the sentiment as its own reason." This anticipates his efforts, which we described in section 2.4, to extirpate the a priori from respectable intellectual life, and goes some distance toward explaining why so very theoretical a work as the *System of Logic* became so large a part of his political activity.

Now, Mill's complaint against apriorism in all its forms is that it elevates feelings into reasons: "we don't like it" is being dressed up in objective-sounding language such as "the moral sense of all right reasoning people disapproves." Mill replaces the appeal to intuitions, that is, on his view, to feelings-in-disguise, with Bentham's hedonic calculus (and later, as we will see, with his own "decided preference criterion"). But of course, and here is the first of those ironies, Bentham's procedure makes feeling—the feeling of pleasure, and the feeling of pain—into its criterion of correctness, and Mill's own replacement, in a more sophisticated way, did likewise. It's very hard to see how Utilitarians could give a proper argument for treating their favorite sentiments as authoritative.[20] If appeals to feelings are dogmatism in disguise, Utilitarianism is as dogmatic as its competition. Mill never seems to have appreciated this theoretical incoherence at the foundation of his view.[21]

Mill's epiphany tells us that the cohesiveness of his project accounts for his identification with it, and Mill's psychological theory does allow him to explain this aspect of the change in his own motivations. But a second irony is that Mill could not see the coherence-building psychological process that brought him to endorse a Utilitarian life project as practical deliberation.

Here's why. Mill had accepted his instrumentalist views of practical rationality, views which he never abandoned, from Bentham and his father.[22] Consider a toy argument that might unpack an explicitly coherence-driven decision: making everything fit together is a decisive consideration; the Principle of Utility is the keystone that makes everything fit together; so I will adopt the Principle of Utility. That's not a means-end argument. To adopt the Principle of Utility because it is the keystone that makes everything else cohere into an intellectually unified structure would be to engage in what is nowadays thought of, in the practical or moral domain, as inference to the most coherent plan, and in the theoretical or scientific domain, inference to the best explanation (sometimes also called "abduction"). Moreover, Mill became well known during his lifetime as an opponent of William Whewell, the nineteenth century's most prominent advocate of coherentist inference, and he argued vigorously against inference to the best explanation.[23] So Mill's life had crystallized around an intellectual move that was the analog, in practical life, of one that he argued at great length was illegitimate in theoretical life; he was thus unprepared to see appeals to coherence in practical reasoning as a legitimate form of argument.[24] Mill became committed to his project because it made everything fit, but making everything fit didn't count for Mill as a reason (and, a fortiori, it didn't count as a reason for adopting a project).

The blind spot is inevitable, and not just an oddity of Mill's intellectual career. Once coherence is added as an independent form of justification, supporting a further and legitimate mode of reasoning, it is hard to see why a life would take the form of a project; recall that we arrived at project lives by imposing the requirement that the justifications that structure a life have to be solely means-end. If someone took there to be other sorts of practical reasons—in particular, that a person's unifying his beliefs, desires, and other elements of his mental life counts as inference—surely the justificatory structure of his life would incorporate them, and the life would take on a very different shape. Someone who is leading a project life may find the coherence of his own life personally compelling, but if he's reasonably aware of his intellectual resources, he won't take that to be among his reasons for the project.[25]

Judgments of coherence are—usually—one of those kinds of support for a commitment that slip between the horns of the dilemma: reasons, or not? I gave a toy argument a few steps back that invoked the coherence generated by the Principle of Utility. But generally the coherence of a view does not figure into our reasoning in that way; rather, it is nothing over and above the way the reasoning runs. Mill said that later on in life he

found the fabric of my old and taught opinions giving way in many fresh places, and I never allowed it to fall to pieces, but was incessantly occupied in weaving it anew. I never, in the course of my transition, was content to remain, for ever so short a time, confused and unsettled. When I had taken in any new idea, I could not rest till I had adjusted its relation to my old opinions, and ascertained exactly how far its effect ought to extend in modifying or superseding them. (I:163–165/A 5:13)

The arguments Mill invented in reweaving his views *were* his contribution to the coherence he valued so highly and found so convincing; but those arguments did not invoke coherence directly, either in their premises or by way of a Peircean inference rule.

3.6

The psychological theory we have just surveyed doesn't seem properly equipped to handle aesthetic responsiveness, and some of its shortcomings become evident when we start to think about whether it can really do justice to the longish passage we quoted at the beginning of the chapter. First of all, on that theory, the default explanation of an associative connection between ideas is lengthy repetition, preferably of real-life experiences. Mill's epiphany shows us associative connections being burned in by reading a book, and reading it once.[26] Although Dumont's Bentham was somewhat repetitive, he wasn't repetitive enough to give the default explanation a grip; the associations "burst upon" Mill because he found the vision impressive, and impressive due to its aesthetic power. That sense seems to have been partly a feeling of fittingness, induced by the cohesion of the Benthamite vision, partly a recognition of the sublime, due to its sheer reach, and partly also a matter of the dissolving clarity produced by Bentham's calculus. The experience Mill recounts is on the face of it a counterexample to Millian psychology.[27]

What's more, it would be a misstep to think that the sort of aesthetic uptake that is tantamount to taking ownership of, in this case, a political program, is accounted for by supercharging a node in a network of ideas. In the recent debate over superlative attribution, the liveliness of an attitude and its ownership have been made out to be simply different things. (The trite example of the drug addict who is desperate for his next fix, but who thinks of himself as a slave to desires he cannot control, plays a central role in this literature.) I'm not so sure about the firmness of that distinction myself; Mill seems to be on to something when he takes *feeling alive*—as we'll see him do in coming chapters—to be engagement. But that's a suggestion we should be willing to explore only if the contrast between being enlivened and deadened isn't exhausted by the crude impressions of pleasure and vividness we've seen the psychology supply.

Mill does not seem to have acknowledged this overtly—on the contrary—but he must have been bothered by the psychology's poor showing when it came to aesthetics, because it was a topic to which he found himself returning. Thus in a note to his second edition of his father's *Analysis of the Phenomena of the Human Mind*, Mill takes up the objection that attempts to "resolve Beauty into association ... confound the Beautiful with the merely agreeable," and after a parrying move which won't concern us here, Mill replies:[28]

in the case of our feelings of Beauty, and still more, of Sublimity ... the theory which refers their origin mainly to association, is not only not contradictory to facts, but is not even paradoxical. For if the perceptions of beauty and sublimity are of a more imposing character than the feelings ordinarily excited in us by the contemplation of objects, it will be found that the associations which form those impressions are themselves of a peculiarly imposing nature.

If ... things which excite the emotions of beauty or sublimity are always things which have a natural association with certain highly impressive and affecting ideas ... we need no other mode of accounting for the peculiar character of the emotions, than by the actual, though vague and confused, recal [sic] of the ideas.

there are some ingredients which are universally, or almost universally, present, when the emotions have their characteristic peculiarity; and to which they seem to be mainly indebted for the extraordinary power with which they act on the minds which have the greatest susceptibility to them.... The question would still remain for psychologists, why the suggestion of those ideas is so impressive and so delightful. But ... it is no mystery, for example, why anything which suggests vividly the idea of infinity, that is, of magnitude or power without limit, acquires an otherwise strange impressiveness to the feelings and imagination.... [C]ompleteness and perfection of which our experience presents us with no example ... stimulates the active power of the imagination to rise above known reality, into a more attractive or majestic world. This does not happen with what we call our lower pleasures.[29]

We will in due course encounter the contrast gestured at in that final sentence, between higher and lower pleasures. For now, Mill is experimenting with accounting for the sense of sublimity by way of the contents of the ideas you have when you experience higher pleasures: you're reminded of something that is either perfect or infinite. But this suggestion runs aground on a couple of elementary confusions.[30] First, an associationist has no explanation for an idea having such a content (we certainly never *see* infinite or perfect things, and so the theory of ideas won't help).[31] Second, the infinitary content consequently doesn't explain how such an idea comes to be highly pleasure-charged or vivid. Without the missing explanation, we can't simply allow Mill's claim: if you take an upper-division undergraduate mathematics class, you are likely to spend hours a week thinking about infinitary objects, but it is rare to see students in such a class finding it a deeply moving experience. When Mill agrees with his father that "the exposition in detail of the associations which enter into our various feelings of the sublime and beautiful, would require the examination of the subject on a scale not suited to the character nor proportioned to the dimensions of this Treatise," he is as much as admitting that he hasn't actually managed an analysis of those feelings.[32]

It is hard for us to recapture their attitude, but for Mill and his fellow associationists, their psychological theory was Science with a capital "S," and the laws of association were on a par with Newton's laws of motion. Mill would have acknowledged that there was a great deal of work still to be done (the analog of deriving treatments of one physical phenomenon or another from the laws of motion), but also would have been certain that a fully satisfactory treatment of aesthetic responsiveness on the basis of the laws of association was just a matter of time. From our vantage point, we think otherwise, but we do not do particularly better ourselves. Neither we nor Mill are equipped to be articulate, intelligent, and thoughtful about what was moving him when he was moved aesthetically, and we will have to look for workarounds as we proceed gingerly through what turns out to be tricky territory.

Mill's problem was not just an antiquated psychological theory; rather, it is another instance of what is starting to be a familiar pattern. Thinking intelligently about, say, art requires fluency with a formally distinctive category of reasons, a kind that typically can't be recast as arguments that force you to accept their conclusions. Now, when you criticize a novel by pointing out the ways in which it trades on the sentimentality of its readers, you are trying to show that their emotional and aesthetic response to it is an error; the error does not consist in a failure to choose effective means to the reader's ends, and it is not an error that is naturally assimilated to a mistake about prosaic matters of fact. Mill was an instrumentalist, which meant that he had only one way of criticizing an emotional response: desires for means can be mistaken when the means are poorly chosen, given one's ends.[33] An instrumentalist is ill-equipped to think his way through aesthetic responses, because he cannot articulate the trains of reasoning that (even when they don't compel assent) both support and undercut them.

The problem will normally go deeper than the formal equipment; someone with an appreciation for and intellectual command of the sorts of reasons deployed by art critics will be unlikely to sign on to a life whose shape makes sense provided you are a person who accepts only means-end considerations as reasons for action. Now we have already seen why the inhabitants of project lives will normally be, implicitly if not explicitly, instrumentalists. So the problem is, again, not just Mill: it's pretty much part and parcel of living a project life that you won't be thinking articulately about its aesthetics, and in particular, about the aesthetic motivations for living a life that is unified and coherent in that particular way. We should not hold it against Mill's being a best-case project life that he sometimes has a tin ear when it comes to art, literature, and the aesthetics of lives; that just comes with the territory.[34]

3.7

I've been suggesting that Mill was unprepared to talk his way through the motivations—motivations that he in fact found compelling—for a life that was unified in the manner recommended by Wiggins. That means that he was intellectually blind to what are probably the philosophically most important reasons for having a project life in general. Still, Mill might have had other justifications for taking on this project in particular, and we should assess the likelihood that they went some of the way toward accounting for his emotional stake in the project.

If we are looking for a justification for Mill's life project, and if the Utilitarian project was built around the Principle of Utility, we might suppose that the explanation we are seeking must be Mill's argument for the Principle. As I mentioned earlier on, Mill gives such an argument, in chapter 4 of *Utilitarianism*; however, there are a number of reasons to doubt that Mill's proof of the Principle of Utility is what we are looking for.

First, *Utilitarianism* was written late in life. Published in 1861, it was drafted over the 1850s, and unless we can date the thinking it expresses to much earlier, it will not explain Mill's much earlier personal stake in Utilitarianism.

Second, most any life could be configured around any number of possible projects, and so, for any project, we can ask, Why *this* one? Now, recall a point which Wiggins made and which I am happy to endorse: that, if anything is valuable or matters at all, then, normally, there are *more* valuable things than can be fit into a life. Think of all the urgent causes and attractive endeavors which you could pursue: you cannot pursue them all. A justification for thinking that something is valuable or important is not yet the explanation for its mattering *to you*. You might have an argument that the cause of the moment is very important, and even an argument that many people ought to devote themselves to it, without having yet addressed the question of whether and why *you* should be one of them.

Mill's proof of the Principle of Utility is an argument that purports to explain why utility is desirable. Even if it shows that there should be many devoted Utilitarians, it doesn't yet show that any particular person ought to adopt the Utilitarian project as his own. And so it isn't the explanation for which we are seeking, of why *Mill* devoted himself to Utilitarianism.[35]

Third, in the course of his proof, Mill tells us that

If the end which the utilitarian doctrine proposes to itself were not, in theory and practice, acknowledged to be an end, nothing could ever convince any person that it was so.[36]

If you must already find utility desirable, in order for Mill's proof to be persuasive, the proof cannot be the reason that you came to find utility desirable in the first place. And if it must already be *your* end, for the proof to be convincing, the proof can't be what accounts for utility being your end in the first place.

Lastly, Mill's proof of the Principle of Utility has a peculiar status within the history of moral philosophy, where it is something on the order of the field's Leaning Tower of Pisa. The argument contains two apparent fallacies, fallacies that are so obvious and clumsy that it is almost impossible to believe that Mill could have committed them in such a carefully considered and composed essay (and this is why I haven't reproduced the proof here).[37] Almost since it first appeared, busloads of philosophers have come to visit the site of the apparent architectural mistake, and every couple of years, someone comes up with another attempt at reconstructing the argument so that it works.[38]

Now, I have never seen a reconstruction of Mill's proof that would plausibly produce emotional conviction. Suppose that in the end some ingenious historian can show that the train of thought works. The historiography shows that it was never *obvious* what the argument's force was; but to be emotionally compelling, it *would* have to be obvious, rather than slippery, delicate, and very, very clever. No one invests a whole life in a project on the strength of the sorts of argument the secondary literature has attributed to Mill.

3.8

Mill's emotional stake in his Utilitarian life project, at any rate in his mid-teens, closely tracked what we identified as the philosophical motivations for seeing the meaning of a life as a project. He himself was theoretically inarticulate about those motivations; we had to provide the associationist reconstruction of his epiphany on his behalf, and we can now make an educated guess as to why: the mismatches between how he remembered the experience, what his psychology could fully reconstruct, and what he could officially acknowledge as a good reason were too large. That inarticulateness, I am in the course of arguing, will typify project lives; anyone who has structured their life this way will not normally be in a position to consider what will strike more open-minded readers as the better reasons for doing so. Nonetheless, that is not anything like a decisive objection to making a project out of one's life; it was never a requirement on having a meaningful life that you be able to provide a lucid account of why having a meaningful life is important, or of why you are taking some project in particular on board.

I earlier introduced, as a worry which someone today might have, the suggestion that Mill's life project couldn't be superlatively attributed to him. That way of setting up the discussion is likely to have suggested that the concern is anachronistic, and couldn't have been Mill's. But while there is nothing in Mill's theorizing that looks like the architectures of personality which recent philosophers have used to give content to the insistence that you didn't *really* want it, or that you really *did* do it, Mill has a use for the distinction, which will turn out to be important later on in our argument, between "a person whose desires and impulses are his own," and "one whose desires and impulses are not his own" (XVIII:264/OL 3:5). To anticipate, Mill's own term for what makes the difference is "originality."

I will return to the question of what sustained Mill's emotional commitment to his project, but first I want to consider how Mill became disenchanted with the specifically Benthamite version of it.

4 Mill's Postdoc

Children still raised on Charles Dickens, together with the many adults who also enjoy reading him today, are unlikely to know that *Hard Times* was a thinly disguised caricature of the Mills. When it was published, however, everyone who was anyone understood who was supposed to be whom. Louisa Gradgrind represented the young John Stuart Mill, and her father, Thomas Gradgrind, was meant to be recognized as James Mill.[1]

In endorsing one popular impression of the Mills, the novel presented, as Mill's own predicament, an objection to the project view related to the one which I introduced in the previous chapter: that if a child is inducted into a project early enough to ensure that it encompasses his entire life, he will turn out to have had no childhood. Louisa Gradgrind complains to her father:

'What do *I* know … of tastes and fancies; of aspirations and affections; of all that part of my nature in which such light things might have been nourished? What escape have I had from problems that could be demonstrated, and realities that could be grasped?'

'You have been so careful of me that I never had a child's heart. You have trained me so well that I never dreamed a child's dream. You have dealt so wisely with me, Father, from my cradle to this hour, that I never had a child's belief or a child's fear.'[2]

Mill's education, I'm about to argue, brought him to a turning point in his life project, and the runup to it must have made him feel much like Dickens's depiction of Louisa Gradgrind. But Dickens misidentified the source of Mill's problem, which is a very different and almost inevitable side effect of having a life project in the first place.

4.1

The nineteenth century's romantic reinvention of childhood (still part of our own culture, and let's be wary of it) allowed Dickens to fill out his diagnosis. Childhood is the period of blossoming, unconstrained imagination; Mill's "starved imagination keeping life in itself somehow" was a side effect of the Utilitarians' educational program, which Dickens exhibited as consisting entirely of rote memorization; today's version of the prejudice that Dickens is exploiting is the idea that nerds don't have emotional lives.[3] The head of the Gradgrind family (who, again, is doing duty for James Mill) is described as "a man of realities ... facts and calculations ... a kind of cannon loaded to the muzzle with facts ... prepared to blow [his elementary school students] clean out of the regions of childhood at one discharge"; and we're shown a particularly brutal classroom scene in which hapless children are drilled on their facts, facts, facts.[4]

Whatever Dickens may have gotten right about the Utilitarians, he got Mill's education entirely wrong. Knowing what we do about the adult John Stuart Mill's accomplishments, the Gradgrind parody is implausible on the face of it: you don't produce an exquisitely refined and endlessly inventive philosopher just by making someone memorize facts.[5] If that were all there was to it, it would be inexplicable that Mill turned out to be the enormously productive, intelligent, and creative thinker he did. And indeed that isn't the upbringing that Mill himself recollects.[6]

James Mill consistently brought his underage son on board his own research projects. For instance, John Stuart helped read proof for the *History of India*; the younger Mill's homework on Ricardo (and more generally economics) was used by his father "as notes from which to write his *Elements of Political Economy*"; when the time came for the older Mill to write the *Analysis*, he had his son read, discuss, and summarize Locke, Helvétius, and Hartley.[7] James Mill helped kick off the new *Westminster Review* by producing a hostile piece on the competition; his son tells us:

Before writing it he made me read through all the volumes of the [Edinburgh] Review, or as much of each as seemed of any importance ... and make notes for him of the articles which I thought he would wish to examine ... (I:93, 95/A 4:2).

Although a large component of his upbringing was no doubt conditioning—and this is a topic to which we'll return—much of Mill's *real* education consists in his having been, from a startlingly early age, his father's research assistant. The outcomes in this case are a heartening confirmation of the theory behind American graduate education, namely, that you educate researchers by apprenticing them to researchers; it also suggests that it's possible to extend this approach much further down the educational food chain than it currently is.

In one way or another it was a side effect of this apprenticeship—although we haven't yet seen this payoff of Mill's education in action—that he learned to argue. He tells us that "the first intellectual operation in which I arrived at any proficiency, was dissecting a bad argument, and finding in what part the fallacy lay"; this was "an intellectual exercise in which I was most perserveringly drilled by my father" (I:23/A 1:12). Because it will turn out to be important, let me pause briefly to say what this means.

As the weary instructors of our critical thinking and logic classes know all too well, most people, and even most academics, do not know how to work with argument. For the most part, they cannot recognize arguments when they encounter them in texts; they cannot construct effective arguments; they cannot identify the components of arguments or correctly explain how the parts fit together; they cannot figure out what is wrong with an argument. To reiterate, it was one of the genuinely impressive accomplishments of twentieth-century Anglo-American philosophy to have made competence in argumentation part of the standard skill set of the discipline; during the nineteenth century, professional philosophers were no better at it than the average layman of today. John Stuart Mill exercises this portfolio of skills to a standard that only the very best of our students and colleagues meet; my classroom experience is that you can give paragraph after paragraph of Mill's prose a quick knock on the side, and one after another they will disassemble themselves into step-by-step natural deduction exercises. The point we'll need presently is this: once you have this skill set, it normally shapes your taste; underargued, or badly argued, or crudely argued political and philosophical writing comes to strike you as, in extreme cases, cringeworthy.

By the time he reached his mid-teens, Mill had studied his way through the equivalent of a PhD ... or two. As we've seen, he had been an active participant in his father's cutting-edge historical and psychological research. In terms of subject matter, the coverage, while weak in mathematics and the hard sciences, was otherwise quite extensive.[8] He had been trained in precisely the opposite of rote memorization; his father made a practice of not giving him answers, and instead required him to figure almost everything out pretty much on his own: "Anything which could be found out by thinking, I never was told, until I had exhausted my efforts to find it out for myself" (I:35/A 1:22). He had learned how to argue, to the standards of twentieth- and twenty-first-century philosophers. Bentham and James Mill had inadvertently produced a much better all-round intellectual and philosopher than themselves.

With the PhD-equivalent under the hood, Mill was ready for the next stage of his academic apprenticeship: a large exercise, not fully original, but in which he would be allowed a great deal of autonomy, and in which he could work at integrating his carefully cultivated skills in writing, argumentation, and the like. In other words, it was time for his postdoc, and here's his retrospective report on it.

About the end of 1824, or beginning of 1825, Mr. Bentham, having lately got back his papers on Evidence from M. Dumont (whose *Traité des Preuves Judiciares*,[9] grounded on them, was then first completed and published), resolved to have them printed in the original, and bethought himself of me as capable of preparing them for the press; in the same manner as his *Book of Fallacies* had been recently edited by Bingham. I gladly undertook this task, and it occupied nearly all my leisure for about a year, exclusive of the time afterwards spent in seeing the five large volumes through the press. Mr. Bentham had begun this treatise three times, at considerable intervals, each time in a different manner, and each time without reference to the preceding: two of the three times he had gone over nearly the whole subject. These three masses of manuscript it was my business to condense into a single treatise; adopting the one last written as the groundwork, and incorporating with it as much of the two others as it had not completely superseded. I had also to unroll such of Bentham's involved and parenthetical sentences, as seemed to overpass by their complexity the measure of what readers were likely to take the pains to understand. It was further Mr. Bentham's particular desire that I should, from myself, endeavour to supply any *lacunae* which he had left.... I also replied to the objections which had been made to some of his doctrines, by reviewers of Dumont's book. (I:117/A 4:15)

Mill's description is carefully politic, and let's render it into plainer language; I apologize for being too American even to try for an in-period, British rendering.

When Mill was eighteen (so, a couple years after his epiphany), Bentham had a favor to ask, and it must have gone something like this: "John, you know, there's this book I've tried to write three times, and wasn't ever able to finish. Why don't you take these three enormous piles of handwritten manuscript, fold them together, clean it all up, and we'll publish it. It'll be great for your career." Mill couldn't very well say no to the great man, and it was in any case a genuine opportunity: a contribution to a substantial publication. His father must have encouraged him; Mill senior had written up a lengthy abstract of this very book, and probably he had originally intended himself to do the task his son was taking on.[10] Mill then produced the five-volume *Rationale of Judicial Evidence* (1827), totaling some 3,300 pages, which we saw him describe as "occup[ying] nearly all my leisure for about a year" (I:117/A 4:15). Having myself tried the exercise of transcribing Bentham's nearly illegible handwriting into fair copy that you might plausibly send off to a publisher, I can advise you not to take the word "leisure" to suggest a part-time hobby or relaxed pastime; that Mill was able to finish it off in this time frame is nothing short of remarkable.[11]

The year Mill turned twenty brought the onset of his Mental Crisis, and as you no doubt expect, I'm going to suggest that the timing wasn't a coincidence. We're going to take a close look both at the Crisis and at some of what people have had to say about it. Right now, by way of introduction, here is a slightly abridged version of Mill's own much-quoted description of it:

From the winter of 1821, when I first read Bentham ... I had what might truly be called an object in life; to be a reformer of the world. My conception of my own happiness was entirely identified with this object.... I endeavoured to pick up as many flowers as I could by the way; but as a serious and permanent personal satisfaction to rest upon, my whole reliance was placed on this: and I was accustomed to felicitate myself on the certainty of a happy life which I enjoyed, through placing my happiness in something durable and distant, in which some progress might be always making, while it could never be exhausted by complete attainment. This did very well for several years, during which the general improvement going on in the world and the idea of myself as engaged with others in struggling to promote it, seemed enough to fill up an interesting and animated existence. But the time came when I awakened from this as from a dream. It was in the autumn of 1826.... [I]t occurred to me to put the question directly to myself, "Suppose that all your objects in life were realized; that all the changes in institutions and opinions which you are looking forward to, could be completely effected at this very instant: would this be a great joy and happiness to you?" And an irrepressible self-consciousness distinctly answered, "No!" At this my heart sank within me: the whole foundation on which my life was constructed fell down. All my happiness was to have been found in the continual pursuit of this end. The end had ceased to charm, and how could there ever again be any interest in the means? I seemed to have nothing left to live for. (I:137, 139/A 5:2)

Mill's friend, protege, and biographer, Alexander Bain, put the lengthy "dejection" down to "over-working the brain," and, looking at the *Rationale*, it's not an unreasonable initial hypothesis. But I don't in fact think that's all, or even nearly all, of the explanation.[12]

Notice this very terse remark in the *Autobiography*: "My name as editor was put to the book [that is, the *Rationale*] after it was printed, at Mr. Bentham's positive desire, which I in vain attempted to persuade him to forego."[13]

First, let me again render that into my down-to-earth American idiom, and in due course I'll argue that what I'm about to give you *is* the right rendering. At one of the final prepublication stages, Bentham becomes aware that Mill has left his name off the title page of the finished book, and sends him a note telling him that he's done a lot of work and should have his name on it. Mill modestly replies: "Oh, no—this is *your* book! I just did copyediting; I really don't deserve that sort of credit ... and I also wouldn't want to look like I'm trying to take credit." Bentham says: "No, I insist." Mill tells him that really he doesn't deserve it, *really*; Bentham absolutely insists; in the end, Mill's name appears, but not actually on the title page; you will find it at the end of the editor's Preface.[14]

Mill is polite, but academic readers recognize what's just happened. This is the moment when you tell your collaborator that it's really *his* work, because you've realized that you don't want to be associated with it, and the reason you don't want to be associated with it is that it's embarrassingly *bad*. I'm going to defend that reconstruction of the course of events in a moment, but first, and to anticipate, here's the cause (although likely only a partial cause) which I'm about to propose for Mill's Mental Crisis: his teenage emotional commitment to the Utilitarian political enterprise is threatened by the very, very low intellectual quality of Bentham's thought and writing.

4.3

We saw the sixteen-year-old Mill experiencing a life-changing epiphany the time he encountered a book by Bentham. How could the same author have produced two so very different reactions on occasions just two years apart? The materials used by Dumont and the manuscripts on which Mill worked were not nearly all the same, but there was nonetheless a good deal of overlap. Bentham's views hadn't changed much; and while Mill was a couple of years older, at a time of life when people mature rapidly, he was evidently still very much the same person as his slightly younger self. And anyway, where do I get off making dismissive judgments about the quality of the work by an acknowledgedly important figure in the history of philosophy and the political and legal history of Great Britain?

If you take time out to read Dumont's *Traité* and Mill's rendition of Bentham side by side, here's what you'll find. Dumont took a great many liberties with his original; he attempts to convey Bentham's ideas, but (evidently partly because Bentham himself wouldn't supply complete manuscripts, or answer Dumont's many questions about what he thought and meant) the resulting work speaks in the voice of a worldly Frenchman,[15] it emphasizes the systematic structure of Bentham's views (especially the organizing idea that all that really matters, when you're designing laws and the institutions that go with them, is the balance of pleasure over pain), and, perhaps most importantly, it is relatively short.[16] Now Mill, as we'll see in a moment, seems to have taken few liberties with the manuscript in front of him: he made choices about which version to use, but the very length of the *Rationale* suggests that, whenever possible, he used *all* of them.[17] He took his job to include rewriting Bentham's sentences, and occasionally he added supporting materials, but on the rare occasions when he felt he needed to correct Bentham, the correction appears as an editor's footnote; so he was unwilling to tamper with the content himself.[18] Perhaps this was because he felt himself to be a great man's underlaborer; perhaps because Bentham was discussing aspects of courtroom procedure that were simply undocumented—in order to know about them, you would had to have spent a great deal of time in court, or talking with lawyers—and so Mill would likely not have felt confident making more than very minor changes to the text in front of him.[19] We no longer have the manuscripts from which Mill worked (and Bentham had the practice of destroying manuscripts once the material had actually been published). But when we look at the *Rationale*, what we see must be very close to what Mill saw, and this is confirmed by the large amount of quite similar manuscript material which we do still possess.

What we see in the *Rationale* is startlingly different from Dumont's rendering of Bentham; I'll mention just a handful of the more striking contrasts. First, there is almost no properly utilitarian argument. Bentham has many ideas about how things ought to be done, but he does not appeal to anything on the order of a hedonic calculation to justify his proposals (and on most of the occasions, not all that frequent overall, that the term "utility" comes up, it clearly means "usefulness," and not the feeling of pleasure).[20] Second, Bentham's proposals often sound reasonable to us: for example, he argues that when taking testimony, you should ask the witness questions in person (as opposed, say, to sending him a letter to answer), you should be allowed to ask followup questions, and when he answers, someone should write it all down. But where Dumont makes this sort of point in a paragraph, the *Rationale* devotes 434 pages to it.[21] Finally for right now, Bentham is much given to pointless taxonomizing.[22] The overall impression produced by the writing—anyway, this is how it struck me, and I would expect it to strike you this way also—is of philosophically uninteresting, intellectually flat, endlessly repetitive crankiness.[23]

The impression the materials made was probably worse than the finished product which Mill has left us indicates. If you sit down today with the many boxes of Bentham's carefully preserved handwriting, you will find, for instance, one after another almost-identical table of contents, meant for the same book, and one after another almost-identical preface, also for that same book ... for folder after folder after folder. These are not drafts, as we normally understand the notion: stages in which previous material is being reworked and improved.[24] Rather, Bentham seems to have commenced writing, morning after morning (he worked until his three o'clock breakfast), by starting in, yet once again, on whichever book it was, beginning, as usual, at the beginning. (He apparently did the same thing in the evening as well: while being shaved, presumably with a straight razor, he would dictate to a secretary.)[25] And, each morning (or evening), the words came out pretty much the same way. Looking at the manuscripts, I had something like the reaction—and I expect that Mill's was similar—of the character in Kubrick's *Shining* who discovers that her husband's novel-in-progress consists entirely in repetitions of the sentence, "All work and no play makes Jack a dull boy."[26]

What really matters, of course, is not how it strikes you or me, but how the young Mill responded to it. And here we have his subsequent testimony to go on as well.

Somewhat over a decade later, Mill penned a biographical essay titled "Bentham" (X:77–115). The tone manages to be laudatory, but inspection confirms the substance of the assessment I've just given. Describing his mentor's prose, Mill tells us that "he fell into a Latin or German structure of sentence, foreign to the genius of the English language. He could not bear, for the sake of clearness and the reader's ease, to say ... a little more than the truth in one sentence, and correct it in the next. The whole of the qualifying remarks which he intended to make, he insisted on embedding as parentheses in the very middle of the sentence itself" (X:114). Bentham, Mill more than allows, is not much good at careful argument: "We must not look for subtlety, or the power of recondite analysis, among [Bentham's] intellectual characteristics. In the former quality, few great thinkers have ever been so deficient" (X:80). Reiterating that "we often must [reject] his practical conclusions," Mill goes out of his way to praise "Bentham's method ... as the method of detail, of treating wholes by separating them into their parts.... Hence his interminable classifications" (X:82f). Mill seems to identify Bentham's procedure with Plato's Method of Collection and Division; he says that "Bentham was probably not aware that Plato had anticipated him in the process to which he too declared that he owed everything" (X:88). For the moment, the relevant observations are two: this is a part of Plato's work that nonspecialists tend to ignore, for the simple reason that we don't think much of the Method. And although Mill seems to praise it, this is not how he argues himself.

Mill is in retrospect also disappointed on matters of substance, although it is hard to know how much of that response to attribute to his younger self. Bentham overlooked the importance of character formation in ethics.[27] His philosophy is capable "of organizing and regulating the merely *business* part of the social arrangements" (X:99). Even these arrangements are unacceptable, because he never noticed that entirely empowered majorities would be likely to oppress minorities (X:106–108). His moral philosophizing was bound to be defective, because he both ignored the work of previous philosophers, and was insufficiently imaginative to compensate without their help for "the incompleteness of his own mind as a representative of universal human nature" (X:91f). And while Mill insists that any one person would be an incomplete such representative, Bentham was an extreme case, someone who had never grown up: "a boy to the last," his understanding of other human beings was "the empiricism of one who has had little experience" (X:92). "It is," Mill remarks in a final note, "indispensable to a correct estimate of any of Bentham's dealings with the world, to bear in mind that in everything except abstract speculation he was to the last, what we have called him, essentially a boy" (X:115n).

We can still hear the echo of those "intellectual results beyond all computation" which the young Mill saw "stretching out into the distance," now almost entirely stripped of the sense of the sublime: his older self tells us that "the field of Bentham's labours was like the space between two parallel lines; narrow to excess in one direction, in another it reached to infinity" (X:100).

Looking back, the more mature Mill did find something he could wholeheartedly praise, and that real praise is reserved almost entirely for Bentham's willingness to stand on his own convictions when faced with institutionalized abuses.[28] "He alone was found with sufficient moral sensibility and self-reliance to say to himself that these things . . . were frauds, and that between them and himself there should be a gulf fixed. To this rare union of self-reliance and moral sensibility we are indebted for all that Bentham has done" (X:81). To borrow a phrase from the *Rationale*, Bentham's role was to be someone who "speaks out and calls things by their names" (vol. i, p. 388n); he was the child who proclaimed that the emperor had no clothes. His example taught others to do likewise: "It is by the influence of the modes of thought with which his writings innoculated a considerable number of thinking men, that the yoke of authority has been broken, and innumerable opinions, formerly received on tradition as incontestable, are put on their defense, and required to give an account of themselves."[29]

The young Mill had been prepared to be a Utilitarian political activist, and on encountering Bentham's ideas in Dumont's rendering of them had embraced that mission. But faced with the actual written manuscripts of the Marx of Utilitarianism, John Stuart Mill had, I am suggesting, a horrifying realization, and I'll put it in today's idiom: that he had been raised by—and into—the Flat Earth Society. I've described his reading of Dumont's edition of Bentham as his teenage epiphany, but Mill in fact turns out to have had a second epiphany, one that was not nearly as uplifting as the first.

4.4

In two hundred years, no one is likely to remember the founder of the Flat Earth Society, much less devote a life of scholarship to editing his writings. Benthamites, then and now, think much better of Bentham than I am suggesting the young Mill did. How are we to reconcile the conflicting assessments?

Bentham was in fact capable of graceful, powerful writing, and a good deal of Bentham's influence was due to it. The material on evidence was crabbed, obsessive, and tedious; so part of the problem was that Mill's sample of the raw materials was unfortunate.[30] The problem was no doubt compounded by a further cause of the uptake Bentham received. Much of Bentham's output made its way to the public by way of other intellectuals, such as Dumont and James Mill, who rewrote what they were given, and in doing so, imposed on the final product a much more attractive authorial persona; it would be a mistake to think of Dumont as having translated Bentham from an already existing English original: rather, Dumont *composed* a work "by Bentham."[31] However, Mill was aware of the provenence of Dumont's *Traité*, and in his struggle to make passable prose out of the source materials for the *Rationale* was only too likely to have decided that he was seeing the real Bentham behind the facade supplied by another author.

Much of the subsequent enthusiasm for Bentham has to do with the obvious merits of many of his practical proposals. An anonymous contributor to the *Times Literary Supplement* provides an overview which conveys what sort of improvements fall under this heading:

He stood for the reform of the representative system in Parliament; he demanded municipal reform; he prayed for the mitigation of the terrible criminal law, for the abolition of transportation, and for the improvement of prisons.... He clamoured for the removal of defects in the jury system, pleaded for the abolition of grand juries ... demanded the abolition of imprisonment for debt, the sweeping away of the usury laws, the reform of the law of evidence, the repeal of religious tests ... the reform of the Poor Law, ... the training of pauper children, ... the establishment of a national system of education. He demanded an extension of the idea of savings banks and friendly societies, cheap postage without the object of national profit coupled with post office money orders. He insisted on a complete and uniform Register of Births, Marriages and Deaths, a Code for Merchant Shipping, full Census returns, the circulation of Parliamentary papers, the protection of inventors. He demanded local Courts, uniform and scientific methods of drafting Acts of Parliament, a general register of real property, of deeds and all transactions, and last, but certainly not least, the passing of public health legislation.

[I]n addition ... [h]e demanded the creation of public prosecutors and of advocates for the poor.

To us to-day [this is 1925] practically the whole of it in principle, if not in effect, is admitted. It makes quite dull reading.... But ... when Bentham set forth his polity all these things were impossible, absurd, ridiculous. Great intellects waved them away.[32]

These proposals stand on their own; one doesn't need to read hundreds of pages of Bentham, or connect them to the remainder of Bentham's intellectual system, in order to appreciate their force.

Finally, Bentham's followers are impressed by him because they think he was *right*. But whether Utilitarianism was right was not Mill's problem; rather, it was that although he continued to think that Bentham was right, he was dismayed by the quality of the presentation.[33]

Why enthusiasm before, and depression after? When, on reencountering Bentham's ideas, Mill became desperately disillusioned with the project, it was a matter of finding Bentham's version of the Utilitarian project to be in (intellectual) *bad taste*. As in Mill's first epiphany, this was an *aesthetic* response, and in the first place to the crudeness and vulgarity of the workings of Bentham's mind. Mill would not have been intellectually equipped to explain what had happened to him. We've observed that associationism, which provided Mill with his conceptual vocabulary, is not articulate about matters of taste; and it is in any case unobvious how a judgment of taste could count for a Utilitarian as a reason for action. That is, Utilitarians were instrumentalists, and took reasons to be provided by pleasures and desires, so they could certainly treat not liking something anymore as a reason no longer to pursue it. But Mill's judgment had a content that was not merely dislike, and the apprehension that his life project was unworthy of his commitment was not a thought a Utilitarian can officially have. All this means that we should not expect Mill himself to have come up with, or to have been prepared to endorse, the story I've just told, even if it is correct; which in turn means that we will have to think through very carefully the relations between these motivations and the explanations for his breakdown that Mill subseqently constructed.

A moment ago I distinguished Bentham's views from his presentation, and I now need to adjust the claim I was making.[34] Mill did stay a Utilitarian, and continued to fight for representative democracy, freedom of speech, and many such components of the Utilitarian platform. But because Bentham's formulations of the theoretical core of the ideology, of the policy proposals, and of his arguments for them were much too crude for his young protege, as we will see, over the course of the coming decades Mill rewrote them all—of course changing the content in subtle and not-so-subtle ways. (Imagine a portraitist who is unhappy with some other painter's treatment of a subject; it's not that he disagrees, exactly, with what the first painter saw, but when he does the portrait over, although the subject is the same, the image is rendered very differently. What Mill did with Bentham was a little like *that*.) When it comes to aesthetic assessments, that distinction between content and presentation is unprincipled.

Analytic philosophy was founded on a distinction between propositional content and mere presentation, the latter category being variously characterized as emotive flavoring, "pragmatics" and so on; propositional content is to be assessed for truth, for inferential validity, for coherence, and generally, for anything that matters philosophically. The contrasting aspects of a view or a text or an utterance, thought of as mere packaging, are, in principle, not supposed to determine whether one believes the content. And so when Mill was derailed by Bentham's writing-in-the-raw, he was exhibiting a response for which our own philosophical tradition has no room. But Mill is not alone, because reactions of this kind guide every intelligent philosopher. How seriously one is able to take a journal article or a book depends (in part, but *correctly*) on its *voice*.[35]

We inheritors of that distinction are in no position to dismiss the observation. During the founding phase of analytic philosophy, the day was not carried by compelling arguments. After all, such arguments could only be expected to make their appearance after full command had been achieved of the movement's distinctive modes of argumentation, and that unsurprisingly happened only a generation or so into its history. Rather, the first analytic philosophers were able to have their philosophical innovations taken seriously by cultivating a shared style and tone of voice. In analytic philosophy today, we see professional training and other institutions placing ever more emphasis on packaging, and consequently devoting ever less energy and effort to content. When analytic philosophers talk as though only propositional content matters—generally in precisely that carefully cultivated voice—the pragmatic contradiction should make us think twice.

Mill's subsequent nervous breakdown has prompted a great many attempts to explain its philosophical import; I will discuss a recent treatment in the coming chapter, and will piece together Mill's own picture of what happened to him in the two chapters following. Right now, I am putting on the table the obvious first-cut explanation for that "irrepressible self-consciousness": Mill had emotionally disinvested in his life project because he came to appreciate just how intellectually shoddy it was. Because Mill was by this point a much more serious intellectual and philosopher than his mentors, he perceived a quality problem which passed them by entirely. I should emphasize that the argument for this account of Mill's Mental Crisis is not yet complete. What makes this reading compelling, in my view, is the aftermath at which I just gestured: that so much in the way of Mill's subsequent efforts were devoted to improving the quality of the project. That part of the argument will fall into place in due course.

To anticipate, Mill's response was not to walk away from his upbringing—as perhaps most adolescents deciding their parents have feet of clay would. Instead, he chose to reinterpret the doctrine and the platform so as to make it *worthy* of his allegiance, and transformed Utilitarianism from a movement that could be effectively lampooned by *Hard Times* into a sophisticated and urbanely presented ideology, one capable of sustaining up of 150 years of philosophical interest.

4.5

A life project occupies the preponderance of a life. Now, it is a severely defective human life that does not pass through several stages of emotional development; if the life project reaches back into one's childhood, as it did in Mill's case, then the project must span youth and adulthood, but even someone coming to a life project rather later than Mill will—if the project does not prove ephemeral, and if he continues to grow and mature—pursue the project during more than one emotional phase of a life. Thus a project large enough to occupy a life must be suitable to different stages of emotional development.

Now, a project that compels emotional commitment from a child or a youth is unlikely to interest a later and more mature self. (And of course vice versa: the sixteen-year-old Mill would not have been gripped, philosophically or personally, by the much more nuanced and apparently less radical version of the project worked up over his adult life.) True, there are exceptions: Bentham seems to have remained faithful to one version of his own project over the course of his working life; but then, Mill subsequently characterized Bentham as a perpetual child (X:92). Leaving such exceptions to one side, a life project must—at any rate from the point of view of the person who adopts it—undergo revisions over the course of a life. There are many ways this can happen: the person whose project it is may revise it himself, as in Mill's own case; the project may be designed by others so as to reveal greater depth and subtlety over time; as in the case of friendships, it may be built around a person who is also changing over time and, one hopes, also becoming more grownup.

Accordingly, we should not take Mill's having become disillusioned with the Benthamite version of the project he inherited to discredit the project as a whole. What we are seeing is one variation on an almost inevitable bump in the road, namely, that because a life project extends over the course of a life, the person whose project it is experiences growing pains while pursuing it. If maturation isn't over with childhood, the problem isn't merely a contingent idiosyncrasy of Mill's; instead, it is a structural feature of enterprises of this kind, and John Stuart Mill, we're going to see, dealt with it in an exemplary manner. But now it's time to take a closer look at that crisis of confidence, at what Mill said about it in his *Autobiography*, and at how some subsequent philosophers have tried to make sense of it.

5 How to Write a Letter of Recommendation

In the last chapter, I suggested that Mill's Mental Crisis—his much-discussed bout of depression and existential angst—was triggered by a realization which his theories of mind and rationality did not equip him to acknowledge, namely, that the project that he had been bequeathed, and which had served as the meaning of his life, had a quality problem: it was too crude, too ungainly, and too obsessive to merit that sort of role. If that is right, we should expect Mill's own diagnosis of the episode to be itself at least somewhat off base, and that is what I am going to argue for first. The reason for doing so is not simply to set the record straight: identifying the expedient which in fact addressed and disposed of the problem he erroneously took to be the source of his difficulties will exhibit a further structural feature of project lives.

I will begin by laying out Mill's own explanation for his Mental Crisis, and flagging a handful of reasons for not taking it at face value. Then I will turn to what proved to be the motivational anchors for his lifelong Utilitarian activities: a sequence of authority figures that included his father, James Mill, his companion and, eventually, wife, Harriet Taylor, and finally Taylor's daughter by her first marriage, Helen Taylor. I will talk my way through Mill's unrealistically worshipful opinions of his authority figures, and argue that putting people (or political parties, or holy texts) on a pedestal is a hard-to-avoid concomitant of project lives. That will allow me to explain the controversial collaboration between Mill and Taylor, and to place the distinctive style of philosophizing that emerged from it as a characteristic side-effect of treating a project as the meaning of one's life.

5.1

There is a precedent for the sort of study of Mill I am undertaking here. In an exceptionally thoughtful discussion, Candace Vogler points out that the lengthy paragraph in which his *Autobiography* explains the onset of his Mental Crisis is simultaneously a narrative description of the Crisis, a causal explanation of it, and a deductively tight argument that, if Mill's philosophical views at the time were correct, you *ought* to have a nervous breakdown. That is, Mill later came to understand himself to have been living out an argument over the course of his breakdown and subsequent recovery. Although I'm going to try to convince you that that argument in fact mischaracterizes Mill's Crisis, Vogler's sensitive reconstruction of Mill's attempts to come to a psychological and philosophical understanding of his first depressive episode can serve as a model for the deployment of biography as philosophical argument that I'm aiming for here.

The argument Mill understood himself to be living through went as follows.[1] As we already know, Mill was both instrumentalist and associationist: all reasons for action identify actions as means directed to satisfying one's desires; all ends or desires, except the hardwired bodily pleasures, are "the results of association: . . . we love one thing and hate another, take pleasure in one sort of action or contemplation, and pain in another sort, through the clinging of pleasurable or painful ideas to those things, from the effect of education or of experience." The pains and pleasures produced by education are the effects of associations that are "artificial and casual"; "[t]he pains and pleasures thus forcibly associated with things, are not connected with them by any natural tie." However, the power of analysis—Mill owes us an explanation of this, which it's not clear he ever gave, but for the moment, and recalling Mill's training in the nuts and bolts of argumentation, let's understand it as clear thinking—dissolves casual and artificial associations, "those which are . . . a *mere* matter of feeling." It follows that analytic habits will dissolve all ends, desires, and pleasures except "the purely physical and organic." With a caveat we will come to, the purely physical and organic pleasures provide insufficient motivational raw material to anchor projects large enough to sustain a life. So when you think clearly about your reasons for action, you will see that you have no reasons to pursue projects large enough to sustain a life.

Let's pause to reconstruct the associationist model of the cognitive process limned by the argument. Mill's utilitarianism, both early and late, differs from older happiness-centered views, like Aristotle's, in that the utilitarians were very aware that different things make different people happy (whereas Aristotle thought of happiness as pretty much the same for everyone). How does each person get his own version of happiness, according to Mill's associationist psychological theory?

Pleasure traverses associative links, and associative links are built up by (mostly) repetition. When life begins, one is equipped with a handful of hardwired pleasures, such as satisfying hunger; so imagine a psychology with only such pleasures as the initial state on which a stimulus operates. When you are an infant, you become hungry, and your mother feeds you. This happens repeatedly, and an associative link gets created between the idea of being fed, and the idea of your mother. Pleasure traverses the link, and becomes associated with the idea of your mother. So now you like your mother: you enjoy her presence, and not merely as a means to satisfying your hunger; her presence has become part of what counts, for you, as happiness. Now imagine that your mother wears straw hats; it happens repeatedly that when you see her, you see her wearing a straw hat; an associative link comes to be built between the idea of your mother and the idea of straw hats; pleasure traverses the link; now you like straw hats; they, too, have become part of what counts, for you, as happiness. Now, and returning to the sort of examples we used to illustrate associationist training in chapter 3, imagine that when your mother parks you in front of the television, there happens to be an advertising campaign in which someone wearing a straw hat drinks a particular brand of beverage. Ads screen repeatedly, and so an associative connection is formed between the idea of straw hats and that particular soft drink. Once again, pleasure travels down the link, and now you have acquired brand awareness: Coca-Cola, perhaps, has also become part of what, for you, counts as happiness.

Some of these connections are causal and instrumental; for instance, it was your mother who fed you, and so as an infant your getting fed depended on your mother being on the spot. However, other associations are *just* associations. This is what Mill means by the contrast between a "natural tie" and "artificial and casual" associations. If you're analytically trained, you discriminate one from the other: you realize that you had a reason for your mother to be around (she fed you), whereas Coke merely *reminds* you of straw hats; drinking a Coke is not a way of getting a straw hat. And once you realize this (but supporting this empirical claim in the way that Mill needs would mean giving the associationist analysis of how analytic thinking works), the associative link stops transmitting the pleasure.

As analytical attention focuses on link after link, the process through which happiness-for-you was etched into your mind is gradually undone. First you no longer enjoy Coke; then you no longer enjoy straw hats … and pretty soon your happiness consists just in the presence of your mother and in getting fed; indeed, at this point, you only care about your mother *because* she's feeding you; you no longer like her presence intrinsically, that is, you no longer like *her*.

What's left is not a lot to live by. Hunger, thirst, a few other hardwired pleasures, and the means of satisfying them may be enough to keep your full attention if you're starving. In an advanced industrial or post-industrial economy, where just getting enough to eat and drink is a part-time activity, that's not enough to direct or occupy a life.[2] If a project served as the meaning of your life, as you cease caring about much of anything, it collapses, leaving you wondering, with Mill, whether you are "bound to go on living, when life must be passed in this manner" (I:145/A 5:5).

There is a subsidiary argument in play in the vicinity of the passage we are examining.[3] The primary object of the Utilitarian social reformers was to reform society and government so as to have "every person ... in a state of physical comfort," and brought to possess the education and intellectual training required for full participation in a democratic society. Now, there are two conditions through which the effects predicted by the previous argument are in practice forestalled. First, when basic bodily needs aren't being met, the pleasures and pains associated with them can be sufficiently intense to allow them to bear the motivational weight required for life projects. And second, most people aren't trained to think analytically. However, if Utilitarian reformers were successful, those conditions would cease to obtain. And so the success of Utilitarian social reform would bring about a Millian mental crisis in most members of the reformed society: life would be pleasureless and without meaning. Recall that the Utilitarian criterion of success is provided by the greatest happiness principle, and that Utilitarians identified happiness with pleasure. It follows that the Utilitarian project is self-defeating; the problem that Mill identified as the source of his Mental Crisis wasn't just personal, but a theoretical incoherence in the political platform, and thus in the project to which he had committed his life.[4]

5.2

On the reading I've just recapitulated, the real problem is the instrumentalism. If you're an instrumentalist—and you wouldn't, as we've repeatedly pointed out, end up with a project-shaped life if you weren't—your means-end reasons form chains that ultimately bottom out in desires whose objects aren't a means to anything *further*. Just because, on the instrumentalist way of seeing things, there's only one kind of practical reason, and just because we've come to the end of *those* reasons, those desires literally have nothing to be said for them. (In Vogler's way of putting it, they're *arbitrary*.) That turns out to be psychologically unsustainable: you can't stake your life in its entirety on reasons that look to you like this, and this inability is what Mill's argument is attempting to capture.[5]

However, while this reading of Mill's lengthy diagnostic paragraph is evidently correct as far as it goes, its context makes it hard to believe that it can really be the whole story of the turning point in Mill's life project, or that it can even be a part of the story that is not highly misleading when considered on its own. Part of the problem is that we've already seen what triggered Mill's Crisis, and it had to do with the merits of Bentham's formulation of the Utilitarian program; as far as the argument we've just reviewed is concerned, merits and demerits shouldn't make any difference, because analysis will dissolve *any* objective that isn't actually hardwired into you. The rest of the problem is that Mill almost immediately puts other parts of the story on the table, and these further stretches of narrative don't on the face of it fit together with this one.

First, Mill seems to tell us that his Crisis was resolved by coming to understand what we now call the Paradox of Hedonism. Insomniacs can't get to sleep by trying; you can't forget something by an ongoing effort of will. There's a film, *The Sure Thing*, in which one of the characters informs another that spontaneity has its time and its place; but of course if you are only spontaneous at the appointed time and in the appointed place, you're not spontaneous.[6] The pursuit of happiness is like these self-frustrating programs of action: you can't be happy by trying to be. Mill tells us:

The experiences of this period ... led me to adopt a theory of life, very unlike that on which I had before acted, and having much in common with what at that time I certainly had never heard of, the anti-self-consciousness theory of Carlyle. I never, indeed, wavered in the conviction that happiness is the test of all rules of conduct, and the end of life. But I now thought that this end was only to be attained by not making it the direct end. Those only are happy (I thought) who have their minds fixed on some object other than their own happiness; on the happiness of others, on the improvement of mankind, even on some art or pursuit, followed not as a means, but as itself an ideal end. Aiming thus at something else, they find happiness by the way. The enjoyments of life (such was now my theory) are sufficient to make it a pleasant thing, when they are taken *en passant*, without being made a principal object. Once make them so, and they are immediately felt to be insufficient. They will not bear a scrutinizing examination. Ask yourself whether you are happy, and you cease to be so. (I:145–147/A 5:6)

If this is an acknowledgement of the Paradox of Hedonism, it assimilates Mill's depression to a common enough class of phenomena. However, where this passage distinguishes the "enjoyments of life" from other, more "ideal" ends, the diagnosis Vogler has reconstructed doesn't: if that diagnosis works, not just immediate pleasures but long-term goals ought to be undercut by analysis. Mill's response to the Paradox of Hedonism is not a cure appropriate to the diagnosis. And in any case, the Paradox of Hedonism gives us the following recommendation: pursue something other than your own happiness. (If you do, we are encouraged to believe, your happiness will probably fall into place on its own.) But now, recall Mill telling us before his breakdown that he "had what might truly be called an object in life; to be a reformer of the world." He *was* pursuing, not his own happiness, but the general utility, that is, the happiness of others.

I endeavoured to pick up as many flowers as I could by the way; but as a serious and permanent personal satisfaction to rest upon, my whole reliance was placed on this: and I was accustomed to felicitate myself on the certainty of a happy life which I enjoyed, through placing my happiness in something durable and distant.... (I:137/A 5:2)

If Mill was already doing what according to his later lights was exactly the right thing (in the terms we have adopted here: pursuing a project), why does he take this recommendation to be a lesson learned from—and the cure for—his Mental Crisis?

Second, Mill announces that seeing his way past the doctrine of Philosophical Necessity—what nowadays is called "determinism"—accounted for his recovery (I:175/A 5:18). But what does freedom of the will have to do with the problem posed by the diagnosis we're considering: once again, that you care about things because of accreted associations, that when you look hard at the associations, they dissolve, and that you end up just not caring anymore?

Finally for now, Mill tells us that the recovery from his depression was cinched when he read Wordsworth's

famous "Ode," falsely called Platonic, "Intimations of Immortality": in which, along with more than his usual sweetness of melody and rhythm, and along with the two passages of grand imagery but bad philosophy so often quoted, I found that he too had had similar experience to mine; that he also had felt that the first freshness of youthful enjoyment was not lasting; but that he had sought for compensation, and found it, in the way which he was now teaching me to find it. The result was that I gradually, but completely, emerged from my depression, and was never again subject to it. (I:153/A 5:10)

On this reconstruction of Mill's self-diagnosis, why would Wordsworth (and in particular, the Immortality Ode) serve as effective therapy? The point of the diagnosis was that Mill was *right* to have his breakdown: he was undergoing his Mental Crisis because he had realized, correctly, that he had no reason to live. Now the force of poetry is not in general exhausted by what it says; but for what it is worth, the Ode, unlike many poems, is easy enough to paraphrase without loss of content, and nothing it asserts plausibly addresses Mill's argument. So Mill would have had to understand the poem to have been effective in some other way, evidently by immunizing some of the associative connections in his own psyche to analytical erosion. Accommodating such effects would be a challenge for his psychology, and it is hard to see how, if they were, his commitment to the political reforms at the center of the Utilitarian project could have survived.[7]

To recap: over and above the explanation Mill gives for his breakdown, he provides *three* apparently distinct accounts of his recovery. An explanation for how a problem was solved should fit the characterization of the problem; provided that the cause of his breakdown was what he seems to claim it to be, each of these explanations is irrelevant to it, and makes a mystery of the subsequent recovery. An explanation of how Mill understood his Mental Crisis ought to make out each of these pieces to be part of a single and unified explanatory narrative. In the meantime, we should not accept Mill's diagnosis at face value (which is not the same as failing to take it seriously). And of course, let us not forget the null hypothesis, namely, that Mill didn't really have a worked out story about what had happened to him, but rather, like most people recounting their own lives, is floating a series of trial balloons.[8]

In the meantime, we have already advanced a very different first-pass explanation for Mill's Mental Crisis: that he gradually came to realize, not that his ultimate ends, like *any* ultimate ends, were arbitrary, but that *these* ends were underwritten by a body of theorizing that was just plain no good. What the habit of analysis made it all but impossible for Mill not to see (even if his instrumentalism didn't allow him to be articulate about it) was the very low quality of the ideology he had inherited.

5.3

The problem with project lives that we're now thinking about is a variation on an old objection to instrumentalism: that it can be very hard to bring yourself to act on a desire, when you can't see much of a reason for the desire in the first place, and that when it comes to your ground-floor desires—that is, the ones that don't merely pop up as intermediate steps on the way to satisfying further desires—you couldn't see a reason for those desires, because you couldn't *have* a reason. A little more carefully, perhaps simply wanting some luxury good or other will seem to you, anyway if you can afford it, like a good enough reason to get it; but when a great deal of weight is being placed on an objective, you have to have more to say to yourself about why you are pursuing it. When a project is organizing your entire life, you are putting all the weight you have got on the project. But because the project organizes all or almost all of your life, there's nothing outside the project to invoke to explain to yourself why the project matters so much: and this last variation on the problem will be a problem for any life that lives up to Wiggins's demand, that it all add up to one thing, whether the mode of organization is instrumental or not.

Although it's hard to imagine a principled solution anyway to the instrumentalist version of the problem, Mill did improvise a way around it. Mill's most intimate relations were coopted into the role of emotional anchors, and let's fit them into their place in our picture of his life.

A significant part of the *Autobiography* reads like academic letters of recommendation, where everyone is the best student the writer has ever had, where every student's dissertation will change the field he is in, where the work clearly makes a successful case for tenure, and so on. Here is Mill on his father, James Mill:

His place is an eminent one in the literary, and even in the political history of his country; and it is far from honourable to the generation which has benefitted by his worth, that he is so seldom mentioned, and, compared with men far his inferiors, so little remembered.

During his later years he was quite as much the head and leader of the intellectual radicals in England, as Voltaire was of the *philosophes* of France. It is only one of his minor merits, that he was the originator of all sound statesmanship in regard to the subject of his largest work, India. He wrote on no subject which he did not enrich with valuable thought, and excepting the *Elements of Political Economy*, a very useful book when first written, but which has now for some time finished its work [in the meantime, the younger Mill had published his own economics textbook, *Principles of Political Economy*], it will be long before any of his books will be wholly superseded.[9]

Here are some representative snippets, describing Harriet Taylor. She was "the most admirable person I had ever known," someone who "could not receive an impression of an experience without making it the source or the occasion of an accession of wisdom." "I have often compared her ... to Shelley: but in thought and intellect, Shelley, so far as his powers were developed in his short life, was but a child compared with what she ultimately became. Alike in the highest regions of speculation and in the smallest practical concerns of daily life, her mind was the same perfect instrument, piercing to the very heart and marrow of the matter ... in the times when such a *carrière* was open to women, [she would have been] eminent among the rulers of mankind."[10] We've just seen Mill describing his father in the most overblown terms; he wraps up his accolade by telling us that "he left, as far as my knowledge extends, no equal among men, and but one among women" (I:213/A 6:11). Finally for now, there is the inscription Mill had put on Taylor's tombstone in Avignon:

AS EARNEST FOR THE PUBLIC GOOD
AS SHE WAS GENEROUS AND DEVOTED
TO ALL WHO SURROUNDED HER
HER INFLUENCE HAS BEEN FELT
IN MANY OF THE GREATEST
IMPROVEMENTS OF THE AGE

FIGURE 5.1 The tomb of Harriet Taylor and John Stuart Mill. (Photo: Adria Quiñones).

AND WILL BE IN THOSE STILL TO COME
WERE THERE BUT A FEW HEARTS AND INTELLECTS
LIKE HERS
THIS EARTH WOULD ALREADY BECOME
THE HOPED-FOR HEAVEN

Mill was later buried in the same grave, and his own inscription appears on the side of the tombstone, looking a little like a footnote. (See Figure 5.1.)

To be sure, no one expects honesty from the sort of encomiums delivered at funerals. But when it is put side by side with the rest of Mill's descriptions of Taylor, it becomes apparent that he meant it.[11] Mill had an impossibly high opinion of his companion and wife: what he believed about her couldn't possibly have been true, because it isn't true of anybody.

Finally for now, he describes his stepdaughter in identical tones:

my stepdaughter, Miss Helen Taylor, the inheritor of much of [Harriet Taylor's] wisdom, and of all her nobleness of character, whose ever growing and ripening talents from that day to this … have already made her name better and more widely known than was that of her mother, though far less so than I predict that if she lives, it is destined to become … of what I owe in the way of instruction to her great powers of original thought and soundness of practical judgment, it would be a vain attempt to give an adequate idea. Surely no one ever before was so fortunate, as, after such a loss as mine, to draw another such prize in the lottery of life—another companion, stimulator, adviser, and instructor of the rarest quality. Whoever, either now or hereafter, may think of me and of the work I have done, must never forget that it is the product not of one intellect and conscience but of three, the least considerable of whom, and above all the least original, is the one whose name is attached to it. (I:264–265/A 7:27)

This last is something of a reality check on the seriousness with which we can take Mill's descriptions. Certainly people have been impressed, in one way or another, with James Mill and with Harriet Taylor. But no one has ever thought that Helen Taylor was an important or impressive figure. If, unlike today's letters of recommendation, we can presume that Mill is expressing his honest opinions, we have little alternative to concluding that he must have been personally unacquainted with the very people who had the most influence on his own life, and with whom he had the most day-to-day contact over the course of it.[12]

Mill's father, wife, and stepdaughter each served as authority figures during different stages of Mill's life. We have already seen the sort of direction that James Mill provided to his son over the period of his childhood and youth. I will shortly take up the relationship between Mill and Taylor, which requires more extensive discussion. After Harriet Taylor's death, Helen Taylor, her daughter by her marriage to John Taylor, had a great deal to do with the body of writing that is left to us under the name of John Stuart Mill. For example (but it's an important example), late in his life, she managed, and answered, Mill's correspondence: letters addressed to John Stuart Mill received replies (and *substantive* replies), above his signature, replies that had been written by Helen Taylor. In a letter, the younger Taylor describes herself as "go[ing] over [Mr. Mill's writings] five or six times, putting in words here, stops there; scratching through whole paragraphs; asking him to write whole new pages in particular places where I think the meaning is not clear; condensing, enlarging, polishing, etc."[13]

Those Mill scholars who do accept the estimate which I am starting to sketch of the authority that Taylor, her daughter, and Mill's father exercised over Mill's decisions, authorial and otherwise, generally also accept the following explanation for it.[14] James Mill had imposed a training regimen on the young John Stuart Mill that had habituated him to working at the dictates of another. His psyche had been shaped—in just the way that associationism would predict—so that effective functioning required someone in the role of authority figure. During his first nervous breakdown, he identified his problem as not having an internal source of motivation or direction: "I was thus, as I said to myself, left stranded at the commencement of my voyage, with a well equipped ship and a rudder, but no sail" (I:143/A 5:4). And in the "Early Draft" of his *Autobiography*, he revealingly remarked: "I was so much accustomed to expect to be told what to do, either in the form of direct command or of rebuke for not doing it, that I acquired a habit of leaving my responsibility as a moral agent to rest on my father, my conscience never speaking to me except by his voice" (I:613). After James Mill vacated the role, Taylor replaced him, filling the slot in Mill's life that James Mill had shaped to himself.[15] And when she died, her daughter moved into the vacant position in turn.

If that explanation of what is evidently a pattern in Mill's life were correct, there would not be much of general interest to be learned from it. Most people haven't been shaped into personalities that require an external source of initiative. But my own view is that the implicitly associationist explanation has the direction of explanation backwards. What we are actually seeing is a difficulty with life-sized projects being played out in Mill's personality.

A project that is coextensive with a life will tend to swallow all the means-ends reasons that one has available. If it does, what is left over to justify the overwhelming importance of the project as a whole? How can you explain why you are devoting your life—your *whole* life—to it? In the framework we have taken from Wiggins, the demand that all your reasons cohere, conjoined with instrumentalism about practical reasons, puts enormous pressure on a single point, the guiding characterization of the project as a whole: here, the Greatest Good of the Greatest Number. It does turn out, as Mill's initial diagnosis reflects, to be psychologically impossible to put that much pressure on an unsupported desire—or, more generally, on a commitment that is not backed up by *something*.

Where scholars have thought that Mill had the project life he did because he was responsive to authority, I think it's rather the other way around. Because Mill's life was structured as a project, it *had* to be responsive to authority. Unable to acknowledge the force of his aesthetic responses, he seemed to himself to lack decisive reasons for taking on and sticking with the Utilitarian project. And so Mill fell back, almost inevitably, on a substitute (again, and again ironically, one that his own theory of rationality could not accommodate). He would take the word of suitably admirable figures that this *was* what he should be doing. The specifically Utilitarian direction of his life was given by James Mill, and Harriet Taylor provided the imprimatur for many of the subprojects that filled in the Utilitarian frame.

If we are correct, we finally have a fully convincing answer to the worry that Mill had his project foisted on him by authority figures. It was his prior emotional stake in the project that accounts for his having adopted them *as* authority figures. For it to be psychologically possible to accord someone *enough* authority to underwrite a commitment of this size, Mill had to be able to see his father, wife, and stepdaughter as impossibly impressive: so much wiser than he was, such moral heroes, and such historically important figures as to be much, much larger than life.[16]

Given how much weight has to be rested on the source of a life project, we are seeing how a realistic view of that source is almost bound to be displaced by a delusional understanding of some very large, very significant part of one's life. That need not necessarily be an individual; during the first part of the twentieth century, perceptions of the Communist Party seem to have been frequently enough controlled by this side effect of project lives. But the direction of explanation, from investment in the project, to unrealistically inflated assessments of an authority capable of vouching for it, will be characteristic of project lives. We have observed that, in general, only someone with an explicitly or implicitly instrumentalist view of practical rationality is likely to have a project life. Whatever the merits of taking the endorsement of a personally impressive figure as a reason to adopt and stick with a project or an end, an instrumentalist cannot construe the impressiveness or the endorsement as a *reason*: reasons for action, instrumentalism holds, are all and only means-end. It follows that people in the course of project lives will exhibit blind spots when it comes to the reason-giving role their authorities occupy.

5.4

I want now to turn to the form taken by Taylor's and Mill's intellectual collaboration, that is, to address the question of Harriet Taylor's role in the writing that was published under Mill's name. I would normally try to sidestep a gossipy debate on which too many academics spend too much emotionally heated argument; however, in this case it is necessary in order to trace out one further feature that is characteristic of certain sorts of project life, and, in addition, to fill in our picture of Mill's own life-as-project.[17] I should emphasize that the topic I'm taking up is highly controversial.

The positions taken in this tinderbox controversy tend to be predictable from the emotional stakes. Academic males who identify with Mill are likely to insist, often vehemently, that Taylor didn't have much to do with Mill's philosophical output in any way that mattered, and that Mill's without-whom-not acknowledgements are the pro forma thank-yous for spouses that you find in the prefaces of three-quarters of all academic books.[18] Feminist scholars scouring history for role models are likely to insist, equally vehemently, that Taylor was Mill's coauthor, in the most straightforward sense. Over and above the effects of gender identification, there seems to be a tendency to confuse an assessment of whether Harriet Taylor was likeable, and whether she was a nice person, with an answer to the very different question of what role she had in the production of the body of work that (to put it as neutrally as I can) is published with John Stuart Mill listed as the author. Finally, and here the professors' professional biases are coming into play, the question is implicitly being treated as an academic priority dispute. In such disputes, what is being decided is who gets credit for first publication. (Who really wrote it, and who plagiarized?) But what *counts* as being an author is getting taken for granted, and the possibility that there was an unusual division of intellectual labor, one which would preempt a resolution of that priority dispute, and which might require rethinking what counts as authorship, has been taken off the table unnoticed.

Briefly, then, when people express opinions on this topic, it's usually just their emotions and prejudices speaking, and there's nothing like a scholarly consensus. I will do my very best to avoid falling into the trap, but you should take my efforts—like those of just about everybody who writes about it—with an appropriately sized grain of salt; maybe it's just my gut feelings speaking, too.[19]

Here is the basic biographical frame. Born in 1807 (which made her slightly more than a year younger than John Stuart Mill) to a family whose head of household was a physician, at eighteen Harriet Hardy married a pharmacist named John Taylor, and had three children, Herbert, Algernon ('Haji'), and Helen ('Lily,' in 1831). She met Mill in 1830, through a Unitarian clergyman playing intellectual matchmaker; her marriage went through complicated times, and after a while settled into an arrangement in which Taylor and Mill spent a great deal of time together. Both Mill and Taylor suffered from tuberculosis, then the romanticized disease known as "consumption"; Taylor's health started to deteriorate around 1848, although both other illnesses and nineteenth-century medical treatments may have contributed to her decline, and she eventually died of it, in November 1858. Perhaps because of the controversy we are about to take up, it is often hard to get Harriet Taylor herself in focus, once we get past such indisputable biographical elements. Taylor seems to have prompted violent emotional responses in her contemporaries which color and evidently distort their portraits.[20] (See Figure 5.2.)

The trap notwithstanding, here's how I understand the writing to have been produced. With a handful of exceptions, in which Mill "acted chiefly as amanuensis to [his] wife," that is, took dictation, it's not that the text published under Mill's name is written by Taylor.[21] Taylor and Mill both have distinctive prose styles, and after a while it's not that hard to tell them apart; Mill wrote (most or almost all of) what he signed his name to. And it's also not that the arguments were due to Taylor. As I have already had occasion to mention, Mill was a real anomaly in nineteenth-century Britain, someone who by our standards had a professional philosophical competence with argumentation. Taylor didn't have Mill's very unusual training, and we have enough of her writing to be fairly sure that this wasn't a part of her skill set. But that doesn't preclude Taylor's playing a very important role in Mill's writing. On the contrary: Taylor may not have constructed the arguments, but she (often) told Mill what to argue *for*; with an important qualification I'll get to shortly, the *conclusions* are Taylor's.

To a first approximation, the form of the collaboration seems to have been this. Taylor would make up her mind what she thought about some issue, and then Mill would make up an argument for her view and write it up. Taylor decided what subjects Mill would write on, and at one point seems to have made up a list of the book and essay projects that Mill would execute.[22] While she was alive, she closely supervised the product, not letting anything out the door that she wasn't happy with. She edited his drafts, and had him rewrite passage after passage, often many times, until she was satisfied with them. And when, as sometimes happened, she

FIGURE 5.2 Harriet Taylor.
From Arthur Hardy, History of the Hardy Family in South Australia. Courtesy of State Library of South Australia.

changed her mind, the published views changed with it.[23] Mill was, though I'll qualify this claim momentarily, quite deferential: he may have had an argument for *p*, but if Taylor decided that it was going to be not-*p*, he would make up an argument for not-*p*. As we know, and will shortly see firsthand, he was very good at making up arguments.

5.5

One reaction people are likely to have to the picture we've just sketched of the Mill-Taylor collaboration is that, if it's true, Mill can't have been an original and deep thinker. If Mill wasn't the outstanding philosopher and intellectual that he seemed, does he really deserve the attention we are giving him? Partly because I don't want that concern to derail my claim that Mill is a best-case project life, I am going to take time out to explain why we shouldn't assume that if the conclusions were chosen by Taylor, Mill isn't an interesting philosopher. But a few steps further on I'll also explain why it's an oversimplification to put it that way.

A surprisingly large part of the practice of philosophy is retelling the history of philosophy, and it's an important metaphilosophical question—I mean, a philosophical question about philosophy itself—why this is so. Now, the many professional philosophers who think of themselves primarily as historians, writing books about Kant, Hume, Mill, Aristotle, etc., present themselves as trying to tell you what the great dead men thought. Yet when you read the better historians, you often enough run into exciting philosophical ideas; these are frequently ideas that you not only had failed to notice while reading the texts they are explaining, but which every interpreter for hundreds and sometimes a couple of thousand years had failed to notice. You also find that historians disagree on what the great dead man said and thought. Because the interpretations disagree so dramatically, not all of the ideas they attribute to the historical figure can actually be his own (at least, if he was more or less consistent). It is hard not to draw the conclusion that the better historians are inventing new ideas, which they are somehow reading into their texts. Historians (the better ones, anyhow) are doing original philosophy in the guise of history.

Such philosophers are like oysters: just as oysters proverbially need grains of sand around which to form their pearls, so these historians need a text to anchor them while they think their way through a menu of philosophical problems. What they produce, when they are anchored in this way, can be original and deep and novel, rather than merely what the philosopher they are interpreting already said and thought.

I suspect that what looks like a quirky psychological handicap is prevalent in the world of academic philosophy for more or less the reasons that Mill behaved this way. It's an unfortunate aspect of the sociology of academia that students become philosophy professors through apprenticeships during which they often become used to deferring to authorities. And those apprenticeships (and so, their lives in philosophy) are often embarked upon with very little reflectiveness in the first place: for the most part, our philosophy professors have *stumbled* into philosophy, typically choosing their specializations within the field on the basis of such extraneous considerations as compatibility with a prospective dissertation adviser, or his presumed ability to give them a leg up in the profession. Like Mill, they are unable to give compelling reasons for adopting the career-sized project they have taken on, and, like Mill, they cope with it by anchoring their project in an authority: a body of texts, in such cases, rather than, as in Mill's, a series of living human beings.

As we will see, the philosophical system that Mill left us is magnificently inventive. So perhaps we should think of Mill as being like these historians of philosophy. Instead of producing readings of Aristotle, or Kant, or Plato, he produced readings of the pronouncements of Harriet Taylor—as well as, earlier and later in his life, of James Mill, Jeremy Bentham, and Helen Taylor. In doing so, he found creative ways of spinning what they told him; he found muscular and often surprising arguments to support the creatively reinterpreted conclusions, and ingenious ways of fitting them together. The historiography of philosophy instructs us that this sort of exercise is (sometimes) a way of thinking original and powerful thoughts; so it proved in Mill's case, and he himself once asked: "Do we not ... see that as much genius is often displayed in explaining the design and bringing out the hidden significance of a work of art, as in creating it?" (I:333)

Not everyone who lives his life as a project philosophizes. But among those who do, we should not be surprised to encounter the philosophical oyster: project lives tend to produce authorities for themselves; it is natural for deference to an authority figure to appear as the tendency to couch one's own views as explications of the pronouncements of the authority. It is, however, important not to underestimate the degree of autonomy that philosophizing—and choices—of this kind can exhibit. Just as historians of philosophy are evidently inventing their own ideas, which they attribute to the figure they purport to be interpreting, so Mill sometimes managed to gloss the views of his own authorities into very nearly their contraries, when he decided that the opinion he had been mandated was, for one reason or another, mistaken.

That means that the apparent deference to the authority figures in such an intellectual life can be misleading. When Mill tells Taylor, "I should like every one to know that I am the Dumont & you the originating mind, the Bentham, bless her" (XIV:112), we remember how much of the shape and style given to Bentham's fragmentary and obsessively composed manuscripts was due to Dumont. And there is still more elbow room than even that observation allows. As we'll see in due course, Mill thought it was very important to see both sides of an issue, and so when he invented arguments on demand, he would usually be trying to balance them against opposing arguments.[24] Finally, while Mill did adopt an exaggerated posture of deference toward his authority figures, these were authorities that he had chosen for himself—in the case of the first of them, as we have seen, by retroactively endorsing the project into which he had been raised, and in Taylor's case, in the course of selecting a romantic partner.[25]

Thus I am not suggesting that Mill merely argued for positions handed down to him by others; the more complicated state of affairs was that although Mill found it necessary to see his father, and then his wife and stepdaughter, as authority figures, he managed to construe them, much or most of the time, as endorsing—and even as dictating to him—ideas, activities, or versions of their proposals at which he had arrived himself.

Our first lesson from the argument that Vogler finds in Mill is evidently that project lives must have anchors, willy-nilly, and that, when it comes to those anchors, there will be a strong tendency for the owner of the project to lose his grip on the reality in front of him. A second upshot of our discussion is that philosophy can be performed as exegesis, and that this too will be typical of (philosophizing) project lives. In some earlier foreshadowing, I indicated that Mill responded to his realization that all was not well with the project that he had inherited by improving it. We can now expect that improvement to have taken the form of *reinterpreting* the theoretical position of his mentors. To explain his reinterpretation, we need to arrive at a clearer picture of the problem that Mill thought he had to solve, and to do that, we have to determine what his final diagnosis of his Mental Crisis really was. Over the coming two chapters, I will take up that task, starting off with Mill's suggestion that his solution to the problem of free will was crucial to his having emerged from his first round of depression.

Right now, because there are a good many balls in the air, let's quickly take stock of where we are. I am happy with the way Vogler reconstructs the argument which Mill advanced as the diagnosis of his Mental Crisis. But we should not mistake it for the correct account of what was going on during that episode; on the contrary. I've just suggested that Mill resolved the problem at the bottom of that argument by adopting authority figures—that is, via what was by his own lights a completely unprincipled device. Mill identified a number of other issues, none of which were what I have been trying to convince you was in fact the occasion for the Crisis; his subsequent efforts were devoted both to those *and* to the real cause of his Mental Crisis. We're about to consider his very interesting, and more-than-serviceable responses.

6 Logic and the Problem of Necessity

Describing the tail end of his famous Mental Crisis, or perhaps its less-well-known sequels, John Stuart Mill tells us: "during the later returns of my dejection, the doctrine of Philosophical Necessity"—what we now call determinism—"weighed on my existence like an incubus."[1] Even allowing for a Victorian literary vocabulary, this is an emotionally charged moment in Mill's writing; an incubus, you will recall, is a supernatural sexual predator. And in a draft of a letter to Florence Nightingale, Mill crossed out, perhaps as too personal, a remark on "the chapter on Free Will & Necessity" in the *System of Logic*, of which he said: "I have always attached much value [to it] as being the writing down of a train of thought which had been very important to myself many years before, & even (if I may use the expression) critical in my own development" (XV:706n).

With signage like this, we should not underestimate the importance of freedom of the will in making sense of Mill's life and thought. Over and above its biographical interest, a philosopher as subtle and innovative as Mill might be expected to have important ideas about the problem of free will. Nevertheless, Mill's treatment of the topic is so badly neglected that I have found most philosophers to be unaware that he had one. Perhaps this is because parts of the treatment are unmarked, and distributed over much more of his written work than the chapter he could not quite bring himself to press on Nightingale; perhaps because a hasty reading of the chapter is likely to make his ideas seem more familiar and less interesting than they are.[2] Mill's treatment of freedom of the will is of special interest to us as an illustration of the manner in which he inflected his inherited life project to address his own very personal concerns; chief among those, I will eventually suggest, was the philosophical claustrophobia which I mean to show was an effect of identifying his life with a unifying project.

Mill understood the traditional arguments about free will to have been driven by the conflation of two very different theses, and consequently he worked his way through the problem in two stages. The first, which I will take up in this chapter, was a treatment of determinism that, quite surprisingly, required a novel solution to the problem of induction; this solution in turn invoked a theory of the history of science, and a radically revisionist account of deductive logic. To anticipate the next chapter, the second stage developed a more contemporary approach to freedom of the will, one which construed the free and unfree will in terms of structural features of a personality. Both will be opportunities for an introduction to Mill's signature style of systematic philosophy.

6.1

Let's rehearse a fairly standard version of the problem of induction (by which I mean a version that gets presented to undergraduate classes nowadays: the point now is not nuance). *Induction* here means inference that takes us from observed features of our empirical world to as-yet-unobserved features of it. For instance (and using a very crude induction-by-enumeration as a surrogate for induction generally), the sun rose this morning, it rose yesterday morning, it rose two mornings ago, and so on. So, we infer, the sun will rise tomorrow morning. (Figure 6.1.) Induction (construed broadly, rather than merely as induction-by-enumeration) is absolutely essential if we are successfully to navigate the world, and the problem of induction is to explain why it is that conclusions of the sort we just drew are at all legitimate.

To see why this *is* a problem, notice that our toy inductive argument looks like it has a missing premise, without which the conclusion does not follow. It is hard (and Mill agrees that it is hard) to formulate the missing premise cleanly, but the force of it must be something on the order of a general claim to the effect that the future will resemble the past (or more generally that unobserved cases will resemble observed cases). Following Mill, and just to have a name for it, let's call the missing

1. The sun rose this morning.
2. The sun rose yesterday morning.
3. The sun rose two mornings ago.
   . . . and so on.
4. So, the sun will rise tomorrow morning.

FIGURE 6.1 An induction by enumeration.

1. If many As are Bs, the rest are. (A dummy version of the Law of Universal Causation.)
2. If many inductions are valid, the rest are.
3. Induction *a* was valid.
4. Induction *b* was valid.
5. Induction *c* was valid.
   ... and so on
6. The rest of the inductions are valid.
7. An induction is valid *means*: if many As are Bs, the rest are.
8. If many As are Bs, the rest are.

FIGURE 6.2 A viciously circular argument for the Law of Universal Causation.

premise the Law of Universal Causation.[3] How is the Law of Universal Causation itself to be established?

There are evidently two possibilities. The Law of Universal Causation could be a necessary truth, something on the order of a theorem of mathematics. But this is implausible, for it would then be necessary that if the sun has risen on previous mornings, it rise tomorrow; and that the sun will rise tomorrow is surely contingent, something that might or might not happen (and that might or might not happen even if the sun has always risen in the past). On the other hand, the Law of Universal Causation could be an empirical fact. But we are using "induction" as our generic label for inferences to empirical fact; so the argument for the Law of Universal Causation will contain the Law of Universal Causation as a premise. But in that case, it is evidently question-begging and viciously circular: "If, then, the processes [of inductive argument for the Law of Universal Causation] require that we should assume the universality of the very law ... is not this a *petitio principii*?" (VII:563; see Figure 6.2, and notice that the conclusion at step 8 repeats the premise at step 1.) To explain Mill's treatment of induction, however, we first have to explain—as briefly as possible—his theory of the syllogism.[4]

6.2

Both traditional and contemporary philosophical logic agree on this: deductive inference—viz., inference that gives you an ironclad guarantee that the conclusions are true if the premises are—is the core of logic. Deductive logic represents first-class reasoning; induction is reasoning, to be sure, but looks second-class by comparison (because the guarantee seems weaker, but also because, as a panoply of paradoxes reminds us, it is not well understood). A good deal of cognition (such as analogizing), which ordinary people treat seriously enough, is often not even counted as second-class reasoning, but gets stripped of the title of inference entirely.[5]

Mill disagreed. He held the surprising view that syllogisms, the rendering of deductive inference he had inherited, weren't reasoning or inference at all. (He did, however, agree about the importance of using syllogisms: "a large portion of our

1. All men are mortal.
2. The Duke of Wellington is a man.
3. So the Duke of Wellington is mortal.

FIGURE 6.3 A familiar syllogism.

1. Albert was a man, and he died.
2. Bernie was a man, and died too.
3. Charlie was a man, and he died as well.

$$\vdots$$

4. The Duke of Wellington is a man.
5. So Duke of Wellington is going to die also.

FIGURE 6.4 The real inference masked by the syllogism.

knowledge," he says, "is thus acquired" [VII:185].) Syllogisms, Mill argued, would be question-begging if they were taken as properly so-called inferences. To see why, consider a very traditional example of a syllogism, one that proceeds from the premises that all men are mortal, and that the Duke of Wellington is a man, to the conclusion that the Duke of Wellington is mortal (Figure 6.3). Now an argument begs the question if one of the premises presupposes or asserts its conclusion. The major premise of our exemplary syllogism asserts, of all the things which fall under the first concept (all men) that they fall under the second (they're mortal). So what the major premise is really asserting is the (very long, maybe infinitely long) conjunction: that A is mortal, and B is mortal, and C is mortal ... (where A, B, C, etc. are all the men). The Duke of Wellington was a man, and so a claim about his mortality will appear in one of the conjuncts in that long conjunction; that is, one of the things the major premise of the exemplary syllogism is asserting is that the Duke of Wellington is mortal. But that is of course the conclusion of the syllogism.[6]

In effect, then, you've already asserted the conclusion when you asserted the major premise, because the conclusion is hidden in the major premise. After all, suppose someone didn't believe the conclusion: suppose he didn't believe that the Duke of Wellington was mortal; suppose that it really was an open question for him. (That's why he needs an argument: to convince him on this point.) Then he won't, or shouldn't, agree to the major premise, since it should also be an open question for him whether all men *are* mortal. (What about the Duke?) Mill concludes that if syllogisms *were* reasoning, they'd be *terrible* (because viciously circular) reasoning. So they're not reasoning at all.

The real inference, Mill claims, is from particulars to particulars: from the fact that A is mortal, and that B is mortal, and that C is mortal ... (where A, B, C, etc. are all the men you've previously observed to be mortal, i.e., to have died), and that W is a man (where W is a new, hitherto unobserved instance), to: W is mortal.[7] (See Figure 6.4.)

The major premise of the syllogism—the general or universal statement—isn't, Mill maintains, actually part of the inference at all. Rather, it's something on the order of a memorandum you've written to yourself, reminding you of what you're willing to infer from the evidence you've seen:

> The memorandum reminds us, that from evidence, more or less carefully weighed, it formerly appeared that a certain attribute might be inferred wherever we perceive a certain mark.... But when we conclude that the Duke of Wellington is mortal, we do not infer this from the memorandum, but from the former experience. (VII:194–195)

> If a person is asked a question, and is at the moment unable to answer it, he may refresh his memory by turning to a memorandum which he carries about with him. But if he were asked, how the fact came to his knowledge, he would scarcely answer, because it was set down in his note-book: unless the book was written, like the Koran, with a quill from the wing of the angel Gabriel. (VII:186)

In other words, the "major premise" of a syllogism is not really a *premise*. This is a startling move. The central task of philosophy of logic is ordinarily taken to be the explanation of the *must* of deductive logic: of the force that moves you from the premises of a valid inference to its conclusion. But where you might have thought that the validity of syllogistic inference was known a priori, and that it was a self-evident truth of logic, it turns out to be not even a truth of logic at all: there *is* no validity of syllogistic inference to explain. All there is is a notetaking technique, something on a par with dayplanners, datebooks, and organizers. Inference, properly so called, is without exception *inductive* inference.[8]

6.3

We can now do a first pass over Mill's solution to the problem of induction. That inductions work is what licenses us to use them. There is a long track record of inductions working, and so, by an inductive argument, we can infer that the next induction will (likely) work. This would be question begging if the claim that inductions work—more or less, the Law of Universal Causation—were a premise in the argument for the conclusion that the next induction will work. But it is not: in such an argument, it has the role of a major premise in a syllogism, namely, that of a reminder, one which helps us keep track of the force of the real premises of the argument; it is not, that is, really a premise at all. And since it is not a premise, it is not a question-begging premise either.

Here is Mill's own explanation:

In what sense, then, can a principle, which is so far from being our earliest induction, be regarded as our warrant for all the others? In the only sense, in which (as we have already seen) the general propositions which we place at the head of our reasonings when we throw them into syllogisms, ever really contribute to their validity.

The uniformity of the course of nature ... the ultimate major premise of all inductions ... will ... stand to all inductions in the relation in which, as has been shown at so much length, the major premise of a syllogism always stands to its conclusion; not contributing at all to prove it, but being a necessary condition of its being proved.

The assertion, that our inductive processes assume the law of causation, while the law of causation itself is a case of induction, is a paradox, only on the old theory of reasoning, which supposes the universal truth, or major premise, in a ratiocination, to be the real proof of the particular truths which are ostensibly inferred from it. According to the doctrine maintained in the present treatise, the major premise is not the proof of the conclusion, but is itself proved, along with the conclusion from the same evidence.[9]

Is this a satisfactory solution to the problem of induction? Or is it just a clever trick? Bear in mind that some of Mill's views are no longer intellectually available to us; we no longer understand deduction syllogistically, and if I am right about how Mill's ideas fit together into a larger architecture, we will not be able to directly endorse or appropriate the further moves that depend on his outdated view of the forms of deduction. Nonetheless, that we can no longer help ourselves to his solution doesn't entail that it *was* only a clever trick. In spirit it is almost exactly R. B. Braithwaite's quite respectable mid-twentieth-century attempt on the problem.[10] Braithwaite distinguished rules of inference from premises, claimed that there were well-supported inductive arguments for induction, and that these were not viciously circular because the conclusion did not appear in the list of premises (but only as a restatement of the force of the underlying inference rule). Braithwaite seems to have been entirely unaware that he was following in Mill's footsteps; when he looked for historical anticipations, the philosopher he came up with was Charles Sanders Peirce.

But Mill did better than Braithwaite. Where Braithwaite has nothing more to support his distinction, and the use he makes of it, than bald and reiterated assertion, Mill has his theory of deductive logic. And the fit is so neat that it is hard not to suppose that Mill's theory of deduction was not meant as a standalone: that it was in fact tailored to provide a solution to the problem of induction.

6.4

We now need to turn to the motivations for Mill's philosophy of logic. Part of the story is already on our plate; it was meant as part of the ideological underpinnings of the Radical or Utilitarian political program. A quick reminder: Bentham and his followers generally took the view that many of the institutions making up the British economic and political system had nothing to be said for them, and the application of Utilitarian cost-benefit analyses would sweep them away. Their opponents, often Church of England apologists, tended to characterize their own claims as not requiring supporting argumentation, inasmuch as they were necessary truths, self-evident and known a priori.[11] After all, the truths of logic and mathematics were agreed to be self-evident and a priori, so why should Tory moral, political, and religious claims be problematic on that account? Mill, adopting the bite-the-bullet attitude that characterized much of his philosophical work, decided to show that logic and mathematics were empirical sciences, just like chemistry and physics: that there *were* no necessary or a priori truths.[12]

There's a further and more purely philosophical characterization of his motivations to be given, however. Mill had been greatly influenced by the French Positivist Auguste Comte. An admirer early on (they parted ways over Comte's views on the "nature" and status of women), Mill eventually wrote a lengthy review of Comte's life and work, meant to popularize it to an English-speaking audience.[13] While he was quite critical of much of Comte's position, he did endorse the following part of Comte's philosophy of science.

Sciences normally progress through three stages, the theological, the metaphysical, and the positive. In the theological stage of a science, gods or other anthropomorphic agents operate as explainers; for instance, in the theological stage of physics, physical objects are understood to move because a god is pushing or pulling them; or again, in the theological stage of psychology, a Homeric hero makes his self-destructive decisions because a goddess has intervened. During the metaphysical stage of a science, the gods, spirits, and so on are replaced by forces; physical objects move because forces act on them, and people make decisions because psychological forces (perhaps drives) sway them. A force, however, is just a depersonalized god, a supernatural agent with a little less character, and so successful sciences eventually progress to the positive stage, in which the forces are eliminated, and all that is left are *patterns*: the laws of physics, which summarize observed regularities, and so allow one to predict, given initial conditions, the future positions of physical objects; or psychological laws (such as, Mill thought, the laws of association) which likewise allow predictions. As sciences mature, they pass from stage to stage, and fully mature science no longer invokes forces of any kind.[14]

Now what of the science of logic (as Mill understood it, namely, as investigating the prescriptive laws of thought)? At an early stage, perhaps so early that we do not really have an historical record of it, conclusions would have followed from premises because a deity intervened to make them follow.[15] At a later stage (our own), conclusions follow from premises with *logical necessity*, a special sort of force or compulsion that *makes* the conclusion true—or that makes you draw the conclusion. That we are still stuck at this stage is evidenced by the peculiar emphasis that philosophers sometimes give to phrases that are supposed to express the 'logical must': if the premises are true, the conclusion has *got* to be true, too. But when logic becomes a mature science, the 'logical must' will be dispensed with: there will be no mysterious, supernatural, almost-theological force on the scene, but simply patterns: when these premises are true, these conclusions are true also.

We can now say what Mill took himself to be doing in his magnum opus, the *System of Logic*: he was moving (or attempting to move) logic from its metaphysical stage to its mature positive stage. The special hardness of the deductive logical *must* was disposed of by arguing, we saw, that there was, tradition to the contrary, really no such thing as deductive inference. And inductive inference was reconstrued in terms of patterns in the phenomena. Phenomena repeat themselves, and we make predictions on the basis of the repeating patterns, in something like the way that, following the patterns in the Persian rug, we predict that the same pattern is to be found under the sofa, where we cannot now see it.[16] Fortunately, the activity of making predictions of certain kinds, and having them come out true, itself forms a pattern, and we come to predict that further such predictions will be borne out. But nowhere in all of this is there a *must* or a *has to* that requires the sort of explanation that philosophers of logic so naturally find on their agendas. The deep solution to the problem of induction is to show that there is no problem, because what is being asked for is an argument for an inductive logical must. But the idea that a logical must—inductive or otherwise—is needed is a vestige of an immature stage of the science of logic.[17]

6.5

The doctrine of "Philosophical Necessity" is that, "given the motives which are present to an individual's mind, and given likewise the character and disposition of the individual, the manner in which he will act might be unerringly inferred" (VIII:836f); that is, it is a claim about the probable success of a class of inductive inferences. Mill thinks that this claim is obviously true, and that the contrary view is an implausible philosophical invention motivated by the notion that determinism is "inconsistent with every one's instinctive consciousness, as well as humiliating to the pride and even degrading to the moral nature of man" (VIII:836)—roughly because, if everything you do is in principle predictable, it can't really be up to *you*. Mill's ground-clearing engagement with the problem of freedom of the will was an attempt to show that determinism needn't be experienced as particularly demoralizing.[18]

We have already encountered Mill's associationist psychology, and so we can say fairly directly what is surprising about Mill's response to determinism, namely, that Mill thinks that the *problem* is that determinism is depressing, and that's a matter of associations, which can be fixed. Words like "Necessity" (or "determination") make you think of coercion; that is, they are associated with something on the order of images of being dragged around by a rope attached to your neck, or perhaps having your arm twisted behind your back by the schoolyard bully. Mill points out that necessitarians tend to be fatalists, even though this is not an entailment of the position; "[t]he associations derived from the ordinary sense of the term [Necessity] will adhere to it in spite of all we can do" (VIII:839). The idea of prediction is associated with the idea of necessity; the idea of necessity is associated with the idea of coercion; the idea of coercion is associated with the idea of pain. So when you think of your own predictability, your mind traverses the chain of associations, and you find the thought painful. But if we get rid of the *idea* of "Necessity," then the chain of associated ideas is broken; there will be nothing to carry your mind to the idea (and feeling) of pain. And so Mill is "inclined to think that [his opponents'] error is almost wholly an effect of the associations with a word; and that it would be prevented, by forbearing to employ, for the expression of the simple fact of causation, so extremely inappropriate a term as Necessity."[19]

Forbearing to employ the word (and more importantly, expunging the idea), when what is in question is inference, is just taking the step from the metaphysical to the positive stage of the science of logic. Logic, Mill has already argued, is entirely inductive; it is equivalent to the study of causation. Logic in its positive stage "repudiates ... the feeling of some more intimate connexion, of some peculiar tie, or mysterious constraint exercised by the antecedent over the consequent" (VIII:837f). Inductions trace predictively valuable patterns in nature—if *this* happens, then *that* happens next—and that is all they do. If you are able to keep Mill's deflationary understanding of logic in mind, the bad associations will fade away, and even though your actions will be in principle entirely predictable, *you'll* be fine.

Mill's account of deduction, I suggested, was meant to dovetail with his solution to the problem of induction; both of these were jointly a way of moving logic into its positive stage; and that, we now see, enabled Mill's treatment of freedom of the will.

6.6

The worry that your actions are jointly determined by the stimuli that impinge upon you and your character, and that your "character [was] formed ... by agencies beyond [y]our control" (I:175/A 5:18) was, for John Stuart Mill, not the distant or fanciful preoccupation it is for today's introductory philosophy classes. Mill had been home-schooled; recall that he grew up sharing a table with his father, who spent much of that time working on his *History of India*. James Mill divided his attention between his own work, his child's homework (Mill remembers having to interrupt him to ask Greek vocabulary questions [I:9/A 1:4]), and—we must suppose—administering rewards and punishments (praise and blame, for the most part) intended, precisely, to shape little John Stuart's character.

Associationist psychology, to which we have been introduced in sections 3.3 and 5.1, entailed that people's choices and actions are predictable in principle; traditional arguments against freedom of the will pointed out (as they do today) that if there is this sort of predictability-in-principle, it follows that your choices are determined by features of your environment which are external to you and, if one steps far enough back, prior to your very existence. Now "in principle" is, for most people, just that: we cannot observe people's characters—the accreted mental traces of their experiences—directly, and we cannot observe their histories closely enough to reconstruct them; even, Mill writes, an "oriental despot" could not command the resources needed for this sort of spying (VIII:865). But Mill had been brought up to have what he came to call a "confirmed character,"[20] one whose contours had been very closely observed while they were being formed, and which had been made pretty much public: his choices were predictable, not just in principle but, for too wide a range of choice situations, in practice. What get abstractly described in philosophy classes as the features of one's external environment which determine one's behavior wore, in Mill's case, the forbidding and very vivid face of his own father. The thought that one's will might not be free was, in John Stuart Mill's case, inseparable from the thought that he had not escaped parental control.[21] And even once his father had passed on, Mill would have been quite aware of how those around him construed the deference he showed Harriet Taylor; the issue would not have abated of its own accord.

We will return to this *ur*-scene from Mill's childhood. In the meantime, it will serve as a stopgap answer to the inevitable question: why was the philosophizing we have just seen so evidently driven by the feeling that he was not really free? Let's turn now to a handful of observations.

We have just seen Mill's mature philosophical style, and in fact our overview has traversed a great deal of ambitious, high-octane theory construction. That Mill had produced so very much in the way of theory means that a substantial part of his life project had been reallocated to a sort of philosophizing that was—as least on the face of it—quite distant from the urgent political concerns that organized the project as it had been bequeathed to him. We are seeing an initial (but nevertheless sizable) way in which Mill reconfigured his life project, and his swerve from the path laid out by his mentors is further circumstantial evidence that what it had been lacking, in his eyes, was theoretical acuity and depth.

Second, that philosophical style is systematic: many different philosophical positions, on many apparently very distant topics, are engineered so that one provides premises in the argument for the surprising account of the other.

Analogies are often asymmetrical, and here is one of them: although David Lewis was never anything like the John Stuart Mill of the twentieth century, Mill was the David Lewis of the nineteenth.

The arguments such system-building makes possible have a sort of sweep that is quite unusual in contemporary philosophy. Here the trajectory of a single argument carried us from philosophy of logic, to the problem of induction, to a theory of the history of science, and then to associationist psychology, all in the interests of a solution to the traditional philosophical problem (usually placed under the rubric of metaphysics) of freedom of the will. Moreover, the different positions which Mill constructed in these—as we think of them nowadays—different subspecialities of philosophy were startlingly iconoclastic (as was the position he adopted from Comte, if indeed he did adopt it, as opposed to inventing it independently). They were typically arrived at by rejecting a premise no one had so much as imagined questioning, then resetting the parameters of the problem, that is, deciding afresh what would count as a solution to it, and, finally, working up a novel position, from scratch, to meet those constraints. One unfortunate side effect of Mill's philosophical depth and sheer originality has been that his most powerful work has not infrequently gone unrecognized. For instance, for contemporary philosophers of logic, Mill's treatment of deductive logic is so far out of the ballpark that, even if they are acquainted with it (most of them are not), they do not know what its philosophical agenda was. His solution to the problem of induction is so deeply revisionist in its understanding of what the problem is that it is widely believed these days that Mill was not trying to solve the problem of induction at all.[22] And recall that I began the chapter by observing that Mill's solution to the problem of determinism remains largely unremarked.

We will later on have a use for the fact that it took Mill much of a lifetime to work out the intellectual machinery deployed in the argument we have just sketched. In the meantime, we can observe that what helped him out of his Mental Crisis could only have been its central idea. We still do not know, however, how this idea helped to resolve the Mental Crisis, nor how it was connected with the initial diagnosis which we reviewed in chapter 5, nor how it is to be squared with the other announced resolutions of the Mental Crisis—though, having by now seen Mill's signature style, we can expect all of these to fit together rather neatly. It is time to turn from Mill's groundclearing exercise to his constructive account of freedom of the will.

7 Mill's Incubus

We've now seen how Mill understood the traditional arguments about free will to have been driven by a confusion, and how he devoted a great deal in the way of intellectual resources to making the case that determinism is not something we ought to find distressing. But determinism, Mill came to think, masked a very different but real problem which, adapting one of his turns of phrase, I'm going to call *moral unfreedom*. Moral unfreedom *should* be distressing, and when we get to the bottom of the problem posed by Philosophical Necessity, we will find moral unfreedom, and not the more traditional concern, to have been Mill's incubus.

Because moral unfreedom is neither metaphysically inevitable nor inevitable in practice, steps can be taken to forestall it. As he emerged from his Mental Crisis, the content of Mill's life project shifted accordingly. That project officially consisted in the pursuit of the general utility, and its pursuit was supposed to ensure Mill's own happiness, that is, his private utility. The first consequence of Mill's reinterpretation of the problem of freedom of the will was a new and more sophisticated explication of the concept of utility, one that framed his further changes to the project's substantive content.

7.1

Let's introduce the notion of moral unfreedom by stepping through the following passages, which, however, I'm presenting out of order:

A person feels morally free who feels that his habits or his temptations are not his masters, but he theirs: who even in yielding to them knows that he could resist; that were he desirous of altogether throwing them off, there would not be required for that purpose a stronger desire than he knows himself to be capable of feeling. (VIII:841)

[I]n common use [the term Necessity] stands for the operation of those causes exclusively, which are supposed too powerful to be counteracted at all ... [But] human actions ... are never (except in some cases of mania) ruled by any one motive with such absolute sway, that there is no room for the influence of any other. (VIII:839)

We feel, that if we wished to prove that we have the power of resisting [any particular] motive, we could do so.[1] ... it would be humiliating to our pride, and (what is of more importance) paralysing to our desire of excellence, if we thought otherwise. (VIII:838)

Moral unfreedom consists in monomania. Putting the characterization a bit more formally than Mill himself did, the will is free—that is, morally free—when, for any motivation you have, there are psychologically available to you further motivations which you could marshal to trump it. Because the phrase is slightly misleading to twenty-first-century ears, it is worth adding that the notion is not restricted to what we would think of as moral matters.[2] Moral freedom is a state of character: a near-equilibrium, in which one's motivations are in relative balance with each other.

Why would Mill have been concerned with moral unfreedom? We saw Mill being quick to imply that monomania is unusual. For most people worried about freedom of the will, getting clear about determinism (and, in particular, seeing that it's not the same thing as fatalism—as helplessly ending up doing what you're condemned to do, whether you want to or not) is the end of the story, because they do not have to worry about what is, after all, a psychiatric disorder. If Mill was nonetheless preoccupied by moral unfreedom, we need to entertain the possibility that, rarity notwithstanding, he thought himself to be—or have been—morally unfree. And so to explain how Mill could have seen himself as possessing a character trait tantamount to monomania, we will take a detour through his psychology. However, our entry point will be, not his overtly psychological writings, but a passage in his ethics.

7.2

Mill introduced a new device into the utilitarian conceptual toolkit, the distinction between higher and lower pleasures: if a preponderance of those who have experienced both of two pleasures prefer any of one to any amount, however great, of the other, then the former is a higher pleasure. "Pleasures" is the Millian way of talking about goods generally, and so Mill is telling us that some goods, and some reasons, are lexicographically (I'll just say "lexically") ranked over others. A lexical ranking—contemporary terminology, not Mill's—is one that resembles alphabetization in the following respect: letters in the second position only make a difference to the alphabetical ordering of two words if the letters in the first position are the same; if the first letter of one word is "a," and the first letter of another word is "b," the former will come earlier in the dictionary, no matter what their remaining letters are. Analogously, if one kind of pleasure is lexically ranked over another, then varying amounts of the latter, outranked pleasure will make a difference to the overall assessment of two options only if both options deliver the same in the way of the former kind of pleasure. Bear in mind that this is a *formal* characterization: as far as the definition goes, anyway, a "higher" pleasure isn't necessarily a "classier" pleasure. Substantive characterizations of the higher pleasures have to be argued for separately.[3]

Mill introduced the higher pleasures in the course of setting up what is nowadays called the *decided preference criterion*: the appeal to the preferences of the more experienced to determine what option you ought to consider more desirable. Very typically, he was trying to get more than one philosophical job done at a time; we will give the decided preference criterion more extended discussion in due course, but for now, let's pause to distinguish two of those jobs.

Mill, we know, was an instrumentalist; that is, he believed that reasoning about what to do was solely a matter of means-end reasoning. We've seen that instrumentalist choices bottom out in desires that you aren't in a position to justify. The flip side of that consequence is that the desires that serve as inputs to your means-end reasoning cannot themselves be corrected by reasoning. That is, if instrumentalism is true, you can't give an *argument* whose conclusion is that you're making a mistake about what you want.

Now, many moral philosophers today (like many nonphilosophers who implicitly have these views) can't quite swallow this upshot of the view. Sometimes that's just squeamishness: people can want just *anything*; moral philosophers are mostly professors, these days, and lead quite sheltered lives; people leading sheltered lives often don't have the stomach for saying that it's practically rational to do one or another awful-sounding thing, if it gets you something you happen to want. But there's a more principled problem as well, namely, that you can get what you wanted and still be disappointed, and conversely, that you can be pleasantly surprised by something you hadn't wanted—or, as we say it colloquially, hadn't known you wanted. Surely rational choice anticipates such changes of heart when it can, and so today informed-desire (or informed-preference) theorists correct the inputs to deliberation, by taking as their standard for the correctness of your desires and preferences what you *would* want if, say, you knew more. The inputs to your practical deliberation are being corrected, alright, but not by *reasoning*, which makes the device officially compatible with the instrumentalist restrictions on what reasoning can be: the counterfactuals about your desires are being treated as brute data, in much the way that in less complicated versions of instrumentalism, your raw desires are treated as brute data.

Mill appealed not to counterfactual desires and preferences—the desires and preferences you would have under more optimal circumstances—but to the preferences of others who *do* know more. It's clear, however, that both devices have a common function, namely, to correct those desires (or preferences), noninferentially. Call this the *corrective* function of the higher pleasures. I'll take up corrective uses of the higher pleasures in chapter 8, but notice in the meantime that a preference's being correct, as witnessed by the preferences of other, more experienced people, does not entail that you exhibit the preference.[4]

Because the corrective function of the decided preference criterion makes use of the actual preferences of actual people, the distinction between the higher and lower pleasures also characterizes the operation of certain pleasures or desires or preferences in particular psychological economies. This *descriptive* use of the notion of higher pleasures prescinds from whether they are or are not correct preferences. My concern at this point is the descriptive rather than the corrective notion. That is, I am about to discuss what operates as a higher pleasure for someone: what he would not, as a matter of psychological fact, trade off for all the—and here you can fill in the blank with a suitable contrasting good—in the world. For the remainder of this chapter, when I mention higher and lower pleasures, I will mean, with only clearly marked exceptions, the objects of such uncorrected lexical preferences.

Being a higher pleasure is, on Mill's definition, a relational property: a pleasure is higher with respect to a specific contrasting pleasure. This means that, as far as the definition goes, a pleasure could be higher with respect to another pleasure, while being lower with respect to a third. In *Utilitarianism*, however, Mill writes as though pleasures fall into two *classes*, the higher and the lower, and that raises two questions for us. One is historical: why did Mill come to talk of the pleasures as higher and lower, plain and simple? Right now I want to address a second question, namely, what to make of the further possibilities to which the relation of being a higher pleasure points.[5]

There are many structures that an unconstrained two-place relation might induce, but I am going to concentrate on just two of them. First of all, some pleasures might turn out, as a matter of psychological fact about some particular individual, to be higher than (that is, lexically preferred to) pleasures that are already themselves higher with respect to other pleasures. Second, some psychologies of this sort might exhibit a *highest pleasure*, by which I mean, a pleasure that counts as higher with respect to any other possible object of choice, including other higher pleasures. I should emphasize that this terminology is my own extension of Mill's; he does not talk of "highest pleasures" himself.

7.3

The young John Stuart Mill had been raised to be a political activist, in the service of a radical movement whose declared objective was the Greatest Good for the Greatest Number. He had been brought up to give the general utility lexical priority in his decision-making. His life had been organized as a single large project, in which every, or almost every, activity or enterprise served to advance the Utilitarian political agenda.

Ignore for a moment a possibility that will shortly become important for the argument: that you do something, not because you want to, but out of sheer habit. If we are ignoring it, then, in Mill's psychology, what motivates you must be a desire.

A personality controlled by a highest pleasure is just one that won't sacrifice any of its highest pleasure for any amount of anything else. So to have an objective that trumps any other reason that might present itself *is* to have a "highest pleasure." (Once again, it's a *formal* notion: something can count as a "pleasure," or a "higher pleasure," or, in our extension of Mill's vocabulary, a "highest pleasure," even if it doesn't *sound* like a lot of fun.) The young Mill's mind was a psychology built around a single priority, namely, the organizing end of the Utilitarian political platform. So if we want to see what happens to a personality that is organized around a highest pleasure, we ought to take a close look at Mill himself.

We are told that "the train of thought which had extricated [Mill] from [the problem of freedom of the will[6]] ... forms the chapter on Liberty and Necessity in the concluding Book of [the] *System of Logic*" (I:177/A 5:18). In the final section of that chapter, Mill supplements the associationist psychological theory that he had inherited from his father with an additional piece of apparatus.

In that earlier account, we saw, action was explained by desire; to desire was to associate pleasure with the object of desire.[7] But, Mill pointed out,

a motive does not mean always, or solely, the anticipation of a pleasure or a pain....

As we proceed in the formation of habits, and become accustomed to will a particular act or a particular course of conduct because it is pleasurable, we at last continue to will it without any reference to its being pleasurable. Although, from some change in us or in our circumstances, we have ceased to find any pleasure in the action, or perhaps to anticipate any pleasure as the consequence of it, we still continue to desire the action, and consequently to do it.

A habit of willing is commonly called a purpose [notice that Mill is defining a technical term]; and among the causes of our volitions ... must be reckoned not only likings and aversions, but also purposes. It is only when our purposes have become independent of the feelings of pain or pleasure from which they originally took their rise, that we are said to have [and here comes another definition of a technical term] a confirmed character.[8]

Here Mill is augmenting the older psychological machinery. There are now two ways of explaining action: desire (on the older associationist understanding of it), and habit, the fossilized remains of action on the basis of desire (understood that older way, as equivalent to anticipated pleasure). Just to have a way of keeping the terminology straight, I'm going to continue using the term 'desire' with the older meaning, even though in this passage Mill allows himself to use it in a more generic sense.[9]

We are now ready to connect our initial exploration of the higher pleasures with Mill's discussion of freedom of the will. Moral unfreedom consists in having a motivation that you couldn't resist, even if you wanted to. It's natural to imagine this as a redescription of a lopsided pattern of desires. But such a motivation could also be produced if a pattern of choice became frozen into "a habit of willing." And we can expect that to happen when the relevant type of choice is made repeatedly and always in one way.

A character for whom there are *several* pleasures (an important special case: for whom there are several *higher* pleasures) that are not lexically ranked with respect to one another will, when faced with competing pleasures, presumably choose sometimes one, sometimes the other. But a personality structured around a highest pleasure gives lexical priority to a single object of choice; that is to say, it always makes one type of choice (between its highest pleasure and anything else) in the same way. A personality structured around a highest pleasure should thus be expected to end up morally unfree.

We saw that, as an adolescent, John Stuart Mill's personality was structured around a single, overriding objective; in his psychology, that objective functioned as a highest pleasure. Thus, for Mill, the threat of moral unfreedom was all too live. His modified associationist psychology predicted that someone living a life such as his own would eventually come to be "ruled by ... one motive with such absolute sway, that there [would be] no room for any other"—a state of mind that we saw Mill describe as "mania."

7.4

In our philosophical tradition, a 'free will' sounds like a good thing, and an 'unfree will,' like a bad one. But we have just seen Mill give 'freedom of the will' a novel sense. So why should his 'moral unfreedom' amount to a theoretical or even a personal disaster?

In fact, that question often enough gets the reply that it is no disaster at all: on the contrary. Mill's concern, differently labeled, has come in for a good deal of recent philosophical attention. Daniel Dennett evidently admires

Martin Luther's pronouncement, "I can no other," as the natural expression of a system of motivations in which one motivation always has priority. Harry Frankfurt's extended discussion of "practical necessity" is equally admiring, as is John McDowell's discussion of "silencing," as is Bernard Williams's treatment of much the same phenomenon under the label of "moral incapacity." What Mill thinks of as moral unfreedom has, under other names, been widely taken for the sine qua non of a decent human life.[10]

And, after all, why not? It consists in having a confirmed character of a certain sort. Having a confirmed character is being psychologically capable of going ahead with courses of action you know you're not going to enjoy; that in itself is no more than being a grownup. The particular sort of confirmed character that Mill had become was someone who made an overriding objective of the general utility. If fighting for the Greatest Good of the Greatest Number is laudable, why the distress at the disposition to do so becoming psychologically entrenched? Even if it became *so* psychologically entrenched that Mill could no longer deviate from it, wouldn't that just amount to having an unswervingly virtuous character? Barry Goldwater once insisted that extremism in the defense of liberty is no vice; why isn't singleminded determination in the pursuit of the greatest happiness, great virtue?

Consider for a moment a further consequence of Mill's hedonic psychology. Changes in your desires or pleasures are predicted by the laws of association, as, roughly, the effects of the impact of experience on the system of associations that constitute your character. To return to a very simple example introduced in section 5.1: if, in your current affective configuration, you enjoy seeing and wearing straw hats, and if straw hats are for a while regularly accompanied by bright blue feathers, you will come to enjoy, and so to desire, bright blue feathers. Now, most of your experience is, as far as anyone can tell, mere happenstance. (Who *knew* that blue feathers in straw hats would become a trend?) So what you find to be pleasant and painful, and so, what you desire or dislike, will, normally, change over time. Call the sum of your likes and dislikes your *hedonic profile*. Then we can say that, according to the psychology that served Mill throughout his intellectual life, your hedonic profile evolves under the impact of experience—much of which is, for all intents and purposes, random. If we select a person's hedonic profile at a time as his base state, then, normally, we will expect his profile to drift away from that base state; the more time elapses, the further the profile will depart from it.[11]

Drift is not the only way that hedonic profiles alter. We saw that Mill's account of his own Mental Crisis emphasizes the effects of introspection: a dramatic shift in Mill's hedonic profile was produced by what is perhaps an unusual cause, his carefully trained ability to see through the associations that were responsible for his desires and pleasures. The undermining trains of thought had roughly this sort of content: "I only like straw hats because it's an effect of my conditioning. That's not a very good reason. I guess I really don't like straw hats, after all." Mill thought that too much hard-eyed self-examination had left him a motivational wasteland.

We had our doubts about that: I argued that the young Mill had first committed himself to the Utilitarian program and then disinvested in it as the result of a series of aesthetic responses—the elation of the sublime followed by disappointment in Bentham's obsessive table-thumping—and while Mill himself was not in a position to be articulate about his emotional development at these junctures, they exhibit another manner in which hedonic profiles can change.

Finally for now, you might think that being very clear about the reasons for your preferences would serve to anchor them. For instance, and to take Mill's own case, if he understood himself to have absolutely decisive reasons for his Utilitarian commitments, then shouldn't his Utilitarianism have stood fast against the deconditioning effects that we have just described? However, in section 8.2, we will see Mill describe the processes that undercut even the most thoroughly supported commitments; it turns out that even the best reasons in the world fail to maintain the stability of a hedonic profile. What matters for present purposes is that hedonic profiles are liable to change; Mill's introspective self-analysis was merely one of several possible causes. His psychology predicts that even without it, his hedonic profile would have changed anyway.

Let's ask, then, what is bound to happen to a confirmed character, one whose choices are structured around a highest lexical priority. On the one hand, the effect of having a highest pleasure, Mill discovered, is to lock one's ends and activities into place: "the will, once so fashioned, may be steady and constant, when the passive susceptibilities of pleasure and pain are greatly weakened, or materially changed" (VIII:843). On the other, associative connections are constantly being reshaped by experience—and other things. We expect an individual's hedonic profile to alter over time.

As hedonic profiles evolve, for whatever reason, they are likely to drift away from any locked-in priority. If a confirmed character stays stable, and a person's hedonic profile shifts, eventually that person's purposes and what he enjoys will no longer match. "Will," he tells us, "is the child of desire, and passes out of the dominion of its parent only to come under that of habit. That which is the result of habit affords no presumption of being intrinsically good" (X:239/U 4:11). And so, to have a highest pleasure means, paradoxically, eventually having not much pleasure at all.

Mill's Mental Crisis is routinely described as a depressive episode, and certainly the fifth chapter of his *Autobiography* contains lengthy passages that sound like reports of clinical depression. But when he realized that he did not care about the supreme goal that had structured his life, the problem was not simply that he became depressed. If Mill's affliction *had* only been clinical depression, it would not have been nearly as bad as it was, and it would not have shaped Mill's life and philosophizing as it did.

The deeper problem was that, although he was depressed and unmotivated, he could not *act* depressed. His hedonic profile had undergone a dramatic shift, and was now sharply out of step with his activities, which went on, it must have seemed, almost of their own accord. People who are depressed mope around, can't get out of bed in the morning, and give up on the enterprises for which they have no heart; if Mill had been able to do any of this, he would not have been as desperate as he was. Instead, having realized that he simply did not care about his party's platform, he could not cease working to advance it. The pace of his labors did not slow perceptibly, and hardly any of his acquaintances seem even to have realized that anything was wrong.[12]

The young Mill's personality was built around a highest pleasure—a single lexical priority. Having locked his ends and activities into place, and having then undergone a shift in hedonic profile, caring about nothing he did, he found himself the helpless passenger of his own life, which lurched onward beneath him like an out-of-control robot.

Because associationists analyzed desires as ideas of the objects of desire associated with the idea of pleasure, Mill's hedonistic psychological theory did not allow him to distinguish between what he found pleasant and what he wanted: "desiring a thing and finding it pleasant," he insisted late in life, "are ... in strictness of language, two different modes of naming the same psychological fact" (X:237/U 4:10). But his moral psychology also did not distinguish between what he wanted and what he cared about, what was important to him, what mattered to him, and what concerned him. That means that Mill was unable to express the full gravity of his predicament.[13] Allow that profiles of *concern* shift as well; for all kinds of reasons, what matters to you changes over time. If the pattern of activities and choices you make is locked in, and is unable to move in tandem with your altered sense of what is important to you, eventually you will find yourself, like Mill, pursuing goals about which you no longer care, and which do not matter to you.

Mill described his moving encounter with Wordsworth's "Intimations of Immortality" as helping him emerge from his distraught emotional state, and if I am correct in my reading of what was at the bottom of it, we can say why that particular poem resonated so deeply in Mill's psyche. Mill tells us that "along with the two passages of grand imagery but bad philosophy so often quoted [those lines about "trailing clouds of glory," and so on], I found that he too had had similar experience to mine" (I:149–153/A 5:9–10). And indeed, what we find Wordsworth describing is a course of life (which he makes out to be the normal progress of human existence) in which one becomes motivationally hollowed out, and one's activities, shaped by "imitation" and "custom" to "the inevitable yoke," proceed independently of one's motivational engagement with them. The affective immediacy of childhood is dimly remembered, from the perspective of the adult's alienated personality constructs, as the "time when meadow, grove and stream,/ The earth, and every common sight,/ ... did seem/ Apparelled in celestial light,/ The glory and the freshness of a dream."[14] Poetry, Mill wrote some seven years later, "is the delineation of the deeper and more secret workings of human emotion, [and thus] is interesting only to those to whom it recals what they have felt, or whose imagination it stirs up to conceive what they could feel, or what they might have been able to feel had their outwards circumstances been different" (I:345f). Mill must have felt Wordsworth to be allegorizing the catastrophic mismatch of volitional and hedonic profiles: "The things which I have seen I now can see no more."[15]

7.5

There is more than one way to tell the story of how Mill came to experience that mismatch, and let's return to what I was calling the *ur*-scene of Mill's education for an alternative version of the narrative—one that is, I think, both independently plausible, and compatible with the account I have just given.[16]

As we have seen, John Stuart Mill was brought up under the extremely close supervision of an associationist psychologist, whose approach to his eldest son's education was almost certainly shaped by his theoretical views. The close control of reward and punishment, for the most part praise and blame, would have been used to shape the child's character, and the practically inevitable effect of such an upbringing would have been to make *pleasing his father* into the very young John Stuart Mill's highest pleasure.

As the son grew into youth, and then into adulthood, he developed new interests: a stake in the Utilitarian political project, and personal ambitions that were closely interwoven with it. Mill found himself hoping for a public and political career, one that might realistically lead to a seat in Parliament; to make that possible, he would have to attend university. Leaving home to pursue his studies would have had the additional benefit of releasing him from his father's monitoring—that is, from a situation which, by the time he had become an adolescent, must have been well-nigh unbearable. We can classify these developments as hedonic drift.

James Mill vetoed going to college, on the grounds that Oxford and Cambridge were religious institutions. In the meantime, he had parlayed his *History of India* into a senior management position at the corporation that ran India on behalf of the British government. This put him in a position to find John Stuart Mill a job at the British East India Company . . . where the son's direct supervisor would continue to be his own father. I expect that, had he been sufficiently determined, the younger Mill could have declined the position. But too much practice at conforming to his father's wishes had made the disposition to do so an aspect of a confirmed character. His habits of compliance overrode his changed hedonic profile, and he took up the career in colonial administration which he would follow for most of his adult life.[17] Moral unfreedom was a fraught subject for Mill not least because it was inextricably bound up with regret.

In Bentham, utility is a qualitatively homogenous sensation, something whose quantity it makes sense to try to maximize. Thus, for a Benthamite utilitarian, decision-making is, in principle, an arithmetic exercise, and so to make utility (whether one's own utility or everybody's) one's overriding end, to come to have it as one's highest pleasure, is to commit oneself to determinate answers to choice problems. It is thus also to undergo the training effects of encountering the same choice problem repeatedly: when it's being made correctly, the same choice will always get made in the same way.[18]

By the time we get to the argument for the Principle of Utility, in chapter 4 of Mill's *Utilitarianism*, what 'utility' means has quietly changed—quietly, because the form that Mill's loyalty to his mentors and party leaders took included this way of handling his disagreements with them. Recall that Mill argues there that utility is the only thing that is desirable, on the grounds that any apparent counterexamples, such as money or virtue, that are not merely desirable as a means to something else, but desired on their own account, are thereby parts of utility. As we have observed, that argument makes sense only if utility is understood to be something on the order of a basket of all the intrinsically desired or desirable goods.[19]

Benthamite utility functioned as a full-fledged and very rigid end, determining courses of action that could properly proceed in only one way—or in a very narrow range of ways. Millian utility functions as a very different kind of end (or rather, as we will see in a moment or two, "end"). Because utility is just a collection of items in a basket, the guidance that end gives is guaranteed to be univocal only when the priority relations and the ways of making tradeoffs among the components of utility are fixed.[20] But how often will that happen?

Recall the decided preference criterion, the idea that you appeal to the preferences of the more experienced for guidance in figuring out what those priority relations are. For others' preferences to give you useful guidance, as opposed to amounting to mere noise, they have to—anyway, most of them—agree. That means that the prescriptive or corrective use of a higher pleasure is possible only when most or almost all experienced judges have been conditioned to have the *same* preferences with respect to the relevant contrasting pleasures. But recall that much of the impact of experience on the pattern of associations that constitutes a mind is for all practical purposes random. It follows that shared priorities, such as the (corrective) higher pleasures, require a very demanding sort of explanation, one that simply won't be available most of the time. We will shortly see how these explanations go, because Mill took great pains to show that liberty and justice are higher pleasures, and the elaborateness of those arguments will confirm that last claim.

Generalizing, while there may be a handful of very firm constraints, the priority relations of the components of utility, as Mill reconceived it, for the most part won't be fixed. That means that Millian utility will often give *equivocal* guidance, and that means in turn that you can pursue everybody's utility in a great many different ways without going wrong.

For example, it may be that neither of two higher pleasures is lexically ranked over the other, and we may have to manage tradeoffs between them. As our illustration, let's use the two higher pleasures we've just mentioned, liberty and justice. If you live in Berkeley, you are free to make a number of minor lifestyle choices that are not permitted in Salt Lake City. However, a couple decades back, the Berkeley municipality was found to be setting the parking meters to give short time, presumably in the interest of ticket revenue. As Mill understands justice, this is an infringement of justice that, as far I know, one does not encounter in Salt Lake City. If you have to choose where to live, which of these mixes of liberty and justice should you prefer?

The decided preference criterion suggests appealing to the preferences of the experienced. If it turns out that all, or almost all, of those who have lived in both cities have strong views, and pretty much all the same views, then that tells you what your preference ought to be. If it turns out that opinions are varied, or not particularly emphatic, then both mixes of these higher pleasures should be regarded as allowable options, and you can reasonably consider living in either city. (At this point, you might well defer to your own uncorrected preferences.)

What it means to pursue Millian utility is thus very different from what it means to pursue Benthamite utility. First, because the same end, that is, the same basket of goods, can be pursued in many different ways, there is a great deal of choice left up to you in deciding how to pursue it. Bentham had thought that the Greatest Good of the Greatest Number was best expedited by a campaign for legal reform. Although Mill was quite qualified to follow in Bentham's footsteps (he had read law with John Austin, and you'll remember that he edited Bentham's *Rationale of Judicial Evidence*), he left that project largely to others, and chose utility-promoting enterprises which better suited his own concerns and temperament.[21] You can stick to *this* sort of end, while nonetheless adjusting what you do to match a changing concern profile.

Second, because choices that serve this "end" needn't always be substantively the same choice (you serve utility now by choosing liberty over justice, later by choosing justice over liberty), the exclusive pursuit of utility needn't produce the conditioning effects we suggested Mill had become so very anxious to avoid. Together, these results tell us that there is a way to escape our earlier argument, the one that took us from having a highest pleasure to having a morally unfree character. If one's highest pleasure is an "end" that formally resembles Millian utility in being a basket of ends, the priority relations among which are only sparsely defined, then one can endorse it as one's overriding objective because it is only verbally and not substantively one's end.[22]

Mill availed himself of this option in a very interesting way. He describes a number of lessons he believed himself to have learned from his Mental Crisis: most importantly, that "the internal culture of the individual" was "among the prime necessities of human well-being," and that, under this heading, "the maintenance of a due balance among the faculties ... [was] of primary importance" (I:147/A 5:7). A "due balance among the faculties" is what it takes to be morally free; it means in the first place that no motivation inevitably trumps all one's other motivations, whether one by one, or in concert.[23] Another way to put it is that characters ought to be shaped so that they can have *higher* pleasures, but no substantive high*est* pleasure: a satisfactory personality has a number of substantive and independent priorities, no one of which trumps *all* the rest.[24]

And so, instead of Benthamite legal reform, Mill turned to thinking through institutions that appear to us in retrospect as the framework of a liberal society. But Mill wasn't what today's political philosophers think of as a liberal (that is, someone who is scrupulously neutral when it comes to what their fellow citizens are like and are after), because the point of those institutions was to shape people's characters. The characters Mill's proposed reforms were meant to produce, I want to suggest, were (among other things) personalities capable of reallocating their energies among different higher pleasures, as their hedonic profiles shift: characters whose wills are morally free.

Let's use *On the Subjection of Women* to illustrate the point, rather than *On Liberty*, which I will discuss in the next chapter; this will allow us to correct an impression made by one of Mill's asides. Recall that in the course of introducing the notion of moral freedom, Mill contrasted it with "mania," and did so in a turn of phrase that conveyed the thought that moral unfreedom was rare. However, now that we know how moral unfreedom is produced, we see that this cannot have been Mill's considered view. His portrait of the education and circumstances of the women of his day should lead us to expect that femininity, more or less, will become the first highest pleasure of a person who is subjected to them: "it would be a miracle if the object of being attractive to men had not become the polar star of feminine education and formation of character" (XXI:272/SW 1:11). We should then anticipate that changing hedonic profiles will leave those women trapped in volitional postures that are the shells of their early hedonic profiles. If that is right, the arguments of *Subjection of Women* are meant to promote a legal and social framework in which women's wills can be free.[25]

In adjusting his conception of the Utilitarian program to accommodate the lessons of his Mental Crisis, Mill was doing the very thing we have just described: readjusting the mix of activities, within his pursuit of his overall Utilitarian project, to match his hedonic—and concern—profile. Like victims of abuse who devote their later lives to running shelters, or like self-made men who spend their fortunes on scholarships for the poor, Mill cared very much about making sure that no one would ever have to go through what he had. The design and implementation of social reforms intended to cultivate balanced characters was thus an enterprise he found emotionally compelling, and by choosing to pursue it, he was reshaping his life around his own very personal concerns, and thereby making it a life he inhabited, rather than one he merely occupied.

7.7

Earlier on, we found ourselves wondering how what looked to be the Paradox of Hedonism figured into Mill's resolution of his Mental Crisis; the problems were that Mill seemed to have already taken the medicine he was prescribing, and secondarily, that the diagnosis competes with what he advanced as his primary account of the breakdown. If we wanted, we could call Mill's problem the Paraparadox of Hedonism, and now we are finally in a position to explain it. In order to allow a Utilitarian's activities to track his changing hedonic profile, utility has to be understood to be a basket of goods, and the priority relations between those goods cannot be too completely defined. That means that a person's utility is no longer substantively an end; you cannot pursue it, because when its components are not prioritized with respect to one another, it is typically unclear when a choice serves one's utility, or rather contravenes it.[26] What you *can* pursue are those component ends; and so "happiness ... [i]s only to be attained by not making it the direct end. Those only are happy ... who have their minds fixed on some object other than their own happiness" (I:145–147/A 5:6). That object might be, as in Mill's own case, "the happiness of others, [or] the improvement of mankind," and in such analogously structured cases, although Mill does not emphasize the point, the pursuit of that object will be replaced by the pursuit of one or another component of it: of liberty, or gender equality, or political representation. The happiness of others, just like your own happiness, will thus fall into place, when it does, as a side-effect of the well-structured means-end pursuit of a fully demarcated end. What Mill has discovered is not after all the Paradox of Hedonism, as it has since come to be understood. Your happiness is only sufficiently well defined to serve as the starting point for means-end reasoning if you are, or are on your way to becoming, morally unfree, and if you are, you will sooner or later find yourself miserable, not just because you are not getting what you want, but because you will for the most part be doing something in which you have no personal stake. If your happiness is more loosely defined, then you cannot take steps toward *it*, but only toward more well-defined ends, whose attainment can be thought of as contents of that basket of goods which your happiness is.

In our earlier discussion of Mill's Mental Crisis, we identified a number of apparently incompatible components of his understanding of what was responsible for the Crisis and for his emergence from it. Those pieces of the puzzle fall into place around Mill's two-stage resolution of the problem of freedom of the will—and in particular, his reconception of what that problem was. We turn now to the ways in which Mill reconfigured his life project to accommodate that understanding.

8 Justice, Freedom of Speech, and Other Higher Pleasures

Mill was very concerned to improve the quality of his life project. The one he had inherited was, he had come to realize, intellectually shoddy, and not very well thought through; his own rigorous training had made him too scrupulous simply to accept it as it was. Unlike most adolescents who discover their parents to be merely human, with all the flaws and faults that entails, instead of abandoning the project his father had bequeathed him, he devoted himself to reformulating it into something that would deserve his allegiance. That reformulation itself became a substantial component of the project: his attempts to articulate the problem of moral unfreedom involved him in rethinking such subjects as philosophy of logic, the problem of induction, and so on, which is to say that we have already seen a part of the recast life project.

I now want to examine a further upgrade Mill made to the theoretical backbone of the Utilitarian program. One complaint repeatedly directed against the Utilitarians was that they were committed to abridging political liberties under a number of easy-to-envision circumstances. The early Benthamites thought of themselves as democrats, and defenders of political liberty rather than its enemies, but their own arguments were quite weak, and mostly put on display their inability fully to appreciate their opponents' points.[1] Mill chose to show how it was that Utilitarians really *were*—that is, had to be—defenders of liberty.

The complaints he was responding to were reiterated long after his death, which means that his attempt to address them has not been understood or appreciated, and thus a bonus of working through this part of Mill's intellectual biography will be an improved grasp of this centerpiece of Mill's political philosophy. More importantly, for our own purposes, we will be seeing how Mill filled in the psychology at work in his treatment of freedom of the will, and thus deepened his conception of moral freedom; we will also come to see how further parts of his life project were tightly integrated with one another, and motivated by a deep concern with what Mill called *originality* or *genius*.

In chapter 7, I suggested that Mill had put himself in a position to select the subprojects that filled in the content of his life project on the basis of how emotionally engaging he found them. Why did he gravitate to the subproject of articulating the scope and grounds of liberty within the Utilitarian world-view, when he was adjusting his newly flexible project to track shifts in his own profile of pleasures and concerns? Here is no doubt part of the answer: as a child, John Stuart Mill was practically never allowed to do anything because he wanted to, or chose to, or felt like it. He did everything because he was required to, and that's a likely motivation for the arguments Mill subsequently constructed, for the freedom to do anything you want that doesn't actually harm anyone else.

8.1

The Principle of Utility, which served to mark out Mill's life project, is that "actions are right in proportion as they tend to promote happiness, wrong as they tend to produce the reverse of happiness" (X:210/U 2:2). The Principle of Liberty is set out in *On Liberty*, which still stands as the canonical formulation of the uncontroversial heart of modern liberalism. (Or rather, that is how it has been regarded, but we will shortly be in a position to entertain second thoughts.) The latter principle "is, that the sole end for which mankind are warranted, individually or collectively, in interfering with the liberty of action of any of their number, is self-protection," and Mill continues:

the only purpose for which power can be rightfully exercised over any member of a civilized community, against his will, is to prevent harm to others. His own good, either physical or moral, is not a sufficient warrant. He cannot be rightfully compelled to do or forbear because it will be better for him to do so, because it will make him happier, because, in the opinions of others, to do so would be wise, or even right. These are good reasons for remonstrating with him, or reasoning with him, or persuading him, or entreating him, but not for compelling him, or visiting him with any evil in case he do otherwise. To justify that, the conduct from which it is desired to deter him, must be calculated to do evil to some one else. The only part of the conduct of any one, for which he is amenable to society, is that which concerns others. In the part which merely concerns himself, his independence is, of right, absolute. Over himself, over his own body and mind, the individual is sovereign. (XVIII:223f/OL 1:9)

How could anyone have supposed that it was possible to sign off on both these principles at the same time?

Aldous Huxley's *Brave New World* is probably the most famous of what is by now a long line of literary and cinematic objections: humans are social creatures, and so the happiness of one person depends on the cooperation of others; why expect the optimizing patterns of coordination to appear unenforced? (Left to themselves, Huxley reminded his readers, people fight *wars*.) If what you're after is maximizing everybody's happiness, you should be drastically curtailing people's freedom of action and freedom of thought.[2] Moreover, Bentham had thought that, by and large, people make choices that conduce to their own happiness; Oscar Wilde objected, and Huxley seconded the objection, that Bentham's psychology was too crude to be realistic on this point. In fact, from a hedonic perspective, and quite likely from any reasonable perspective, human beings' choices—*especially* when they are driven by a sophisticated pursuit of pleasure—are often catastrophically bad.[3] Wrapping up our sampling of the litany of complaints, James Gunn, in a more recent novelistic treatment, supplemented the traditional objections with a more subtle difficulty. Liberty is a benefit only to creatures that are not just agents in principle, but in practice as well: who get off their duff and actually *do* things. Most people, he suggested, if given the choice between agency and daydreaming, will choose not to make choices or do things for themselves. What they find to be most pleasant—alternatively, what they choose, when they're familiar with the options—is where the greatest utility lies; evidently, the Principle of Utility endorses the life of daydreaming. Now, if you don't practice being an agent for long enough, you cease to be one; thus a society run for long enough on Utilitarian standards will eventually be a society of non-agents, to whom liberty is irrelevant.[4]

Historians of philosophy are trained to see conflicts like this one as textual puzzles: the exercise is to resolve the apparent inconsistency by locating additional claims or arguments within Mill's writings which will allow the Principles to be squared with each other. In the exegetical practice to which this sort of puzzle solving belongs, such a solution is the finish line; when you have found a theoretically coherent position to ascribe to the body of texts, the work is over and you can stop. Our own interests lie further down the road, but we can make headway on them by taking up the textual puzzle on the traditional terms. Since *On Liberty* explicitly acknowledges "utility as the ultimate appeal on all ethical questions" (XVIII:224/OL 1:11), that in turn means that we are in the market for additional premises with which to derive the Principle of Liberty from the Principle of Utility. Now Mill announces that the argument proceeds in two similarly motivated but distinct phases: the first argues specifically for freedom of thought and expression; the ensuing discussion makes the case for freedom of choice generally. So we will follow him in reconstructing the two stages of his argument separately, and we will take a break in between them to work up an analysis of another famous and related argment, to the effect that, for a utilitarian, justice ought also to be an indefeasible commitment.

8.2

The overall structure of Mill's argument for freedom of opinion, speech, and the press, as it is laid out in the second chapter of the *Liberty*, is as follows. Any opinion you might have is either true, half true, or false. If your opinion is true, it needs to be contested to keep it alive. If your opinion is half true, it needs to be contested to have it completed. And if your opinion is false, it needs to be contested so it can be changed.[5] Since any opinion you have needs to be contested, and since you're probably not going to do the contesting yourself, you have a very strong interest in others having the liberty to disagree with you.

One branch of this argument is second nature to the educated inhabitants of present-day democratic states: that nobody is infallible, and that the best chance of arriving at the right view about anything is to be had by letting the differing opinions compete in the marketplace of ideas, are platitudes even when they are not believed deeply enough to govern action. Because Mill's treatment is very densely argued, we need to be picky about what we allow onto our agenda; I am going to leave these familiar considerations to the textbooks, and confine our attention to the less familiar parts of the argument. I'll start with the branch that allows your opinions to be true, and we'll return to the possibility that your opinions are half true.

Mill claims that freedom of thought, and "liberty of expressing and publishing opinions," which "is practically inseparable from it," are necessary, because if one's beliefs are not contested, one will sooner or later cease to have them; his recapitulation of the argument runs as follows:

unless [the received opinion] is suffered to be, and actually is, vigorously and earnestly contested, ... the meaning of the doctrine itself will be in danger of being lost, or enfeebled, and deprived of its vital effect on character and conduct: the dogma becoming a mere formal profession.

Thus, Mill holds, even those who are absolutely confident in their religious beliefs and authorities should not want their religion established: if it is, there will eventually be no actual believers, as opposed to regular churchgoers who mouth the "formularies," "phrases retained by rote."[6]

A claim regarding the conditions under which beliefs fade away is evidently psychological, and if we want to know why Mill held it, we should turn to his psychology. As we already know, his psychological views are laid out in the *Analysis of the Phenomena of the Human Mind*. And so we will not be surprised to find the evanescence of belief coming in for thorough consideration in the editor's notes.[7]

When one first learns to read, one is aware of the letters on the page; after one has become proficient, one no longer notices the letters, or, often, even the words, but only the content of what one has read. Mill considers three explanations for the phenomenon: that "the lost ideas pass through the mind without consciousness," that "they pass consciously through the mind and are … then instantly forgotten," and that "they never come into the mind at all, being, as it were, overleaped and pressed out by the rush of subsequent ideas." He allows that each of these, properly understood, is a genuine possibility, but leans strongly toward the third.

The effect follows from the laws of association. Consider an oft-repeated series of mental states, A, B, and C. Even if the initial associative connections were between A and B, on the one hand, and B and C, on the other, frequent repetition, if there is "nothing to make the mind dwell on" B, will produce an associative connection directly between A and C: "B will cease to be excited at all; and the train of association, like a stream which breaking though its bank cuts off a bend in its course, will thenceforth flow in the direct line AC, omitting B." Consequently, and returning now to *On Liberty*, the beliefs of a mind moving in habitual paths will "degenerate into the mechanical," "the words … cease to suggest ideas," and the beliefs simply drop out of one's mental life.[8]

It doesn't matter, as far as Mill's account of the phenomenon goes, whether B (the deleted intermediate mental state) is a belief, or some other mental state, such as a desire or intention. On Mill's way of thinking about it, desires, intentions, hopes, and—as far as I can see—actual enjoyments will drop below the radar of one's attention if they only figure into completely routinized trains of thought. And I do think that we can confirm anecdotally that the scope of the phenomenon extends to ends. One of my own ends happens to be obeying the local traffic laws; for me, it is a final end, that is, I do it not just to avoid getting ticketed, and not just to avoid accidents, but rather because it seems like the thing to do. When I was just learning to drive, this end was a focus of my attention and remained vividly before my mind. But for the most part, driving has become completely habitual; the end of conforming to the traffic laws, and the steps I take to it, are a scarcely noticed background to my coffee and Danish, my conversation with my passenger, and my attempts to borrow her phone. Merely being an end—even a final end—seems to have no staying power at all against the sort of automatism that Mill is analyzing.

A belief can be kept in play, Mill thought, by being made to figure in trains of thought that are not habitual or routinized. This will happen most effectively when the belief is under attack: "if [an opinion] is not fully, frequently, and fearlessly discussed, it will be held as a dead dogma, not a living truth"; "it almost ceases to connect itself at all with the inner life of the human being." But if it *is* fully, frequently, and fearlessly discussed, it will be held as a living truth rather than a dead dogma; that's what the American constitution's First Amendment is really for. During that developmental stage of a religion in which its doctrines are live, its adherents, in the course of arguing for them, "have weighed and considered [its fundamental principles] in all their important bearings," which is to say that the variety of trains of association in which the beliefs figure is great enough to maintain them as "a power in their minds." When the belief is itself at issue, it will not drop out as intermediate stages of a train of thought are likely to, and when new arguments against it must be met by new counterarguments, the occasions for bringing the belief to mind will not be well enough rehearsed to be replaced by shortcuts. And so a "livelier impression of truth [is] produced by its collision with error."[9] Freedom of speech and of the press are necessary for debate, which is necessary to prevent one's ideas from fading into mere words, "the shell and husk only," that is, to prevent mind-deadening boredom: thus Mill's argument.[10]

In the special case of freedom of speech, the problem of explaining how Mill could have insisted on both of the Principles comes to this. Put plainly, the Principle of Liberty has it that I must be allowed to say what I want, no matter how unhappy it makes other people. The Principle of Utility has it that if enough people are made sufficiently unhappy by what I want to say, I ought to be prevented from saying it. Allow the conclusion for which we have just seen Mill argue, that liberty of thought and expression are necessary if one's beliefs are not to have detours permanently constructed around them, and fade from consciousness. Now if we take on board the further premise that most pleasures, and certainly the most important of them, are dependent on the presence of full-fledged beliefs, it will turn out that the maximization of utility *requires* the intellectual liberties. This added premise is not, I think, implausible: when a student is overjoyed at having gotten an A, his pleasure depends on his believing that he got an A. If freedom of speech is required to keep *anyone's* pleasures live, then other people don't much benefit by a regime that silences one person, however inconvenient and annoying his speech is, at the expense of also silencing everyone else.

The argument has only carried us so far. As we have it, it's not obvious that *limited* freedom of thought and expression—say anything you like about football, just leave the politics alone—wouldn't suffice for passionately held beliefs and the pleasures that depend on them. Maybe Mill was theoretically handicapped by never having been in a pub during a World Cup game, but whatever the argument's shortcomings, it is of interest to us for several reasons.

First, this not atypical representative of Mill's often surprising arguments suggests that those arguments themselves do not merely have the usual function, that is, establishing conclusions, ideally once and for all: in this case, a practical conclusion amounting to a commitment to free speech. If the argument is any good, no single such argument *could* permanently tie down a commitment of this sort (or, for that matter, even a purely theoretical conclusion): that is, it could tie it down *logically*, by showing it to be true or practically required, but it couldn't tie it down in your ongoing mental life. The argument's very novelty and surprisingness falls into place as having the inevitably transient function of keeping Mill's own attention directed to liberty. Mill is not only improving the intellectual quality of his life project by making sure that the conclusions are better supported by better premises; he is acting to preempt the prospect of being bored literally out of his mind.

Second, Mill's arguments serve to remind us why it is that every generation needs to refight the important philosophical battles. Just for instance, as his discussion predicts, the Utilitarian arguments against intuition were forgotten, and throughout the twentieth century, analytic philosophers treated their intuitions as the touchstone of correctness, without any awareness that there were troubling objections to the practice—objections which a responsible philosopher would need to address before engaging in it. Those objections are in the process of being rediscovered by today's experimental philosophers, who have no idea that they are reinventing Mill's wheels. Mill may be history, but because we forget our history, taking the trouble to understand Mill may teach us a good deal that is—at least to us—new.[11]

Third, even if the argument is not conclusive, Mill is introducing the sorts of consideration which he puts to work in his full-on argument for freedom of choice, and liberty to act on those choices. Accordingly, with our reconstruction of the warmup argument on hand, let's proceed to his defense of freedom of action.

8.3

The First Amendment, which is very much in the spirit of Mill's view, is nowadays interpreted to mean Freedom of Speech, No Matter What, and not, Freedom of Speech, Unless It's Especially Irksome or Inconvenient. And Mill insisted that liberty more broadly construed takes priority over any amount whatsoever of the goods that might be gained by sacrificing it. The only device in his bag of tricks that allows a good to be ranked over other goods in this way is the distinction, already encountered in our discussion of moral freedom, between higher and lower pleasures. So we should expect Mill's argument for a liberal political order to invoke this distinction.

The standard and almost correct formulation of Mill's distinction between higher and lower pleasures runs as follows: if all (or anyway most) of those who have experienced both *A* and *B* prefer any amount, however small, of *A*, to any amount, however large, of *B*, then *A* is the higher pleasure.[12] This definition of a higher pleasure does nothing to explain to us *why* the particular pleasures Mill claimed to be the higher ones *are*. But if Mill's arguments turn on the claim that experienced judges, as a matter of psychological fact, lexically rank some pleasures over others, we should expect there to be a psychological explanation for lexical rankings generally. We should further expect Mill to have had in mind psychological arguments that the particular pleasures which he took to be higher would indeed be lexically preferred to competing pleasures.

In fact, Mill is methodologically committed to producing such explanations. Mill's moral and political arguments are meant to show that what he takes to be the higher pleasures remain so even in novel social environments, in particular, in the improved social arrangements which Utilitarians hoped to bring about; he is not merely trying to demonstrate that liberty is a good only in our imperfect political world, but that someday it will no longer be needed. If the claim that liberty was a higher pleasure was just an observation (perhaps of the choice behavior of suitably experienced judges), it would count as what Mill called an empirical law. But "until an uniformity can ... be taken out of the class of empirical laws, and brought either into that of laws of causation or the demonstrated results of laws of causation, it cannot with an assurance be pronounced true beyond the local and other limits within which it has been found so by actual observation."[13] In other words, unless his claims about the higher pleasures can be underwritten by his psychology, Mill cannot use them as he does in his political arguments. So we must assume that he thought they could be.

How, according to associationist psychological theory, could something come to function as a higher pleasure in somebody's life? The treatment of the phenomenon we are examining appears in the *Analysis*, perhaps disconcertingly, as Mill's explanation of how one becomes a miser. A miser is someone who values money over anything he could buy with it; that's why he hangs on to the money. So a miser acts as though money is a higher pleasure. James Mill writes:

Wealth ... afford[s] perhaps the most remarkable of all examples of that extraordinary case of association, where the means to an end, means valuable to us solely on account of their end, not only engross more of our attention than the end itself, but actually supplant it in our affections.[14]

Here is the explanation of the phenomenon given by Mill *fils*:

when a grand cause of pleasures has been associated with a great many pleasures, and a great many times, the association acquires a peculiar character and strength. The idea of the cause, as cause, is so lost among the innumerable ideas of the pleasures combined with it, that it seems to become the idea of pleasure itself.... Many are the instances in which the association of pleasures with money constitutes so vehement an affection that it is an overmatch for all others.[15]

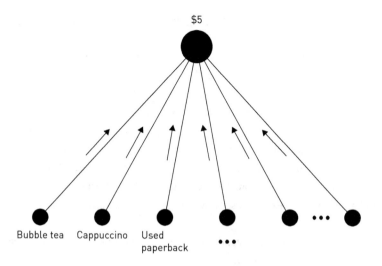

$5

Bubble tea   Cappuccino   Used
paperback

FIGURE 8.1 How to become a miser.

The miser constructs associative links between his idea of, say, five dollars and of each of the many things he could buy with five dollars: a bubble tea, a cappuccino, a used paperback, and so on. (See Figure 8.1.) Since each of those items is a pleasure (that is, the idea of it is pleasant), the feeling of pleasure traverses those associative links and attaches itself to the idea of the five dollars. Consequently, that idea becomes pleasant also, which is to say that the miser now desires his five dollars. But because the idea of the money is accumulating feelings of pleasure transmitted over *each* of the links, it ends up being a *more* pleasant idea than the ideas of any of the goods one could purchase with five dollars. That is just to say that the miser desires the money more than anything he could buy with it; when offered a choice between money and what it can buy, he will prefer the money.[16]

The love of wealth over all else is a *mistake*, "an effect," James Mill tells us, "of misguided association, which requires the greatest attention in Education, and Morals," and the opinion was endorsed by his son: the "true value . . . [of] riches . . . [is] the worth, for comfort or pleasure, of the things which they will buy."[17] Money is not actually a higher pleasure. The formal criterion, recall, is that money would count only if a majority of suitably experienced people were misers. Just about everybody who lives in a money economy is suitably experienced, having, on some occasions, traded his money for commodities, and on others, hung onto it. But misers are a vastly outnumbered minority, and the reason is that the associative links from the idea of the money to the ideas of purchasable goods represent an exclusive or: if you buy one item with your money, you have used it up, and you cannot buy anything else with the money you have spent. The miser is behaving as though the money could be exchanged for *all* of the purchasable goods together.

Because a given amount of money can only be exchanged for one item priced at that amount, it is not worth more than one such item. While the idea of money may have been, at some stage of each person's education, associated with the myriad commodities that money can buy, sooner or later most of us learn that you get only what you pay for: the five dollars ends up buying us what are only five dollars worth of goods. After this lesson has been repeated sufficiently many times, the idea of five dollars ends up associated with the pleasure of a single five-dollar purchase; misers are rare because the relevant patterns of means-end association follow causal connections, and when the misapprehension of the causal structure that gives rise to the very highly positively connected idea of money is corrected, the pleasure ceases to be connected enough to be lexically preferred: "Analytic habits ... strengthen the associations between causes and effects, means and ends, but tend altogether to weaken those which are, to speak familiarly, a *mere* matter of feeling."[18]

Now that we understand how higher pleasures are implemented psychologically, we can say what a higher pleasure is going to come out being: it will work like money to the miser, only, unlike a miser's attachment to money, it will not be a mistake. Before taking up the question of what such pleasures could be, let's briefly register where John Stuart Mill would have encountered preferences that were lexically ranked in the way he took the higher pleasures to be, and why he would have been so impressed as to rely on them for theoretical heavy lifting in *On Liberty* and elsewhere.

Return to the pedagogical *ur*-scene: his father is working at home, writing his *History of India*. At the other end of the table is his son, John Stuart, doing his Greek homework. He reads Plato, Pope's translation of the *Illiad*, Gibbon's *Decline and Fall of the Roman Empire*, and William Robertson's *History of Scotland*. He has a full-time personal supervisor: hardly ever out of James Mill's sight, his father continually makes him do one thing after another: conjugate Greek verbs, solve mathematics problems with inadequate explanation, summarize chapters in history books, and much more of the same.

Each time little John Stuart fails a task, or is frustrated at it, his father sternly and abruptly corrects him, and (recall how close his father's psychological theory was to behaviorism) other rewards and punishments are no doubt administered, all on the basis of praise and blame.[19] *Blame* is being associatively connected with all those brief unhappy moments. So the feeling of pain will traverse those many links, and after a while, blame (or maybe *his father's* blame) is going to be—further extending the terminology we've been given—a 'higher pain': something Mill would do anything to avoid. As his father put it, discussing the "association [that] constitutes ... the feeling ... of Praiseworthiness, and Blameworthiness ...: In some men it exists in so great a degree of strength, that ... every other feeling of their nature, is subdued by it."[20] While praise might have been turned into a higher pleasure in the same way, we are told that Mill's "recollection of such matters is almost wholly of failures, hardly ever of success" (I:35/A 1:22): James Mill must have rarely praised his child.

You will notice as well that the associationist account that we gave of Mill's teenage encounter with Bentham's *Traité* makes it out to share the psychological structures of a higher pleasure (compare Figure 8.1 with Figure 3.1). Because the coordinating idea of the Utilitarian project was connected to so many prospects for improvement, that idea itself became more enthralling than any of them. And thus John Stuart Mill first learned about the higher pleasures, about how lexically ranked preferences were formed, and about how effective they could be. It would have been the drawn out and painful lesson of his childhood that there are experiences which, once lived through, prevent one from trading off competing options. (After enough of such training, you'd do *anything* rather than expose yourself to even a little bit of this kind of correction.) And it would have been the sudden and uplifting lesson of what I was calling his epiphany that one highly connected objective could, by virtue of its position in one's mental life, overshadow the pleasures connected to it. The turn to psychologically entrenched lexically ordered preferences, and Mill's conviction that they could make a dependable armature for a utilitarian but liberal social order, was most likely an echo of his own formative years.

8.4

I earlier suggested that the standard formulation of the decided preference criterion does not quite get Mill right, and I can now say why. There is an old joke about a drunk in a bar to whom a genie grants three wishes. His first wish is for a bottomless pint of Guinness, and the drunk is so pleased with the outcome that he asks for two more of the same. If higher pleasures are, paradigmatically, nondepletable resources that are seen to serve indefinitely many further ends, then one has a higher pleasure or one does not, but one does not exactly have *more* or *less* of it. Mill introduces the notion of higher pleasures in the following passage:

If one of the two [pleasures] is, by those who are competently acquainted with both, placed so far above the other that they... would not resign it for any quantity of the other pleasure which their nature is capable of, we are justified in ascribing to the preferred enjoyment a superiority in quality, so far outweighing quantity as to render it, in comparison, of small account. (X:211/U 2:5)

Notice Mill's careful choice of wording: the lower pleasure comes in quantities, but there is no mention of any quantity, great or small, of the preferred (and therefore higher) pleasure. It is a mistake to think of higher pleasures as coming in *amounts.*[21]

The central and most important higher pleasures are, we should expect, nondepletable means to an indefinite range of goods. What do these look like, when no mistake is involved, and why does Mill care about them so much? To see what such a higher pleasure might be, let's turn to a further warmup argument, this time from the final chapter of *Utilitarianism*.

The distinction between higher and lower pleasures is introduced in chapter 2 of *Utilitarianism*, where Mill also introduces what was widely felt to be a pressing objection to the view:

Utility is often summarily stigmatized as an immoral doctrine by giving it the name of Expediency, and taking advantage of the popular use of that term to contrast it with Principle. (X:223/U 2:23)

We are told that an utilitarian will be apt to make his own particular case an exception to the moral rules, and, when under temptation, will see a utility in the breach of a rule, greater than he will see in its observance. (X:225/U 2:25)

Prescott recounts how Hernando Cortés allowed his soldiers to torture the deposed Aztec monarch Guatemozin, in order to extract from him the location of hidden Mexican gold. The prisoner was subsequently executed, apparently on trumped-up charges, and this despite Cortés having promised the former sovereign, on his surrender, to treat him "with all honor."[22] We know that Cortés was no utilitarian, but the complaint is that, as far as these decisions went, he might as well have been. The lost gold benefitted no one, and if recovered would have brought enough happiness to the Spanish Conquistadores to outweigh the disutility produced by torturing one or two men. The cumulative inconveniences of having to keep a close watch on a still popular and charismatic enemy leader outweighed the benefits—and even the benefits to that leader himself—of keeping him alive.[23]

Mill's response was to protect the "important branch of expediency called justice" from utilitarian cost-benefit calculations by showing it to be a lexical priority. Justice consists in honoring rights, rights being those expectations which society ought to defend, come what may. Now, all non-momentary goods depend on the possession of rights: "nothing but the gratification of the instant could be of any worth to us, if we could be deprived of everything the next instant by whoever was momentarily stronger than ourselves." This dependence makes us feel very strongly about the abrogation of rights, and not just of our own rights: we feel "a thirst for retaliation" whenever "the machinery for providing [the rights] ... is [not] kept unintermittedly in active play." The feelings are "so much more intense than those concerned in any of the more common cases of utility, that the difference in degree ... becomes a real difference in kind ... assum[ing] [a] character of absoluteness." Thus, the possession of such rights is a higher pleasure. And thus, justice will be preferred to any of the other common cases of utility; it is always the preferred option, from the utilitarian point of view.[24]

Justice (security in our expectations, in knowing that the rules are fixed, even when it's inconvenient to others) is a means to all other nontrivial pleasures, and so the feeling of pleasure traverses the many associative links representing those means-end connections. It accumulates at the idea of justice, eventually becoming more intense than the pleasure associated with any of the ideas at the other ends of those links; justice accordingly turns out to be preferred to any of the particular goods for which it is a necessary precondition. The psychological structures thus resemble those of the miser. But notice that, unlike any finite amount of money, justice is a nondepletable good: when justice has secured one further pleasure for you, you have (as Locke once put it, albeit in a rather different connection) "enough, and as good, left." The mistake the miser is making is, in this case, no mistake at all.[25]

Mill did seem to think of great literature as a higher pleasure, and we can now say why that was not unreasonable. A standard complaint, that no one is always going to give up eating for reading Thackeray, is evidently miscast: Thackeray isn't normally a generic means to eating, and so Thackeray and eating don't stand to each other in the relation we've been examining. However, it is the distinguishing mark of great literature that you can always find something new in it; in associationist terms, there are always more associations to be built to further ideas. Unlike our previous examples, the associations need not depend on causal connections; but like our previous examples, the further ideas are often enough pleasurable in their own right. An experienced reader will correctly come to regard such a work as an inexhaustible source of literary pleasure, and eventually, value it more than the pleasure of any one good read.

Looking back, we can now see that if freedom of speech and the press are preconditions for keeping in mind the ideas on which one's pleasures turn, then we ought also to expect such freedom of expression to prove to be a higher pleasure also—or to amount to a necessary precondition for something else, such as having lively and vivid beliefs, that turns out to be the higher pleasure. Just as you would not trade in *Vanity Fair* for any number of airport-bookstore thrillers, so you would not sacrifice your ability to express (and so to have) your beliefs on behalf of any one of them, no matter how strongly you were convinced of it. Normally, when freedom of speech and of the press are repressed, it is on behalf of particular protected beliefs, and so the argument amounts to a de facto effective defense of these freedoms even before we consider competing conveniences of other sorts. But once we take into account the ways in which almost all our most important pleasures depend on our beliefs, the argument looks to make the intellectual freedoms indefeasible, even to a utilitarian.

Before turning to the argument for liberty more generally, which Mill has informed us is going to be modeled on this one, let's quickly notice two things. First, if we have gotten the argument right, Mill's way of making room for thinking and talking about things differently is an expedient for making sure one isn't locked into any single mindset. And second, Mill looks to have been experimenting with a psychological explanation of the experienced awfulness of being locked into that one mindset, and of merely occupying rather than living your own life. We are in the middle of a very academic exercise, but we want to stay fully aware of what we are seeing: at the bottom of his defense of the intellectual liberties is John Stuart Mill trying his hardest to figure out what had gone so terribly wrong with his life.

9 Taking Liberties with Utilitarianism

"After the means of subsistence are assured," Mill tells us, "the next in strength of the personal wants of human beings is liberty; and (unlike the physical wants, which as civilization advances become more moderate and more amenable to control) it increases instead of diminishing in intensity, as the intelligence and the moral faculties are more developed" (II:208). The chapter of *On Liberty* in which the central argument for freedom of choice is provided bears the title, "Of Individuality, as One of the Elements of Well-Being," and in his *Autobiography*, Mill describes *On Liberty* as a whole as "a kind of philosophic text-book of a single truth ...: the importance, to man and society, of a large variety in types of character, and of giving full freedom to human nature to expand itself in innumerable and conflicting directions" (I:259/A 7:20). "Individuality is the same thing with development," and liberty is the precondition of "originality" and "genius" (XVIII:267/OL 3:10f). Somewhat uncharacteristically, Mill does not develop one or even several intertwined arguments turning on these concepts, on the related notion of "individual spontaneity," or the importance of "'the highest and most harmonious development of [man's] powers to a complete and consistent whole.'"[1] Instead, perhaps following through on some of his early strategizing with Taylor—he told her, "We must cram into it as much as possible of what we wish not to leave unsaid" (XIV:332)—Mill as it were heaps up the ingredients of a number of arguments into a pile, without assembling them for his reader.

Here's how we'll proceed. First, I am going to put together a train of thought from elements picked out of the pile, one showing that because originality is a higher pleasure, and because lack of liberty squelches originality, liberty is a precondition for an indefeasible good. Let me reemphasize that this train of thought is by no means the only argument that can be teased out of the heap; nonetheless, the close attention that Mill paid to originality will be the guide we need in order to understand both what Mill made of his life project, and what went irremediably wrong with it.[2] We are in the middle of reconstructing some of Mill's reasons for adopting the views for which he is most famous, but we don't want to lose track of our real interest, namely, the way in which he reconfigured his Utilitarian life project as a response to his Mental Crisis.

Originality wears more than one aspect in Mill's writings—though it is not exactly that the term is being used to mean more than one thing. On the one hand, originality often eventuates in novelty: "new truths" and "new practices" (XVIII:267/OL 3:11). On the other, an intellectual effort need not produce novelties to qualify: in an early essay on "Genius," Mill tells us that "the capacity of extracting the knowledge of general truth from our own consciousness ... is *originality*; and where truth is the result ... Genius" (I:332). Let us put to one side the idea that originality is a matter of going where no man has gone before, and allow it to signify, with Mill's official pronouncements, figuring things out for yourself.[3] What we have been calling his first teenage epiphany evidently belongs under this heading:

Every one, I suppose, of adult years, who has any capacity of knowledge, can remember the impression which he experienced when he *discovered* some truths which he thought he had known for years before. He had only believed them; they were not the fruits of his own consciousness, or of his own observation; he had taken them on trust, or he had taken upon trust the premises from which they were inferred.

[W]hoever thinks at all, thinks to that extent, originally.... Whosoever does this same thing systematically—whosoever, to the extent of his opportunity, gets at his convictions by his own faculties ... —that man, in proportion as his conclusions have truth in them, is an *original thinker*, and is, as much as anybody ever was, a *man of genius* ... (I:332)

Just as originality is not in the first place a matter of having done something that was previously undone, so genius is not a matter of getting good scores on intelligence tests; as Mill is using the notion, it is presumably possible to be cognitively disabled, and nevertheless to exhibit genius, because you do things *your own* way, meaning, the way you have figured out for yourself.[4]

Once the argument from originality has been assembled, I will turn back to the argument for the intellectual liberties, which we took up in the previous chapter. I'll take up the branch that was left to one side in our first pass over it, and argue that the considerations in play there should convince us that Mill's interest in liberty more broadly has to do with the way that it fosters moral freedom—that is to say, freedom of the will.

Having these moves on our plate will be an occasion for a more nuanced reassessment of Mill's Utilitarianism, and I'll take time out to give it a shot before reviewing the upgrades to his life project, and asking what makes them fit together into a unified and cohesive whole.

9.1

Recall the distinction we introduced in section 7.2, between the descriptive and corrective versions of the contrast between higher and lower pleasures: to show that, as a matter of fact, a certain type of psychology experiences a good as a higher pleasure is not yet to show that it ought to be treated by others as a higher pleasure. I'm going to pick out two contrasting psychologies, the analytic and poetic minds, and explain why each will end up treating originality as a higher pleasure. Then I'll say something about how to bridge the gap between that conclusion, and the further conclusion Mill wants, to the effect that originality is—in the corrective sense—a higher pleasure.

In another early essay, "Thoughts on Poetry and Its Varieties," Mill explains how poetic and analytic minds differ. There is a great deal of biological and specifically neurological variation from one human being to another, and one side effect of it is variation in how strongly people are disposed to feel their emotions.

Where feelings are relatively weak, the mind is 'analytic'. In this case, figuring things out for oneself means drawing conclusions; these may be beliefs, but in the practical case will amount to intentions or decisions.[5] Associative connections are built up that track patterns which repeat themselves in one's experience: if you see first *A*s and then *B*s, after a while, when you see (or come to think of) an *A*, your mind will leap ahead to the idea of a *B*. Those transitions amount to inductions, which are, in Mill's logic, the sole form of genuine theoretical inference. Alternatively, you can be trained to follow "the artificial classifications which the understanding has voluntarily made for the convenience of thought or of practice" (I:357). The upshot is a mind whose trains of thought are largely inferential: in moving directly from idea to idea, an analytic mind in the first place traverses cognitive pathways which track first-this-then-that patterns in the world. Since, on Mill's view, practical reasoning is means-end reasoning, and a means is a cause of an end, when analytic minds figure out what to do, they are by and large arriving at their conclusions inferentially as well.

When someone tends to have very strong emotions, however, "agreeably to the law of association by which ... the strongest impressions are those which associate themselves the most easily and strongly, these vivid sensations [are] readily recalled to mind by all objects or thoughts which had coexisted with them."[6] In a 'poetic' mind, consequently, "[a] thought will introduce a thought by first introducing a feeling which is allied with it. At the centre of each group of thoughts or images will be found a feeling; and the thoughts or images will be there only because the feeling was there. The combinations which the mind puts together ... will be indebted to some dominant feeling, not as in other natures a dominant thought, for their unity and consistency of character—for what distinguishes them from incoherencies."[7]

The inductive pathways etched into an analytic mind by repeated experience transfer the liveliness (in the case of beliefs), or the pleasure or pain associated with one's premises, to one's conclusions, with little or no loss of vividness or strength on the way. To figure things out for oneself is in part to reason from premises one already fully believes; those premises are therefore fully vivid—or, if they are pleasures or pains, intensely felt. Consequently, the conclusions at which one arrives will be vividly apprehended and thus capable of supporting full-fledged pleasures (and pains—but notice that when the conclusion is practical, what is in question will more often be pleasure than pain, because one tends to choose pleasures when one can).

It evidently follows that figuring things out for oneself, when one has an analytic mind, both feels good on its own, and supports further pleasures. Let's work up a low-key, albeit philosophically artificial example of the phenomenon. Imagine two high school seniors who are as alike as you please, and in particular who share a configuration of antecedently available desires. One of them takes up the question of what he is going to do after high school, and figures it out for himself: from a longing to sail the seven seas, and grim views about what it takes to survive in today's economy, he determines that he will pursue a career as a maritime engineer, the first step of which will be an apprenticeship in a Hamburg shipyard. The other arrives at the same decision, but in a very different manner: he consults the school's guidance counselor, who administers interest inventories and aptitude tests, and produces the recommendation on which the student acts. The Millian claim, which sounds plausible enough in this case, is that the former will find both his choice and subsequent career more satisfying, other things equal, roughly because he will be more passionate about it. By our earlier argument, such consequences should make an agent with sufficient practice in figuring things out on his own come to experience this sort of intellectual self-reliance as itself a higher pleasure.

My own impression is that—perhaps because Mill was not himself a poet, as he understood it—he did not properly debug the analogous argument, to the effect that poetic natures ought to prize originality just as much as analytic minds. But it is easy enough to tell the story for him: imagine that during youthful stints as park rangers in the redrock desert, two people have come to associate the blue-green tinge of the sagebrush on a cloudy day with the exhilaration of hiking briskly through the spring outdoors, simply because that was how they felt at the time. (And to keep it simple, let's not now reconstruct more of the poetic personalities' clusters of ideas organized by this feeling.) Once again, we can suppose the paired individuals to be as alike as you please. One of them chooses to remodel his living space, and selects that shade of bluish-green as a motif, because it evokes those feelings and memories. The other happens to have the very same shade picked out for him by a professional interior decorator. The Millian claim, which again sounds plausible enough, is that the former will enjoy his remodeled home more than the latter, because his choice has been enlivened through his having traversed the relevant associative connections himself.

Mill is quite aware that many people will find the notion that originality, in this sense, is a higher pleasure to be quite implausible: as academic readers will have frequently had occasion to remark, most students (and they're presumably representative of most non-students) *hate* figuring things out for themselves. Mill's way of putting it is that the Englishmen of his time are conformists: "the English, more than any other people, not only act but feel according to rule."[8] But recall the corrective use of the decided preference criterion: we are to take as our point of reference the preferences of those who have experienced *both* of the options which we mean to prioritize. Those who figure things out for themselves, whether they have analytic minds or poetic natures, can agree on the importance of orginality, on the basis of hands-on practice. Conformists are unacquainted with that side of the comparison, and so, even if conformists are the vast majority, here we should be guided by the shared preferences of the intellectuals and the poets.

Let's tie up a loose end, while we're at it. Mill describes the systematic reconsideration of his own views during his twenties thusly:

Much of this, it is true, consisted in rediscovering things known to all the world, which I had previously disbelieved, or disregarded. But the rediscovery was to me a discovery, giving me plenary possession of the truths not as traditional platitudes but fresh from their source: and it seldom failed to place them in some new light, by which they were reconciled with, and seemed to confirm while they modified, the truths less generally known which lay in my early opinions, and in no essential part of which I at any time wavered. (I:175/A 5:18)

In chapter 3, we considered the objection that Mill's life project was not really his own—that it was not, as we put it, superlatively attributable to him in the manner that preoccupies analytic moral philosophers today. As it turns out, Mill had his own view of what is required for "plenary possession" of a truth (and presumably of other attitudes and of activities): originality. What it is to *really* think something, as opposed to *merely* thinking it, is to think it through and understand it for oneself.

If originality proves to be a higher pleasure, and if lack of liberty squelches originality, then liberty will have turned out to be a precondition for an indefeasible good. Let us consider whether there is a Millian way to support the second premise of that argument, and, by way of a shortcut, let's introduce the idea of futility, as the thought that you're not going to be allowed to say what you think, or go through with the choice you think it would be best to make, regardless. (Alternatively but equivalently, the anticipation that if you do say or act as you believe best, you're going to be punished.) That idea is obviously unpleasant, and even painful.

Now, if you live in a society where liberties are severely restricted, and so where doing things differently, and doing them your way, is not going to be tolerated, then if you do figure things out for yourself, you will repeatedly bump up against that fact: there's a way things are done, and it's not going to change. To do so is not only to learn that your figuring things out for yourself is, in this or that instance, futile; after a while, the idea of figuring things out for yourself will elicit almost immediately the painful thought of futility. That is bound in the first place to take the lively and pleasurable edge off the conclusion of one's train of thought, and, as the negatively valenced feelings flow back along the chain of associations, to dampen even the tendency to initiate an original train of thought, whether practical or theoretical. "Endeavour," says Mill, "is even more effectually restrained by the certainty of its impotence, than by any positive discouragement" (XIX:410/RG 3:23). Thus, after a while, an agent in an unfree society will stop figuring things out for himself, and we have recently acquired an idiom that captures this state of mind nicely: he doesn't want to even go there.[9]

There is a way this argument needs to be qualified. The sense of futility is produced by encountering restrictions on action. But obviously you can't dispense with all restrictions on action (or even on speech). Nature herself provides many of them, and a utilitarian will be led to endorse socially enforced restrictions on action, as when Mill supports what has come to be called the harm principle (the idea that the state may prohibit actions directly causing harm to others). Evidently there will always be *some* restrictions on what one can and may do, and so the argument, if it is to work, must take the training or conditioning on which it turns to be a matter of degree and extent. The conclusion, therefore, must be a requirement that as much freedom be kept available to the agent as possible, and in any case enough for the training that teaches you that you can do what you have chosen to overshadow the training that teaches you that you can't. Quite possibly, clarity of the boundaries between what one can do and what one can't also matters (and this may explain Mill's interest in such demarcating conditions as the harm principle). After all, plausibly, if there are sufficiently clear-cut boundaries between what you can and can't do, the conditioning that associates following out one's train of thought with futility will restrict itself to what is found on one side of them.

I haven't tried to quite make the finish line of the textual puzzle; in particular, I haven't tried to show that the argument we have put together was something that Mill had squarely in mind when he set out to show the compatibility of the Principles of Utility and Liberty. Again, in navigating my way through this argument, I have been picking out considerations which Mill presents, and treating them as though the box they came in was printed "Some Assembly Required." Nonetheless, because the ingredients of this argument are clearly enough elements of whatever it was that Mill did have in mind, we have enough in place to take our next step. It's time to persuade you that promoting moral freedom is fairly high up on the agenda that Mill was pursuing in *On Liberty*. The constraints on governmental and other institutions for which Mill is arguing should, by his lights, jointly tend to shape motivationally balanced personalities.

The requirement that governments permit as much freedom of action as is reasonably possible—that is, freedom within the limits of the harm principle—is explicitly meant to allow budding motivation to develop. And whatever precisely the psychological account of the process is meant to be, the idea is worth running with. Taking a close to home example, the sustained commitment that anchors a career devoted to philosophy often enough starts out in a scarcely formed curiosity that is just strong enough to get one to enroll in a first philosophy class. If one isn't permitted to take the class, or perhaps more importantly, if one's philosophizing is squelched by a teacher who will not allow one to develop philosophically interesting thoughts, that initial philosophical inclination is all too likely to wither and die. But with both the liberty to take the class, and the liberty within the class to try out objections, alternative positions, and arguments for both of them, the initial motivation may become more knowledgeable (about, say, what a philosophical way of looking at a question is like); it may be supplemented by interests in newly encountered ideas or books or figures; gradually, it may be deepened into a sense of competence with philosophical ways of thinking.

If we are attempting to connect liberty to moral freedom within Mill's way of thinking, there is still a problem. While the argument supporting our last claim is supposed to show that liberty is needed to prevent motivations from being flattened out, it does not on its own show that whatever motivations are developed are likely to be suitably balanced. On the contrary, one might think: surely it is the liberty to do as one pleases, and turn oneself into, say, someone who *only* philosophizes, while neglecting family, civic entanglements, and the obligations of public and political life that accounts for the proliferation of morally unfree personalities.

But we've noted that Mill presents the arguments of chapters two and three of *On Liberty* as parallel but distinct; they are alleged to turn on analogous considerations, and the former is presented as a more straightforward warmup for the latter. If I'm seeing how those arguments are meant to work together, Mill has a response to the objection I've just introduced. To exhibit it, I need to embark on a digression which will clear up that third branch of Mill's argument for freedom of speech and of the press. I expect this to *feel* like a digression, but please bear with me: that very response will later serve as an illustration of a point I'll need to make, once the time comes to say what became of Mill's life project.

9.4

Recall that the frame of Mill's argument for the intellectual freedoms identifies three possibilities: any opinion you might have is either true, half true, or false. Why did he feel it necessary to clutter a straightforward dilemma with an extensive discussion of the middling case: of those beliefs that are neither true, nor false, but merely half true? After all, why isn't the possibility of part-falsity already covered by the final case: false opinions which need to be contested in order to be corrected? To explain what Mill is up to, I will quickly sketch one of several ways in which his discussion of scientific method was meant to improve the intellectual underpinnings of the Utilitarian platform.

Some sciences, Mill points out, are highly systematized, in such a way that lengthy inferences can be assembled from shorter ones; these are the "Deductive or Ratiocinative Sciences" (VII:209), with Euclidean geometry serving as his paradigm case. To effect this sort of systematization, we "construct the science from the fewest and simplest possible inductions [the axioms], and … make these, by any combinations however complicated, suffice for proving … truths, relating to complex cases."[10] To remind us that this is technical vocabulary, I'll keep Mill's capitalization for all of the terms in this family.

Now, of the Deductive Sciences, some exhibit composition of causes, and others do not. The model for composition of causes is, "in dynamics, the principle of the Composition of Forces" (that is, summing vectors to get resultants); formally, causes compose when "the law which expresses the effect of each cause acting by itself … also correctly express[es] the part due to that cause, of the effect which follows from the [causes] together" (VII:370f). Sciences which exhibit composition of causes treat causes which can cancel each other out: "A stream running into a reservoir at one end tends to fill it higher and higher, while a drain at the other extremity tends to empty it…. [I]n cases such as these … the two causes which are in joint action [may] exactly annul one another" (VII:372); this means that your calculations may be mistaken if you have overlooked a contrary cause.

We can contrast these sorts of sciences with Deductive Sciences in which there is no composition of causes. If you add 5 and 7 to get 12, you do not have to worry that perhaps a countervailing cause is draining off some of the total unnoticed, and that in *this* case, $5 + 7 = 9$. This latter sort of science affords no room for what so constantly occurs in mechanics and its applications, the case of conflicting forces.... In mechanics we continually find two or more moving forces producing, not motion, but rest.... There is no similar state of things in geometry.... What is proved true from one geometrical theorem ... cannot be altered and made no longer true by reason of some other geometrical principle. (VIII:887f)

Mill calls the mode of treatment appropriate to a science like mechanics the Physical Method, and that appropriate to sciences like arithmetic or geometry the Geometrical Method.

For domains in which a great many different kinds of cause interact, Mill recommends the Deductive Method. (Bear in mind that not all 'Deductive Sciences' are suitable for the 'Deductive Method'; because Mill's various uses of "deductive" differ from our own, it is easy to lose track of his terminology.) In special cases, a core of initial principles—he seems to think of Newton's Laws of Motion as a model—can be established inductively;[11] often, however, they will have to be handed down as results established by a methodologically simpler science, as when associationist psychology is to supply the initial principles for "ethology," Mill's projected science of character. Further results are derived from these initial principles, in the manner of any Deductive Science. (Here we can think of the ways in which, from Newton's laws, we work up treatments of planetary orbits or automobile collisions.) But because the causes represented in the treatment might be overridden, we treat them as "tendencies" (VIII:898), and the conclusions "are therefore, in the strictest sense of the word, hypothetical. They are grounded on some suppositious set of circumstances, and declare how some given cause would operate in those circumstances, supposing that no others were combined with them" (VIII:900). The reality check is "Verification," that is, comparison of the results of the science to "Empirical Laws." As I remarked earlier on, this phrase is misleading to today's ears; Mill means what we call phenomenological laws, rough and ready generalizations "which observation or experiment has shown to exist, but on which [one] hesitate[s] to rely in cases varying much from those which have been actually observed" (VII:516f).

In very complex domains, in particular and especially, that of social science, merely calculating a composition of causes in the manner of mechanics does not in practice suffice. Instead, an entire science is to be peeled out of the domain and systematized, on the understanding that the treatment exhibits only one aspect of the highly interconnected phenomena; the conclusions drawn within such a treatment will have to be checked against the phenomena and the results of complementary sciences to see whether in one case or another they are overridden by other tendencies. For example, economics helps itself to a simplifying assumption, that people are motivated by solely "economic" considerations (they want to make as much money as possible for as little work as possible). But the conclusions drawn in particular cases may be overridden by phenomena assigned to that to-be-established science of ethology; in many countries (Mill seems to have France especially in mind), "in conducting the business of selling their goods over a counter ... [men] care more about their ease or their vanity than about their pecuniary gain."[12]

In the *System of Logic*, Mill takes time out to criticize "the interest-philosophy of the Bentham school." Bentham's "mistake was not so much one of substance as of form": he applied the Geometrical Method in domains whose sciences require the Deductive Method. That is, when he derived a conclusion from idealized or oversimplified initial principles, he forgot to allow that the conclusion might, in simpler or more complicated ways, have to be modified or overruled. In the example Mill gives, Bentham treats human beings as governed by self-interest, and draws conclusions about how the behavior of rulers can be yoked to the interests of the ruled. These conclusions are right as far as they go, but they have to be corrected to take account of further causes that Bentham overlooked: that human beings in general, and rulers in particular, are also governed by habit and local custom.[13]

I earlier argued that Mill was disheartened by Bentham's writings, and that he reformulated the Utilitarian political program and its theoretical underpinnings so as to retrieve his own youthful commitment. So notice that we are seeing how Mill managed to understand himself to be rescuing rather than rejecting Bentham.

The Deductive Method allows the result of one treatment to be complemented, adjusted by and even overridden by considerations belonging to a different treatment (or even a different science). Bentham's error, as Mill thought, was that of treating the Geometrical Method as appropriate in social-science subject matter. That allowed Mill to correct Bentham's policy dictates, while granting that the arguments that Bentham constructed for them were right as far as they went. In his essay on Bentham, in one of those attempts to make a criticism sound as nice as possible, he remarked that "there is hardly anything positive in Bentham's philosophy which is not true: ... when his practical conclusions are erroneous, which in our opinion they are very often, it is not because the considerations which he urges are not rational and valid in themselves, but because some more important principle, which he did not perceive, supersedes those considerations, and turns the scale."[14] At the age of sixteen, Mill had taken on a lifelong commitment to a cause, one which he was not going to abandon; his work in philosophy of science turns out to meet a very personal need. It allowed him to understand himself as *improving* the Utilitarianism he had inherited, rather than merely *replacing* it.

9.5

Our digression concluded, and returning now to the argument for freedom of speech in *On Liberty*, we can finally see why Mill thinks that half truths deserve special treatment and attention: they are the normal product of Deductive Sciences in which there is composition of causes, and it is especially these sciences whose deliverances will figure into public policy debates.[15] But we can also see what the upshots of freedom of speech ought to be for the moral freedom of the citizenry. The Deductive Method leads its practitioners to expect their opponents' conclusions to complement their own, and to think that the correctly adopted policy is likely to be one that reflects and accommodates the apparently conflicting arguments. In any suitably complex domain (pretty much any political subject matter, but not only those), a normal outcome of hearing your own opinions contested ought to be folding the opposing view, and the arguments for it, into your own: extracting the grain of truth (or, one hopes, much more than just a grain) in each way of seeing things.[16]

Now, many such arguments have affective or motivational elements as components. Coming to appreciate those views, and adapting the arguments for them into suitable parts of your own intellectual repertoire, will foster those motivations, when they are already part of your mental life—in something like the way that, in our earlier example, someone's fledgling curiosity about philosophy was likely to flourish in a well-run classroom. Moreover, doing so may well introduce those motivations into your emotional life, if they were not there already. Mill had a reason to think so that is now unavailable to us, to wit, that within the theory of ideas, sympathy is a technical notion: to understand what someone is feeling is to experience a weaker copy of the feeling yourself.[17] This means that following someone else's train of thought closely enough to understand what is moving him is literally to experience his motivations yourself. We construe sympathy differently, but we can accept that often enough it does work out that way: you acquire some version of those motivations.

We can borrow that third chapter of *On Liberty* as an illustration. Vogler points out that it is very hard to make sense of the argument as appealing—which by instrumentalist lights it ought—to its audience's extant desires.[18] Mill himself concedes "the indifference of persons in general to the end [of the free development of individuality] itself" (XVIII:261/OL 3:2), and, when it comes time to appeal to inventiveness and novelty, realizes that he will need to convince "the sort of persons who think that new truths may have been desirable once, but that we have had enough of them now" (XVIII:238/OL 2:16). Nonetheless, suppose that an authoritarian, in the spirit of the Deductive Method, is attempting to accommodate the ideas and arguments of *On Liberty*; we can imagine someone with, as Mill elsewhere puts it, "the tone of mind, which is less eager to hold up to obloquy the errors of an adversary, than conscientiously to examine what portion of truth exists in those errors, and gives them their plausibility."[19] If he thinks his way through Mill's train of thought, he is likely enough to come to have a new interest in inventiveness, in what sort of person a society produces, and so on.

In just the way that you are kept mentally active by the intellectual liberties of others, so you are edged toward moral freedom by their liberties more generally.

Your own choices will not normally make a great deal of sense unless they take account of what other people around you are opting to do; that means you have a pervasive incentive to figure out what they're up to, and that very often means understanding their motivations. The operation of sympathy produces images of those motivations within your own field of motivation. And this amounts to widening the range of motivations on which you can draw, when the time comes to consider whether you will act on any one of them.[20]

Putting the pieces together, if one accepts Mill's reasons for insisting on freedom of speech, freedom of the press, and the liberty to do whatever one decides to (with the most minimal restrictions manageable), then one should also see those very institutional constraints as strongly tending to produce moral freedom. The need to integrate the many opposing half truths that populate the discursive landscape makes one see the point of the arguments for them; getting inside the opposing view acquaints you directly with its motivational and affective aspects. The liberty to pursue interests tends to foster whatever motivations, however nascent, you happen to have. The pressure to cope with the liberties of others will tend to bring it about that you appreciate their motivations, and sometimes in a way that can motivate you. And so the upshot will be a personality in which many very different motivations have been developed: one in which, for each motivation, there are others that one could draw upon to resist it, and successfully.[21]

Finally for now, Mill's *Essay on Representative Government* has learned the lesson of the Mental Crisis, that the shaping of character is of the greatest importance; his primary objective, in the design of democratic institutions, is the effects they will have on the personalities of those who occupy them. The aspects of character that Mill attends to in this work are, first, the need for impartiality and for a citizen "to feel himself as one of the public"; and second, the ability to take broad views of one's society—as Mill puts it, "giv[ing] largeness to their conceptions ... [and] sentiments" (XIX:411f/RG 3:24). This is not by any means the only agenda of the *Essay*, but those broad views are a further way of rebalancing lopsided motivational portfolios.

When Mill reworked components of the Utilitarian platform and of its intellectual supporting framework, he was not simply making it more intelligent, more mature, and generally impressive, in a way that Bentham's version of it had not been. (That is, he was not just fixing its aesthetic problems.) He had learned the importance of moral freedom from his own Mental Crisis, and he chose to reconfigure the Utilitarian project, as he was pursuing it, around the systematic redesign of the basic institutions of society; the agenda of that redesign was the promotion of freedom of the will. This is a surprising move, and one that deserves the attention of today's political philosophers. In the discourse of political liberalism, we have almost lost the thought that the point of political institutions is to make better people. Perhaps the reason is that the sort of person it would behoove a liberal to try to fashion would be one who had, precisely, a free will, and the tendency to think of freedom of the will as a matter of metaphysics rather than of personality precludes asking what it would take to come to have (more of) it. Mill is a valuable corrective on this point.

The move is textually surprising as well, since Mill tells us at the very outset that "the subject of [*On Liberty*] is not the so-called Liberty of the Will, so unfortunately opposed to the misnamed doctrine of Philosophical Necessity; but Civil, or Social Liberty" (XVIII:217/OL 1:1). While that is true as far the conclusions he argues for go, it is also misleading, in that it keeps out of sight his interest in arguing for them.

9.6

We tend to think of utilitarianism, the moral theory, as one thing, and Mill's exercises in political philosophy, such as *On Liberty*, as something else entirely; it's not surprising that his readers are quick to assume that the different enterprises conflict. But Utilitarianism was a political movement, not in the first place a moral theory; Mill's very refined articulation of the moral theory was put in place as a way of integrating the various planks of the Utilitarian platform, and we can now see how Mill is reformulating the version of the program he had inherited so that liberty is part of it. In particular, *On Liberty* is spelling out what utility consists in; only partially, of course, because further and very similar spelling out is allocated to, for example, *On the Subjection of Women*.

In our present practice, our moral theories compete against one another to accommodate more of our moral intuitions. But not only would it be a mistake to read our professional distinction between political and moral philosophy back into Mill, imagining that our intuitions come sorted ahead of time into, say, the moral, the political, and the religious would also be to treat an artefact of our disciplinary turf wars as an important methodological constraint. (We have already remarked on the irony of using intuitions to assess a theoretical enterprise whose point was to provide an alternative to appeals to intuition.) Our own arguments over which moral theory is correct are for the most part very thin, and one likely explanation is that our practical concerns have come to be so thoroughly siloed.

If we want to critically assess utilitarianism, the moral theory, we should instead consider what its pros and cons are once it is spelled out into a political and social program. With any luck we will find weightier things to say than merely that we find ourselves inclined to agree or disagree.

Notice, first, that there is a glaring pragmatic contradiction in the neighborhood of the argument we have been reconstructing; offhand, Mill looks like a refutation of his own argument. We have already seen that Mill lived under the constant supervision of members of his own political movement, and when he worries, in *On Liberty*, that "[i]n our times ... every one lives as under the eye of a hostile and dreaded censorship" (XVIII:264/OL 3:6), he could just as well have been describing himself.

For all practical purposes, he lived in a totalitarian micro-state—that is, within a radical political party, which had its own version of what we now call political correctness. He couldn't say things that deviated, anyway too obviously, from the party line, and he took orders: first from his father, who supervised him on a day-to-day basis, and later on, from Harriet Taylor.[22] If liberty is required for originality, and lack of liberty squelches it, Mill should not have been capable of doing the smallest part of the strikingly original philosophizing he did do. Conversely, if his sort of upbringing produces a John Stuart Mill, then if we are after originality and individuality, why shouldn't we be aiming to reproduce *that*?

It might seem that there is a further pragmatic contradiction in the offing. Recall that there are two aspects that originality normally wears, the more familiar being novelty. Mill's intellectual output is highly original in this familiar sense, and it's hard to see how to account for that in terms of Mill's own intellectual apparatus. Following the pathways etched into his network of associations by the causal structure of experience will explain neither his highly individual cast of mind, nor his accomplishments. Causal pathways are the same for everyone, and so—although complexity, especially of the social world, may lead different observers to notice different connections—analytic minds can be expected to share a great deal in the way of views and approaches to problem-solving. If Mill had an analytic mind, how could he have written the *Collected Works of John Stuart Mill*?

Mill does have an answer. Poetic minds construct clusters of association around their feelings, in a manner that makes those clusters pretty much a matter of happenstance: it is for all practical purposes sheer coincidence that someone comes to associate the colors of Escalante sagebrush with a feeling of exhilaration, and just an accident that, in our example in an earlier chapter, a mother wore straw hats. When "poetic natures" make choices, we can expect them to be *different* choices.

Mill repeatedly characterizes one of his authority figures, Harriet Taylor, in the language he uses for describing poetic minds. Poetic minds can convey their own new directions to analytic minds, sometimes by producing poetry that makes the happenstance cluster of associations, and its organizing feeling, affectively compelling, and sometimes, as when they occupy Taylor's role in Mill's life, by their sheer say-so. Once the new direction is given, even an analytical mind will arrive at novel trains of thought, when it is made to figure things out for itself.

Still, now that we have defused the impending pragmatic contradiction, remember that the point of a society governed by the Principle of Liberty was for everyone to have the opportunity to be as original and as individual as Mill himself: it was to make original personalities *routine*.[23] It is starting to seem that it was not the environment which was to be fostered by his political reforms that gave rise to Mill's inventiveness and ingenuity, and to the intellectual novelty that pervades his work. Rather, the enabling circumstance has just been identified as Harriet

Taylor, who was an effective prompt to originality even in oppressive and unfree surroundings. If we buy into Mill's psychological views, it was not in the first place liberty that enabled Mill's genius, but the pairing of an analytic with a poetic mind.

9.7

Continuing with our reassessment of Mill's simultaneously moral and political theory, we have emphasized the way in which institutional structures—not to mention the central concept in the moral theory proper—have been reengineered for flexibility. But if they are meant to accommodate swerves in people's interests and concerns, the revised Utilitarian program serves people who *have* interests and concerns: things they care about deeply and want to pursue. If the spirit of Mill's Utilitarianism is captured by the title of an old Kinks album—*Give the People What They Want*—then it is suitable for a particular clientele: those who *do* want.

That presupposes that there are going to be people who know what they want: who have desires you can take seriously because they are not wishy-washy about them. Here is the point made in a Wittgensteinian accent. A measuring device makes sense only against the background of a great many empirical facts; for example, yardsticks are made of materials that don't stretch; we can lay them up against objects that aren't themselves changing their sizes and shapes too rapidly; if we had to make all of our yardsticks out of dough, or if most of the things we wanted to measure were always mid-morph, we would stop using yardsticks soon enough. The utility construct—how much people are getting what they want—serves utilitarian moral philosophers as a measuring device. So there are empirical background conditions to be met, for it to be reasonable to use the utilities of outcomes as a basis for choice. And the first and foremost of these is people *having* a great deal in the way of goals and desires and preferences; if they turn out not to, you would be well advised to find yourself a different method of evaluation.[24]

But then Millian utilitarianism looks like it's a good way of thinking about choice only for people who are much more goal- and desire-driven than most of us are. Mill anticipated this objection; in *On Liberty*, he complained that his contemporaries for the most part *didn't* know what they wanted; they didn't have strong preferences, but rather merely did as those around them, and complied with what they thought was expected of them. And it is a further irony that in his own life Mill sometimes seemed like that himself.

Once we have this concern in mind, *On Liberty* and *On the Subjection of Women* fall into place as a surprising response to it: Mill intended the institutional structures he was designing to produce the strong-willed agents his method of moral assessment presupposed. That is, Mill was proposing to address the mismatch between his moral theory and the available clientele by creating a clientele to suit the theory. I earlier on gestured in passing at the idea that Mill's political philosophy is treated as an early presentation of our own version of liberalism, but that is in many respects misleading. We are now in a position to see one such respect: contemporary liberals don't think that their job is to manufacture a populace for which liberalism would provide satisfactory political guidance.

We now live, and have lived for some time, inside institutions that are substantially the ones designed by Mill; we have had freedom of the press, more or less the range of other personal liberties he had imagined, gender equality in pretty much the way he specified it, representative governments, and so on for, in a good many places, on the order of a century.[25] And they have not worked as intended: if you look around, you will see people who are, if anything, *more* conformist and *less* original, in precisely Mill's sense of the word, than before. The ingenious arguments notwithstanding, it is quite clear that the moral and political program has failed to create its clientele.

Here is not the place to take up the very interesting question of what went wrong. Whatever the explanation, the Utilitarian program doesn't fit its clients: not its clients when it was formulated, and not the clients it has been producing—in the real world rather than its own imagined future. Now, a moral, social, and political program that doesn't fit the needs of its customers is *inadequate*. And so the time has come to qualify our initially enthusiastic endorsement of the substance of Mill's life project. As with almost everything important enough to matter, there is no simple answer to whether Mill's Utilitarianism—the whole package, the core theory taken together with the surrounding program—was well chosen.

That said, and even with our more nuanced retrospective assessment of his project in hand, he has not forfeited his role as a best-case project life. On balance, our judgment of the political program is still positive, and not mildly but emphatically so. Life is complicated; the best laid plans of mice and men, even when they work out as well as could have been hoped, turn out to be riddled with misjudgment; it is hard to believe that anyone who had a project anywhere near as ambitious as Mill's could expect to do better. Our accomplishments always involve mistakes such as these, and our retrospective assessments of even the best of them are bittersweet.

9.8

Let's take stock. We've just been arguing that Mill's treatment of liberty is shaped by a concern for moral freedom. We saw earlier on that his redefinition of utility itself was meant to make room for moral freedom; I mentioned in passing that when we sort through Mill's feminist arguments, we find the promotion of freedom of the will to be the pivot of the more dramatic among them. And we have seen at length that a great deal of the *System of Logic* is directed first toward that ground-clearing treatment of determinism, meant to make room for Mill's discussion of moral freedom, and then to a theory of scientific method that, we have just noticed, shows why it is that freedom of the press fosters, once again, moral freedom. We arrived at the point of seeing the importance of moral freedom to be the lesson that Mill had extracted from living through his Mental Crisis. Although we haven't by any means surveyed everything he subsequently did, we are now in a position to conclude that the central moral and political elements of the Utilitarian project—and in any case, the components of that project that Mill took upon himself, as his own life project—have been reformulated and adjusted so as to reorient them toward producing the personality trait he had found to be indispensible: not just in himself, but in *everyone*.

I earlier suggested that Mill had misdiagnosed his own Mental Crisis. But the sovereign remedy for what, in my view, *was* responsible for it has been baked into Mill's arguments. Bentham's depressing shoddiness would be fixed only by unrelenting intellectual rigor; that is, by figuring things out for yourself, that is to say, in Mill's proprietary vocabulary, by originality. And now that we have surveyed them, it is clear that these were very original arguments.

Mill cared about originality enormously, and I'm guessing that this was in significant part why; thus we find originality at the bottom of the argument for liberty, and although he does not consider it explicitly, it is clear that he thinks of it as closely connected with moral freedom. Moral freedom is evidently needed for originality: if you figure things out for yourself, and if your train of thought takes you in surprising and even unwanted directions, you must be able to muster the various motivations that allow you to override your desires to end up where you had formerly wanted to go and imagined you were going.

A life project of the sort in which we are interested connects all of its subprojects one to the other; now that we have seen how Mill reconfigured his own life project, we can see that it is still what we were hoping for as a best case and a test case. The project is woven together throughout by the twin concerns of genius and free will.

10 Mill's Aftermath

Woody Allen once ridiculed the notion of achieving immortality through one's works; he wanted, he demurred, to become immortal through *not dying*. Not everyone has agreed; in particular, Bernard Williams, in a very elegant but long-neglected essay, argued that it would be a bad idea. As you continue living, he observed, either your character will stay the same, or it will change. If it stays the same, and you're immortal, you'll end up so bored you'll wish you were dead, and Williams helped himself to a play by Karel Čapek, and to the opera that Leoš Janáček made from it, for his very vivid illustration: the inhumanly disengaged personality of the several-centuries-old Elina Makropulos, who quite believably opts to finally terminate her own life. However, if your character changes, and you're immortal, you will eventually change into someone about whom you now cannot care. And either way, Williams concluded, you have no stake in living forever.[1]

Mill was not immortal, and did not cut his own existence short, but we can nevertheless see how the problem posed by Williams's argument might account for some of the signs of trouble we have already remarked on in Mill's life, and in particular what early on I labeled its perversity. Plausibly, a life-size project is only psychologically sustainable if it's supported by an emotional investment in the substantive content of the project, for example, voting rights, universal education, liberty, etc.; the abstraction, 'utility,' will not suffice. But a project will only figure as the meaning of your life if you're committed to it, and, over time, either the substantive content of the project will stay the same, or it will change. If it changes, especially in ways that are driven by your responses to your ongoing circumstances, then it will pull away from its original rationale; if you are not to cease being committed to it, you will have to come by a new understanding of the project as a whole, which in turn will defaultly require a new source of commitment. In any case, what we earlier called hedonic drift has to be taken seriously; what you find engaging, enjoyable, and important changes over time, for all sorts of reasons. This means that if the project *does* stay substantively the same, you must be overriding hedonic drift; you're sticking with activities—subprojects—you longer enjoy or care about. Thus if your project stays substantively the same, it will be largely composed for the most part of activities you find constraining and irksome. And in large, highly coherent projects, when most of the components are felt to be chores or worse, eventually the project as a whole will be experienced as intolerable. So a life-size project will either fail to sustain your commitment to it, or will eventually be experienced as intolerable. When you can't stand what you're doing, and you can't or won't give it up, a natural response is to behave perversely with respect to what you're doing.

Williams's problem is evidently a variant of the trap with which Mill had wrestled as a youth; as it turns out, endless life is not needed to spring it. But we have reconstructed Mill's ingenious response to it, and it seems, at first glance anyway, to slip between the horns of Williams's dilemma. By relaxing the top-level characterization of one's life project, and by allowing more flexibility in one's selection of subprojects, one's interests and personality can develop, even as one retains one's commitment to that central organizing concern. Mill remained a committed Utilitarian, even though he was no longer pursuing Benthamite legal reform, and instead had turned his attention to gender equality, the foundations of his projected science of character, philosophy of logic, free will, and all the rest of it.

Perhaps we've reached the finish line. It looks like there is after all a way to configure a project as the meaning of your life, one that surmounts the obstacles Mill encountered in his own early life. And along the way, we have seen those obstacles interestingly articulated by one of the most thoughtful philosophers of his century.

In fact, however, Mill's resolution of his Mental Crisis could not have been successful, or so I will now try to persuade you.

10.1

The book you are now reading is not a commentary on Mill's *Autobiography*, but you could still make your way through the both of them side by side without their getting much out of sync. So imagine you are accompanying one book with the other; where have you gotten?

Almost to the end: there is only one chapter of the *Autobiography* we have not really discussed. Thus it's a bit of a surprise that that remaining chapter picks up not even halfway through Mill's lifespan. It covers Mill's *System of Logic*, that is, his main work on metaphysics and epistemology, on philosophy of logic, and foundational philosophy of social science. Although for various reasons we don't think of Mill's *System* as on a par with Kant's first *Critique*, it has the same scope and ambition, and it was the book that established Mill as the leading British philosopher of his generation.[2] The chapter also covers the short teachable classics for which Mill is now famous; his almost incredible election to Parliament (remember, he refused to campaign); it covers what he did there; it covers his later political activity ... in brief, and sparing ourselves the recitation of the full list, with the large exception of his intellectual and personal intimacy with Harriet Taylor, its coverage includes pretty much everything he did during his mature adulthood. And so the peculiar title of that last chapter—it is a "General View of the Remainder of My Life"—is a dead giveaway. As far as Mill was concerned, everything but the youthful preliminaries was mere *aftermath*.

That way of seeing one's life is a sure sign of something's having gone badly wrong, but we are by this point positioned to see how in Mill's case what has gone haywire isn't just *something*. I'll step through three variations on the pragmatic paradox.

First, as we have just reminded ourselves, Mill's reworking of the Benthamite project he had inherited turned on the inevitability of hedonic drift. The point of the reconfigured project was to accommodate those shifts in interests and concerns by allowing just such reworkings. So if his revision of the project was well motivated, there should have been further such revisions. But while there are perhaps further nervous breakdowns (recall that Bain mentions them, but Mill himself does not), there are no further Mental Crises—no massive rethinkings of the shape of the Utilitarian project. Rather, practically everything in the life falls into place, piece by piece, as part of the resolution of his first and only Mental Crisis. Although we are only getting to the final chapter of his *Autobiography* now, we have had occasion to mention many of the activities and accomplishments it describes; one after another of them was taken up in order to complete discussions of *earlier* parts of Mill's life. The real agenda, we argued, of a good many of the institutional structures that Mill devoted his life to designing and promoting was providing room for their inhabitants to reconfigure their lives, in the very manner that he had done so.[3] Mill's own later life should make us wonder whether the project was after all misconceived: if grownups can settle down and stick with a life plan, as Mill did with his, why rebuild your entire society around the need to accommodate midlife crises and other sudden swerves?

Second, the worry is deeper than whether there really is a need to accommodate hedonic drift. We saw that Mill's spelling out of the Utilitarian agenda as including, first and foremost, a commitment to liberty was an attempt to foster genius and originality. We saw that those notions are Mill's way of talking about thinking things through for yourself, and arriving at conclusions that are genuinely your own. So his argument presupposes that thinking things out for yourself is extremely important.

Now allow that when you do think things through for yourself, if you do not simply give up at some point, you will end up rethinking them, and that when you do rethink things, your mind (often enough) changes. Then if Mill understood originality to be as important as that, and if he was living by his own standards, his mind should have kept changing: there should have been further Mental Crises, and with them, further large-scale rethinkings of his life project. And if there had been, the seventh chapter of the *Autobiography* would not have been its last; the story of Mill's intellectual development—of his *Bildung*, in the Romantic way of talking—would have been over only when he was too old and tired to live up to his 'genius.' Instead we are told, at the very outset of the chapter, that "from this time, what is worth relating of my life will come into a very small compass; for I have no further mental changes to tell of" (I:229/A 7:1).

And third, if Mill *was* original, in his sense of the word, there should have been repeated large-scale rethinking of the Utilitarian project, not just on general principle, but for concrete and pressing reasons. Over the course of the discussion, we have identified a number of occasions for it. We observed repeatedly that neither his psychology nor his theory of rationality made sense of or room for the aesthetic responses that had shaped his life; we saw Mill squaring his commitment to his life project with his instrumentalist account of justification by invoking figures in his life as authorities, in a way that by his own lights was entirely unprincipled; we saw Mill awkwardly framing a moral and political theory suited to a nonexistent clientele; we will shortly turn to Mill's endorsement of socialism, and there too we will see that Mill stopped short of thinking it out; we will soon return to that pair of projected social sciences that are conspicuously missing from his otherwise extremely systematic theoretical enterprise; finally, in an appendix, I will sketch how Mill was unable to manage a philosophically satisfactory treatment of personal identity.[4] Mill was aware (although he explicitly acknowledged only some) of these problems, and he never got to the bottom of them. It is very plausible that, had he done so, both the overall Utilitarian project and the parts or aspects of it which he had folded together into his own life project would have had to be changed deeply and dramatically. We have seen Mill's originality on display in the resolution of his Mental Crisis; so it was not that he lacked the ability to follow trains of thought all the way to the very end. If Mill had lived by the ideas that made his reworked life project made sense, we would have seen one after another episode of soul searching, intellectual demolition, and reconstruction, throughout the course of his life.[5]

Now at this point the alert reader will be wondering whether complaining about incoherence in a life does not simply beg the question against both utilitarianism and Utilitarianism. It is characteristic of these ways of thinking to weigh costs against benefits; if a life that looks like some sort of pragmatic contradiction is the price of a political movement's benefitting the mass of mankind, well, that is just the way the cookie crumbles, and Mill is doing, by utilitarian lights, the correct thing. (Don't forget, utilitarianism is focused on the production of happiness, not coherent lives; Utilitarianism, the political program, never made coherent lives one of its platforms; and although many movements do make lifestyle demands of their cadres, Utilitarian ideology does not demand Wiggins-style coherence of its own activists.) Here I want to put to one side objections to the effect that no one has a reason to make *that* sort of sacrifice.[6] Our own interest in project lives arises precisely from seeing how a coherence requirement plays out within a life. So from our standpoint, the question is not whether incoherence imposes unacceptable costs, but rather whether the life ceases to be meaningful, by the lights of the proposal we are considering. What it takes for a life to be meaningful, and whether its being meaningful is more important than large-scale improvements in the general utility, are two different matters.

10.2

We need to pause for second thoughts; maybe we have been unfair in our assessment of Mill's development. Surely there were changes both in the shape of his life project and in its intellectual infrastructure that cannot be accounted for as the implementation of his response to his Mental Crisis. And if there were, maybe there is no pragmatic paradox, even if Mill either did not experience or felt no need to report accompanying hand-wringing.

The live candidate for this role is Mill's turn to socialism, which we remarked on in chapter 5. The Utilitarians had fought long and hard against the Corn Laws—these were trade barriers meant to protect British grain producers—and Mill did start out a liberal in the older European sense: someone who took it for granted that private property and free enterprise were the drivers of economic progress, and so of the Greatest Good of the Greatest Number. In between the first and third editions of his *Principles of Political Economy*, his views shifted; he came to think that how to manage production and how to distribute the wealth were to be treated as distinct questions, that society was to be rearranged to ensure economic equality, and that workers could be motivated by sentiments similar to patriotism, rather than merely by monetary incentives.[7]

However, while hedonic drift is being accommodated, the alteration in interests and concerns is not in the first place Mill's own, but Harriet Taylor's; Taylor seems to have encountered socialist ideas, adopted them enthusiastically, and instructed Mill to revise his economics textbook accordingly. And perhaps for that reason, while Mill complied, there is nothing of the originality in his treatment that we have come to expect from him: although he did produce a handful of arguments in favor of the newly mandated view, we are not by any means seeing someone thinking through an idea all the way to the end. There is no analog of *On Liberty* or *Subjection of Women* or even *Utilitarianism*—I mean, an ingenious argument purporting to show that a Principle of Equality is surprisingly entailed by the Principle of Utility.[8] There is no working out of the institutions of socialism. And there is no attempt to figure out how to square socialism with the other institutional components of Mill's Utilitarian program. A century and a half later, we are vividly aware of the tension between, on the one hand, liberty, and on the other, equality as socialists understand it: perhaps it can be negotiated, but is at least an apparent conflict, one that has to be worked through.[9] You would in any case expect there to have been adjustments to the institutional structures that Mill had already designed. Yet although the conflict had already been noticed in Mill's time, and although he noticed the tension himself, there is no such treatment.[10] Or again, Mill was part of a tradition that was systematically concerned with the effects of social, political, and economic structures on character: he argued for liberty, gender equality, plural voting, and much else on this basis.[11] The effects of socialism on people's personalities surely deserved extended treatment, by these lights, and that sort of attention is almost entirely absent.[12] Instead we have the revised stretch of the *Principles of Political Economy*, a posthumously published draft of some "Chapters on Socialism," and the miscellaneous speech, all of which is, by comparison with almost everything else Mill ever produced, visibly half-hearted.[13]

We can float an explanation or two, but for our purposes we don't need to decide whether we have it right. Perhaps Mill sensed just how far the revisions to his life project would go, and self-deceptively refused to follow out the consequences of adopting socialist principles; that late in life one can lack the energy to redo everything from scratch. Perhaps he simply wasn't invested in what was, after all, someone else's change of heart; we noticed that Mill managed to reinterpret the dicta of his authorities into views and programs that lived up to his philosophical standards, and it may be that when he did not see his way to doing so, while he complied, he just didn't try very hard. Whatever the explanation, the likeliest example of originality in Mill's adult life that was not a working out of his Mental Crisis proves on second glance not to be that at all.

Even if Mill's turn to socialism is not the expected deeply original reconfiguration of his life project—the one that would show Mill not to have been imprisoned in his crusade for fluidity in one's life plans—and even if there is no further and similarly large episode left unmentioned, perhaps what we have been looking for has been under our noses all along, concealed by a methodological error. It is all too easy to take outcomes to be already present in origins, in something like the way that nationalities, which have been gradually developed over a long period of time, are routinely projected back into the distant past (so that the inhabitants of ancient Gaul, for instance, are imagined to be already Frenchmen).[14] When the twenty-something-year-old Mill decided that what was needed first and foremost was the culture of the feelings, and embarked on the enterprise of designing the intellectual and institutional framework for it, he had not yet constructed the intricate edifice I've been describing as the resolution of his Mental Crisis: working that out could only happen over the course of a lifetime. Just as the Greatest Good of the Greatest Number is too thinly specified an objective to be a guide to action as is, so is the next lap of Mill's specification of the Utilitarian project, that it has to be directed toward "the internal culture of the individual" (I:147/A 5:7). In the course of specifying what *that* would amount to, Mill was adding further determinate content to his life project, and that is where we should expect to find the constant rethinking—the originality and genius, as well as the effects of hedonic drift—that ought to have been present in his adult life. It is hard to see (the objection concludes) only because I have made the mistake of reading the final articulation of the completed life project back into its originating moment.

Before fielding the objection, I had better register the limitations of my conceptual equipment. I confessed early on to being an analytic philosopher by upbringing and ethnicity, and the distinction I now need to talk my way through isn't well-handled in our vocabulary. (This isn't the last time we'll need to be up front about such limitations; there will be another round in the next chapter.) When we talk about what people think, want, and so on, we couch our descriptions in terms of propositional attitudes, that is, combinations of a type descriptor for a mental state, along with a proposition; that latter is conceived roughly as a content that has been given the form of an idealized indicative sentence. (For instance, the *belief* [attitude type] that *Mill lived a surprisingly ascetic life, for someone whose theoretical views sound like an altruistic version of hedonism* [content sentence].) The propositional attitude is individuated *as* that combination, which means that when you change the propositional content, you have replaced that propositional attitude by a different one. And that in turn means that it is hard for us (that is, us analytic philosophers) to make sense of the contrast between filling in the content of a project you already have, and changing out that project for a different (and more contentful) one.

Since I'm not in a position to give a principled account of that distinction, an illustration will have to serve, and we have one right in front of us. Mill's turn to socialism looks very different, in just this respect, from the other developments we've discussed in Mill's project. These are, in one way or another, clever, subtle, and inventive ways of filling out a determination that Mill has already committed himself to, that in order to forestall the collapse in motivation that comes of desires, interests, and concerns ceasing to match a fixed pattern of activity, activities must able to track hedonic drift; institutions must be arranged to promote intellectual and emotional engagement with one's activities; and so on. Whereas there's nothing that makes Mill's turn to socialism out to be that sort of response: there's no story on offer as to how rethinking the distribution of wealth, how agricultural enterprises are managed, and so on addresses Millian Mental Crises.

Once we have the illustration to anchor the distinction, it is clear that while Mill continued, with great intellectual agility, to work out the content of his project, as he had recast it when he could no longer live with its Benthamite version, he never went back to the drawing board. His originality—his 'genius'—was exercised only within the confines of his reconfigured project, and when the time came to rethink its parameters once again, or exit the project entirely, he balked.

10.3

Perhaps we are still being unfair to Mill. He accomplished an enormous amount in the span of a single human life, and we haven't come close to surveying all of it. Perhaps the untrammelled originality that strikes me as missing is hidden elsewhere, in the vast reaches of the *Collected Works*, or in the administrative and legislative activities that Mill undertook. Now, if we embarked on a survey of everything Mill did, the present book would become unreadably long. And I am in any case not going to insist that everything on Mill's list of achievements and attempted achievements was directed toward the objective of producing flexible personalities. Mill inherited a multifaceted political and social project, and while he did adjust it, and while it became a great deal more integrated in his hands, a good many of its elements are best accounted for as belonging to an already existing agenda. But let me make one last attempt to persuade you that Mill's energies really were primarily devoted to implementing the resolution of his Mental Crisis—in the course of which I will identify one final problem with the project as a whole. To do this, I will once again discuss, briefly, his *System of Logic*.

We have already shown how much of the *System* can be understood to be in the service of Mill's two-pass account of freedom of the will, which was in turn produced to make sense of his Mental Crisis, and which served as the basis for the institutional blueprints of *On Liberty* and *On the Subjection of Women*—as well as the theoretical adjustments to Bentham that we find in *Utilitarianism*. But the overt program of the *System*, to which Mill turns once he has solved the problem of induction to his own satisfaction, is to build up, layer by layer, the methodological foundations of social science.

That should be unsurprising. A great many arguments in Mill's moral and political theory turn on character. For instance, his *Subjection of Women* argues for feminist reforms on the grounds that they will improve men's characters—a reason not likely to be much invoked today.[15] Mill objected to the secret ballot, because having to stand up for political choices in public would improve voters' characters (XIX:488/RG 10:1–3; XV:558); he insisted that "the most important point of excellence which any form of government can possess is to promote the virtue and intelligence of the people themselves" (XIX:390/RG 2:20). Political and social institutions were to be carefully tailored to suit the collective character of a people at a time, and thus colonial administrations and benevolent despotisms could be justified in those cases where a national character would not support democratic ones (e.g., XVIII:224/OL 1:10; compare I:169, 177/A 5:15, 19).

Mill was fully aware that if these pronouncements were merely pronouncements, they could not do their work in his arguments, which was why he proposed to inaugurate two new social sciences.[16] The first phase of the research project that was supposed to tie his philosophical system together consisted of ethology, the science of character.[17] The followon phase was to be political ethology, the science of collective or group characters. Mill had spent time in France as a youth, and had been impressed by the differences between (as he thought of it) what the French were like and what the English were like; such observations seem to have served as his paradigm of the subject matter.[18] By our lights, Mill was envisioning the Science of Ethnic Jokes.

To most of us, that makes the enterprise seem startlingly misguided. But recall that the most urgent job these sciences were tasked with was resolving the tension between the Principle of Utility and the Principle of Liberty. We did sketch those arguments in a way which gives us some sense of the sort of content ethology was projected to have. In particular, the analysis of the higher pleasures is in retrospect a general theory of the formation of certain types of character. Although we haven't examined it, the third chapter of *Utilitarianism* contains an additional case study in character formation, this time explaining how people will to an ever greater degree come to have altruistic characters.[19] So Mill himself would have had reason to think that the research program was promising; and notice that while the *System of Logic* is being accounted for as meant to underwrite the doctrines of the short political works, those short works serve as illustrations of, and so themselves underwrite the plausibility of, the sciences for which the *System* is providing the methodological foundations. Mill's life project is in many respects very highly integrated indeed.

Mill executed a great deal of preparatory work for his ethological sciences. After devoting the *System of Logic* to working out the correct methodology for social sciences, in which reproducible and controlled experiments are hardly ever possible, Mill wrote his way through his economics textbook, partly, I believe, as a proof-of-possibility: if economics, which faces the same methodological obstacles as ethology, has shown itself a viable enterprise, many of the standard objections to the viability of ethology are defused. The methodology worked out in the *System* required a further science at the foundations of (both political and just-plain) ethology, one with cleanly stateable and independently verifiable principles. Mill's associationist psychology had been allocated that role, and I take it that this was an important reason for revisiting and updating his father's work in the field.

All in all, there was a great deal of effort put into stage setting for the sciences-to-be of ethology and political ethology. While the methodological efforts are at several removes from the substantive results he needed, bear in mind that Mill was writing at a time when the very idea of a social science was a novelty. It quite reasonably became part of his life project to demonstrate that it was possible to obtain those sorts of results legitimately.

So one of the surprises of the body of work that Mill left us is an empty space where the keystone was supposed to be; when we run our eyes down the spines of the *Collected Works*, notably absent from the list of titles is anything along the lines of *The Principles of Political Ethology*. As before, we can entertain various explanations: perhaps Mill just never got around to it; perhaps he was exhausted by his other labors; perhaps the Science of Ethnic Jokes was destined to remain programmatic because it simply wasn't possible; perhaps he thought that Alexander Bain, whom he had mentored, would do the job for him (and indeed Bain did end up writing a volume *On the Study of Character*).[20] Whatever the reason, that part of Mill's life project went missing. In chapter 11 I will have a use for the lacuna, but right now, let's notice a further irony in Mill's intellectual and emotional trajectory.

Mill's Mental Crisis, I proposed, was triggered by his disappointment in Jeremy Bentham. While there were many aspects of Bentham's work and personality that no doubt contributed to it, one was almost certainly Mill's realizing, as he worked his way through the manuscripts that became the *Rationale of Judicial Evidence*, that Bentham was not providing arguments to connect the Principle of Utility with his substantive proposals. There was a hole where the justifications for Bentham's policies and institutional innovations were supposed to be.

Mill did produce much more in the way of high-quality argumentation than Bentham ever did. But it is now clear that at the center of Mill's mature political and philosophical program there is an analogous gap. The pivotal arguments for Mill's policies and institutional innovations turn on claims about the effects that they would have on people's characters, or alternatively, on claims about the effects that existing social arrangements were already having on people's characters. Mill took it that in order to make those claims stick, he would need a social science; that's why he worked so hard to lay the groundwork for it. But that means that, except in special cases, he never ended up in a position to support his policies with the arguments that he thought necessary.

I suspect that Mill never noticed the similarity between the edifices that he and Bentham had erected. But it is hard not to wonder what his own response would have been if he had. Would he have been disappointed in the way his own accomplishments had turned out incomplete? Or as a mature philosopher at the end of his career, aware that one never has all the arguments one would like to lock down one's conclusions, would he have been more tolerant?

10.4

There's been a great deal of foreshadowing of the very large problem that is finally emerging. As we've recently reminded ourselves, Mill led a perverse life, one in which he seemed, on point after point, to behave as though to spite his own official views. Here are just two of the more important of those juxtapositions. Although his over-the-top execution of his carefully thought through revision to the Benthamite life project should have left him personally happy, we've noted that he struck those around him as deeply unhappy and (what is the same thing by utilitarian lights, though perhaps not our own) pleasure-starved. And although he was himself an "experiment in living," and although the ability to experiment in just this way was supposed to produce passionate and strong-willed personalities, he comported himself as one of the conformists he criticized in *On Liberty*, who have no real preferences of their own. I do need to register that the picture we have seen is more complicated than that brief summary, but nonetheless, Mill seems to have been stuck with the very psychological posture whose rejection he had taken on as his task in life.

There was, you will recall, a great deal more of the same; something had gone deeply wrong in Mill's life. I now want to take up the question of just what the source of the problem was.

11 A Very Quiet Tragedy

It has been a long haul, but now that we have talked our way through Mill's life, we can finally read off it the argument we have been anticipating; it is time to assess the proposal we have had on the table since the outset, about what it takes for a life to be meaningful. First, I will ask you to allow me a number of observations, which I will quickly assemble into the argument, interleaved with reminders of the relevant aspects of Mill's biography and intellectual output. Then I will entertain second thoughts: To what extent can we really see those components at work in the story we have recounted? Do we really have to treat them as observations, or can we reinforce them with subsidiary arguments? Does the argument come with an escape hatch? I am going to register more than one way that the argument in the offing is one that philosophers today are ill-equipped to manage, or even articulate. What adjustments to the available philosophical vocabulary would be needed to unpack it?

11.1

First observation: It is a rigorous discipline, in philosophy and elsewhere, to follow trains of thought where they go: and by that I mean, where *they* go, which is not at all the same thing as what you are inclined to think next. Trains of thought can be arguments, and since philosophers are used to the idea of following an argument where it goes, those are the ones that are likely to come to mind first for some of my readers. But not all such trains of thought—I mean, the ones that lead you on, step by step—*are* arguments. As we have seen, Mill was very aware that part of being a strong poet is following one's train of thought out to its destination, and that those poetic trains of thought are often constructed out of idiosyncratic personal associations.[1] And between these extremes, we can find intermediates of all sorts. Often, solving one problem will require solving another, and solving that to require solving yet another, and so on. Here the discipline required to follow a train of thought where it goes is displayed in taking up each of those problems in turn, until one has gotten to the bottom of one's initial conundrum. Doing that may not amount to following an argument; especially when these are philosophical problems, the argument is rather likely to be the *result*: what one produces or finds as one reaches the end point of that train of thought.

Mill was very good at this; looking back, he credited his accomplishments to the "mental habit" of not letting go until he had gotten to the bottom of things:

> of never accepting half-solutions of difficulties as complete; never abandoning a puzzle, but again and again returning to it until it was cleared up; never allowing obscure corners of a subject to remain unexplored, because they did not appear important; never thinking that I perfectly understood any part of a subject until I understood the whole. (I:127/A 4:20)

Although we've identified a number of points on which Mill fell short of this aspiration, nonetheless his treatment of his Mental Crisis, which we reconstructed in chapters 4–7, illustrates what following out a train of thought of that sort looks like, and in fact does so twice over. The first lap gave us one of his interim results, that very terse argument for having a nervous breakdown which we saw in section 5.1. We retraced Mill's further steps, as he faced up to the practical and personal problem posed by his violent aesthetic response to the early Benthamite version of his life project; we saw him implementing, step by step, both a way of handling the problem as he officially understood it, and a response to the problem as he experienced it (even though he was never able to formulate it in a way that reflected his experience, using a theoretical vocabulary he controlled).

Now, here is a further observation: trains of thought can go *just anywhere*. I mean, it is part of, for example, a philosopher's working experience that if you follow the argument, and don't flinch when you see where it is taking you, there is no position so startling but that you might not find yourself having to adopt it—and that position may be on a subject that you had never imagined you would need to have a view about. For example, you will recall that we started out asking about the meaning of life, took up a proposal due to David Wiggins, found ourselves examining the biography of a Victorian political activist and intellectual, and shortly thereafter were considering what free will, the theory of the syllogism, and positivist philosophy of science had to do with one another; when Mill considered that last question, he worked himself into the view, which most philosophers still consider outlandish, that there is no such thing as deductive inference.[2]

These two observations already allow us a lemma of sorts. We introduced the notion of a life project as exemplifying Wiggins's criterion for meaningfulness in a life: that the role of any valuable element within that life is accounted for in a way that appeals to each of its other valuable elements. Thus, a life project absorbs *all* of a life. This entails that if one has a life project, one's time and attention must be devoted exclusively to matters pertinent to the project. Trains of thought, we said, go *just anywhere*. So, even in a project as flexible as Mill had managed to make his, having a life project means *not* following trains of thought wherever they go. Compare William Whewell, another Victorian intellectual whom we have run into in the course of our discussion, and someone who did allow his mind to stray. His own project in history and philosophy of science was certainly quite ambitious, but it did not prevent him from taking time out to write bad poetry, to translate a German novel, to produce a book arguing against the existence of space aliens, to edit a posthumous volume of a friend's economics lectures, and to develop enough of an interest in Gothic architecture to author a book about it.[3] Mill stayed on point, and while he did a great many different things, they all (or just about all) contributed, in one way or another, to the very large project that served as the meaning of his life.

A step and a half back, I characterized the ability to follow out trains of thought as a discipline. If you look around, you will see that it is rare, which I believe should be put down to its being extremely demanding. In the first place, staying hard on the trail involves not being distracted by whatever else may come to mind, in particular, by whatever is easier to think about.[4] Iris Murdoch used to emphasize the dangers of emotionally satisfying daydreams, but what derails you need not be a fantasy: there are also the straightforward comforts of revisiting and rehearsing familiar patterns of thought, whatever they are.[5] Performing the exercise depends on having available the requisite skills; in Mill's own case, an aptitude for argument, first and foremost, but other types of trains of thought will make other demands. Following out a train of thought is surprisingly time-consuming; but there are always errands to be run, and personal and professional duties to discharge. The discipline involves being willing to sacrifice the opinions, evaluations, and agendas one happens to already have, and if one confers with others, it involves encountering resistance—or, what is sometimes harder to get past, sheer disinterest. It involves learning: new information, skills, and habits of mind may be required at any step. Briefly, it involves repeatedly exiting your comfort zone, and thus the phenomenology of following trains of thought is typically that of resisting temptation, of weakness of will—*akrasia*, in the philosophers' lexicon—and of procrastination.

Consequently, those who are able to follow trains of thought wherever it is they go, all the way to the very end, are just those who experience doing so as an obligation, and as overridingly compelling: as something that they *cannot but do*. After all, if one felt one could do anything else, one would; and unsurprisingly, in his rough draft of the passage we just quoted from his *Autobiography*, Mill describes "des clartés de tout" as "a mental necessity with me."[6]

The coherence criterion proposed by Wiggins was demanding: the importance of *any* valuable component of a life must be explained by *all* of its remaining valuable components. Composing a life in this manner entails finding connections between those components, and ways of adjusting them to make them not just jointly compatible, but mutually supporting. However, lives have to be assembled out of materials that are, as far as the person whose life it is is concerned, simply given: one does not get to choose one's parents, or who one's children turn out to be; one has to take the opportunities that come one's way, overcome the obstacles one happens to encounter, manage the crises that come up—and do all of that and more with the personality, abilities, and incapacities one has and the self that one is. We have been examining at length one somewhat unusual extended illustration. The Benthamite project Mill inherited was, like the program of most any political party, a hodgepodge of policies and ideological fragments: a universal franchise, repealing import duties on wheat, getting rid of the usury laws, Malthusian worries about population, freedom of the press, penal reform, the maximization of happiness ... and you will also remember that this is only a sample of a much longer and quite heterogeneous list.

Now, you cannot expect the connections between such found objects to come as an off-the-shelf commodity. Densely connecting these sorts of intractable materials, conformably to whichever view of practical justification one holds—instrumentalism, in Mill's case—so that they add up to the meaningful life, in the Wiggins understanding of that notion, will be an ambitious undertaking: so much so (putting to one side second thoughts I will get to in due course), that one will not find enough in the way of the requisite connections unless one is committed to firmly, thoroughly, and even ruthlessly tracking them down. Over the course of two chapters we saw how Mill managed to square freedom of the press and other liberties with the requirement of maximizing the overall happiness via his ingenious theory of the higher pleasures, and how getting that connection in place was managed by interposing the importance of originality and genius, which were themselves tied to the demand for moral freedom via a sophisticated view of scientific method, which in turn reshaped the large structure of Mill's argument for freedom of the press. To track down *those* sorts of connections means following trains of thought where they go: how else would you find them? That means that only those who have the discipline to follow trains of thought out where they go will even be candidates for having a life project of the sort we are after.

It follows that such life projects will be rare at best. You might have been assuming that what was distinctive about Mill's Utilitarian project was its vastly ambitious political and intellectual scope, together with the mark it made on history, rather than its formal aspect: the principles on which it was organized, and its having filled all but a couple of the rooms in the floor plan of his life. It is, after all, not unusual to see people treating, say, their families as projects, and whether that's a good or bad approach to take to domestic life, projects that unify a life cannot be, it would seem, infrequent. However, if I am right both about what this sort of unification requires and about the resistance of the raw materials, once we take a second look, what we will find is that the components of—to stick with the example—a family-life-as-a-project usually coexist uneasily with each other, and are held together merely by being placed side by side, rather than being integrated in the manner we're considering, where each component justifies the presence of the others. I'll return to this point and provide supporting argument shortly; in the meantime, life projects that live up to the condition Wiggins imposes are evidently uncommon, even though the aspiration is common enough.

The unity of one's unified life may itself not be an aspiration. Remember, the ground rules of utilitarianism do not say anything about unified agency or coherence; the sole concern is everyone's happiness, and so for Mill to have worried about whether his life was unified would have been, in a well-known phrase due to Bernard Williams, "one thought too many."[7] And the unity may or may not be experienced as an obligation. But if a project ends up colonizing your life in its entirety, or even nearly so, it must be irresistibly compelling, in very much the way the intellectual virtues of following out trains of thought must be for those who have them. In Mill's case, the overwhelming importance of the Utilitarian program—supported within the structures of his personality by the people he had adopted as moral authorities—drove out almost every competing activity. Someone who permits that to happen to him finds proceeding with the program to be something he cannot but do.

Pulling these observations together, if one is successful in organizing one's life into a unified project, one must have been ruthless in following out trains of thought wherever they go, all the way to the very end. Someone who is ruthless about doing so experiences it as something that he cannot refuse to do. But to stay on point, to keep one's project on track, requires precisely refusing to do so. And now it seems that anyone who is fully committed to a life project will be subject to conflicting imperatives, in a way that renders the practical posture of the person himself deeply incoherent.

11.2

Williams once advanced an account of tragedy, on which it is an effect of having indefeasible but conflicting obligations: as when Agamemnon was required, in his capacity as admiral of the fleet, to do whatever was necessary to get the ships moving; was required, as a father, not to do anything that would grievously harm his daughter; and was informed that the ships would stay becalmed until his daughter had been sacrificed.[8] If we take this account on board, we can say that Mill's exemplary project life was a tragedy. The argument we have just put in place tells us that its tragic shape was not a coincidence, but the normal or default outcome of assembling such a life. Mill's diagnosis of his Mental Crisis focused on the way that motivations can be *undercut*; we have arrived at a very differently focused diagnosis of the problem that pervaded the remainder of Mill's life, on which it had to do with the way that motivations in a project life inevitably *clash*. It is perhaps of interest that in both processes, patterns of expenditure of intellectual effort play an important role.

Is it fair to assimilate Mill's life—a phenomenally successful career, unmarred by the violence of the tragic stage—to the misfortunes of Antigone and Agamemnon? In his classic treatment of realism in literature, Erich Auerbach argued that we have gradually learned to give the serious literary treatment which was once reserved for the military and political decisions of kings and aristocrats to the lowliest topics and most mundane subject matter.[9] It is a recent cultural accomplishment (and it *is* an accomplishment) that authors such as Gustave Flaubert and Richard Ford can make catharsis-inducing high literature of, respectively, the misadventures of a bored housewife and the daily grind of a divorced real estate agent. Philosophy has been traversing its own version of that trajectory as well, albeit more slowly; where once it was confined to subject matter such as Plato's Forms of the Good and Beautiful, by Wittgenstein we had reached the point where someone was able to ask, in what was nonetheless the register of high philosophy, what it really takes to teach someone to balance his checkbook. Both as philosophers and as readers of belles lettres we should be prepared to accept as full-fledged tragedy the almost invisibly ruined life of a middle-class Victorian intellectual—even when there are no oracles pronouncing to him his miserable but unavoidable fate, no gods intervening in the outcomes, and no climactic scene littered with dead bodies.

Now, one cannot always follow out every train of thought where it goes, and remain a coherent personality.[10] Nonetheless, the conflicting obligations that made Mill's life tragic had to do with following, and with not following, his trains of thought where they led—each of which was experienced as something he could not but do. In today's philosophical discussions of practical necessity, moral incapacity, and the like, we sometimes lapse into assuming that practical necessities dictate what one in fact does: if betraying your oldest friend, or taking bribes, is something you just can't do, then you *don't* betray him, or take bribes.[11] However, that is not the 'cannot but' in play here: when two obligations of this kind clash, at least one of them will go by the board, and in Mill's case, he stayed focused and largely on point, as far as the Utilitarian project was concerned. Rather, one pays a psychic penalty, normally one that becomes visible in one's comportment or behavior. When Williams investigated conflict of obligation, he focused on regret and remorse as its markers, but the ways in which the sacrifice of an indefeasible obligation can play out within a life are arbitrarily varied. For instance, we are told of Agamemnon that

> when necessity's yoke was put upon him
> he changed, and from the heart the breath came bitter
> and sacrilegious, utterly infidel,
> to warp a will now to be stopped at nothing.[12]

Life in the projects is understandably experienced as claustrophobic: you *have* to get out of it, and you *can't*. Mill's response to subordinating his intellectual freedom to the Utilitarian project proved to be the ongoing perversity of his adult life.

What we are seeing is that a life can be tightly unified only if the person who lives it is deeply committed to an intellectual discipline that undercuts that unity. Now, as hard as a tragic life is, I do not want to construe its unhappiness as a decisive consideration against opting for it: some people like being drama queens, punk puts a premium on self-destructiveness, and on occasion someone—we used Oscar Wilde as our example in chapter 1—chooses to arrange his life as a tragedy for the aesthetic effect. These may be bad choices, but I don't think our argument should depend on the (often dangerously moralistic) insistence that they are. Rather, tragedy as we are understanding it marks evaluative and practical conflict within a life.

Tragedy as Williams understands it is a matter of, roughly, conflicting imperatives; the conception of the coherence of a life that we are taking from Wiggins has to do with how you account for the importance to you of one thing or another. But why can't you be torn between two courses of action, such that the importance to you of each is explained by everything else that matters to you? That is, why isn't the argument from tragedy trading on an equivocation, on what it is to "add up to a life"?

The model of coherence we've been using has been assembled from instances of a single relation: that *these* elements of your life matter to you explains why *those* do. But let's build that model out a little more. The sense of Wiggins's proposal also requires that some of the things that matter to you *won't* explain why other things that matter to you, *don't* matter, after all. A life's components add up to a life not just when they support one another, but when they don't undercut each other's importance.

Tragic conflicts are produced by conflicting but indefeasible commitments; after all, if they permitted tradeoffs or compromises, you would simply select your all-things-considered best option. (It would be too bad if you had had to make a tough choice, but it would be water under the bridge, and no need to look back.)

Now, an indefeasible commitment won't make sense to the person who has it unless it is shadowed by a characterization of what it's about, one that makes it clear *how* it sweeps aside potentially competing commitments.[13] Any such characterization cannot but undercut the importance to you of other commitments that also present themselves as indefeasible. For instance, because armies are only effective when their soldiers are willing to die in battle, a conception of military duty, such as the one that must have been in play in Agamemnon's forced choice, will demote familial concerns, along with everything else, to second rank. Returning to Mill's case: an indefeasible commitment to the general utility means that the need to get to the bottom of things could not be an overriding concern; from the utilitarian point of view, intellectual curiosity is just one more preference, and just one more occasionally useful means. Conversely, the indefeasible commitment to getting to the bottom of things makes the general utility out to be just one more thing to be understood without remainder. So if someone is experiencing a tragic conflict, their commitments are mutually undermining; thus they are in violation of our built-out rendering of the Wiggins coherence condition.

Thus, to show that a life constructed as a project presses toward tragedy is to show that the life-as-project is not an available conception of a coherent life. But the point of the constraint that led us to consider project lives was, precisely, coherence: it is not a good choice to attempt to have a meaningful life by unifying it into a project if the result of doing so is to produce a life that is not meaningful, by those very lights. We don't, it turns out, have an understanding of *what it would be* to live out a life that was unified in the way that Wiggins requires.

11.3

A lap or two back, I pointed out that if our observations are on target, life projects of the Wiggins variety are rare, and some of my readers might have responded with sudden indifference to their prospects. If it turns out that we were only considering what might serve as the meaning of life for members of, as it were, a monastic elite, then how such enterprises work out is, as far as us normal everyday Joes go, moot. It turns out that something like that response *is* the correct one, even if you aspire to be a member of that elite; if we do not have a coherent conception of what a project life would be, then the question of whether life projects are a good choice is moot for everyone.

Assured failure is not a reasonable recommendation, but again, all of this does not show that Mill's life was a failure by *his* own lights. Again, although Mill explicitly devoted a great deal of effort to the intellectual coherence of his views, the (anyway, official) reason was not that his objective was coherence for its own sake; on the contrary, he argued vigorously against William Whewell, for whom it was. The unity of Mill's life project was a side effect of devoting himself to an overwhelmingly important mission, the Greatest Good of the Greatest Number;

because, unlike goals with clear finish lines, projects are open-ended, an important project tends to push other activities out of a life, and this was how it came to pass that Mill's life (apparently) satisfied the condition Wiggins imposed.[14]

Wiggins's leading idea was that a meaningful life is one whose parts add up to a life, and we opted to consider a particular way of making that thought concrete by adding to the formal constraint that he devised to express it the further premise that all practical reasons are means-end reasons. So notice that the argument we have now given does not invoke that second, instrumentalist premise at any point. When we started out by suggesting that Mill's life was a train wreck, we couldn't know whether to locate the problem in its instrumental structure, or in its cohesiveness and unity, or in both conditions together. Now we do know: while we have seen that there are disturbing features of his life that can be pinned on his instrumentalism—most notably, his need for authority figures—its tragic aspect is due to its drive toward thoroughgoing integration. We can accordingly expect that any life that was equally tightly organized, in the sense of satisfying, or nearly satisfying, Wiggins's condition for meaningfulness, would be as tragic—although the way it played out would no doubt differ.

But only expect: for reasons I will air in section 12.1, I do not want to claim that we have an airtight argument to the effect that anyone whose life is coextensive with a project will live out a tragedy. In the messy territory of real life, our arguments are almost bound to be defeasible: that is, if they go through, it will be only other things equal, and it's never possible to manage an exhaustive survey of those other things up front. We need to consider what anyway the most pressing forms of pushback to the argument would be, and how they play out.

11.4

Are life projects really as difficult to cobble together as all that? After all, a great deal of the connectedness between the parts of one's life seems to come easily enough: I need exercise, I like the outdoors, and so I hike; I like talking to my friends, so I take them along on those hikes. What's so hard about that? There is a sizable repertoire of ready-made modes of integration: when people take on the family-life-as-project, desires for romance and companionship fit together with an interest in progeny, all in one neat package; when they go to college, education, vocational certification, networking and social positioning, a sports club and the opportunity to live away from one's parents—all these are rolled together into a four-year program for which you can submit a single application.

Now, it would be a mistake to conclude that because some integration comes easily, full integration must be easy, too. If I am reading the problem correctly, the exercise is asymptotically hard: as the motivational posters would say it, the first 90 percent takes the first 90 percent of the effort, the next 5 percent takes the second 90 percent of the effort, the next $2\frac{1}{2}$ percent takes the next 90 percent of the effort. . . .

If what has to be explained by (just about) everything else in your life is (just about) *everything*, then if you have to do the work of finding those connections yourself, the obvious ways of assembling the jigsaw pieces together, and the available ready-made connections, will not be enough; only a vehement commitment to thinking it out for yourself will get that last 10 percent, or last 5 percent. This is why Mill's emotional stake in originality and genius is not, from our perspective, a personal idiosyncrasy; if he had not had some such very deep commitment, he would not have been a suitable medium for investigating such lives.

Nonetheless, and allowing that last point, if the argument turns on its being hard to assemble a large number of found objects in a way that satisfies our very demanding coherence condition—that is, hard in a way that requires an extremely high level of originality, i.e., thinking for yourself—we had better consider some of the various ways of making the task significantly more tractable. Several expedients suggest themselves. We can cut back the number of pieces of a life that need to be integrated. We can make the task much more doable if we are allowed to excise the especially recalcitrant pieces of a life. And maybe we can help ourselves not just to socially available ready-made connections between pieces or elements of a life, but to entire templates: if the template has been engineered to be, as we might put it, Wiggins-compliant; if institutional arrangements are there to produce the sorts of items that fit the slots in that template; then not much in the way of inventiveness or hard thinking is required, on the part of anyway most individuals, in order to have a meaningful life.[15]

Let's travel down each of these exit ramps from the argument that project lives turn out to be tragedies, but only just far enough to assess where taking each of them will land you.

First off, perhaps the simplest way of making the task simpler would be to cut back, drastically, the number of things that are important or matter in a life. If the Wiggins-compliant life requires that the explanation of anything that matters to you invoke everything else that matters to you, we can satisfy that condition trivially, if there is only one thing that matters to you; easily enough if there are two, such that each of them counts as a reason for the other; still pretty easily, if there are only three.... Notice that the life itself need not be overly stripped down; we are not necessarily contemplating the character in the opening scene of *Flowers for Algernon*. Early on in our discussion, we encountered a picture of the human personality according to Bentham, on which people are hedonic engines driven by pleasure and the absence of pain, both being construed as locations along a uniform dimension of sensation. Although this sort of Benthamite individual cares about only one thing, we also saw that he is nevertheless likely to have a great many irons in the fire.

However, while this strategy produces something that is, according to the letter of the condition we are investigating, technically a meaningful existence, it is not responsive to what motivates this conception of the meaning of life. When a philosopher finds coherence or unity of agency attractive, what he is after is complex rather than trivial coherence; he admires the complex but highly coordinated agent, rather than the sort of unity that is achieved by there being hardly anything to unify. (Likewise, when an epistemologist wants a coherent theory of the world, he isn't after a theory containing only two interentailing propositions.) Here we haven't been investigating what lies behind those philosophical motivations—what motivates *them*—but we can still say that the price of this way of defusing the argument is that the source of the initial interest in this conception of meaningfulness is no longer being addressed. Since we borrowed Benthamite psychology as an illustration, let's observe that we can see the problem exhibited in the Benthamite's inability to give a satisfactory account of why utility is important and why it matters to him.[16] If you are that single-minded, your range of concerns is too impoverished to provide the explanatory depth that is anyway one of the things which makes coherence seem like an attractive aspiration.

Second, and turning now to a more sophisticated relative of that proposal, the thought that the tragedy of the project life can be sidestepped if one is able to excise recalcitrant pieces of one's life strikes me as among the most philosophically challenging of the objections we are surveying. What *is* a life, if not those things that matter to you, connected together into a coherent whole? And if that is the way we construe the boundaries of a life, an activity or person or object whose importance you are unable to explain in terms of other elements of a life probably doesn't belong to it; that is, this objection goes, it looks like we get a long way toward satisfying the condition we lifted from Wiggins for free.

And what you don't get for free, this objection continues, you can get for cheap. If you are the one producing those unifying justifications and explanations, then only if there were an antecedent fact of the matter, one beyond your control, as to what counts as part of your life would there be a genuine barrier to simply editing items out of—or for that matter into—your life. Granted, in social interactions the stance is a bit hard to swallow: imagine someone insisting that he has nothing to be ashamed of, and does not need to apologize for what happened yesterday, because he has decided that what happened yesterday doesn't count as part of his life. But what could such a fact of the matter consist in? It is not as though anyone has on hand a criterion for what does and doesn't belong to a life, much less is in a position to show why his proposed criterion is correct. It is not as though there were an invisible glow emanating from the items that populate a life, to which the demarcation has to be responsible; putting an illustration of the objection in the first person, that philosophy is part of my life is a matter of my engaging in it, and of the position I give it among my concerns, rather than a *Diktat* handed down by the Fates. Your life is what you make of it.

I am not going to try to provide the missing criterion, but I think I can make a plausible case, using the materials we are now working with, that what is part of your life and what isn't is not generally up to you. As it happens, Mill attempted to delete a piece of his own life, and his failure is instructive: it very strongly suggests that, for present purposes, what you try to amputate stays attached to you, willy nilly.

In the runup to his marriage to Harriet Taylor, Mill opted to pick a fight with his family, the pretext being their expressions of discomfort with the socially and personally problematic pairing.[17] From that point on, he had for all practical purposes nothing to do with them; in fact, as various commentators have noticed, Mill's *Autobiography* doesn't actually mention his mother.[18] Surely this is what it would look like to slice off an inconvenient piece of your life.

Focusing on Mill's mother, and leaving his siblings aside, if we look more closely, and in particular, look at the closest thing we have to a portrait of Harriet Mill, the attempted excision *doesn't* remove the apparently detached piece of the life—anyway, from what we are now interested in, the scope of the requirement we lifted from Wiggins. That depiction, from Dickens's rendering of the Mill family in *Hard Times*, is something of a caricature, and the real Harriet Mill must have been a more complex character; nonetheless, my guess is that what we see there is Mrs. Mill either as she was described to Thomas Carlyle by her son, or as she struck Carlyle himself. (Recall that Carlyle was likely Dickens's informant.) Here are a few representative snippets:[19]

Mrs. Gradgrind, weakly smiling, and giving no other sign of vitality, looked (as she always did) like an indifferently executed transparency of a small female figure, without enough light behind it.

[T]ruly it is probable she was as free from any alloy of that nature [imagination or "fancy"] as any human being not arrived at the perfection of an absolute idiot ever was.

And on her deathbed, the Harriet Mill character says,

"You must remember, my dear, that whenever I have said anything, on any subject, I have never heard the last of it, and consequently, that I have long left off saying anything."

One of Mill's main concerns, in the *Subjection*, is the way women get ground down in certain kinds of marriages. His model, and the reason he felt so strongly about it, looks to have been his own parents' marriage. His much-put-upon mother doesn't seem to have been the object of domestic violence, but she is depicted as a human doormat.

My sense of it is that Mill unfairly, but not in a way that is unfamiliar, blamed and resented his mother for having put up with his father, and for having allowed James Mill to turn her into the almost completely effaced figure that was Dickens's source for Mrs. Gradgrind. All of that was Mill's motivation for what amounted to disowning her.

Evidently, one of the things that *Subjection of Women* is (really) about is ensuring that other women would not be treated like his own mother. But now, if that *is* a large part of Mill's reason for taking the feminist stand he does in *Subjection*, and if Mill's feminism is tightly connected to various other elements of his overall tightly integrated life project, then when the time comes to trace out the explanations of why the various things in his life that matter to him *do* matter to him, we cannot honestly leave his reaction to his mother's mistreatment off the plate. The lesson is that announcing that—or acting as though—something or other is not really part of your life is not enough to *make* it something that does not matter in your life. Those sorts of denials do not exempt it from the requirement that whatever matters in your life be tightly connected to everything else that matters in your life. So, and now we are finally wrapping up our response to the objection, the difficult task of tying your life together into a coherent package cannot be made easy simply by reclassifying the inconvenient and intractable bits as standing outside of it.[20]

11.5

Continuing to page through plausible defeating conditions for the argument to the tragedy of project lives, here is that third objection. If we cannot manage the complexity of the task by shrinking the number of elements it involves, or by selectively deleting them, perhaps we can spare people the burden of originality by exempting them from fitting together pieces that are, so to speak, originals, and which they have to take just as they come.

If this approach is to have any chance of working, it will have two sides to it. On the one hand, imagine that people are provided with templates for their lives that have a solution to the puzzle of full coherence built into them: the blueprint for such a life contains standardized slots for all of a life's important elements, and specifies how each of them fits in with the others. Like Dickens's sketch of Mill's mother, this is going to be a bit of a caricature, but I'll help myself to the American Dream of the 1950s, in one of its two gender-specific versions: your wife raises your children, and plays hostess when you have the boss over for dinner; your job allows you to support your family, afford your ranch house and your V8 station wagon; your children hold the marriage together, help their mother with household chores, score you bragging points with the neighbors, and excuse your asking for yet another promotion; your car takes you back and forth between your home in the suburbs and the mainframe manufacturing facility in Illium, New York; your suburban home is the ideal environment in which to raise your children, and is impressively respectable in a way that visibly suits the job you have; the bulky television console in the living room reminds you on a daily basis of just how each piece of your life is supposed to look.

On the other hand, because such templates will not effectively structure a life if the roles they designate are not correctly filled, imagine further that institutions are set up to supply candidates for the things that will matter to you, more or less manufactured to spec. People are raised to aspire to those tightly constrained spousal roles; large corporations offer the jobs that allow their employees to buy houses in the suburbs; developers build the subdivisions and put up white picket fences around the houses.

The historical versions of these templates were not designed with Wiggins-style integration in mind, and so we should expect them to deliver at best an approximation to it; but, the objection goes, we could in principle preempt the argument that the project life is a tragic one by prepping the elements of the project life in this way. Living this sort of life will be a little like solving a jigsaw puzzle; the puzzle is designed and manufactured so as to ensure that the pieces in the box *will* fit together: they have been cut from the very picture into which they will be reassembled. Although there may be some intellectual challenge in putting the pieces back in order, nothing like Millian thinking things through to the very end will be needed; for one thing, the complete picture is reproduced on the front of the box.

As will become apparent in the next chapter, in my own view the principled way of fielding the objection would be an exercise much like the one we are now wrapping up: that is, to locate a life in which we can see how the proposal plays out. But since this is not the point at which to start in on a further book-length treatment, here is a stand-in for it.

Mill had his own way of thinking about the issues, and since we've been using him as our stalking horse, let's put that on the table first. In his arguments for liberty, Mill analyses the costs of conformism from a utilitarian point of view.[21] Firstly, human faculties of perception, judgment, discrimination, and so on are exercised only in making a choice. When you do something merely because that's the way it's done, you're not making a choice. So template dwellers don't exercise their faculties of perception and so on, or not very much, and those well-developed faculties are necessary if people are going to turn out well.

And secondly, it is those faculties which give rise to feelings and preferences—more generally, to 'impressions,' in the British Empiricist lexicon. Since those faculties are exercised only in making a choice, and since, when you make your own choices, your feelings control your conduct, strong feelings and a strong character depend on your making choices on an ongoing basis. Conversely, when "inducements to an act" aren't "consentaneous" with your feelings, your feelings and character end up "inert and torpid." Someone who doesn't have strong feelings can't take much pleasure in life—which is to say, in the utilitarian way of seeing things, that he can't really be happy. But of course the "Greatest Good of the

Greatest Number"—the Utilitarian guiding idea—consists in people's happiness. When you act because it's the custom, you're not acting because you literally feel like doing it. And so utilitarianism has to veto always, or almost always, acting on the basis of conformism.

If we are not ourselves utilitarians, we do not have to accept a utilitarian evaluation of the template-driven strategy, and at least the second lap of that argument invokes psychological theory we no longer believe. Nonetheless, it does seem to me that, looking past Mill's attempt to articulate the drawbacks of conformism, we discern considerations that make sense outside the frame of utilitarianism and the antique psychology.

In the sort of prepared template presupposed by the prefab coherence approach, the things that matter to someone, or that are important in his life, occupy those slots in the template. To do so, they must fit the slots. But there are two classes of things that matter to almost anyone, which won't end up fitting the slots, and which jointly cover enough of the territory of a life to make template-based arrangements unworkable as a way of engineering a Wiggins-compliant life.

Some things are such that, the more they matter to you—the more *deeply* they come to matter—the more specific, particular, and idiosyncratically shaped your concern for them becomes. In these cases, as it becomes more important to you, you pay more attention to it; as you do, there turns out to be ever more to notice about it; how you care shapes itself to what you see; and the result is that the way it ends up mattering to you won't be captured by any generally available description of the kind of thing it is.[22] We can see this tendency at work in the life we have been examining; just for instance, as Mill thought more about liberty, feminist policy proposals, and the like, what proved to be at stake for him, namely, moral freedom, was dramatically different from what his comrades-in-arms thought to matter. I want to acknowledge that not nearly everything that is important to someone will be like this: people can take what matters to them for granted, and pay hardly any attention to it at all; in many cases, what more there is to see, as you look at something more closely, is irrelevant to why you care about it; and sometimes there *is* nothing more to see. (E.g., money is an abstract object, and so looking more closely at your dollar won't reveal anything special about *it*.) And I don't want to hang the argument on a suggestion that there's something wrong with being shallow about this or that. But lives do tend to involve elements whose importance exhibits this trajectory.

Next, in a complex society like our own, some things that matter to people will have to come in a vast number of sizes, shapes, and configurations; division of labor makes jobs the nearest-to-hand illustration. The templates we were imagining, which integrate the things that matter to someone into a mutually reinforcing package, are going to be available only if they're designed that way. And because, as we argued, the proposal requires social structures to be arranged to provide a home for the template, if there are many such packages, each integrating—to proceed with the illustration—different sorts of work, their design will have to be coordinated: the proposal requires something like the central planning that was supposed to guide communist-bloc economies, only with rather different objectives. An advanced economy requires there to be so many substantively different things that people do for a living that it is impossible for anyone to so much as understand them all: what there is to care about in one job or another is inevitably, as the Austrian economists would have said it, local knowledge. And so the explanatory connections between elements of the template will have to be generic: in our version of the American Dream, the job allows you to support your family, but nothing is said about the importance to you of what you actually *do* for forty hours a week. So either your developing emotional investment in your work won't be captured by the template, or you will be alienated from your job.

All of this means that when what matters to you is inserted into the slots in such a template, (i) either the fit will be bad, or (ii) the fit will be forced, or (iii) you won't actually care very much or very deeply about it, or (iv) what you really care about will be, precisely, the *fit*. Let's consider these options one by one.

In the first case, the template does not induce the form of coherence that it purports. The relation out of which Wiggins-style coherence is constructed is: *this* being important to you explaining why *that* is important to you. In deploying such a template, the explanatory relations come ready-made. So if the fit between a slot in the template and the shape of your concern is bad, what is being explained is not what you care about, but rather, why someone else might care about something that looks roughly or approximately like what you care about.[23]

Turning to the second possibility, since the world does not grow people, activities, and the like on its own to be the sort of thing that just snaps into the slots in such a template, and since they grow away from the forms they start out having, the institutional efforts that would account for the availability of items to fit those slots—education, mass production, advertising, etc.—in practice come down to a sort of machining, in which the bumps on a person are shaved off and abraded away. Indeed, a great many of those who had to go through it in the 1950s complained that they were round pegs being made to fit into square holes. But we observed that what matters in your life is deletion-resistant, and so we shouldn't be surprised that when the 1950s were followed by the 1960s, one of the complaints of that decade was that the suburban American Dream could not actually have been what it was presented as being. There were too many things that mattered to the people who tried to live it that were being suppressed and papered over, and, the youth of the 1960s insisted, their parents had been living a lie.

Leaving aside our collective memory of the second half of the twentieth century, we have on hand a much more developed illustration of how the first two tines of our four-pronged fork are unworkable. As we saw in the course of our reconstruction of Mill's Mental Crisis, it was the shape of his life being set by some unbending structure—in his case, by his political mentors, but a template for generic interlocking concerns provided by society at large would have done the job just as well—that rendered it intolerable. What Mill experienced as hedonic drift turned his life into one he was helplessly carried along by, as opposed to living. With the vocabulary we have since adopted from him, we can say what Mill found it took to live a life that was owner-occupied: originality, that is, figuring out what your life is to be, and implementing those conclusions, for yourself.

Third, allow that if something matters to you deeply enough for it to reasonably fall within the scope of Wiggins's condition, then, frequently enough, you will either find that there is more and more to say about *how* it matters, and that it is distinctive and idiosyncratic, or you find that what keeps you involved with it (say, what you take to matter about doing your job) is too niche-specific to have been captured by that generic template. A socially available template that would serve to organize your concerns will have to supply thin and generic explanations for why the things that matter to you, do. So if this is how the Wiggins-derived coherence condition is going to be satisfied, those things can matter to you only in those ways. So if what matters to you is after all captured by such a socially available template, then it turns out not to matter to you very much, or very deeply—in fact, it matters hardly at all.

But of course it is scarcely worth organizing the things that do not matter to you all that much, and that are only superficially important to you, into a Wiggins-compliant form. The motivation for the condition was to make the things that matter to you add up to a life; but if you are only organizing things that don't matter very much to you, you still need to, as we say it nowadays, get a life. And returning to the observation that the 1950s were followed by the 1960s, the other accusation leveled by the youth of the period was that the lives of those who had been inculcated into the social forms of the time were *empty* and *hollow*. Surely we should be having second thoughts if the way we opt to evade the argument for the tragedy of the project life has in the recent past given rise to precisely *these* complaints.

Fourth and finally, we can allow that someone's concerns might fit a set of conventions very neatly, provided that what really matters to him is *convention*. Judith Martin, writing in her advice-column persona of Ms. Manners, tells us that brides and babies are beautiful by definition; we are imagining someone whose sense of beauty, along with everything else, is actually correctly represented by that turn of phrase. Notice that in this case, we no longer have a project life; the real stake in what are apparently means-end connections between the elements of the life is in their conventionality, that is, not in their effectiveness, but in this being *the way one does it*. There are normally many different ways of pursuing a goal, and the basis for your selecting any given one of them will be that it is the usual means to your end; that means that what looks like a project life supported by the sort of scaffolding we're considering will prove to be a convention-driven life, one that is lived in a world in which the conventions dictate that lives take on, superficially, the form of projects.

For all we have said so far, the conventional life might still be coherent, in the Wiggins sense. But we are now considering a *very* special case, one that it's legitimate to set aside. The turn to coherence, that is, to the form and organization of a life, was motivated in part by accepting that it would be unreasonable to prescribe any particular content as the meaning of life—as had been possible in earlier, religious world views. To allow that we can have coherence only if what matters to us is fixed is to let go of a consideration without which the turn to coherence would not have made sense.

A couple of paces back, I indicated that the right way to think through the template-driven life would start in, once again, with the right biography. We can now see that it would have to be the investigation of the conformist life which I gestured at briefly in the Introduction: one in which all of the justifications in it appeal to available conventions.

11.6

Still surveying objections to the argument we have laid out, some readers will have been keeping in mind one of the second thoughts I registered a while back: that perhaps the point I hope to make about the *form* of a life has been illegitimately exploiting the particular matter—the substantive content—of Mill's life project; political projects that mean to remake the world are unusual and optional. (Only some readers, since often people who find compelling the idea that a project could be the meaning of your life are thinking of ambitious projects in the first place.) Why couldn't someone have a life project that was low key, even lackadaisical, but which nonetheless satisified the coherence condition we found in Wiggins?

We can now put that worry to rest, by assembling a quick argument from pieces we already have in play. First we need to consider how people come to have the sorts of tightly wired lives that the coherence condition we took from Wiggins requires.

We introduced projects as being instrumentally structured. But the natural way to arrange an instrumentally structured life, if you have the elbow room to do it, is to manage your various enterprises so that they're more or less nonoverlapping; that way one of them doesn't find that the others are getting underfoot. And if you are doing it that way, your various projects will proceed relatively independently of one another. Responsiveness to instrumental reasons normally moves a life toward satisfying the Wiggins coherence condition when that's not possible, that is, when your activities have to share resources.

We've just observed that it's instrumentally bad planning to have your activities share resources, unless you're running up against the (not always entirely sharp) cap on the resources available to you. So high levels of integration in an instrumentally structured life happen at the point where the subprojects as it were start to press up against each other. Implementing resource sharing forces the integration in which a subproject comes to count as part of the justification for the shape of others with which it's coordinated.

Thus project lives will normally move towards Wiggins-compliance only when they run up against limitations on resources. Projects, recall, were introduced as open-ended, and an open-ended activity can be pushed out farther, or less far. So projects can be more or less demanding, and how resource-hungry a project is will depend on how ambitious and urgent it's taken to be. We can conclude that project lives will tend towards Wiggins-compliance only when they are urgent and ambitious. Thus if we're investigating Wiggins-compliant life projects, we will find that (normally, roughly) they turn out to be experienced by their owners as ambitious and urgent. Mill's wildly ambitious, politically urgent project wasn't, by our lights, just a coincidence. The Wiggins-compliant form of a life project requires a particular sort of matter or substantive content.

But couldn't the person we're imagining just *happen* to want to arrange his subprojects so that they're mutually supporting? Why shouldn't it be a personal preference of his?[24]

Consider what will be the upshots of a dilettante's rearrangement of low-key activities into a formally Wiggins-compliant life project, first on the assumption that configuring the life in this way doesn't affect the temperate, less-than-urgent manner in which the enterprise is pursued. (We'll relax that assumption in a moment or two.) We can unpack a move we have already made, stepping through it more slowly; I'll vary the example somewhat.

If something matters to you, there's a *way* it matters to you, which is to be respected in the choices you make: for instance, if your daughter matters to you, you care about making choices that are good for *her*; if you're a soccer buff, you're enthusiastic about well-played games. And in an important class of cases, the more something matters to you, the more articulated and contoured the *way* it matters is. If your daughter matters to you a great deal, you pay close attention to her personality, her idiosyncrasies, the contours of her aptitudes, and so on in making choices that are good for her. Thus, in such cases, the more something matters to you, the harder you have to work to respect the way it matters.

Now, if you address your preference for coherence by arranging the components of your life to support one another, and you don't go overboard about it, there isn't going to be a lot of nuance and articulation. For example, we can imagine that you decide to encourage your daughter to join the soccer team: she needs an extracurricular, and since you have to ferry her to the extracurriculars anyway, you'll be able to watch the practice and the games while you wait. If you *do* go overboard about it—well, picture struggling to find ways to fit together the fractally shaped pieces without forcing: perhaps, you decide, if you invest enough coaching and practice time with her, you can convey to your daughter your love of the sport, in a way that will carry over to a soccer scholarship for college, but then you also have to get her to a place where that college is a good fit for her otherwise.... In that case, you've no longer got a low-key, relaxed life project. Rather, you're starting to look in the relevant respects like J. S. Mill.

It follows that if you don't go overboard about nailing down the coherence, and you arrive at what counts for you as a coherent arrangement of your activities and objectives, then the things you're getting to cohere didn't matter to you all that much. Maybe soccer isn't the best sport or extracurricular activity for your daughter, but you let that get overridden by the convenience of having something to do while you ferry her around. But then, how much *does* she matter to you? Again, you'll be watching high-school soccer, which is not very good soccer. If you cared about soccer a great deal, you wouldn't compromise and watch such amateurish games, week after week. So soccer must not matter all that much to you.

But if the things that matter to you don't matter all that much, you don't get a meaningful life (a kind of meaningfulness worth having) by imposing a Wiggins-compliant form on them. And so a lackadaisical life project, one that becomes Wiggins-compliant because you happen to want things to cohere, doesn't amount to a sort of meaningful life that's worth having.

We were assuming, for the sake of the argument, that an independent interest in a Wiggins-compliant project life would leave its components as low-key as they started out. But that assumption very likely needs to be retracted. When the young Mill, in the course of what we called his first epiphany, suddenly grasped his various Benthamite activist activities and commitments as components of a unified project, the newly organized agenda became overwhelmingly important to him: so much so, that the experience served, or so I suggested, as one of his models for the formation of lexical preferences. (His higher pleasures were important enough to trump *any amount* of a competing lower pleasure.) We did explore the account that Mill's own psychology was able to provide of the dramatic amplification of a person's stake and level of concern produced by increased connectedness, but since we no longer sign onto associationist psychological theory, we cannot take on that explanation as our own. Nonetheless, it would be a good idea to proceed on the assumption that when psychology finally becomes a science done right, it will make sense of what happened to Mill.

The objection on the table was that if a person's stake in his various activities is sufficiently low-key, folding them together into a Wiggins-compliant life project, on the basis of an equally low-key predilection for that sort of coherence, could bypass the pressures of the sort of political utopianism that in Mill's case induced the concealed tragedy that he lived out. But we saw in Mill's own life that this sort of first-pass integration of activities will tend to make one's commitment to the project into which they have been folded more forceful, and the project itself, accordingly, much more ambitious. And the point of the objection was to detour around the ambitiousness of Mill's own life project.

Before affirming that the argument for the tragedy of the project life goes through, I want once again to acknowledge the limitations of our intellectual toolkit as forthrightly as I can. I have been talking about the pieces or elements of a life, and about its scope or reach or extent, meaning not just how long it lasts, but what sort of things it includes. These are by no means well-understood concepts, much less technical terms. The argument depends on a presupposition of several of its premises, that there are places that trains of thought go: on their own, and independently of what the person who is traversing them happens to think next. (He may lose his train of thought, or may as it were shunt himself onto a siding, but the train of thought itself continues, out of his sight.) We philosophers don't know how to make head or tail of this assumption, either. We do have a relatively well-understood theory of correctness of inference, taught in introductory logic classes, and its concept of a valid argument is independent of the psychological activity of any actual individual. But even when the train of thought *is* an argument, any particular argument is normally only one of many pathways through the network of possible arguments. You can all too easily fail to follow your train of thought by straying down the path of an irrelevant argument. And in any case we emphasized that not all trains of thought of the sort we have in mind are arguments.

One of the more important forms a train of thought can take is solving a series of problems. Solving one problem in order to solve another may seem to give these trains of thought the tractable appearance of steps taken toward a goal. But even this overestimates our level of theoretical preparation for handling the notion of a train of thought with a direction of its own. Philosophers work on problems day in and day out, and ought to (but mostly do not) notice that problems are not always goal driven; often problems are introduced not by objectives we are trying to attain, but by noticing, for example, that we are tripping over our own feet as we pursue our objectives, and that it makes no sense to have all of them together; or that we are disappointed when we achieve them; or that our goals are insufficiently ambitious. However, there is no other account of what it is to be a problem waiting in the wings, and remember that trains of thought that consist of a series of problems are also only a special case.[25]

How should we construe our inability to cash out this pivotal presupposition in a familiar philosophical vocabulary? One way would be to see it as an objection, and even a decisive objection, to the argument. However, in this case, where each of us is personally familiar with the sort of thing we are trying to talk about, being brought up short this way rather exhibits the inadequacy of our theoretical resources. Thus it sets an agenda, that of expanding our philosophical toolkit so that we can think fluently about such matters. To put on the table a point I will have a use for in a moment or two, when we do so, we will want to accommodate the thought that trains of thought can be followed honestly, or in a Procrustean fashion—that is, by trying to force them to go where you want to have them go—and that the latter counts as a *failing*.

Next, I suggested that trains of thought can and do go just anywhere, and that this claim too could be given the status of an observation. (Of course, in retrospect it often seems like such a train of thought has stayed right on topic; but that is only because these surprises change the way it is natural to sort out what belongs to which topic.) But can we do better than that? Shouldn't we try constructing an argument for it?

We should be aware of the obstacles to producing that sort of underpinning. First of all, giving an argument for that claim will be possible only if one has a firm philosophical grip on the notion of a train of thought's going somewhere—as it were, of its own volition. We've just admitted to not having that sort of grip. Second, to say that a train of thought might go anywhere is to say that it might go somewhere that—no matter how carefully you had tried to anticipate the topics and claims it would fasten on—turns out to be genuinely surprising. A surprise is something you don't anticipate: it is a you-know-not-what. So it is very hard to give a tight argument that surprises are in the offing.[26]

My own experience is that philosophers accordingly tend to underestimate the importance of surprises, novelty, and just plain messiness when they are theorizing about the basic structures of rationality and human life. But we should not pretend that if we don't know how to manage a theory of surprises, surprises don't matter. That trains of thought can go just anywhere matters very much.

11.8

I have suggested that if Mill stayed on point, and kept his thoughts within the ambit of his life project, he must have been preventing himself from thinking about other things, and so must have been violating his own deepest intellectual commitments. But if he did manage not to stray, what evidence do we have that he so much as wanted to? What was it that Mill ought by his own lights to have been thinking about, and that he balked at taking up?

Can we convince ourselves that this must have been taking place, even without identifying particular views Mill should have entertained but avoided? We saw him constructing a remarkable philosophical system; he appears to have had a view on every philosophical question of his day, and on a great many nonphilosophical questions as well; all those views are mutually supporting, and most of them are quite surprising. As we've seen, if his treatment of freedom of the will, together with his political party's pushback against the Church of England, require a supporting position in philosophy of logic (I:233/A 7:4), sure enough, Mill has, not just *a* position in philosophy of logic, but the one his treatment and party require—a position that strikes even philosophers who appreciate its ingenuity as flatly incredible. If in order to show that the Principle of Liberty can be compatible with the Principle of Utility, he needs a psychological theory according to which people can come to exhibit lexical preferences for generic means, lo and behold, that is the psychology he has. Now, trains of thought go just *anywhere* (and you can treat the step taken in this chapter, that of bringing to bear an account of tragedy on Mill's life, as yet another illustration). When you investigate a problem de novo, putting the pieces of the puzzle together in the way that makes most sense of them, what are the chances that what you come up with will again and again be just what you needed for fitting the subprojects together cleanly? When you look at philosophical questions fair-mindedly, what you come up with is typically inconvenient; Mill's answers to those questions were systematically convenient; therefore Mill must have been Procrustean in his approach to his problems. He must not, after all, have been letting himself follow his own trains of thought wherever they were going.

We have hazarded a guess or two as to where in particular Mill backed off from following his thoughts to the very end. Mill noticed that the Empiricist metaphysics of personal identity, at any rate when taken together with Empiricist phenomenalist metaphysics, was incoherent as it stood.[27] He noticed that his accounts of basic distinctions in the philosophy of mind, for instance, between belief and mere imagination, would not do.[28] And I have already suggested that he must have felt the limitations of his philosophy of mind and theory of content when it came time to think his way through the problems in aesthetics that weighed so heavily on him.[29] But adjusting these very basic parts of his intellectual framework would have required him to abandon his Empiricism. And so he settled for stopgaps: he decided to accept memory as a primitive, to accept that distinction between belief and other attitudes as a primitive, and to gesture admiringly at Ruskin, even though he could not in his own conceptual vocabulary make sense of Ruskin's judgments about art and the arguments he gave for them.[30]

In chapter 10, we noticed that despite all of Mill's preparation for the sciences of character, they never got off the ground. The role assigned to those sciences in Mill's political agenda, and thus in his life project, was to show that the policies he advocated would be effective in the ways he claimed. That means that his life project was only conditionally cohesive: it made sense as a project only *provided* the views about what policies advance what intermediate ends would eventually be borne out by the not-yet-inaugurated sciences of ethology and political ethology. What should we really learn from Mill's backing away at just this point? Perhaps it is in fact so hard to manage full integration of a project life that it can only seem to work if it includes a very large promissory note, of roughly this kind, to the effect that one's views about what fits together with what will be substantiated later. But perhaps he was too unsure of what a science of ethology would show to be willing to explore it further; that is, perhaps relinquishing the enterprise was pretty much what it looks like to sacrifice originality to the need to stay on point, and keep on doing what the Utilitarian life project required.

I think we can also see Mill's ongoing worries about how easily spontaneity or originality can be squelched to express a sense that his resolution of his Mental Crisis had been ineffective, after all. Even though he had explained to himself why his will was, in the only sense that mattered, free, a successor of the problem continued to bother him: correctly, since, as we saw, his adult life never exhibited the changes of direction that, on his own view, it should have. But, as we know, he never revisited that train of thought, and never pushed it farther; if the argument we have assembled is on track, doing so, he is likely to have felt, would have endangered his commitment to his life project as a whole.

All of these suggestions are only meant to make more plausible the argument's consequence: that Mill must have been forcibly reining himself in.[31] But we nonetheless will have to stop well short of the decisive and most direct evidence we would like to have. If I am right, and he repeatedly refused to follow his trains of thought where they went, he will not have left behind him reports of the thoughts that he consequently did not think.

Now that we have the argument on the table, we can also ascertain that it is robust in one way that matters for how seriously we can take it. You might be thinking that what it shows is that no one should strive to have an *absolutely* unified life; but whose life is ever absolutely unified? If the argument does not have consequences for lives that aren't exceptionlessly integrated, it would be too fragile to demonstrate anything that mattered. However, we read the argument off Mill's life, and while Mill's life project did cover just about all of his life, there were exceptions: his day job at the East India Company was only equivocally integrated into his Utilitarianism; and we mentioned in passing that Mill's lengthy country walks and accompanying botanizing were not part of the Utilitarian project—except perhaps trivially, in the way that any form of recreation can serve one's more serious pursuits. It turns out that these exceptions don't matter: the argument goes through anyway. The (apparently) *almost* completely integrated life is just as intolerable, and on close inspection, just as tragically incoherent, as the apparently completely integrated life.

11.9

Because the argument has been conducted so concretely, we have considered only one of the various ways one could build out unity of agency into a concept of meaningfulness. So the alert reader will have been wondering whether the problem we located has to do with that choice. Now would be a good occasion to pause to explore whether adjusting one's account of agential unity a little bit one way or another will make a difference to the outcome.

I don't propose to start in on a survey of the indefinitely many such adjustments one could try out, but let me briefly consider one of them, just by way of giving you an indication of what the exercise I am leaving to the reader would be.

Kant tells us that we are to love our neighbor in a practical rather than pathological sense—meaning, you are commanded to help him out, but not to *feel* any particular way—and you might wonder whether the problem is just that we have been considering lives being unified or disunified, as again Kant might have said it, pathologically.[32] Our argument identified a deep and ongoing conflict in the motivations of the person leading a would-be project life; but maybe what matters is not whether he *feels conflicted*, but what he *does*. Mill managed to stay on point and do what his Utilitarian life project required. Why is there any need to wring our hands about his inner life?[33]

This variation on unified agency seems to me to be a nonstarter, because the depsychologized alternative version of a unified life that we have just floated was briefly lived through by the object of our study, and found wanting. When Mill descended into his famous Mental Crisis, the outwardly coherent structure of his activities remained intact, even as their motivational underpinnings dissolved: recall that the most difficult aspect of it was that, although he no longer cared, he couldn't stop working. And so Mill, in an era during which suicide was generally not excusable even as a last resort, found himself experiencing what any therapist would now recognize as suicidal ideation: "I frequently asked myself, if I could, or if I was bound to go on living, when life must be passed in this manner" (I:145/A 5:5). If Mill found practical-but-not-pathological coherence intolerable in this way, why would we want to pursue it as an alternative to modes of coherence that do unify both the inner and outer life of an individual?

11.10

We have finally put our finger on the problem with which Mill struggled throughout his life. Early on, he misidentified it as a lack of flexibility in his political life project, but as we have seen, it persisted even when the project was made substantially less rigid, and was never successfully resolved.

Put as abstractly as possible, a life that is mobilized to make what is important to the person living it coalesce into the highly integrated pattern recommended by Wiggins slides into internal conflict. That conflict is both motivational and practical, though the practical side of the conflict is exhibited in the first place in one's intellectual activities. The conflict conforms to Williams's explication of the concept of tragedy, and thus the life configured for maximal coherence is incoherent, after all. While the argument for that upshot was defeasible rather than deductive, when we surveyed the live—or the apparently most live—ways of stepping off the boat, we repeatedly found ourselves able to satisfy the letter of the coherence condition only at the cost of sacrificing its spirit. You can tie together the things that matter in your life only if they do not matter very much, or if you pretend to yourself that they matter less, or differently, than they do.

Mill has served us well as a testbed for what is the most popular conception of a meaningful life, both within analytic moral philosophy, and for the secular, achievement-oriented demographic. The meaningful life, so construed, is unattainable, and in attempting it you are likely to inflict a great deal of collateral damage, very likely on bystanders, but primarily, and most unavoidably, on yourself.

12 Concluding Remarks

Now that we finally have all of the argument on the table, it's time to take stock, say what we have shown, and indicate what our next steps should be. But before doing that, let me pause for some retrospective remarks about the argument's methodology; these will take the form of compare and contrast, in this case with the generic method of contemporary analytic moral philosophy.

12.1

That generic method consists of describing a set of circumstances; of inviting one's interlocutor or reader to have a response to it—an "intuition" about it—and finally, treating those responses as data points to which one's analysis is responsible, in roughly the way that a linguist's reconstruction of a grammar is responsible to the linguistic intuitions of native speakers. Indeed, one of the few recent book-length discussions of the meaning of life by an analytic philosopher does take this form. Susan Wolf's *Meaning in Life and Why It Matters* describes a handful of imaginary lives (for instance, someone who plays Sudoku day in and day out), anticipates her readers' responses ("no, such a life isn't meaningful"), and arrives at a conceptual analysis, to the effect that your life has meaning when you're actively engaged in projects of worth.[1] The volume is based on a pair of lectures, and it includes replies by a panel of commentators; these share the methodology, differing only in that the prompts are drawn, not from the philosopher's imagination, but from recent history: the reader is invited to agree that figures like Claus von Stauffenberg and Ted Berrigan led meaningful lives, even though those lives did not conform to Wolf's formula. If you are acculturated into analytic philosophy, you will have been trained to expect my own treatment to amount to an argument on this pattern: a life was presented, to be sure much more elaborately than even Wolf's panelists considered doing, and now we are to ask ourselves whether we feel it was meaningful; that response is to be part of a 'reflective equilibrium,' one that contours the definition of the concept to a suitable collection of such data points.

But this is not what I have been doing. Notice that in the method of reflective equilibrium, you get the hypothesized prompt for free: in our own case, you would be asked to imagine that someone had a life that was coextensive with a project. However, the point of the argument we have given is that you cannot simply suppose that the coherently organized life is available for the imagining: its conclusion was that the project life, intended as an instance of the ideally coherent life, generates incoherences within itself as one attempts to implement it. So what we had before us was not an especially complicated instance of the usual mode of argument (although no doubt you have been having your own reactions to Mill's life as it was laid out, step by step). But in that case, how was the argument supposed to work?

As the professional readers will know, a recently fashionable view in philosophy of science has it that explanation in science consists of laying out the interlocking mechanisms that generate some phenomenon of interest.[2] This is not the place to register my own reservations, which I do have, but I think that a view in something like its spirit—I suppose you could call it *mechanism for ethics*—should be given a run for its money. There will be disanalogies: For one thing, I would not want to advance it as a claim about *all* ethical explanation. For another, what counts as a mechanism to an ethicist should be rather different than what would seem like one to, say, a neuroscientist. And the scientific focus on figuring out how the mechanisms work in well-functioning organisms was displaced, in our argument, by an attempt to figure out how a well-meaning philosophers' adjustment to the machinery of a life can make it go haywire and break down.

The argument we have developed consisted in exhibiting the mechanisms involved in getting a life project off the ground and keeping it in the air; we saw that, in anything like normal circumstances, the operation of the mechanisms that make the life project so much as possible undercuts the special form of coherence that drove our own interest in project lives. That is, the argument turned on seeing what the *workings* of a life project must be, and the upshot was that the idealized project life, in which it occupies the entire life, is carried through wholeheartedly, and exhibits an agent's unified selfhood—and about which one would in the traditional methodology go on to have intuitions—is not so much as an option one can in fact entertain. If the comparison helps, the move is a little like responding to advocates of a socialist utopia by considering what it would take to administer the socialist economy; if you convince yourself that it is impossible actually to administer an economy in the socialist mode, you conclude that no state could be the properly socialist utopia, after all; intuitions as to the desirability of the socialist utopia are then moot.[3]

Biography isn't the way we philosophers—anyway, we analytic philosophers—are used to arguing: very early on you learn that ad hominem arguments are a fallacy. And even if you're not professionalized into philosophy, if you have any contact at all with literary studies, you have conveyed to you, also very early on, the idea that any interest in the author of a text, and specifically in his biography, is an unforgivable sin, this time, the "intentional fallacy." However, if we have committed what is alleged to be an egregious fallacy and an unforgivable sin—retelling a life as an argument, and treating the writings produced by the protagonist of that life as in the first place of biographical interest, that is, as a *part* of the life—that was necessary because the techniques we analytic moral philosophers have been using don't work on our subject matter. (If the necessary argument is on inspection satisfactory, then it will also be time for second thoughts about ad hominem arguments and intentional fallacies.[4])

Why *don't* those techniques work? In the first place, because a method that recovers the contours of a concept makes sense only when people already have well worked out, highly contoured concepts to analyze. We remarked very early on the surface ill-formedness of the phrase "the meaning of life"; that's a symptom and indicator of the fact that here we're not trying to figure out one of those well worked out concepts.[5] It's not just that the notion of the meaning of life doesn't have much of a home in the world of philosophical theory. Much more importantly, it's not *used* in day-to-day tussling with other people—in ongoing assessments of action, say—in the way that assessments of injury are used in excuses, or in blaming people, or in the way that other assessments of value are used in setting goals. When we (ordinary people, I mean, not philosophers) *exercise* concepts, they end up having structure that it's instructive to recover: having a concept shaped like *this* was evidently what was getting its job done—socially, say. But our 'meaningful' thoughts are *so* unexercised and *so* unregimented that sticking with a procedure which at best gets us back the shape of the concept we already have, and which tells us at most what we already think, is pretty much useless. In philosophy, there's a law of conservation of work: when what you already think had no work put into it, finding out what you already think doesn't count as philosophical progress.

Because this is an important methodological point, let's bring it into tighter focus. Conceptual analysis consists in contouring a description of a concept—or perhaps some other intellectual device—to a profile of intuitions, which consist in the first place of responses of the form: the concept does or doesn't apply in an imagined situation. So conceptual analysis reconstructs patterns of responses to imagined situations. Now, people's imaginations are trained by inducting them into a practice, and by their own experience with that practice. So conceptual analysis will reconstruct something worth knowing about only if there is an extant practice that *works*. For instance, if people communicate successfully by speaking German, then the linguistic intuitions of native German speakers inform you of something useful; but if you happen to have linguistic intuitions about a nonsense language, there's nothing useful you learn by systematizing them.

A practice normally works only if there is extensive field testing, of the sort which allows for correcting the participants (i) when they deviate from the conventions of the practice and (ii) when the practice produces suboptimal results. Extending that for-instance, speaking German works because people who don't say things correctly are corrected by others, and also because you're likely to notice failures to communicate, and work out an alternative way to get your information or advice across.[6] It follows that conceptual analysis of 'meaningful', or of 'the meaning of life', only gives you something worth paying attention to if it's embedded in a practice that allows for that sort of correction. But there isn't a lot of use given to that concept, *the meaning of life*. How often do we even find people talking about the subject? Far less, apparently, than they talk about happiness, and the investigation of what makes people happy has scarcely moved since Aristotle.[7] Moreover, when you use the concept in public, for the most part people don't correct you when you make mistakes. Finally for now, even when the concept is used, it's rarely given the kind of application that allows you to notice suboptimal results.

In the background of the idea that our philosophical objective is to elicit the contours of our concepts, we find the conviction that ethics is a priori: it is not an empirical subject matter. By this point, it should be apparent that I think otherwise. It seems to me that most, perhaps all, of moral philosophy is to be learned from experience, and in any case needs to be repeatedly checked against experience. If that is right, the imagined and hypothetical cases *are* insufficient, and the lives of real people indispensible, in an investigation like this one; a departure from the standard, intuition-driven approach to moral philosophy is unavoidable.

Those who take ethics to be a priori assume that that very status is a priori as well; whether ethics is a priori or not is taken to be a priori itself. But it is time to reconsider the status of the status: by this point, we have several thousand years of recorded theory and practice to draw upon, and if we are not going to beg the question in favor of the apriorist assumption, we ought to ask ourselves what the track record shows. We should not rule out in advance a possibility which Mill and his circle regarded as likely, that it will show the insistence on the aprioricity of ethics or morality to be not merely an error, but a moral failing—namely, defensiveness. Insisting that one *just knows* what morality or ethics requires, without looking, has often enough been no more than the sheer unwillingness to allow that ways of thinking and acting one is used to might have to be retracted and left behind.[8]

Our alternative mechanism-oriented approach requires the thoroughly investigated lives of real individuals, rather than the thinly imagined stock characters of most moral philosophy, or even the rapid sketches of characters from the history of literature, art, and warfare used by Wolf's respondents. The biography is neither merely window dressing for the argument at which we eventually arrived, nor simply the stimulus that got us to think of it (part of the 'context of discovery' rather than the 'context of justification,' as old-school philosophers of science used to put it). Once a mechanism is very well understood, or this is anyway what we see in other fields of study, it may well be possible for simulations to arrive at reasonably reliable results; but this state of affairs is the product of exhaustive experimental work, and the investigation of the moral mechanisms at work in human life, and of the meaning of life, is at its very initial stages. Whatever may be possible in a mature field of study, we are not nearly there yet.

Mechanisms generally (and moral mechanisms in particular) do not operate in a vacuum, but rather in a sea of mechanism. Thus they interact with other mechanisms and their surrounding circumstances, and consequently arguments constructed around the workings of a mechanism are defeasible: they only go through other things being equal. The history of engineering shows that the operation of interacting mechanisms has to be studied in the wild if one is to have any chance of getting the defeating conditions of those arguments right—or, more dramatically, even of understanding which mechanisms one has to be paying attention to, and which are just distractions.[9]

We have the discussion we have now completed as anecdotal confirmation: I would not have noticed the factors that produced the train wreck that was John Stuart Mill's life without studying that life closely, but more importantly, I would not have been able to trust the defeasible arguments that in retrospect account for it as far as I do without seeing them play out in that life. To be sure, in an argument like this one, there is the trap of using the evidence for which a hypothesis was meant to account to confirm that very hypothesis. It would be a mistake to stop with our first argument-by-biography. On the contrary, we need many further case studies of this sort if we are going to be confident that we understand the engines that move lives.

The pieces of the argument we are now concluding fit together neatly. The argument-by-biography follows out the workings of a life. But in the last chapter, I invoked, in the course of the argument, the sheer brute resistance of the materials of life to being arranged. Should we worry that when the sort of argument we are completing seems to work, it must be Procrustean, and so must not actually work after all?

The lesson here seems to be that the mechanism-for-ethics approach uses as its testbed a particular *sort* of life: our arguments did not have to be Procrustean, precisely because Mill's life *was*. Most lives won't assemble themselves into arguments, and suitable subjects will be those whose lives took on an explicable shape because there was an argument that they lived out. Mill is atypical, and in deploying the biographical mode of argumentation I am advancing, we have to watch out for selection effects; these arguments make visible to us the workings of highly structured, as opposed to relaxed and casually arranged, lives. If the highly structured lives are internally Procrustean, and consequently fraught, this philosophical methodology will tend to present us with one after another form of unhappiness. We will want to keep in mind that the lives we opt to examine, however revealing, are not a fair sample of all the lives there are.

Return for a moment to the method of conceptual analysis and reflective equilibrium: it should have been clear at the outset that that method can at most clarify the concept you have already been using, and the content that concept already has. But if, as I suggested a turn or two back, the concept does not have enough of a track record of use and debugging to be worth reconstructing as is, and we have an argument that one currently popular spin to put on the notion of the meaning of life makes it a dead end, then we will want to change or replace it. And the method of reflective equilibrium cannot tell us what its successor ought to be. Before we start to consider alternatives and upgrades, we should ask ourselves: what intellectual and practical work do we want this concept to do?

12.2

The meaning of life is of deep concern to many of us, and on this subject, the state of play within analytic philosophy is the proposal we have been examining and can now reject. That proposal amounted to giving the phrase a concrete sense; like freedom of the will, this is one of those puzzles in philosophy where to address the puzzle is in the first place to decide what its central concept comes to: to find something precise to make it mean.[10] Wiggins's proposal, I suggested, was consonant with the stake contemporary analytic moral psychology has in unified agency. But we are now back to square one: we need to consider what to make of the notion of a meaningful life—and of the meaning of life—which is to say, how to firm it up into a concept which we know how to apply to a life, and which appropriately addresses the concerns moving us. I think our first consequence is that it is time to move away from the presumption that the home of the firmed-up concept we are after is a tightly unified life. On the contrary, we have motivated taking a large step back from imagining a unified self to be (anyway fully) achievable, much less a good idea and, if we stop thinking it is, that would mean looking for live alternatives to recent theory of agency, to much moral theory, and perhaps also to our current menu of theories of practical reasoning.

Once we adopt that agenda, we will be seeking a notion of meaningfulness suited to a life that is more loosely structured than Mill's. Since we should choose our philosophical concepts for their usefulness in our lives as we actually live them, or as we might reasonably aim to live them, perhaps we should be looking for a conception of the meaning of life meant to help us regulate and manage lives that are not trying to be imposingly monolithic. I hope to investigate that possibility on another occasion.

In the meantime, we have a very brass-tacks lesson on hand. At the beginning of our examination of the life of John Stuart Mill, I pointed out that the project life which he so impressively exemplified is the most popular form that the secular aspiration to have a meaningful life takes nowadays; usually, I observed, the project is framed as a career. I also gestured in passing at variants that share Wiggins's unity requirement, but replace instrumentally structured justifications with alternatives. We have just argued that neither project lives nor these other variations on the maximally integrated life should be expected to work out. We do not have a clear conception of what success in such an enterprise would actually look like, and we concluded that this sort of life should be expected to play out as a tragedy. So now that we have wrapped up our discussion of life projects, here is the takeaway: Kids, don't try this at home.

Appendix
Mill's Metaphysical Paradox

Mill was the last great British Empiricist, and earlier on I described British Empiricism as a philosophical tradition built around a psychological theory, or rather, two of them: the theory of ideas and associationism. Like earlier Empiricists, Mill understood the theory of ideas to have metaphysical consequences, which when taken jointly amounted to a paradox. One of these was phenomenalism: material objects were, he thought, correctly analyzed as clusters of actual and possible sensation—as "Permanent Possibilities of Sensation." By the same token, however, minds had to be analyzed as streams of impressions and ideas. The paradox was that the phenomenalism made it impossible to sort the impressions and ideas into mind-like clusters.

On the one hand, there is a lesson to be drawn from the fact that Mill thought there to be a problem, and because I put it to use in chapter 10, it is worth putting on the record. On the other, it is somewhat exotic, and for that reason I'm spelling it out in this appendix.

First, some historical background. Mill's Empiricist psychology and philosophy of mind were inherited from David Hume (with minor modifications due to his father and to other intervening figures in that tradition). Now, Hume had noticed that his theories of causation and of personal identity were inconsistent with each other.[1] On Hume's analysis of the self, it is a bundle of 'perceptions,' that is, mental states, connected by relations of resemblance and causation. Part of the ordinary notion of the self is that each person has his own mental states; so it is a condition on the satisfactoriness of our analysis of the idea of the self that we can in principle determine to which selves particular mental states belong. (It's worth observing that this analysis is an application of the theory of ideas.)

Because different people may have qualitatively identical perceptions at the same time—think of two people in different cities, watching showings of the same movie that screen at exactly the same time—resemblance by itself cannot do the work of assigning perceptions to bundles. So we must use the relation of causation to determine which perceptions belong to which bundles. But on Hume's analysis of causation, the causal relation is a matter of (i) spatio-temporal contiguity, (ii) constant conjunction of event types, and (iii) an associated feeling of expectation or anticipation in the observer. (This analysis is also an application of the theory of ideas.)

Paging through these (but waiving temporal sequence for now), perceptions are in "inner space," which is to say that they don't have real spatial locations; in fact, external space turns out, on Hume's view, to be a construction out of the perceptions. So the first subsidiary condition, that of spatial contiguity, cannot be used to determine which of two simultaneously occurring, qualitatively identical perceptions belong to which bundles. But without a spatio-temporal constraint, constant conjunction can't be used to determine which of two qualitatively identical causes is to be assigned to which of two qualitatively identical effects.

Moreover, the feeling of expectation is useless for solving this problem: unless we are already able to assign it to one bundle or another, we can't make it out to be a feeling of expectation that this particular perception (rather than another qualitatively identical one) is going to occur. So the causal relation will not suffice to assign perceptions to bundles, either. All of that entails that we can't make the notion of a bundle of perceptions intelligible, and so we have no satisfactory reconstruction of the idea of the self, after all.

Now, Hume may or may not have seen his own way past this problem; here we don't need to have an opinion about that. But Mill took up personal identity in his *Examination of the Philosophy of Sir William Hamilton*, and identified a version of Hume's problem, which he described as a paradox: "that something which *ex hypothesi* is but a series of feelings, can be aware of itself as a series" (IX: 193–194).

The argument proceeds roughly as follows. What holds together the mental items—the sensations and ideas—that constitute your mind is either physical or mental. But the physical objects are themselves merely 'Permanent Possibilities of Sensation,' that is, constellations of mental items, or so Mill had argued just previously. In fact, these constellations are held together by the fact that you're there to perceive them—so, by you. So what holds the mental items that constitute your mind together must be mental relations, and since we know that memory must be a central such relation, let's take it as a representative example.

The relevant aspect of the binding relation, that is, the relation that constitutes your mind, is this: if a mental item (idea or sensation) is a memory of a previous experience, then both the mental item and experience belong to the same mind. Here we're helping ourselves to a grammatical feature of English: it only counts as your memory if it's veridical, that is, if it is derived from and correctly represents a previous experience, one that really happened to *you*. So, still taking memory as a representative binding relation, a British Empiricist is in a position to explain what holds the mental items that constitute your mind together only if he can explain what makes a mental item a memory of a previous experience. The British Empiricist's theory of mind describes mental states in terms of their qualitative features (i.e., what the mental picture looks like), their vividness, and their associative connections. However, it's clear that qualitative features and vividness won't do the job: for instance, I might have a very vivid image that wasn't properly connected to a previous experience and so wasn't a memory; I might have a vivid image that resembles an image you had once, but isn't a memory of your experience. Evidently, the problem is that these are intrinsic features of the mental items, and we need relational features.

Now, the disposition of one mental state to follow another only counts as an association if both of them belong to the same person. (Recall those two different people watching the same movie.) So although association is trickier, it won't work either: it presupposes a solution to the problem we're trying to solve. And if that's right, *nothing* in the British Empiricist toolkit will work: Empiricism can't explain what holds together the mental items that constitute your mind.

Mill resolved the tension by making a move that was, by Empiricist lights, completely unprincipled, namely by taking memory as a primitive: "I think, by far the wisest thing we can do, is to accept the inexplicable fact, without any theory of how it takes place" (p. 194). The proposal is that when you remember a previous impression or idea, it's being *this* (i.e., *your*) previous impression or idea you remember (and not, say, a similar impression belonging to someone else) doesn't require any further explanation. For Mill, that's an uncharacteristic moment of intellectual squeamishness; to let personal identity go unanalyzed in this way is plain and simple copping out, and the quotation I just reproduced suggests that it felt that way to him.

What matters for our purposes is that had Mill insisted on a fully satisfactory resolution of his paradox, he would have ended up changing his philosophical views dramatically. Like Hume, he took the different parts of his problem—the 'bundle theory' of the self, and the phenomenalism—to follow from the theory of ideas; thus one very likely upshot of reconsideration would have been to abandon it. It's hard to know how Mill himself would have handled having to do that, but when the pragmatists, soon after, dropped the theory of ideas (as being too apriorist), they were suddenly no longer Empiricists. And when Kant wrestled with this problem, the unity of the self became the anchor for his transcendental arguments—that is, for a radical departure from previous modes of philosophy.[2] Mill understood very well that he had a problem, and instead of rethinking his philosophical views from the ground up, he chickened out.

Notes

CHAPTER 1

1. But of course the question does not have to be treated as rhetorical, and Kayley Vernalis once suggested to me that they do: by standing for something.
2. Hare, 1972, is perhaps the most sophisticated treatment in this family.
3. Wiggins, 1991, ch. 3, at p. 95; Taylor, 1981. The other piece I have in mind is Nagel, 1979; it addresses itself to the worry that nothing is valuable *enough* (more or less, that it's all small change), as contrasted with the concern Wiggins was trying to meet, that nothing is valuable *at all*. A short followup can be found in Nagel, 1986, ch. 11.
4. More carefully, the several noncognitivist views about value share the thought that what looks like a possibly true statement about a matter of fact, namely, what's valuable or important, is in fact something else, such as an expression or projection of an emotion, or a concealed command; but there are a number of very sophisticated noncognitivist positions that are too complex to summarize in a phrase or two. Mackie, 1983, ch. 1, and Hare, 1961, are introductory presentations of noncognitivism about value.

    That term 'value' should set off flashing red lights; when it is part of a philosopher's vocabulary, it often ends up meaning an obscure sort of impossible object. Whenever I use it, there will be an obvious and low-key paraphrase in the vicinity, either mentioning particular items as being (or not being) valuable or important, or different ways of being (or not being) valuable or important. And I will use it sparingly: in fact, only as much as is needed to recapitulate the older philosophical back-and-forth that was conducted with the notion.

5. The treatment of values as secondary qualities—that way in which values could be made out to be real—is further developed in Wiggins, 1991, ch. 5, and McDowell, 1998, ch. 7; for some criticism, see McGinn, 1983, pp. 145–55, and Millgram, 1999.
6. Its current defenders call themselves "expressivists"; see Blackburn, 1998, esp. pp. 9f, 68, Gibbard, 1990, and Gibbard, 2003.
7. This doctrine is, like its predecessor, occasionally spelled out and endorsed, e.g., by Wolf, 1997.
8. I'm grateful to Candace Vogler for pressing me on this point.
9. The example is Taylor's, 1981, at p. 143.
10. For an account of practical rationality that emphasizes this point, see Vogler, 2002.
11. Because he has nothing to contrast it with, Williams renders projects formally as desires, with perhaps the suggestion that one would use the word only for larger-scale cases, and when they are smaller and come with closure points, he tends to use the term 'desire' (2001). I expect that this is why he does not require projects to be open-ended in the way we have just described: scale is tacitly doing duty for the formal distinction. I'll return to the distinction between projects and goals, and what work it ends up doing for Mill, in chapter 7. (The marriage-as-project can be found at Williams, 1981a, pp. 14–18; Millgram, 1996, is a discussion of the relations between his internalism and generic instrumentalism.)

Williams attempts to reconstruct the notion of a meaningful life within his relatively subtle version of instrumentalism, using his concept of 'ground projects' (or 'categorical desires'). Some desires have conditional content, and in particular, one's interest in their objects can be conditional on whether one is going to be alive anyway; for instance, a retiree might want to putter around in his garden, so long as he happens to be alive. (But he would not try to live longer in order to do more gardening.) When a desire is not in this way conditional (as when he wants to live long enough to see his granddaughter graduate), it is categorical, and constitutes a ground project. To have a meaningful life, as Williams construes it, is to have reasons to go on living, and by definition these must be ground projects; to have a meaningless life is to have no ground projects, and so no reason to go on.

Millgram, 2015, ch. 4, explains how Williams tried to bring these ideas to bear on moral theory; see also Rosati, 2013.

12. Later on, we will address the issue of whether to extend Wiggins's condition somewhat, so as to require that lives in addition not *leave out* elements needed to make sense of the important things in those lives.

13. Prominent examples include Williams, 1981a, Velleman, 2015, Korsgaard, 2008, ch. 3, Korsgaard, 1996, ch. 13, Korsgaard, 2009, Frankfurt, 1988, Bratman, 2007; for discussion, see Millgram, 2015, ch. 10. Philosophers outside the analytic tradition, especially some of those influenced by Nietzsche, have been much more skeptical about the unified person.

14. John Stuart Mill, whose life we will shortly take up, would probably have agreed, and insisted on real-life examples. He argued that thoughtful biography affords more thorough understanding than the currently popular method of approaching philosophical problems through fiction: "From the data afforded by a person's conversation and life, to frame a connected outline of the inward structure of that person's mind, so as to know and feel what the man is, and how the life and world paint themselves to his conceptions ... is an effort of genius"—by which Mill means, as we will see, understanding arrived at on one's own—"superior, I must needs believe, to any which was ever shown in the creation of a fictitious character" (I:333).

15. Connell, 2010, Connell, 1981.

16. Nehamas, 1985, which proposes that the view was not only Nietzsche's, but was exemplified by him; Nehamas, 1998, attributes similar ambitions to a number of further philosophers, including Socrates, Montaigne, and Foucault. Nehamas has gotten anyway Nietzsche and Foucault wrong. Millgram, 2007, points out that the authorial protagonists of Nietzsche's work are not as tightly constructed as all that; on the contrary, they are meant precisely to exhibit their own incoherence. Foucault, 1984, criticizes the presuppositions involved in Nehamas's recommendation as culturally parochial, and expresses the hope that we will soon move past them, which makes it hard to believe he was adopting the recommendation for himself. However, Anderson and Landy, 2001, make an interesting case that Nehamas himself is trying to conform to the model he provides.

17. Ellmann, 1988, Bartlett, 1988. Notice that the problem wasn't that Wilde chose tragedy as his medium. He was in fact much better at comedy, and we can imagine what his life would have been like had he tried to script it to read like *The Importance of Being Earnest*. Perhaps it would have been aesthetically better, but it still would not have been better *for him*.

18. Dancy, 2004, is a well-known presentation of particularism, although it is advanced as a theory of moral or practical reasons rather than of aesthetics; Sibley, 1959, nicely describes the way particularism characterizes aesthetic assessment. Millgram, 2005a,

ch. 5, argues that what is on offer is a placeholder for particularist theory, rather than the theory itself. Brooks, 1984, is an extended treatment of narrative structures that provides a sense of how thin our theoretical understanding of them is; when Brooks does identify some shared structural features of narrative, they turn out to be instrumental or means-end, and so of a piece with the option I will get to next—rather than, as I have suggested, having the formal characteristics of color harmonies. Velleman, 2009, ch. 7, is a more recent attempt by a philosopher to explain what narratives are and why we find them gripping; on this account, they follow emotion cascades (think of the five stages of grief popularized by Elisabeth Kübler-Ross and David Kessler).

19. Nussbaum, 1990, lays out one way of giving this complaint some bite. What narratives you find compelling is mostly a matter of, to put it crudely, what fairy tales you happen to have been raised on; if you were raised on the wrong sorts of fairy tales, and they shape your life (via your emotions, which Nussbaum thinks have narrative structure), then your life will be ruined.

20. For my take on the question, see Millgram, 1997, and Millgram, 2015, ch. 3. Millgram, 2005a, chs. 6–8, discusses an exception to the sociological generalization I just offered: a philosopher who rejected even means-end justification.

21. While that's the near-consensus view, you shouldn't be deterred from wondering whether it's really true; Millgram, 2006, and Millgram, 2008, entertain second thoughts.

22. Notice that lives structured around a dominant *end* will normally fail to satisfy Wiggins's condition; if only instrumental justifications are available, the agent's ultimate end will be an explanatory dangler. Within a project life, however, any end invokes upstream goals as explainers; moreover, subprojects compete for resources, and must be coordinated to fit into the larger project: in fully explaining your commitment to one end or subproject, you will end up adducing other competing and coordinated components of the project. That leaves the global project itself, although no longer as a valuable item *within* the life; isn't *that* now the dangler? We will take up this concern in chapters 3 and 5.

23. The Radicals, who for some time counted as a left-wing political party, were a broader group that included the Benthamites, or Philosophic Radicals, as its own left wing, and a number of near-Whigs as its right. Thomas, 1979, is helpful background, even though, in his attempt to undermine the characterization of the group as a cohesive movement, he emphasizes differences among them, rather than commonalities.

24. Mill recalls how small the group was even much later, at I:103/A 4:6–7; and in 1865, he reminded a cheering crowd that "When they only counted tens I was amongst them" (XXVIII:15f).

25. For those to whom the contemporary theories are familiar reference points: associationism differs from behaviorism in studying conditioning effects within the mind, and not merely between external stimuli and behavioral responses; it differs from connectionism in that representation was not understood as distributed. Paul Thagard's quasi-connectionist networks, in which each node represents a proposition or goal, are very close in spirit to Mill's associationist models of cognition; his Computational Epistemology Laboratory, at the University of Waterloo, has software available for download that is very useful for getting the feel of how associationist networks behave. For descriptions, see Thagard, 1989, Thagard, 2001.

26. I:163/A 5:12; at one point, Mill tellingly describes himself as "the only mind directly formed by [his father's] instructions" (I:105/A 4:8), and in a typical reaction, Woods,

1961, p. 27, describes the "young son ... [as] almost an experiment in Benthamism, an experiment that somehow did not quite succeed."

27. XXVIII:lv; I:37, 39/A 1:24; see also the excerpt from a letter by John Roebuck cited at Hayek, 1951, p. 31.

   "Reputed": I have heard this from what should have been an authoritative source but, in view of Mill's hiking journals (XXVII:455–637), find it hard to believe. What matters for present purposes was that he ended up as the sort of person of whom one *would* believe it.

28. A point emphasized by Carlisle, 1991.

29. The magazine went through several incarnations; at one point, it was called the *London and Westminster Review*. At times, instead of serving as editor himself, Mill supervised various managing editors.

30. I:81, 83, 123, 125, 129–135/A 3:10, 4:18–20, 23.

31. See, respectively, XXI:349–371; XXI:422–435; I:281f/A 7:47; I:285/A 7:51; XV:787. For background on the Jamaica Affair, see Semmel, 1969; on Durham, see Thomas, 1979, ch. 8.

32. He kept journals of his outings, which take up much of volume XXVII of his *Works*; a surprisingly large part of his correspondence with his wife and stepdaughter consists in reportage of his hikes (although he and they seem to have thought of them as a way of improving his digestion, thus in the first place as a health measure). In the course of his botanizing, he embarked on a never-completed survey of the flora of the Vaucluse region of France (Packe, 1954, pp. 486, 488).

33. For a discussion of Utilitarian legal and economic reforms in India, see Stokes, 1982. For the issues with which Mill dealt on the job, and the positions he took on them, see Zastoupil, 1994.

34. Ishiguro, 1989.

35. Not everyone agrees that they *were* successful: e.g., Thomas, 1979, pp. 446f, tries to explain their "failure to acquire a mass following," and Gash, 1979, p. 46, opines that "had Bentham never lived, most of the reforms popularly ascribed to his influence would probably have come about. ... though Bentham and the utilitarians helped to colour the thought of their age, few pure examples of Benthamite reforms ever found their way to the statute book."

   Partly the disagreement seems to me to turn on temporal scale; the Utilitarians look much more effective from our vantage point than they do if you are confining your gaze to the early and mid-nineteenth century. And partly it is a matter of the sociology of historiography: like other academics, historians are rewarded for controverting what "everyone knows," and so that is what they do.

36. Was Mill's life not after all meaningful? We will be able to give a suitably nuanced answer in chapter 11, but in the meantime we can say this. Part of the process of philosophizing about the meaning of life is giving that phrase a definite sense, and it would be unfair were I unwilling, even temporarily and for the sake of the argument, to assign the phrase the sense that the project view gives it. But if we argue our way to the conclusion that a meaningful life, in this sense, isn't a reasonable objective, that would be an appropriate time to reopen the question of what there is to mean by "a meaningful life" that might yet be of interest to us.

37. Packe, 1954, is a respectable account of Mill's life in the standard format. Although there are quite a number of strong treatments of one or another narrowly focused topic in Mill's writing, I am unable to recommend a survey of Mill's philosophy. That none of the many expositions seem to me satisfactory is itself a puzzle, and down the

road (chapter 11, note 2) I will take a shot at explaining why the vast literature on Mill is so spotty.

38. X:97, and while the posture adopted in one's treatment and the attitude that one takes personally toward one's subject are different matters, for readers who are not satisfied with the former, I will be up front about the latter also. Here I can borrow the words of one of Rousseau's biographers: "By now we are very old friends indeed, and the feeling I have for him is neither love nor hate. I admire him and pity him, as, no doubt, we eventually come to admire and pity almost any human being we have got to know well" (Guéhenno, 1967, vol. i, p. xii).

CHAPTER 2

1. The systematic application was new, but the "greatest good" slogan had precedents: Jonathan Israel reminds us that Saint-Hyacinthe "proclaimed as his supreme political maxim: 'agir tousjours pour le plus grand bien'" (2001, p. 583).

2. The example (as well as the recipe in Figure 2.1) has been just slightly modernized, in that neither Mill nor Bentham is used to working with probabilities in the now-obvious way; *expected* utility is a twentieth-century concept. As you will have noticed in his statement of the Principle of Utility, Mill's fuzzier and more qualitative notion is *tendencies*.

    Of course, in real life there can be less to such cost-benefit analyses than meets the eye; for an example having to do with dams, see Paolini and Vacis, 2000.

3. Bentham, 1817/1983.

4. For a more detailed history of the auto-icon, see Bentham, 2002, and Marmoy, 1958. Such overly dismissive attitudes can backfire philosophically and rhetorically. Anscombe, 1972, used their reasonableness by Utilitarian lights as a challenge to conceptions of virtue that give explanatory priority to a conception of the human good, such as Benthamite utility, that is explicable to someone who does not already possess the virtues. There is, she argued, obviously something wrong with treating dead bodies so casually, and Utilitarians are not in a position to explain what it is; a philosophical view that is structured in this way around an independently comprehensible notion of the human good must be flawed. It is an interesting exercise to think through whether her criticisms stick to Mill.

5. Sayre-McCord, 1996, points out that, in Hume, utility is analyzed as that which produces roughly this reaction: *That's* a neat solution to a practical problem!

    When Mill starts off chapter 2 of *Utilitarianism* by dismissing the "merely colloquial sense in which utility is opposed to pleasure" (X:209/U 2:1), and those people who think the theory is "impracticably dry," it's this older sense of the word he has in mind. In chapter 4, we will get to Charles Dickens's unflattering portrait of the Utilitarians; it perhaps unfairly shows them as fixated on utility as usefulness. Even scholars don't always keep the different notions straight; Albee's *History of English Utilitarianism* (1957) covers Hume, who belongs to the utilitarian (as opposed to the British Empiricist) tradition only by equivocation.

6. Under the heading of fuzz around the edges, see the list at Bentham, 1996, p. 39, which enumerates factors such as intensity, duration, propinquity, fecundity, and purity.

    If what you need is a fungible currency that can be used to assess decisions, why not use *real* currency, that is, money? After all, as Bentham, 1827, vol. v, p. 634, puts it, "*money* [i]s the only efficient cause of interest ... [that] is commodiously measurable"; when you are considering building a dam, you probably *will* use money. There is normally a further reason for the move to a subjective measure of value, viz., the diminishing marginal utility of money. The more money you have, the less an additional dollar is worth to you: if you're a street person, and you find a twenty dollar bill, that's a big deal; if you're Bill Gates, the twenty isn't worth the time you take to notice it. (For the Utilitarian's own way of putting the problem, see Bentham, 1950, pp. 103ff.)

Now ask yourself: when we think of pleasure as a sensation, doesn't that feeling exhibit diminishing marginal utility? Pleasure obviously matters most to people who experience scarcely any of it at all, and hedonism—in the guise that's now relevant, the view that sensations of pleasure are what matters, and the only thing that matters—is emotionally compelling especially to the deprived, and rarely to anyone else. But if that is so, then pleasure has not solved at any rate one of the problems for which the Benthamites had originally turned to it.

7. X:235–236/U 4:5–6.

8. The canonical exposition is still Luce and Raiffa, 1957. Notice that, unlike Mill's and Bentham's versions of utility, the contemporary economist's notion doesn't allow you to compare the utilities of different people. For the history of how the contemporary notion of utility displaced both earlier more-or-less Benthamite versions, and a more substantive notion of well-being popular late in the nineteenth century—on which, very crudely, the more ribs you could count, the lower someone's utility was—see Cooter and Rappoport, 1984.

9. In chapter 7, we will return to the topic; it will turn out that Mill's conception of utility is deeply different from the contemporary notion in a further respect.

10. X:213/U 2:8; but there was a secondary reason for revising the conception of utility. An argument implicit in such well-known later authors as Huxley ran roughly as follows: Utilitarians tell you to do what will produce the most pleasure, where pleasure is understood as a sensation. The most powerful pleasurable sensations are produced by activities like (especially) sex. So utilitarianism will tell you to do as much in the way of such activities as possible. Many sexual activities are *immoral* (or at any rate, crass and unrefined). So utilitarianism will tell you to engage in immoral (or crass and unrefined) activities. So utilitarianism can't be a satisfactory moral theory. (See also note 26, later in this chapter.)

As we will see, Mill's alternative preference-based analysis gave him a way of responding to such objections on their own terms—some pleasures are "higher"—and it is usually introduced in the classroom as such a response. However, I expect that Mill did not find this motivation theoretically urgent, because the argument is question begging: if the utilitarian criterion is correct, a utilitarian should not concede the argument's final premise, that sexual activities and the like *are* immoral. Likewise, Bentham had famously insisted that, "prejudice apart, the game of push-pin is of equal value with the arts and sciences of music and poetry" (1838–1843, vol. ii, p. 253). If push-pin really *does* produce as much pleasure as poetry, why shouldn't a utilitarian dismiss as elitist prejudice the charge that push-pin is intellectually uninteresting and unrefined?

That said, Mill was not only a theoretician but a political activist; the theoretical problem may not have been urgent, but we should not suppose that meant that the political challenge posed by the objection was not.

11. In principle, Benthamites are committed to taking into account what is felt by *every* creature capable of experiencing pleasure and pain, which means, not just humans, but many animals. That Benthamite conclusion has not received much attention until very recently, but is now advocated by Singer, 2002. (Bentham is both the first philosopher whom Singer's book mentions, and is invoked as someone who "pointed

to the capacity for suffering as the vital characteristic that gives a being a right to equal consideration" [p. 7].) Animal-rights activists of this bent seem unaware of the problems with Bentham's views that motivated Mill's more sophisticated version of utilitarianism.

12. Although there's now a respectable subdiscipline of social psychology, "hedonic psychology," it doesn't do much better; mostly it uses Likert scales. (Subjects check off, on a scale of 1 to 7, how they feel; often enough, the scales are illustrated with smiley and frowny faces.) Some of the more interesting results—Gilbert, 2005, is a recent popular overview—suggest that there isn't enough consistency to treat what's being performed as *measurement*.

13. For a vividly told version of the episode, see Reeves, 2007, pp. 1f.

14. For example, he ended up advocating voting procedures meant as workarounds for the flaws that he saw winner-take-all elections to have (I:262f/A 7:24f and XIX:448–466/RG 7).

15. See, e.g., Mill's letter to Theodor Gomperz, at XIV:238f.

16. "A priori" is how philosophers say that you can know it up front, without going out to look; "synthetic," for present purposes, means that such knowledge isn't confined to truths-by-definition and the like. (For Kant's contrast between analytic and synthetic, see Anderson, 2015.)

 Kant had also criticized hedonistic approaches to moral theory, and in my view the difficulty he raises—that we cannot understand what our happiness consists in concretely enough to use it as a guide to action—is still among the deepest objections to utilitarianism (1785/1981, Ak. 418, with some foreshadowing at 399). Mill seems not to have appreciated the force of Kant's concern, and does not seem generally to have been a good reader of Kant's moral philosophy. For instance, he clumsily misreads Kant's Categorical Imperative at X:207/U 1:4.

17. Kant had also defended—as "Postulates of Pure Practical Reason"—the existence of God, the immortality of the soul, and an afterlife in which everyone would get their just deserts. My sense is that the intellectual public was aware of this, without particularly tracking the subtle distinction between Kantian 'postulates' and synthetic a priori knowledge. So Kant's moral theory also contributed to an overall impression that the new German philosophy could be drawn upon when support for conservative positions became necessary.

18. In *Beyond Good and Evil*, Nietzsche amusingly characterizes the very similar uptake that Kant received in Germany: "'How are synthetic judgments *a priori possible*?' Kant asked himself—and what really is his answer? *'By virtue of a faculty'* ... The honeymoon of German philosophy arrived. All the young theologians of the Tübingen seminary went into the bushes—all looking for 'faculties'" (1886/1966, sec. 11).

 Mill's essay on Coleridge identifies him as one of the primary importers of German apriorism into England (going so far as to call the doctrine "Germano-Coleridgian"); it gives a sense of the level of nuance in appropriating these ideas that the British intellectual world had managed at that stage. On the one hand, Mill carefully registers a sophisticated qualification to the "doctrine [of] Coleridge, [and] the German philosophers since Kant," the doctrine being that "among the truths which are ... known *à priori* ... [are] the fundamental doctrines of religion and morals, the principles of mathematics, and the ultimate laws even of physical nature ..." Although these are "truths, not cognizable by our senses," they "are not indeed innate, nor could ever have been awakened in us without experience." On the other hand, Coleridge "claims for the human mind a capacity ... of perceiving the nature and properties of "Things in Themselves,'" which is to badly misunderstand what Kant thought to be possible (X:125f).

19. For a clear and perceptive discussion of how those arguments work, see Anderson, 2001.

20. Story credit: John Rawls.

21. You can find one variant of the anecdote in Brunner, 1968, p. 559.

22. Ever since Kripke, 1980, philosophers have been careful to distinguish necessary truths and a priori knowledge. Since Mill and his contemporaries didn't, for the most part neither will we. For Mill's own description of the tactical choice, see I:233, 269f/A 7:4, 34.

23. And this was how Mill came to be known across the Channel: shortly before his death, in a widely read work, Lange, 1950, Book I, p. 210, called Mill "the most distinct empiricist among the chief logicians of our time."

 I mentioned earlier that Mill was unusual at the time in knowing how to construct an argument. Most of Mill's demolition (in volume IX of the *Collected Works*) of a well-known academic philosopher, whom no one has heard of since, consists in showing, at tedious length, that Hamilton was unable to keep track of the parts of an argument.

24. If the reader is not himself in the business, he may be wondering how philosophers could have been wasting their time on such exercises, and may consequently also be wondering if I have not caricatured the method to the point of complete misrepresentation. While there is some caricature involved in any description as terse as this one, I don't think I'm misrepresenting the practice. Bear in mind that there had originally been a justification for the methodology. After about the midpoint of the twentieth century, philosophy was claimed, in the English-speaking world, to be an enterprise of conceptual analysis, and such intuitions were thought of as analogous to the linguistic intuitions of native speakers used to reconstruct the grammar of a language. Some later philosophers understood themselves to be reconstructing "folk theories" of one subject matter or another, and their own intuitions were treated as evidence for what those theories were. However, the methodology survived the demise of the philosophical self-conception.

25. For instance, Weinberg et al., 2001, suggest that philosophical "intuitions" vary by cultural background and social class.

26. That fact was reflected in the public debate to which Utilitarianism gave rise. A number of Utilitarian dystopias, most prominently Huxley, 1932/1998, suggested that the Utilitarians were committed to promoting mindless debauchery; Wilde, 2005, made the French Decadents out as having shown that refined pleasures can easily turn destructive and dangerous, and that hedonism committed one to cultivating physical and psychological illnesses. And, more recently, Kubrick, 1971, pressed the first two of these complaints, while attempting to rebut the Utilitarian reply we will shortly see, that the demands of social order could be squared with antisocial pleasures and preferences by a program of associationist conditioning. I'll return to these objections to the Utilitarian program in section 8.1.

27. When Mill remarks on "the vulgar notion of a Benthamite ...: [someone who was not] a lover of poetry and of most of the fine arts," and describes a fellow traveler, John Roebuck, as having "very quick and strong sensibilities," rather than "being as Benthamites are supposed to be, void of feeling" (I:155/A 5:11), he is further reflecting that public impression of his youthful self.

28. Bain, 1882, p. 134; as we will see in chapter 3, Mill was perhaps overstating matters; what I will end up describing as the first of two teenage epiphanies must have been a

memorably exhilarating high. (I'm grateful to Svantje Guinebert for pressing me on this point.) Nevertheless, that it could seem to Mill that way in retrospect is striking.

29. Bain, 1882, p. 64n, reports: "tea, bread and butter, and a boiled egg." Later on he adds: "To have seen his simple breakfast at the India House, and to couple with that his entire abstinence from eating or drinking till his plain dinner at six o'clock,—would be decisive of his moderation in the pleasures of the palate" (p. 149).

Sometimes people don't actually taste their food, and in such cases, bland fare shouldn't suggest asceticism. But evidently Mill did taste his: later in his life, while staying in France, he occasionally did acquaintances back home the favor of shipping them French wine, and when he did, he was perfectly happy to assure the recipient that he had tried it and liked it (XV: 853, 856; I'm grateful to a reviewer for pointing me to these letters).

30. See Anderson, 1991, for some discussion of this notion, and the suggestion that we regard Mill this way.

31. A typical example, taken from Ralph Waldo Emerson: "Woman, with her instinct of behavior, instantly detects in man a love of trifles," and after putting "the new chivalry in behalf of Woman's Rights" down to "a certain awkward consciousness of inferiority in the men," he pronounces: "Certainly, let her be as much better placed in the laws and in social forms, as the most zealous reformer can ask ..." (1971–2013, III:87f).

When an editor referred to the essay, "Enfranchisement of Women," as "the article on Woman," Mill in turn described (to Taylor) the use of the capitalized abstraction as "vulgar" (XIV:177).

32. See XXX:37, 59; if it were necessary to replace the then-current system, he thought, the one that was "intrinsically the best, would be ... public competition," i.e., competitive entrance exams (XXX:60).

33. See XXX:37, 61, 166, 182, 202; notice that there are two very different points getting run together, the first being that government employees are not on the job long enough to learn their way around it, and the second being that India was very unlike England or other British colonies, and intimate acquaintance with the society would be necessary for intelligent decision making. The considerations are reproduced in XIX:568f, 574f/RG 18:14, 19–21; the Company was served by "persons who have acquired professional knowledge of this part of their country's concerns; who have been trained to it *in the place itself*, and have made its administration the main occupation of their lives" (my emphasis); and objecting to "the appointment of persons ... from motives of convenience" as opposed to "the choice of ... candidates by competitive examination," Mill points out that the latter has the benefit that "there are no personal ties between the candidates for offices and those who have a voice in conferring them." For Mill's discussion of populations for which democracy is unsuitable, see XIX:413–421/RG 4.

34. And Mill had also managed to get a brother hired to a junior clerkship (XXX:xviii). In the course of testimony to a House of Lords select committee, Mill was pointedly asked whether "there [was] not a tendency ... to the service of India becoming a sort of caste of particular families and particular connexions" (XXX:37); Mill replied that "It will happen under any system that persons who have served *in* India will look by preference to Indian appointments for their sons" (my emphasis), thus managing to understand the question as not being about his own family.

On the lack of first-hand experience of the subcontinent, when pressed, Mill awkwardly "agreed in the opinion that those who were entrusted with the chief power in India should not in general be persons who had passed their lives there," and "that those who were at the centre of government in England really knew India, as a whole, better than those who were in India" (XXVIII:233, 236).

See also Bain, 1966, p. 344; James Mill was "asked if a person could form a judgment of the natives without being personally acquainted with them." James Mill's social history of India (1858), although respectable enough at the time to lead to a senior position in the East India Company, is outrageous in many respects, one of which is its insistence that it is no disadvantage to an historian not to be personally acquainted with the country about which he is writing, and not to be able to speak—or read!—its languages (vol. i, pp. xx–xvii).

35. Packe, 1954, p. 271; I:255/A 7:18n.

CHAPTER 3

1. The phrase comes from the title track of LCD Soundsystem, 2007.

2. Bentham, 1830 (originally published in 1802); the 1840 translation by Richard Hildreth can be found in Ogden's edition (Bentham, 1950). (I'm grateful to Philip Schofield for helping me sort out the various *Traités*.)

3. Shklar, 1969, p. 219.

4. If you make a Venn diagram out of contemporary discussions of freedom of the will and of practical rationality, you will find this conversation, ongoing since the 1970s, located in the intersection. The early attempt is from Frankfurt, 1988, ch. 2; the further references I have provided in chapter 1, note 13, cover some of this ground. Thalberg, 1978, esp. p. 215, is a survey of the first wave of the literature, expressing skepticism as to the psychological realism of such treatments. Millgram, 2015, secs. 10.1–10.2, summarizes a recent and representative entry in the back-and-forth.

5. For a less compressed rendering of the point, in the context of an argument that displays how one can make use of it, see Millgram, 2015, p. 105.

6. Nozick, 1981, pp. 4–6, is a well-known and critical description of this philosophical demand of argument.

7. Sibley, 1959, p. 445, is making this point when he brings his discussion of aesthetic concepts around to the observation that "we cannot prove by argument that something is graceful." (I'm grateful to Sarah Buss for pushing me on this.) de Sousa, 1990, pp. 253ff, relatedly points out that arguments—he labels them "lovers' arguments"—whose intended conclusion is someone feeling something are generally futile.

The inadequacy of our theoretical apparatus is a brisk reminder of the shortcomings of compartmentalization within the discipline of philosophy as we have it today. As late as the nineteenth century, a serious all-round philosopher understood that he had to have worked out views in aesthetics, because he would need them in his philosophical theorizing on other topics. But we analytic philosophers have since internalized the notion that aesthetics is a ghetto, one that is of no real interest to other areas of philosophy, even though it is, perhaps for historical reasons, housed within philosophy departments. As should be apparent, in my own view that notion is a mistake.

8. For the laws of association, see Mill, 1869, ch. 3; quick reviews of some of them can be found at VIII:852/VI.iv.3 and IX:177f.

Earlier British Empiricists had made the extra vividness, or vivacity, or intensity—the precise terminology varied—into the official criterion used to distinguish sensations from ideas: an idea was qualitatively just like a sensation, only less lively. And they had tried to distinguish beliefs from ideas that one was merely entertaining in the same way; a belief is qualitatively just like a daydream or a supposition, only more vivid. Mill realized that this wouldn't do, and decided that these distinctions would have to be psychological primitives ("ultimate and primordial," Mill, 1869, vol. i, p. 412n); nonetheless, he seems to have thought that, by and large, sensations *were* more vivid or intense than ideas, even if the intensity wasn't what *made* it a sensation.

9. We can think of pleasure and pain as flowing down the associative links, and that is probably how Mill and his circle did think about it in practice. But there is an alternative way of describing the process that is by their lights the technically correct one. If the idea of A is associated with the idea of pleasure, and if the idea of A is also associated with the idea of B, then the thought of A brings B to mind, and the thought of A also brings pleasure to mind. That means that B and pleasure are being brought to mind side by side, and on the associationist account, repetition will suffice to associate the idea of B with the idea of pleasure directly. For our purposes we can ignore this nicety.

10. More carefully, a desire consists in the idea of pleasure associated with the idea of the object of the desire. Mill took this definition over from his father, and noticed that it wouldn't do as was (Mill, 1869, vol. 2, pp. 191f; see p. 258 for a similar definition of "motive"). Even if you specify that the object of the desire lies in the future, what you get looks like hope or wish or even just expectation, rather than desire. However, Mill never adjusted the account of desire he had inherited to handle the objection.

11. Mill, 1869, vol. ii, pp. 353f, 355n, 357n: the first passage in the note by John Stuart Mill describes Hartley's views; the second gives the adjusted version that he himself endorsed.

12. Anecdote credit: Aubrey Spivey.

13. Two historical points: First, there's a reason that Locke, Berkeley, and Hume, but not James Mill or John Stuart Mill, are remembered as the notable British Empiricists. T. H. Green, a Victorian Hegelian, influentially presented Hume as the culmination and termination point of British Empiricism, its reductio ad absurdum, and the point from which Empiricism underwent *Aufhebung* into Kantian transcendental idealism. A not unwanted rhetorical side effect of the story was that Green's contemporary competitors who, like Mill, still worked in the Empiricist tradition could be dismissed as driftwood on the sands of history: philosophers who just hadn't gotten the point, and who hadn't realized that it was all over. Green's highly tendentious organization of the history of philosophy has bypassed protest by being written into the curriculum; courses on "British Empiricism," since Green, include Locke, Berkeley, and Hume, but not, for instance, Hartley, or Mill, or Bain.

Second, in the earlier Empiricists, as we are on the verge of recounting, associationism was paired with the so-called theory of ideas: a theory of the contents of mental states. Recall that ideas are, roughly, mental pictures copied from sensations (or assembled by reshuffling bits and pieces of mental pictures copied from sensations). The content of an idea thus is derived from the sensations it copies. Although the theory of ideas was philosophically very important for earlier figures in the tradition (such as Hume: see, e.g., Millgram, 2005a, chs. 6–7), Mill was well along the way to abandoning it (VII:97–108/I.v.4–7). While he never completely got beyond it, and while it will come up on the edges of our discussion, it doesn't do much work for him; I will accordingly be able to confine the use I am going to make of it to the appendix.

That's just as well: associationism has intellectual inheritors today, but the theory of ideas is, for many reasons, no longer a live position. Copying and qualitative resemblance isn't a satisfactory account of content (Putnam, 1981, ch. 1); Mill himself observed that "scarcely any picture, scarcely even any series of pictures, tells its own story without the aid of an interpreter" (I:352). In the early twentieth century, gestalt psychologists became interested in phenomena that this kind of account doesn't handle very well; think of the "duck-rabbit," Necker Cubes, or "Magic Eye" pictures. (You can find a survey of some of these phenomena in Verdi, 2010.) The theory of ideas assumes that one is conscious of one's mental states, whereas Freud made that seem like an unwarranted assumption: states of mind can be *un*conscious. Finally for now, in the theory of ideas, ideas are copied from sensations. Mid-twentieth-century ordinary language philosophers argued against the notion that perception actually involves *things* like sensations (or "sense-data") that were there to be copied; this view was diagnosed as something on the order of a grammatical mistake (Austin, 1962, Wittgenstein, 1998).

14. The revival is due to experimental philosophy—recall from chapter 2, a recent movement that appeals to work done by psychologists in the first place to explain opinions on matters philosophical. However, although the experimental philosophers are reinventing some of Mill's wheels (in particular, Mill's criticism of appeals to intuition), there is no central psychological doctrine that plays the same role in their work that associationism or the theory of ideas played for the British Empiricists. Experimental philosophers are more like scavengers, helping themselves to whatever bits and pieces of the psychology literature they find they can use.

15. Mill, 1869; James Mill began writing it about the time of his son's epiphany; eventually, a reading group organized by the son worked its way through the manuscript. When Mill *fils* edited the 1869 edition, he persuaded Alexander Bain and George Grote, whom we still remember, along with one Andrew Findlater, whom we don't, to contribute additional commentary and updates; consequently, one has to check the tail ends of the notes to determine whose opinions are being presented. Bain's and Grote's notes don't necessarily represent Mill's views; in fact, Grote was working on an attack on utilitarianism when he died.

16. A second source that belongs under this heading is Mill, 1992.

17. Given the subject matter of Bentham's discussion, we must suppose that Mill's "knowledge and beliefs" include his views as to what was important, what mattered, and what was valuable. For Mill, all of those are modeled by associating pleasure with an idea. That is, in Mill's associationist psychology, these beliefs are also, technically, desires.

    I'm simplifying the story for the moment by treating attitudes like pained impatience with opponents as pleasure at the thought of getting them out of the way.

18. Troy Booher originally pointed this out to me.

19. Some philosophers distinguish the former ("constitutive") sort of means from the latter ("causal") sort of means. For our purposes, both of these fall under the rubric of instrumentally organized components of a project. For brief discussion of the distinction, see Millgram, 2008, p. 734.

20. One way to see the problem: the decision to treat pleasure and pain (sticking just with the Benthamite version for a moment) as the final arbiters is itself a choice, and so an argument for it will either appeal to greater pleasures produced by making utilitarian choices—or not. If the argument does bottom out in this sort of appeal to pleasure and pain, then it begs the question; but if the argument takes some other form, it is thereby a pragmatic contradiction: that is, it proceeds in one way, but its conclusion is that it should proceed not in

that way, but in another. (If your philosophical background is continental rather than analytic, "identifying a pragmatic contradiction" is the analytic way of saying "deconstructing.")

There's a further variation on this irony in the uptake of Mill today. Utilitarian moral philosophers routinely argue for their view by trying to show that it matches our intuitions. But utilitarianism was originally introduced in order to provide an *alternative* to appeals to intuition, which the early Utilitarians insisted were corrupt through and through. (I will follow up on this point in section 9.6.)

21. However, Millgram, 2015, ch. 5, discusses a way Mill could have softened the circularity, through the application of the decided preference criterion to itself.

22. For instance, here is Mill quoting his father's "Fragment on Mackintosh": "all action, as Aristotle says, (and all mankind agree with him) is for an end. Actions are essentially means" (Mill, 1869, vol. 2, p. 262n).

23. For an overview of the Mill-Whewell debate, see Millgram, 2014; Fisch, 1991, is a recommended treatment of Whewell's philosophy.

24. In fact, Whewell's philosophy of science (1847) introduced concepts that would likely have served Mill better than his own methodological views did. Whewell held that the intellectually most difficult part of successful theorizing is coming up with the Idea (his capitalization) that unifies facts into a new theory; the hardest part of Kepler's demonstration that the planets travel in elliptical orbits was thinking of ellipses in the first place. Whewell was adapting Kant, as he was read then, into a surprising (but scarcely remembered and underappreciated) philosophy of science; he understood Ideas (and here's a bit of shorthand for those to whom the notions are already familiar) as making possible the analog, in the history of science, of Kant's syntheses of cognitions into larger cognitions. Whewell's term for this sort of synthesis is "colligation"; for instance, apprehending the observed positions of Mars as points on an ellipse is a colligation. Once the colligation of facts has been managed, those older facts are reconceived; the facts are "see[n] *through*" the Idea (vol. I, p. 40). Principles can subsequently be extracted from the Idea which appear to be necessary and a priori—even though the theory could not have been established nonexperimentally.

Mill's understanding of the concept of utility might well have been improved had he thought of it as an Idea enabling the moral version of a Whewellian colligation. Utility binds together diverse goods that come to be seen as constituents of or contributors to it; from the Idea of utility can be extracted (or so Mill thought) the a priori requirement that it be maximized. And thinking of utility as a colligation would have made a great deal of sense of the moment in his early life that we have been calling his epiphany.

25. A complication: To an instrumentalist, simply pointing out the coherence does not amount to an argument, but he can still explain why coherence is desirable, provided he can show it to be a means to a further already acknowledged goal. Since what goals you have is, on the instrumentalist way of thinking, an idiosyncratic and very contingent fact about *you*, these means-end arguments will not normally amount to reasons for *just anyone* to prefer coherence. There may be occasional exceptions to that rule of thumb; perhaps Mill was in a position to give a psychologically driven argument for having a very coherent life, namely, that the sort of feedback effects we were examining a moment ago are hedonically enlivening. But he seems never to have entertained this argument, or any variant of it.

26. "Default": recall that, according to Mill, pleasure and pain make stronger associations form faster. So if you survive even one plane crash, you may no longer be able to make

yourself get on a plane. But however reading Bentham in French translation felt, it is not recalled as anything like being in a plane crash.

Possibly many of those connections were in place at the outset of the episode—his "previous education had been, in a certain sense, already a course of Benthamism"—but they were being suddenly and dramatically strengthened.

27. Of course, Mill himself is a much larger counterexample; as Woods, 1961, p. 29, remarks, "if teaching could not only mould but make the character, then John Stuart Mill should have grown up to be the perfect Benthamite, the first citizen of the future utilitarian State."

28. Mill, 1869, vol. ii, pp. 252–255n, and briefly to recap that parrying move: Mill points out that "a complex feeling generated out of a number of single ones [may be] as unlike to any of those from which it is generated, as the sensation of white is unlike the sensations of the seven prismatic colors." He is gesturing at his theory of "blended ideas," and at the account of "Chemical" sciences developed in the *System of Logic* to support it. (For very helpful discussion, see Vogler, 2001, ch. 4.)

However, what makes a science "Chemical" is that combinations of causes produce qualitatively different effects that cannot be anticipated without quite direct experimentation. That is: in mechanics, you can sum vectors to predict the outcome of two forces acting on an object of a given mass; but if you put the green powder into the yellow liquid, it is from your point of view a brute fact that what is left in the beaker is a red solid (VII:373/III:vi:1). To formally assimilate the sudden appearance of the qualitatively different feeling of the sublime to the processes studied by chemistry so understood is to give up on explaining it.

29. Mill takes himself to be learning from Ruskin, 1906, vol. ii, to which he ascribes "profounder and more thoughtful views respecting the beauties both of Nature and of Art than any psychologist I could name." However, the evidently heartfelt praise notwithstanding, you will not find Ruskin to supply theoretical apparatus that can be used to make sense of Mill's experiences within an Empiricist framework, as opposed to candidate prompts for the feelings of beauty and sublimity, "illustrated with great force."

(Accordingly, when Donner, 2011, p. 147, describes Mill as having argued "that Ruskin succeeds 'in showing that the things which excite,'" etc., that is a misassessment: because they do not share enough in the way of conceptual machinery, Mill is not in a position to *argue* that Ruskin has succeeded; in fact, he merely *states* that Ruskin has done so.)

30. I'm grateful to Kristina McIntyre for these incisive observations.

31. Spelling that point out just a bit: Sticking with infinite objects for the moment, in the theory of ideas, an idea of, say, an infinitely large object is in the first instance a quasi-pictorial copy of something you've seen. But you've never apprehended an infinitely large object (you could, at most, have seen a vanishingly small part of one), and, if you think about it, you wouldn't know how to go about drawing one: because no picture you could draw would *count*. And while the theory of ideas allows complex ideas to be assembled from simpler parts, in this case the complex idea would have to share the structure of the English "in·finite"; it's no clearer how to get the abstract idea of finitude from the ideas of the various finite things one does encounter.

32. Mill, 1869, vol. ii, p. 254n.

33. When we consider Mill's mature views, this will turn out to be an approximation to a more complicated claim; I will adjust it to accommodate the so-called decided preference criterion once it has been introduced.

34. But Mill didn't *always* have a tin ear; the evidence is to be found in his hiking journals and his letters to his wife. Although the earlier descriptions of the landscapes are flat and mechanical, by his 1831 walk through Yorkshire and the Lake District (XXVII:501ff) he is thoughtfully explaining the aesthetics of the scenery. Interestingly, his own psychological theory does not seem to get invoked at any point.

35. Although if he were confused, it might have been the explanation; Frankfurt, 1999, p. 159, points out that sometimes people pursue goals because they are important, even though they are not important to *them*. We will eventually see Mill trapped into doing something like this himself, in chapter 7.

    Perhaps Utilitarianism is a special case: the general utility consists in the agglomeration of everything anybody wants, and Mill's argument for the Principle of Utility purports to show not only that utility is desirable, but that *only* utility is desirable. However, even that is not enough: that utility encompasses all that is desirable does not entail that one should make the Utilitarian project one's own. Whether the general utility is best promoted by everyone, or even *anyone*, taking it on as an objective is an empirical question, and, indeed, a good deal of subsequent discussion has turned on whether "Government House utilitarianism" might be a consequence of the theory: if utility is best promoted by keeping the theory an esoteric doctrine, known only to a handful of behind-the-scenes administrators, or even to no one at all, then utilitarianism would require that most or all people not become Utilitarians. (We've reviewed the argument that only utility is desirable in section 2.2; for Government House utilitarianism, and the possibility that utilitarianism is a self-effacing theory, see Williams, 1973a, pp. 134f, 138f.)

36. X:234/U 4:3; notice that Mill is not applying the distinction we are bringing to his texts and his life, between a goal or end, and an open-ended project.

37. Briefly, the argument seems to equivocate on two senses of "desirable," and seems to treat inferences of the following form as valid: What's good for every individual on the team (being the captain, say) is good for the team taken as a collective (everyone on the team should be captain).

    Perhaps Mill simply did commit the fallacies. But, against that supposition, Mill was the logician who had written what turned out to be the preeminent logic textbook of the latter half of the nineteenth century, and, as was the custom for such books at the time, the *System of Logic* contained a survey of fallacies. Mill discusses the very mistakes he seems to be committing in his Proof. And he cannot have been simply unaware of the appearance of a mistake when he was writing *Utilitarianism*, because he as much as announces that the workings of his argument require some special explanation: the chapter in which it appears is titled, "Of What Sort of Proof the Principle of Utility is Susceptible."

38. I have tried my hand at this myself. For the attempt, see Millgram, 2005a, ch. 2; for discussion of a textual bug, which suggests that the reconstruction is at best half-right, see pp. 13–16. If you're a first-time reader wondering what the argument actually is, the paper reproduces it and spells out the alleged fallacies at greater length.

CHAPTER 4

1. Dickens, 1854/1981; the novel is dedicated to Thomas Carlyle, and Carlyle had been friendly with Mill early on; the dedication makes it probable that, after they stopped getting along, Carlyle served as Dickens's informant. (I'm grateful to Stephen Menn for pointing out the connection to me.)

    The gender switch was a common theme of such caricatures. Mill became identified with the feminism of his day (eventually the author of *On the Subjection of*

Women, he was a suffrage activist), and editorial cartoons depicted him in women's clothing.

2. *Ibid.*, p. 95; her father replies, "It has always been my object so to educate you as that you might, while still in your early youth, be (if I may so express myself) almost any age."

3. Mill seems to have bought into this picture to some degree himself: compare his description of his teenage self "as a mere reasoning machine" (I:111/A 4:13).

4. Dickens, 1854/1981, p. 2; the demand for "Facts" is the opening line of the book; that last description of Louisa Gradgrind comes at page 12. Why does Dickens characterize the Utilitarians as, first and foremost, insisting on facts, rather than as promoters of the Principle of Utility? I expect that it's partly an understandable mistake: remember, "utility," in Hume and Adam Smith, had had to do with what was *useful*, not pleasure or happiness; the emphasis on facts in *Hard Times* is a matter of conflating two senses of "utility." Moreover, in political debate the Utilitarians struck the posture of (as we would say it today) evidence-based policy, rather than (and here's the phrase they used to dismiss their opponents) "vague generalities" (X:90, I:113/A 4:13).

5. I'm grateful to Sandra Osborn for pressing this point.

6. Even Dickens's conviction that Mill's childish imagination must have been "starved" won't withstand scrutiny. Mill recites a reading list full of just the sort of panavision history and swashbuckling heroism that appeals to young boys; his father "was fond of putting into my hands books which exhibited men of energy and resource in unusual circumstances, struggling against difficulties and overcoming them" (I:11/A 1:5). Mill tells us straight out that he responded to it in the ways young boys are expected to (for instance, "the struggles between the patricians and the plebians ... now engrossed all the interest in my mind which I had previously felt in the mere wars and conquests of the Romans" [I:17/A 1:9]). In an introduction to Mill's *Autobiography*, John Robson states that "the most common reaction to the *Autobiography* has been one of astonishment, mixed with either awe or horror, at his education" (1989, p. 4). The horror reflects badly on those who experience it, in that it suggests that they cannot imagine reading with enjoyment prose that requires adult levels of literacy, or perhaps that they have an especially condescending view of the literature suitable for children: illustrated volumes of the adventures of talking animals and the like. The astonishment, however, not only reflects badly on us, but tells us what went wrong with the Utilitarian political program; Mill fought for universal education because he assumed it would be on average of very high quality, that is, comparable to his own.

7. I:27/A 1:15; I:31/A 1:19, I:71/A 3:4. This was probably not what Albee, 1957, p. 261, meant when he called Mill's childhood a "unique pedagogical experiment," but the description fits.

8. Apparently James Mill had not taken mathematics classes while in college, and this component of the home-schooling curriculum would not have been up to his otherwise very high standard. Bain observes that "the subject was not, at that time, obligatory on students for the Church" (James Mill was in training to be a preacher), and that "[James] Mill lost a great deal by not attending" Playfair's classes: "he could not have been so accomplished a mathematician as he was a classic" (1966, p. 15).

9. Bentham, 1825, is an (apparently unauthorized) English translation.

10. Bentham, 1838–1843, vol. vi, pp. 1–187.

11. Even at the time, his correspondents complained about Bentham's handwriting: "vos billets," Dumont gently chided him, "demandent des heures pour être déchiffrés" (Bentham, 2006, p. 181).

12. Bain, 1882, p. 38. It's perhaps worth noting that Mill's characterization of his "object in life" is very close to that of Wilhelm von Humboldt, who was one of his intellectual heros. Here is Humboldt's version of the ambition to a life project:

> It is in the prosecution of some single object, and in striving to reach its accomplishment by the combined application of his moral and physical energies, that the true happiness of man, in his full vigour and development, consists. (von Humboldt, 1996, p. 2)

13. I:199/A4:15; in an 1837 addendum to the preface, in Bowring's reprinting of the *Rationale*, Mill remarks that

> His name [that of the "original Editor"] was subsequently affixed, contrary to his own strongly expressed wish, at the positive desire of the venerable author, who certainly had a right to require it. (Bentham, 1838–1843, vol. vi, p. 203)

The addendum refers as well to the "anonymous Editor," and manages to not actually mention Mill's own name.

14. This must have been an awkward moment, because although the Mills and Bentham lived around the corner from each other, the back and forth was conducted as correspondence, most of which we still have. Here's the long version from which I drew the colloquial summary (Bentham, 2006, pp. 347–349):

> It is a matter of no small surprise to me [Bentham begins] to see the title page without your name to it. Nothing could be more clearly understood between us than that it should be there....

> I certainly did not understand you [Mill replies] to have expressed any desire that my name should be in the title page. Nevertheless, if you positively require it, I am willing that it should be so rather than that you should imagine I had taken less pains with the work under the idea of its being ... anonymous. But I confess I should greatly prefer that my name should be omitted ... if my name were annexed to it people would think that I wished to make a parade either of your good opinion [of] me, or of the few notes which I have added ... & I should be very sorry to be suspected of wishing to obtain a reputation at a cheap rate by appearing before the public under the shelter of your name.

> [Bentham replied curtly in two notes:]

> Your name is of far too great importance to the work to be omitted in the titlepage to it.

> P.S. Name at end of the Preface.

15. Dumont was in fact Swiss, but that's the right description nonetheless.

16. Emphasis on the "relatively": the French totals 1214 pages of text, exclusive of front and back matter, and the English translation runs to some 555 pages. But this is still a great deal shorter than the *Rationale*, and it has much greater breadth of coverage.

    In his earlier work, after mentioning that "Lyonet wrote a quarto volume upon the anatomy of the caterpillar," Bentham averred that although "morals are in need of an investigator as patient and philosophical [he has] not courage to imitate Lyonet." He continued: "I shall think it sufficient if I open a new point of view—if I suggest a surer method to those who wish to pursue this subject" (1950, p. 33). One way to describe the difference between the *Traité* and the *Rationale* is that, in the latter, he did, in the end, imitate Lyonet.

    To get a sense of how Bentham treated his editor, see, for instance, his letter of April 5, 1799, complaining about having to retrieve missing pages; Bentham says: "Observe that the manufacturing of this Chaos was not my own doing, and if it vexes you, think how much more it must vex me" (1984, p. 142). For an indirect acknowledgement of how much Dumont has had to put up with, here is Bentham, once more: "I ... said to you, that, if within ten days ... I did not send you a copy ... I should be disappointed. I am disappointed accordingly; which is what you, who have so long known me, will not wonder at" (2006, p. 179).

17. Indeed, at one point, Mill apologetically announces that he has included two chapters which are near-duplicates of one another (vol. iii, p. 333n; freestanding citations in this format will be to Bentham, 1827).

18. That said, it needs some qualification. Bentham's writing is simultaneously choppy and overloaded—under the latter heading, I mean that copying out, for instance, just the title of one of his tables gives you a half-paragraph—and is occasionally simply illegible. So anyone writing up his prose will have had to interpolate words and phrases, and not infrequently to make up his own mind as to what Bentham was trying to say; likewise, anyone copyediting Bentham will have to make up his mind what can be left out. Moreover, at various points, Mill found the manuscripts to be simply incomplete. He complains in the editor's notes: "This and the following section were left by the author in the state of mere fragments"; "The paragraphs ... inserted by the Editor ... appeared necessary to complete the section, which is composed of mere fragments ... which the Editor was obliged to connect together as he best could"; "The papers from which the above remarks ... have been compiled, were written by Mr. Bentham at different times, and left by him in a very incomplete and fragmentitious state.... The remainder of this chapter ... is the result of a partial attempt to fill up the void which had thus been left in the body of the work" (vol iii, pp. 422, 374, 573f, emphasis deleted).

19. I'm grateful to Philip Schofield for this observation.

20. Here's the sort of thing I mean: Arguing against "the ceremony of an oath," Bentham remarks that "it places the Almighty in the station of a sheriff's officer" (vol. i, p. 366). Or again, Bentham points out that Christians cannot consistently treat hearsay evidence as inadmissible; after all, their own religious beliefs are based on hearsay (vol. iii, p. 532n). Those are the sort of point-scoring you might find in Voltaire, but they're not appeals to the Principle of Utility. In many ways, Bentham belongs a great deal more to the Enlightenment than we remember.

    (However, there is a certain amount of this in Dumont's rendering of Bentham as well; e.g., arguing against attempts to derive parental rights over children from the notion that "the son naturally belongs to the father, because the matter of which the son is formed once circulated in the father's veins," Bentham considers a circumstance in which "the corn of which your body is made formerly grew in my field." By an analogous argument, "how is it that you are not my slave?" (pp. 75–76))

There are rare exceptions: for instance, an appeal to cost-benefit calculation (though not one that explicitly invokes utility as Bentham officially wants us to understand it), at vol. ii, p. 521; or again, in proposing that a register be kept of cases in which "makeshift evidence" is used, he argues that reviewing the register will "exhibit the aggregate quantum of the benefit on the one hand, and of the mischief on the other," and allow future legislators to revise the judicial code on the basis of the track record (vol. iii, pp. 545f); or again, at vol. iv, pp. 36f, 278, 479–481. (The term is mentioned—but it's not clear in which sense—at vol. iv, p. 393n, again at p. 471, and again at vol. v, pp. 416, 457, 735 and 744.)

However, in vol. v, the frequency with which utility is invoked picks up: "the principle of utility" is used in its proper sense on p. 60; Bentham's utility-driven account of justified punishment is rehearsed at pp. 141–143; the Principle of Utility is in play when we are told what "humanity" amounts to on p. 233; on p. 298 the point is made that comparative utilities matter, whereas traditional legal categories (such as the classifications "civil" and "criminal") don't; on p. 303 we are given a definition of immorality in terms of the tendency to lessen the quantity of happiness in society; and there are similar references at pp. 326f, 330–32, 344, 587, and 628n. Mill tells us that over the course of the year-long homework assignment, his own writing style improved, to the point where it "became, at times, lively and almost light" (I:119/A 4:16). The change is noticeable only in the final volume (not throughout, however), and the relatively frequent invocations of utility are confined to those more gracefully written stretches of text. I suspect that we owe them to Mill rather than Bentham; at the stage when as editor he became willing to impose his voice on the writing, he also found himself able to adjust the content.

If, as John Plamenatz once remarked (Halévy, 1972, p. xvi), the "ends of policy" which Bentham identified "were not happiness but other things which he believed (without troubling to prove it) make for happiness," and if the "principles," which he intended to be "used as guides in making policy ... (though he thought otherwise) have nothing to do with promoting the greatest happiness of the greatest number, conceived as a sum of pleasures," the problem, from the point of view of a sophisticated Benthamite, is not that most of Bentham's arguments are not made out in terms of sums of pleasures and pains. Benthamites were and are committed to identifying intermediate principles and ends. (I'm grateful to William Twining for pressing me on this point.) The problem is rather that those intermediate principles and ends are supposed to be anchored to the Principle of Utility, and the young John Stuart Mill working through Bentham's manuscripts would have found no evidence that they were.

21. Book III, at vol. ii, pp. 1–434.

22. A shortish sample, picked more or less at random, can be found at vol. iii, pp. 612–618. I should emphasize that the problem was not the presence of taxonomies (recall Mill's "strong relish for accurate classification," from his description of the earlier epiphany), but rather, as Bain, 1966, p. 143, dryly put it, "distinctions without adequate differences."

23. Mill's contemporaries balked at the finished product as well. One reviewer, who as a matter of fact thought well of Bentham's project overall—for instance, he seconds the point about testimony we just touched on, noting that "if there is a point that may be considered indisputable as a general maxim, it is the superiority of

vivâ voce examination over prepared and written questions"—complained about "a repulsiveness of style as mysterious as the bricks of Babylon, [which] set[s] lay-readers so completely at defiance," and he reproduces "specimens of the style" that "form as unsuitable ornaments [in a work meant for the edification of posterity] as the grinning faces and burlesque forms with which monkish builders have studded our magnificent cathedrals"; he pointedly observes that "ignorance of the views of other men is not indispensible for the correctness of one's own; and that it is possible for opinions that are not insolently expressed, to be yet honestly, boldly, and successfully maintained"; and he remarks on Bentham's "eccentricities and impracticableness," which "thrust him out of the rank where [his] genius ought to place him," of "frequent absences of a plain work-a-day sense," and "flaws, which strike across this great work a vein so deep and coarse that there is scarce a page together which we have read with unmixed pleasure" (Empson, 1828, pp. 459, 482, 516–19).

24. Compare Bentham's own later description of the process of writing the *Rationale*: "all the time of scribbling it the second time I never looked at what I had scribbled the first time: nor while going over the field a third time . . . never did I . . . take the trouble of bestowing a glance on what I had done at either of the two preceding times. . . . I suffered the pen to run on in the track upon which it had entered" (2006, pp. 336f).

25. Wheatley, 1855?, pp. 9, 34–36.

26. Kubrick, 1980.

27. X:98, and compare XIX:390f/RG 2:21, where Mill looks back on Bentham's project of redesigning the judicial system. Mill explains that "the . . . good qualities in the governed . . . supply the moving force which works the machinery"; accordingly, it's necessary to pay attention to both the character of the citizens and the formal arrangements, and the unspoken complaint is that Bentham had concerned himself only with the latter.

28. Mill's example of such an abuse is legal clients having to "pay for three attendances in the office of a Master of Chancery, when only one was given" (X:81).

29. X:78, and it is this, together with Bentham's knack for rethinking the nuts and bolts of institutional structures, which I think accommodates the brief retrospective assessment in the *Autobiography*:

The *Rationale of Judicial Evidence* is one of the richest in matter of all Bentham's productions. The theory of evidence being in itself one of the most important of his subjects, and ramifying into most of the others, the book contains, very fully developed, a great proportion of his best thoughts. (I:119/A 4:16)

That is, Mill's praise is sincere, but very carefully scoped, in rather the way that today's letters of recommendation will enthuse about what they can, and leave gently to one side what they can't. Mill has explained how Bentham's insensitivity to issues having to do with development of character severely restricted his competences as a moral philosopher; thus, "whatever can be understood or whatever done without reference to moral influences, his philosophy is equal to"; thus "it is fortunate for the world that Bentham's taste lay rather in the direction of jurisprudential than of properly ethical inquiry"; thus when "he found the philosophy of judicial procedure, including that of judicial establishments and of evidence, in a more wretched state than even any other part of the philosophy of law [and] carried it at once almost to perfection," sorting out the "jumble" of legal theory and practice, that *would*, after all, have been the "richest" part of his output, containing "his best thoughts" (X: 99, 98, 104, 102).

30. There are exceptions: e.g., the chapter on improbability and impossibility (Bentham, 1827, vol. iii, pp. 258–384) is decently written and develops a recognizably philosophical view, which comes with supporting arguments. (For example: by the law of the excluded middle, a proposition is true—and so a fact is the case—or it is not; probability comes in degrees; therefore, probability must be psychological, rather than a feature of the objective world.) But this stretch of text is most striking for the contrast it makes with the remainder of the *Rationale*.

31. Acknowledged in his own somewhat awkward explanations at the beginning of the "Discours préliminaire" to Bentham, 1830, at vol. i, pp. iff.

Ogden, remarking on the looseness of Dumont's rendering of the manuscripts, describes "his work [as] chiefly that of a journalist who happens to know the mentality of a public which the specialist fails to reach" (Bentham, 1950, xxxvii). Dumont himself had warned: "I have translated not the words, but the ideas," and he allowed, "I have sometimes made an abridgement, sometimes a commentary." He described the task at length in ways that make it sound much like the ordeal Mill underwent: "When I have found many treatises relative to the same subject, but composed at different times and with different views, it has been necessary to reconcile them … I have stripped [outdated material], like an abandoned house, of everything worth preserving. When [Bentham] has delivered himself up to abstractions too profound, to metaphysics … I have endeavoured to give more development to his ideas, to illustrate them by applications, by facts, by examples…. I have been obliged to write out some entire chapters …" (quoted at p. xlviii).

When the reviewer invoked in note 23 objects to "[t]he slovenly and careless confidence with which [Mill's] office of editor has been performed," part of his dislike has to do with the young Mill's own lack of legal training and experience, but a good part of it is a response to Mill's unwillingness to cut down the manuscripts as ruthlessly as had Dumont: "Not a single unsightliness seems to have been removed" (Empson, 1828, pp. 462n, 465n).

32. Anonymous, 1925, p. 902; Ogden, whose own somewhat abbreviated quotation of it directed me to the passage, attributes it to an "eminent authority" (Bentham, 1950, pp. ix–x), and, writing when and where he did, may well have known enough to do so.

33. Hilton, 2006, p. 331n, conveys the usual outsider's view—"John Mill's severe nervous breakdown in 1826-7 is generally attributed to a loss of faith in Utilitarianism"—which is just about flat false.

34. This is the complicated qualification I promised in the previous chapter, to my assertion that Mill's second-order attitudes remained constant over the course of his epiphany.

35. I'm grateful to Kimberly Dill and C. Thi Nguyen for conversation on this point.

CHAPTER 5

1. I:141–143/A 5:4; my recap follows Vogler, 2001, ch. 3, but she is of course not to be held to my formulation.

2. Childrearing is the obvious counterexample to the claim that hardwired desires won't occupy a life. Was the problem just that Mill didn't have a family?

Perhaps not: Victorian childraising practices were very different from our own. Middle- and upper-class families routinely farmed out their children to wet nurses and nannies, and turned them over to be educated by, respectively, boarding schools and tutors. Lower-class children received a bare minimum of attention until such time as they could be put to work as chimney sweeps and factory hands—among the many other roles that we are aghast at seeing filled by such a workforce. (See Thompson, 1988, for some of the economic history.) Bringing up children was—as perhaps throughout most of humanity's past—not nearly as time-consuming as it is in most of the West today.

The real puzzle is to explain how childrearing came to occupy such a central role in our own lives. Here is a frame for the puzzle: over most of the twentieth century, full-time American housewives spent a constant fifty or so hours per week on their domestic duties (Cowan, 1983, pp. 159, 178, 199–200, and see p. 232 for further references). At the outset of that period, housewives not only lacked the labor-saving appliances we take for granted today, but performed tasks we no longer regard as housework at all, such as making soap. That was possible in part because child care took up a great deal less time than the present allowable minimum. (Calvert, 1992, see esp. pp. 6f, 124f, surveys ways in which nineteenth-century children's furniture, clothing, and other devices were meant to immobilize children.) As other chores were whittled back, whether by being mechanized or by being outsourced, standards for child care rose to make up the difference. (I'm grateful to Janet Abbate for discussion on these topics.)

3. I:149/A 5:8.

4. If not just the "physical and organic" ends (along with ends derived from them by means-end reasoning) were "natural," the corrosion would be blocked. And so on various later occasions Mill turned to expanding the range of analysis-resistant pleasures or desires; the move is occasionally highlighted in discussions of Mill's moral theory (e.g., Skorupski, 2006, pp. 76–78). I'm going to be claiming that the argument to which this strategy responds was a red herring, which means that we won't need to do a full-on reconstruction of this part of Mill's intellectual machinery. Nonetheless, let's consider in passing what could be done with it.

What's important at this juncture is not to succumb to confusion about levels of explanation. When he explores this option, Mill attempts to come up with psychological theories that will explain "natural" pleasures; that a pleasure "comes naturally" is not that account, and thus to describe an attitude as "natural," hence analysis-resistant, is a placeholder for a psychological explanation, not an alternative to one. This emerges clearly enough when Mill advances his claim that "the social feelings of mankind [or] the desire to be in unity with our fellow creatures" is "a powerful principle in human nature," one that is "a natural basis of sentiment for utilitarian morality," and that would not "yield by degrees to the dissolving force of analysis," or end up being "analyzed away" (X:230f/U 3:9–10). He canvasses two explanations, namely, that the desire is hardwired (like hunger, or perhaps the disposition to care for one's children), or that it is produced by conditioning, and opts for the latter: "my own belief [is that] the moral feelings are not innate, but acquired." (Mill spends much of the chapter explaining the complex social processes through which that happens.) However, he is careful to allow that the social feelings might be either, and that's reflected in his choice of comparisons: "they are not for that reason the less natural. It is natural to man to speak, to reason, to build cities, to cultivate the ground, though these are acquired faculties" (X:230/U 3:8). N.B.: Mill does not take resistance to analysis to entail being ineradicable; responding to William Ward, he wrote, "You ask what are the natural instincts that civilisation has strikingly & memorably conquered. I answer, nearly all"—after which he gives a brief list (XIV:26f).

We earlier noticed Mill's interest in a psychological account of a particular class of pleasures: unanalyzable, because "chemically blended," states of mind (ch. 3, note 28). This is a more flexible resource than just adding items to a short list of hardwired desires, because the blended states of mind can apparently have arbitrary contents, that is, be about anything at all. The flexible resource comes with the explanatory costs mentioned in the note just indicated, which also stick to the more rigid strategy of extending the list of content-specific built-in desires.

But there is, from our own point of view, an additional cost to appealing to a list of analysis-resistant "natural feelings." When the items on the list are tied to a specific range of contents, they can't be recruited to underwrite anything like the full range of reasonably adopted life projects. Continuing the example, suppose that it is in fact "one of [somebody's] natural wants that there should be harmony between his feelings and aims and those of his fellow creatures" (X:233/U 3:11), but that the project which he is pursuing involves innovation, disruption, and a willingness to disregard the feelings and aims of one's fellow man—as when Robert Crumb took up drawing comics that many people found offensive, or as when Travis Kalanick decided to upend the taxi industry. Then the naturalness of that particular sentiment could not be drawn upon to forestall the erosion of commitment to the project.

5. How seriously should *we* take the argument? On the one hand, the psychological theory it invokes is after all defunct, and if we reject it, we don't have to think that one's arbitrary final ends are bound to be undercut. On the other, Vogler plausibly argues that the associationism is not an independent premise, but rather an antiquely accented expression of the instrumentalist conception of rationality; if we today are instrumentalists, we will end up accepting a psychological theory that can be substituted into the argument to produce substantially similar results.

However, Sean Reichert (personal communication) has observed that if the argument works, Mill's problem ought to solve itself. Analysis, after all, is admittedly a skill we're educated into. So analytical thinking must consist in traversing "artificial and casual" associations of ideas: those associations of ideas should be dissolved by analysis as well. An over-analytic education should be a problem only temporarily; if it gets out of hand, you need only redirect your analytic attention to your analytic skills.

And in any case, it's hard to believe that analysis is as effective at dissolving artificial associations as Mill's argument requires. It's easy enough to put someone off their food by suggesting such associations ("your pasta looks like *worms*"), and merely understanding that there is nothing more to it than that is often insufficient to restore the victim's lost appetite. Still, as I observed in note 4, I am about to argue that Mill was misdiagnosing his predicament; we don't need to arrive at a final assessment of his argument.

6. Reiner, 1985.

7. Vogler explores this option thoroughly, and makes a convincing case that Mill experimented with ways of making room in the psychology for the healing effects of poetry. On James Mill's account, a complex idea or train of thought contained as parts the simple ideas from which it was formed. An analytically trained mind was one that habitually decomposed complex thoughts and trains of thoughts into their parts. But if there were complex ideas whose ingredients *blended* to produce qualitatively new states of mind, they would not have parts to be extracted by analysis. (Compare the example which I quoted at chapter 3, note 28.) And a thought blended

with a feeling into a complex idea would have analysis-resistant motivational force. On Vogler's reading, Mill decided that poetry was suitable for conveying blended ideas; poems compress ideas together, and their semantic density prevents one's mind from breaking down the thoughts they evoke into parts. Accordingly, Mill proceeded to emend his father's psychology to allow blending. As a systematic philosopher, Mill was both a moral philosopher and a philosopher of science; Vogler plausibly makes out Mill's introduction of a distinctive category of "Chemical" sciences in the *System of Logic* to be a way of allowing a psychology of qualitative "blending."

As Vogler has herself pointed out (in unpublished material), the problem this fix poses for the rest of Mill's project is that, if poetry does what Mill suggested, the arguments against just about any of the institutions that the Utilitarians hoped to sweep away could be met by a poem. Take, for instance, *The Subjection of Women*: much of its argument consists in just the kind of analysis that "chemically" blended ideas were supposed to forestall. But Mill would certainly not have wanted to allow that a poem's producing a blended (and so both motivating and unanalyzable) idea of feminine submissiveness—perhaps in the style of Sir Walter Scott—could count as a legitimate response to the analysis.

A secondary problem is that the semantic density account of the effects of poetry is very implausibly applied to *this* poem; as I remarked, it is straightforward to give a verse-by-verse paraphrase of Wordsworth's Immortality Ode (and I have had many semesters of classes do just that, without especial difficulty). It is not as though the ideas the poem evokes somehow come too fast and furiously to be kept clear and separate in one's consciousness.

8. And we should not forget this possibility, either: that none of these overintellectualized reconstructions of the course of events have much to do with a clinically routine bout of depression. (I'm grateful to Candace Vogler for reminding me not to lose track of this option.)

9. I:211–213/A 6:11; in a letter to Lytton Bulwer, he describes his father's death as "the event which has deprived the world of the man of greatest philosophical genius it possessed" (XII:312).

10. I:193–195/A 6:1. However, the comparison to Shelley may be double-edged. Treating him as an exemplary poetic temperament, Mill had characterized him thus: "For him, voluntary mental discipline had done little: the vividness of his emotions and of his sensations had done all. He seldom follows up an idea; it starts into life, summons from the fairy-land of his inexhaustible fancy some three or four bold images, then vanishes, and straight he is off on the wings of some casual association into quite another sphere" (I:359).

11. See, just for instance, the entirely typical, but entirely over-the-top descriptions in letters to Louis Blanc and Pasquale Villari (XV:601, 604), or the tail end of the famous dedication of *On Liberty*: "Were I but capable of interpreting to the world one half the great thoughts and noble feelings which are buried in her grave, I should be the medium of a greater benefit to it, than is ever likely to arise from anything that I can write, unprompted and unassisted by her all but unrivalled wisdom" (XVIII:216).

12. In *The Subjection of Women*, which can be treated as something of a window into Mill's relationship with Taylor, Mill remarks that "one can, to an almost laughable degree, infer what a man's wife is like, from his opinions about women in general" (XXI: 278/SW 1:21). Because *Subjection* was finished after Taylor's death, she was not in a position to do a final line-by-line review; the published version is relatively unguarded, and commentators have been quick to turn the observation on Mill

himself. (E.g., Stefan Collini's Introduction to vol. XXI of Mill's *Collected Works*, at p. xxx.)

One pivotal argument of the *Subjection*, developed at great length, is that we can't argue for our present institutions by appealing to facts about women's "nature," because we (men, the enfranchised audience who would have to be convinced to change those institutions) aren't in a position to know anything about women's characters. (Nonetheless, having argued that no one is in a position to say what women are like, Mill's exposition takes a sudden swerve, and he goes on to tell you, without argument, a good deal about what women are like anyway; these remarks, which I will pass over, are taken up by the treatments I mentioned a moment ago.) The claim for which Mill actually argued—that men know hardly anything about women, and that men scarcely know who their wives really are—strikes me as one of those statements about women-in-general that do tell you about the wife of someone in particular. As we've just concluded, Mill had no idea who the person at the other end of what he called "The Most Valuable Friendship of My Life" actually was.

13. The letter was sent to Kate Amberly, and is quoted at Packe, 1954, pp. 480, 481.
14. Not always: for instance, Mazlish, 1975, is a psychoanalytically inflected alternative.
15. A popular biography from a half-century back provides an amusing purple-prose version of this view: "Her [Taylor's] comments, though usually sweetly admiring, were also quite unforseeable. This, to [Mill], was an attraction. It supplied the mixture of fear and delight that he had grown used to under his father" (Borchard, 1957, p. 53).
16. Early in his career, Mill occasionally assumed something like this posture toward the correspondents whom he had adopted as intellectual father figures; see, e.g., letters to Comte and Tocqueville, at XIII:434, 552.
17. I *will* take off the table another such question, that of Mill's and Taylor's sex life, and whether or not Mill died a virgin. While this is conceivably relevant to a criticism Wilde made of Mill—what did Mill know about *pleasure*?—the generally low quality of the discussion and the obsessive interest of its participants make it a counterproductive topic. (For an overview of Wilde's complaint, see Millgram, 2010.)
18. See, just for instance, Pappe, 1960.
19. A quick advisory: to form an opinion that's worth having on this subject, you will need to read what we have left of the writings that are uncontroversially Harriet Taylor's. There's less than there might be, because she asked Mill to destroy her letters when she died, but we still have enough to make up a sizable volume (Mill, 1998). So if you *do* want to argue about this, I suggest you read this book cover to cover. Hayek, 1951, interleaves what we have of the Mill-Taylor correspondence in a way that makes it straightforward to follow the back-and-forth, and is also a valuable resource.
20. Just for instance, here is Thomas Carlyle, at various points in his correspondence with his wife: "a living romance-heroine, of the clearest insight, of the royallest volition... of questionable destiny"; "she affects, with a kind of Sultana noblemindedness a certain girlish petulance"; "I for my share can see no wholesomeness in the witchery of the woman"; in 1836, after describing Mill as "Wasted thin, and with the miserablest twitchings, and St-Vitus work going on about his face: the hair of his head is fast falling out this long while," he diagnoses: "I reckon it to be the fruit of that Taylor-Platonica affair mainly." And subsequently: "Mrs Taylor it is whispered is with him, or near him. Is it not very strange, this pining away into desiccation and nonentity, of our poor Mill, if it be so, as his friends all say, that this Charmer is the cause of it?" Similarly, we have Jane Carlyle, describing Taylor as "a dangerous looking woman ... engrossed with a dangerous passion," and "the fascinating half

angelical half demonical *Mrs* Taylor" (Carlyle and Carlyle, 1977–1981, 7: 245f, 270; 8:15, 103, 291, 328; 9:67). Going back to the purple-prose biography of note 15, here is a later such thumbnail sketch, representative of the sort of thing one finds: "Little did anyone suspect the thoughts that were hidden in the elegantly dressed, dark, small head, the turmoil that was stirring under Harriet's shapely bosom" (Borchard, 1957, p. 41).

21. XXI:102; compare XXI:393.

22. XIV:152. My take on the matter is close in some respects to that of Himmelfarb, 1990, although I wouldn't want to endorse her neoconservative subtext. She holds the purpose of *On Liberty* to be that of providing the ideological underpinnings for *The Subjection of Women*, which she thinks was a project more of Taylor's than of Mill's. The suggestion is that the *real* author of *On Liberty* is a woman, and its *real* topic is women's issues; the unstated and unfair implication is that it can be dismissed.

23. A famous and politically important incident of this kind is discussed at Himmelfarb, 1990, pp. 227–233; compare Packe, 1954, pp. 306–315. I'll have a use for it later on, in section 10.2.

24. I'm grateful to an anonymous reviewer for pressing this point.

25. Mill does exhibit a great deal of deference in some of his correspondence, so here also it's worth remembering that, to the extent that he treated Comte, Tocqueville, etc., as authorities, these were authorities-by-adoption also. We should also keep in mind that his magnum opus, the *System of Logic*, does not seem to have been supervised by Taylor or anyone else.

CHAPTER 6

1. I:175/A 5:18; Bain, 1882, p. 32, takes Mill's "later returns" to mean further breakdowns, and he had the advantage over more recent readers of being well-acquainted with Mill personally. He tells us that Mill was "seized by an obstinate derangement of the brain" in 1836 (p. 42), and that "he had another relapse of his indisposition" in 1844 (p. 79). Bain seems to be of two minds as to how much continuity there was between Mill's breakdowns; on the one hand, he thinks that "we can plainly see in [his first] 'mental crisis' the beginning of the maladies that oppressed the second half of his life in a way that could not be mistaken" (p. 38); on the other, Mill "had many illnesses [after the second], but I do not know that anyone [sic] was so markedly an affection of the brain as on this occasion" (p. 44). If Bain is right—but the natural way to read Mill's own presentation is as referring to the latter parts of his first breakdown—it would suggest that the issues the Crisis raised did not cease to be immediate and pressing concerns in Mill's later life. Although Mill's *Autobiography* gives a good deal of airplay to his first breakdown, it gives little or none to his relapses; he tells us that after reading Wordsworth, he "gradually, but completely, emerged from [his] habitual depression, and was never again subject to it" (I:153/A 5:10). (He does mention, ambiguously, "a later period of the same mental malady," at I:143/A 5:5.) Because that may mean that Mill is suppressing part of the story, Bain is perhaps the more reliable source.

2. Those who are aware that Mill has something to say on the topic tend to think that he is repeating Aristotle, or discuss Mill's views on freedom of the will unsympathetically. For instance, Carlisle, 1991, p. 294, complains that Mill "would not recognize that a verbal feint does not resolve the conflicting claims of freedom and necessity."

3. VII:323–325. Because contemporary metaphysicians tend to understand causation differently from Mill, it's worth being explicit about what he means by it:

"invariability of succession ... between [a] fact in nature and some other fact which has preceded it;... To certain facts, certain facts always do, and ... will continue to, succeed. The invariable antecedent is termed the cause; the invariable consequent, the effect" (VII:327).

4. The problem of induction is usually attributed to Hume (1888/1978, pp. 86–94), and the reader should be aware that the current orthodoxy—due to a revisionist reading on the part of Scarre, 2002, and Scarre, 1989, ch. 4—is that Mill was simply unaware of this part of Hume, and was not trying to solve the now-familiar puzzle. I lay out my reasons for thinking Scarre mistaken in Millgram, 2009b, sec. 6, and Millgram, 2014, p. 114n6.

   Mill in fact seems to have paid close attention to Hume, and particularly to his skepticism, calling him "the profoundest negative thinker on record ...: a man, the peculiarities of whose mind qualified him to detect failure of proof, and want of logical consistency, at a depth which French sceptics, with their comparatively feeble powers of analysis and abstraction, stopt far short of, and which German subtlety alone could thoroughly appreciate, or hope to rival" (X:80). The problem of induction is one of the related difficulties that Kant took up, and is very likely intended.

5. I'm grateful to Kate Elgin for a back-and-forth on this point.

6. VII:184; you will notice that Mill has substituted the Duke of Wellington (that is, a then-living person) for Socrates, who appears in the more standard recitations of the exemplary syllogism, but who was long dead. This marks Mill's understanding of the point of inference, which is to make predictions about the unobserved, paradigmatically about the future.

7. VII:186f, or again, VII:201. A natural response to Mill's complaint, nowadays, would be to reiterate the distinction between soundness and validity: whether the conclusion follows from the premises does not depend on whether a premise can be known to be true independently of establishing the conclusion. While Mill is quite aware of this distinction (e.g., IX:354, 367; VII:321n), on exhibit here is a psychologistic view of logic, on which it is a practical discipline, one that gives guidelines for reasoning. On such a view, usability is a paramount qualification for a would-be guideline. (Thus it's not entirely appropriate that, in the course of presenting almost precisely this response, Peirce, 1992, p. 61, emphasizes his antipsychologism.)

8. Mill summarizes his treatment in the *System of Logic* in a footnote to his edition of the *Analysis* (1869, vol. I, p. 427): "I have maintained ... that Ratiocination does not *consist* of Syllogisms; that the Syllogism is not the analysis of what the mind does in reasoning, but merely a useful formula into which it can translate its reasonings, gaining thereby a great increase in the security for their correctness."

   A couple of tangential points: First, if syllogisms are data extraction devices, we might wonder how Mill knows that they extract the information stored in a major premise reliably. Mill does not seem to have considered this question explicitly, but there is only one answer he could have given: we have a great deal of experience with syllogisms, and we have learned, inductively, that they are entirely reliable in this regard.

   Second, we might also wonder about plain old modus ponens—that is, an inference of the form, 'if p, then q; p; so q.' It does not require the quantificational apparatus built into the syllogistic, and the Stoics, for instance, were already aware of the inference pattern. (I'm grateful to Lanier Anderson for raising this question.) Is a modus ponens not really an inference, either? Again, Mill does not discuss the question, but it is clear what his answer to it would have to be. How do we come to know the conditional premise, 'if p, then q', of a modus ponens? Not in the way suggested by its semantics: construed as a material implication, 'if p, then q' is true when p is false or q is true, but if you already know that q is true, then you do not need the modus ponens, and if you already know that p is false, you cannot use the modus ponens. Evidently, you come to know that 'if p, then q' by, say, observing previous p-like circumstances followed by previous q-like circumstances. That is, once again, the major premise of a bit of deductive reasoning records and encodes observations of particulars, and these are the real premises of the reasoning in which a modus ponens is invoked.

9. At VII:307, VII:308, and VII:572; however, for a later complication, see IX:482n.

10. Braithwaite, 1960, ch. 8.

11. Whewell, 1854, and Whewell, 1862, were representative targets; Mill objects to Whewell's moral theorizing in these terms at X:167–201. There is a delicate question, which I do not want to take up here, as to how uniformly apriorist Church of England apologetics actually were. Whewell himself seems to occupy a puzzling middle ground, on which truths that are in retrospect necessary, and which, once acknowledged, are visibly not merely empirical claims, nonetheless could not have been arrived at through any means other than lengthy experience. However, I think this characterization of Mill's motivations survives the complications the question introduces; he does not, for instance, seem to have appreciated the nuances of Whewell's position.

12. Recall our earlier pass over these points in section 2.4. The idea that arithmetic and logic are empirical sciences is generally regarded as, well, daffy, but it's important not to be dismissive. Notice that a very interesting change has happened when it comes to geometry. When Mill argued that geometry was an empirical science, he sounded just as daffy as when he argued for the same conclusion about logic and arithmetic. But that geometry is an empirical science is now the received wisdom.

13. X: 263–368; compare VIII:928.

14. Is this a coherent endpoint? Ravetz, 1979, p. 205, complains, of Mach's very similar proposal, that "banishing the concept of 'force' from mechanics as an anthropomorphic relic leaves the field of statics as 'the science of nonexistent motions.'" Moreover, it's actually a tricky question whether Millian psychology lives up to positivist standards, given the role that "intensity" (or forcefulness or vividness) of sensations and ideas plays in it. However, I won't pursue these questions here. See also the related discussion of metaphysical accounts of volition at VII:353ff, esp. from the last paragraph of the lengthy quote from Reid (p. 358).

15. Perhaps Malebranchian occasionalism was a more recent relative of this sort of picture; again, possibly a view ascribed to Descartes by Florka, 2001, esp. pp. 67, 90, 105f, 107, 116f, on which God has chosen the metaphysical structure of the world, and is thereby responsible for the laws of logic, can give us some of the flavor of this Comtean stage.

16. This is an adaptation of an example due to Jenann Ismael. Let me add a reservation to my earlier agreement that we are still stuck at the metaphysical stage of logic: Mill's positivist aspirations for logic suit a natural way of looking at model theory. So perhaps we have, after all, come a good way along the path that Mill pointed out.

17. In the *Autobiography*, Mill states that his "theory of Induction was substantially completed before [he] knew of Comte's book," but acknowledged that he "gained much from Comte, with which to enrich [his] chapters in the subsequent rewriting" (I:217/A 6:14); later he reiterates that "much matter derived from Comte" was subsequently

"introduced into the book in the course of rewriting" (I:231/A 7:3). In the note to A 7:1 (I:255), Mill returns to the subject of his intellectual debt to Comte, this time insisting once again that "the first volume [of the *Logic*], which contains all the fundamental doctrines of the book, was substantially complete before [he] had seen Comte's treatise... it is only in the concluding Book, on the Logic of Moral Sciences, that [he] owe[s] to him any radical improvement in [his] conception of the application of logical methods." And in a letter to Spencer, he reiterates: "I myself owe much more to Comte than you do, though, in my case also, all my principle conclusions had been reached before I saw his book" (XV:934f). Regardless of who owed what to whom, the fact that Mill repeatedly felt he needed to return to the question of how much he owed to Comte tells us how closely connected he took their views to be.

For readers already familiar with Hume on induction, we can now briefly compare Mill's treatment with his. Hume's texts are notoriously unstable, but with that caveat, one of the poles they flip-flop between is radically skeptical. (The other pole is usually described as "naturalistic.") Hume's content analysis of causal judgments shows that the idea of a (by Comte's lights, metaphysical-stage) force derives its content not *from* such a force, but from an impression of reflection; the suggestion is that something very important is missing. (We don't have any *justification* for induction, but custom lets us carry on without justification.) By contrast, Mill is not skeptical; the point is that what we have *is* justification, and it is only metaphysical-stage prejudice that would make one think otherwise.

18. For a very clear introduction to the problem of determinism, see Bok, 1998, ch. 1.
19. VIII:839; compare I:177/A 5:18: "I perceived, that the word Necessity, as a name for the doctrine of Cause and Effect applied to human action, carried with it a misleading association; and that this association was the operative force in the depressing and paralysing influence which I had experienced." (Notice that what is involved in the association is said to be the word or the term; perhaps this is meant to allow us to bypass the Humean question of what the content of the *idea* of necessity could be.)

Two points are worth emphasizing: First, Mill is quite aware of the standard rendering of the problem of freedom of the will; see, for instance, his discussion of Sir William Hamilton's views on the topic at IX:437–469 (and n.b. the pointer to his own take on it at 439n). Second, the explanation of the depressing aspect of determinism cannot be complete as it stands. As a matter of psychological fact, necessity is as much associated with logical or mathematical proofs as it is with the predictability that preoccupies theorists of freedom of the will. Almost no one finds mathematical necessity depressing (the "underground man" of Dostoevsky, 2008, at pp. 15f, 34, is an odd exception). Thus Mill still owes an explanation for why the further and painful associations arise almost only in the latter case.

20. We will see this concept introduced on pp. 95f.
21. Mill acknowledged the popular impression of him "as a 'made' or manufactured man, having had a certain impress of opinion stamped on me which I could only reproduce" (I:163/A 5:12). Alan Ryan, in his capacity as guest editor of a volume of the *Collected Works*, tersely sums up this widely shared understanding of Mill's concern: "In his youth, Mill had obviously been very vulnerable to the accusation that his character had been made for him, and not by him, and that he was an artefact of James Mill's designing" (IX:lxii).
22. As discussed in note 4 to this chapter.

1. Mill adds, at this point, "that wish being, it needs scarcely be observed, a *new antecedent*"—the point being that there is no violation of the natural order of which determinism is the putative consequence.

2. In the older usage of "moral," the phrase "moral sciences" corresponds roughly to our "social sciences."

3. For an explanation of lexicographic orderings, see Weisstein, 1999. The distinction is presented and put to work in *Utilitarianism* (X:211/U 2:5), which was published a good deal later than the *System of Logic*; consequently, we must bear in mind, in tying the pieces of our story together, that when Mill wrote the chapter of the *System* that explicitly addressed the problem of freedom of the will, he did not yet have the terminology I am laying out—which does not imply that he did not have the conceptual apparatus, or anyway a precursor of it.

4. For critical discussion, see Millgram, 2005a, pp. 68f, 82ff nn 27, 28, 31; Enoch, 2005.

5. I'll return to the first question in note 24. Conceiving of the contrast in this way meant that Mill never adjusted the definition of higher pleasures to accommodate the arbitrary hierarchies of higher pleasures which we're about to consider, and I'll return to that issue in chapter 8, note 21.

6. In particular, from "the [dilemma] ... of thinking one doctrine true, and the contrary doctrine morally beneficial."

7. Recall the discussion in chapter 3, note 10.

8. VIII:842f; compare X:238/U 4:11: "in the case of an habitual purpose, instead of willing the thing because we desire it, we often desire it only because we will it.... Many indifferent things, which men originally did from a motive of some sort, they continue to do from habit." Or again, "when what was at first a direct impulse towards pleasure, or recoil from pain, has passed into a habit or a fixed purpose, then the strength of the motive means the completeness and promptitude of the association which has been formed between an idea and an outward act" (IX:468).

9. Mill himself later sorted out the terminology along these lines: "The distinction between will and desire ... is an authentic and highly important psychological fact; but the fact consists solely in this—that will, like all other parts of our constitution, is amenable to habit, and that we may will from habit what we no longer desire for itself, or desire only because we will it. It is not the less true that will, in the beginning, is entirely produced by desire; including in the term the repelling influence of pain as well as the attractive one of pleasure." (X:238/U 4:11)

10. Dennett, 1984, p. 133; Frankfurt, 1988, chs. 7, 13, Frankfurt, 1999, chs. 9, 14; McDowell, 1998, ch. 3, Williams, 1995. The liveliness with which these notions are invoked suggests that if Mill does turn out to have something to tell us about moral unfreedom, we should not assume his conclusions to be of merely antiquarian interest.

   To be sure, these accounts differ a great deal both from one another (e.g., Watson, 2002, sec. 6, compares and contrasts Williams's and Frankfurt's versions of practical necessity) and from Mill's. In particular, they do not typically share Mill's end-like (or purposive) conception of the form and content of what it is one cannot but do. Still, I think the problem I am about to exhibit in Mill can, suitably modified, be raised for each of them.

11. However, that expectation is defeasible: the home of a fixed habit is a controlled environment, and such an environment might tamp down the randomness in one's experience; a well-designed project will provide positive feedback for task completion, and those intermediate rewards can help keep you invested in it; you

can discover new aspects of an activity to like; if the shift in profile is gradual enough, won't the habits have time to catch up? So we won't want to overestimate the effects of hedonic drift. (For discussion on this point, I'm grateful to Zach Ascherl, Dan Brown, Phoebe Chan, Megan Heath, and an anonymous reviewer.)

12. Packe, 1954, p. 80; however, there were perhaps signals that would have tipped off observant bystanders. As a youth, Mill was in the habit of writing letters to the editor, and there is a lengthy break between his missive of September 16, 1825, and that of June 6, 1827 (XXII:103–107).

13. I'm grateful to Ken Gemes for pressing me to clarify this point.

14. Wordsworth, 1958, vol. iv, pp. 279–285. Paul, 1998, is a reading of Mill's Mental Crisis that emphasizes the cultivation of sympathy, and thus echoes one element of the Ode's resolution. However, Mill was far too secular to have endorsed the religious elements of Wordsworth's train of thought, and failing to do so gives "primal sympathy," "the soothing thoughts that spring/ Out of human suffering," and "the philosophic mind" the look of a second-rate consolation prize. For this reason, I think we have to look beyond the turn to sympathy in making sense of Mill's response.

15. One might wonder whether it is safe to tie Mill's uptake of the poem so directly to its argument: doesn't poetry that stands the test of time, as has the Ode, require subtler treatment? However, we can leave to one side the question of whether our own reading of the poem should stop with what we have taken from it. Looking back, in an essay on "Poety and Its Varieties," Mill tells us that "in Wordsworth, the poetry is almost always the mere setting of a thought... what he is impressed with, and what he is anxious to impress, is some proposition, more or less distinctly conceived; some truth, or something which he deems such.... His poetry, therefore, may be defined to be, his thoughts, coloured by, and impressing themselves by means of, emotions" (I:358). Because what Wordsworth was capable of, in Mill's view of him, was "feeling enough to form a decent, graceful, even beautiful decoration to a thought which is in itself interesting and moving" (I:359), we can take the anchor for Mill's response to his work to be the interesting and moving thoughts.

16. I'm grateful to Candace Vogler for pressing this line in conversation.

17. The account I am presenting here draws on Carlisle, 1991, which is recommended reading for those with an interest in the subject. Kinzer, 2007, pp. 36f, 63f, 131, lists the scarce occasions on which Mill defied his father. One of these pertained to a personal matter, and even in this case, as Kinzer nicely puts it, "The first reported instance of such frank opposition would also be the last." Others were ideological, and James Mill's "eldest son could not muster the courage for a candid reckoning of the differences that had grown up between them."

18. Bentham, 1950, pp. 1, 102, tells us that the "efficacy" of the Principle of Utility depends on, inter alia, "find[ing] the processes of a moral arithmetic by which uniform results may be arrived at," and that "it is necessary to have a moral thermometer to make perceptible all the degrees of happiness and misery" (although he acknowledges that this sort of ideal precision is not in practice fully realizable).

19. X:235f/U 4:5–6; you will recall that the argument is reconstructed in section 2.2.

20. Oddly enough, something like that is true even when one's own utility is at issue. Although Mill's psychology more or less guarantees that, faced with two options, either one or another of them will seem more pleasant to you, or they will seem equally pleasant, the corrective function of the decided preference criterion is to make room for the idea that you might be mistaken about what you really want. Your confidence that the objects of your desires will not prove disappointing is

to be underwritten by the preferences of other and more experienced judges. When unanimity on the part of the external referees is lacking, or your own hedonic expectations are controverted by their consensus, you may quite reasonably wonder whether what you feel yourself to prefer is really part of your own utility.

21. He did continue to *root* for those reforms, when it looked like they were being implemented in India: XXX:21.

22. Millian utility is too easily regarded as a halfway house between the older conception, on which it is a sensation, and today's von Neumann–Morgenstern utility functions, on which utility is a construction out of revealed preferences. On this way of seeing him, Mill shares with us the idea that utility is constructed out of preferences, lacks the mathematical sophistication to deploy preferences over probability mixtures, and disreputably preserves the sensation of pleasure in his psychological theory of how those preferences are implemented. That turns out to be quite misleading, and there is a short way to say how. VNM utility functions require preference relations that are complete: for any two elements a and b of the agent's choice set, either the agent prefers a to b, or he prefers b to a, or he is indifferent between a and b. Millian utility does the job that Mill needed precisely because experienced judges do not agree on their preferences over many of the elements, and thus, because the (prescriptively relevant) preference relations are drastically *in*complete.

23. That turn of phrase is usually read as being about balancing reason with feeling, and that is Mill's message here. But if I'm right about what Mill took the problem to be, we should see generally flat affect as a special case. When there is not much in the way of motivation to marshal, it is easy for lone motives to be irresistable.

24. That is, we now can see why Mill does talk about higher and lower pleasures as though they were two unstructured classes of goods: that would be the most straightforward version of the sort of psychological configuration to which we should aspire.

25. For this suggestion, I'm indebted to Rae Langton. I owe the more general idea that freedom of the will is part of the agenda of *Subjection* to an unpublished manuscript by Luana Mueller.

Briefly recapping the argument Mueller has noticed in Mill, bullying someone produces short-term rewards such as compliance, attempts at appeasement, flattery or deference, anyway when you can get away with it. So when someone generally gets away with it, bullying will become a higher pleasure. (We will see the structural feature of higher pleasures that underwrites this inference in chapter 8.) Higher pleasures are lexically preferred: they always get chosen over their alternatives. So once it's a higher pleasure, bullying husbands will always chose bullying. And what always gets chosen turns into a habit, and eventually, becomes automatic, something you can't stop doing. So eventually, husbands who are able to get away with bullying won't be able to break the habit. Since Victorian marriages let husbands get away with long-term bullying, Victorian marriages turned men into bullies who couldn't break the habit. But if you can't break a habit—if you can't stop—your will is (morally) unfree. So the problem with Victorian marriages was that they deprived men of their free will.

Notice, first, that the argument focuses on the benefits of gender equality that, Mill insisted, would accrue specifically to men—the voters whom he needed to convince. Second, you might be wondering how Mill could have objected to Victorian marriage, because it undercut moral freedom, but insisted that Mormon polygamy was covered by the Principle of Liberty, because it was voluntary and thus permissible (XVIII:290f/OL 4:20). Evidently, even choices that are morally unfree, or that lead to moral unfreedom, can count as voluntary, at any rate in that they have to be respected by others—as in the case of monogamous marriage, as Mill took it to function in his day and age. And third, still apropos polygamy, keep in mind that what Mill was objecting to was bullying, women's inability to own property and so on—the "rivetting of the chains"—and not, in the first place, the allowable configurations of spouses.

26. I take this upshot to clarify a remark Mill makes in his second essay on Bentham, that "we think utility, or happiness, much too complex and indefinite an end to be sought except through the medium of various secondary ends" (X:110). However, let's register two caveats.

First, evidently we are looking at a phenomenon that is something like a matter of degree: of *how much* the rankings of components of one's utility can be relaxed before it becomes practically impossible to treat one's utility as, substantively, an end. Some crafts, for example, medicine, architecture, and even, perhaps, philosophy, have goals resembling Millian utility in substantively amounting to and functioning as a cluster or basket of goals, the priority and tradeoff relations among which are only occasionally defined. For instance, although the defining goal of architecture is (I suppose) to design and erect good buildings, one architect may prioritize style over convenience, where another prioritizes functionality or price. Nonetheless, different conceptions of good building have a large common denominator, and so it is possible to teach architecture students generically useful means to building good buildings. Or again, philosophical styles differ, but some tricks of the trade will be useful whatever sort of philosophical style you end up adopting, and accordingly there is a repertoire of skills that one can reasonably teach in a philosophy graduate program. (I'm grateful to Roger Crisp for questions on this point.)

Second, in what was evidently meant as the segue from the *System of Logic* to his *Utilitarianism*, Mill suggests that there is an Art of Life, and that utility ("the happiness of mankind, or rather, of all sentient beings") is its defining goal or "general principle." If I am right, this is a misstep on his part: Mill does understand an 'Art' to be built around a "desirable object" or "end to be attained" (VIII:944, 949, 951). But as we have seen, he also came to understand that what structures a life had better not be any single goal, desirable object, or end.

CHAPTER 8

1. See, for instance, Bentham, 1950, p. 95: "The care of his enjoyments ought to be left almost entirely to the individual." This sounds like Bentham is coming down on the side of certain liberties, anyway, but shortly thereafter he tells us:

Security ... has many branches, and some branches of it must yield to others. For example, liberty which is a branch of security ought to yield to a consideration of the general security since laws cannot be made except at the expense of liberty.

We cannot arrive at the greatest good, except by the sacrifice of some subordinate good. All the difficulty consists in distinguishing that object which, according to the occasion, merits pre-eminence. For each, in its turn, demands it; and a very complicated calculation is sometimes necessary to avoid being deceived as to the preference due to one or the other. (p. 98)

In other words, liberties (or more generally, forms of security) are to be prioritized on a type-of-case by type-of-case, or even case-by-case, basis: not a very reassuring stance, as such calculations are sensitive to the variable circumstances.

2. Mill himself inadvertently supplies a template for these sorts of arguments. In *Subjection*, he suggests that opponents of feminist reforms act as though they are thinking: women will not bear and raise children unless they are compelled to do it; it is absolutely necessary that the job get done; therefore, women must be compelled (XXI:281/SW 1:25). Mill did not imagine that anyone would admit in public to believing the first premise of that argument, and he did not fill in the specifically utilitarian justification for the second. But it is easy to see how other arguments of this general form might be advanced.

   Huxley folded many such arguments into his novel, some turning on the Benthamite identification of pleasure with happiness, and some not. I'll quickly recap an instance of the latter variety. Intelligent people are only happy when they have stimulating, demanding, challenging, creative jobs; put in menial jobs, they become frustrated and miserable. But there are many menial jobs that have to be done—many more than there are not-so-intelligent people—and very few stimulating jobs. If the percentage of intelligent people in the population stays as is, many people will be frustrated and miserable. Utilitarianism tells you to do whatever it takes to make as many people as possible happy. So utilitarianism tells you to adjust the number of intelligent people downwards, to match the number of stimulating jobs; Huxley's implementation suggestion was to have the government stunt the neurological development of fetuses by injecting them with alcohol and formaldehyde. But because you shouldn't just leave the match between person and job to chance, the government must further impose a caste system, in which the severely cognitively disabled persons produced in this way are required to perform the menial tasks.

3. Recall our brief survey in chapter 2, note 26.

4. Gunn, 1961, Part III. A further and more decisive objection is intended also. Utilitarianism is a moral theory, i.e., a theory about what choices to make; thus utilitarianism will eventually make itself irrelevant to the inhabitants of a society governed by it. And Gunn may also be suggesting that because full-fledged liberty provides the option of inactivity, and so enables the development of the preference for it, extreme liberty is self-undermining.

   I don't propose to take up Gunn's criticisms here, but it does seem to me that they have never been properly addressed, I expect due to the literary format in which they were presented, and the disciplinary affiliation of the author.

5. XVIII:228–259, esp. at pp. 252ff.

6. At, respectively, XVIII:225f, 258 and 247f/OL 1:12, 2:43 and 2:26–27.

7. Mill, 1869, vol. 1, pp. 106–110, 231–232.

8. Ibid., vol. 1, pp. 109f; XVIII:267/OL 3:11; XVIII:247/OL 2:26. Mill slides back and forth between describing the vanished ideas as having been bypassed, and as having faded away, that is, having diminished in liveliness and vivacity. While he does not defend the transition, it is, by his lights, defensible: the laws of association connect frequency of conjunction to intensity of impression (VIII:852); as an idea comes to

be more often bypassed, it is less frequently conjoined with other ideas, and so its intensity drops.

Beliefs can figure into more than one train of thought, and, even when routinized, different trains of thought may be differently abridged. So we should take Mill's argument to require other-things-equal qualifications at various junctures.

9. At XVIII:243/OL 2:21, XVIII:248/OL 2:27, XVIII:249/OL 2:28, XVIII:229/OL 2:1; cf. XVIII:249/OL 2:29: "a much livelier feeling of the meaning of their creed." The phrase "livelier impression" recalls the vocabulary of earlier British Empiricists (and there's a more explicit allusion at VIII:852); Hume, for instance, made belief out to be a matter of the liveliness of ideas, thinking that lively ideas could approach the liveliness of an impression, i.e., a sensation. However, recall (from chapter 3, note 8) that Mill himself officially abandoned the psychological doctrine that would have underwritten such a use of the terminology.

10. XVIII:247/OL 2:26, but boredom evidently comes in more than one variety. Robert Louis Stevenson's "Ordered South" contains another relative of the phenomenology we are now considering; his consumptive's downward spiral moves through "a patriarchial impersonality of interest" to a "dullness of senses [in which] there is a gentle preparation for the final insensibility of death" (1992, p. 9). A characterization of a further but similar sort of boredom can be found in Frankfurt, 1999, p. 89:

Being bored entails a reduction of attention; our responsiveness to conscious stimuli flattens out and shrinks; distinctions are not noticed and not made, so that the conscious field becomes increasingly homogenous. The general functioning of the mind diminishes ... [and] approach[es] a complete cessation of significant differentiation within consciousness; and this homogenization is, at the limit, tantamount to the cessation of conscious experience altogether.... [Boredom] threatens the extinction of the active self.

All of these are rather different from the sort of boredom which involves nervous, fidgety agitation.

11. The phenomenon is not confined to philosophy, of course. Bentham had complained that insisting on rights as the bottom line could amount to no more than trying to write prejudices into law. Sure enough, the discourse of human rights today has returned to the state of affairs he was criticizing, in which anyone who feels something would be a good idea tries to talk it up into a human right.

Return for a moment to the irony we noticed in chapter 3, that the Utilitarians introduced the Principle of Utility as an *alternative* to arguments from intuition, while today's utilitarians argue for the Principle mostly by trying to show that it matches their intuition profile. It's evidently the round of memory loss we're noticing right now that has prevented us from seeing today's discussion as Mill would have seen it.

Why does the shift in methodology matter? Let's quickly remind ourselves of the relevant bit of Mill's report of his teenage epiphany. Bentham was rejecting

the common modes of reasoning in morals and legislation ... as dogmatism in disguise imposing its sentiments upon others under cover of sounding expressions which convey no reason for the sentiment, but set up the sentiment as its own reason.... Bentham's principle put an end to all this ... all previous moralists were superseded ... here indeed was the commencement of a new era in thought. (I:67/A 3:3)

Utilitarianism was a movement, not just a moral theory, and it was a radical movement: the point was to sweep old institutions away. Old institutions have intuitions on their side; people find whatever they're used to intuitive. So radicals need a criterion of choice that's independent of people's intuitions. When you find yourself trying to defend utilitarianism, the moral theory, by relying on your intuitions, you're buying into a version of the theory that can't possibly do the job for which it was invented. We have allowed an artificial distinction between professionalized moral theory, on the one hand, and political philosophy in the service of activism, on the other, to become much more entrenched than it should be. We will shortly consider how one can assess the theory when the Chinese wall is discarded.

12. X:211, 213f/U 2:5, 8, 10.

13. VII:525; we'll introduce the concept properly in section 9.4.

14. Mill, 1869, vol. 2, p. 215, which also adduces power and dignity as examples; John Stuart Mill endorses them as "almost perfect" (p. 233n). See also vol. 2, p. 188 (on "money ... hugged as a good in itself"), and p. 233n on how "persons, things, and positions become in themselves pleasant to us by association; and, through the multitude and variety of the pleasurable ideas associated with them, become pleasures of greater constancy and even intensity, and altogether more valuable to us, than any of the primitive pleasures of our constitution ... as the love of wealth ...."

   The point of the extra documentation here and below is to demonstrate that the account of miserliness is not just a throwaway; it turns up again and again, and it was evidently important in the younger Mill's thinking. Indeed, it turns up so many times that William James later complained about "the somewhat threadbare instance of the miser who has been led by the association of ideas to prefer his gold to all the goods he might buy therewith" (James, 1956, p. 94).

15. Mill, 1869, vol. 2, p. 266; he notes the qualitative difference in the resulting feeling at p. 321. Here is his father's version of the explanation:

Money, for example, instrumental in procuring the causes of almost all our pleasures, and removing the causes of a large proportion of our pains, is associated with the ideas of most of the pleasurable states of our nature. The idea of an object associated with a hundred times as many pleasures as another, is of course a hundred times more interesting. (vol. 2, pp. 206f, endorsed yet again by the son at p. 236n)

Discussion of the psychological phenomenon in question is not confined to the *Analysis*. In his *Principles of Political Economy*, John Stuart Mill gives a related explanation for the once-popular economic doctrine of mercantilism:

As it is always by means of money that people provide for their different necessities, there grows up in their minds a powerful association leading them to regard money as wealth in a more peculiar sense than any other article; and even those who pass their lives in the production of the most useful objects, acquire the habit of regarding those objects as chiefly important by their capacity of being exchanged for money. A person who parts with money to obtain commodities, unless he intends to sell them, appears to the imagination to be making a worse bargain than a person who parts with commodities to get money; the one seems to be spending his means, the other adding to them. Illusions which, though now in some measure dispelled, were long powerful enough to overmaster the mind of every politician, both speculative and practical, in Europe. (III:505f)

Here is further discussion in *An Examination of Sir William Hamilton's Philosophy*:

association can generate new mental affections. Let us take, as one of the obvious examples, the love of money. Does any one think that money has intrinsically, by its own nature, any more value to us than the first shining pebbles we pick up, except for the things it will purchase? Yet its association with these things not only makes it desired for itself, but creates in many minds a passionate love of it, far surpassing the desire they feel for any of the uses to which it can be put. (IX:284n)

16. Mill does not emphasize the supplemental reinforcement we are given for riches, power and reputation, but being wealthy has many social rewards, over and above the actual purchases it enables one to make: in particular, "it adds to our Power and Dignity" (Mill, 1869, vol. 2, p. 208). These additional rewards ought to have a further conditioning effect.

Is all this enough to account for a miser's *generally* preferring money to what money can buy? After all, no one has had the opportunity to build up associative links of the sort we have just described around the ideas of *each* sum of money. The bridge between the steps of the argument, in Mill's mind, is almost certainly the notion of a tendency, which plays an important role in his philosophy of science. What the miser is learning about, and coming to value, is money's *tendencies*. (For a contemporary discussion of the notion, see Cartwright, 1989; section 4.5 takes up its Millian antecedents. I'm grateful to Candace Vogler for reminding me of this part of his view.)

Still, could it actually be true that misers exhibit a lexicographic preference for money over *everything* else? They don't just starve to death, so mustn't they be buying food, paying the rent and so on? In this conception of miserliness, one eats to live, and one lives in order to squirrel away more money; expenditures are to be understood as in the service of that higher pleasure.

17. Mill, 1869, vol. ii, p. 215; III:810. His son further endorses his father's view in a letter to Gomperz, where he recommends "arguing questions [in economics] at first on the supposition of barter, in order to adjourn the difficulties which arise from the wrong and confused associations which cling to the idea of money" (XV:859).

18. I:143/A 5:4; notice that what I just described as a misapprehension need not involve a miser *believing* that he can buy more than his money is worth.

    ATMs disburse one's cash, again and again and again, but we don't ever, as far as I know, find ATM-misers, people who'd give up the money the ATM provides for ATM access privileges. On Mill's account, there should be at least some such people. The moral: don't forget that this is the *history* of psychology, not necessarily a plausible psychology for us.

19. The younger Mill quotes his father on the role of praise and blame in parental pedagogy in the *Analysis* (vol. 2, p. 314), and remarks, in a tone that conveys the deep impression it made on him, on "the desire [James Mill] made [the minds he came in contact with] feel for his approbation, the shame at his disapproval" (I:105/A 4:7). Compare also I:141/A 5:4 on his teachers' overreliance on "the old familiar instruments, praise and blame, reward and punishment."

20. Mill, 1869, vol. 2, p. 298f. Compare his remarks in a letter to William Ward: "it might well be, that the innumerable associations of pain with doing wrong which have been rivetted by a long succession of pains undergone ... (especially in early life), may produce a general & intense feeling of recoil ..." (XV:649). (However, Mill goes on to contrast this sort of conditioning with "the normal form of moral feeling ... a state of society is so eminently natural to human beings that anything which is an obviously indispensable condition of social life, easily comes to act upon their minds almost like a physical necessity.")

21. Perhaps this is a further reason that Mill was willing to treat the higher pleasures as a class: since they do not come in amounts, Mill may have concluded that they do not trade off against each other. If this *was* what Mill was thinking, however, I'm not happy with it: different higher pleasures do trade off against one another, and instances of the very same higher pleasure can trade off against each other (as when you have the option of sacrificing some people's liberty to allow liberty to many others); many people surely have preferences over such tradeoffs, and Mill discusses one such tradeoff himself, at XVIII:266/OL 3:9.

    And notice that if Mill had explored the hierarchies of ever-higher pleasures made possible by the two-place relation, he would have wanted to reintroduce a suitable notion of more-and-less to underwrite those comparisons. I expect that would have been doable—for instance, a generic and nondepletable means can have narrower or wider application—but because Mill himself did not go down this path, neither will we.

22. Prescott, 2000, pp. 607, 621f, 647–649.

23. During the twentieth century, the device most used to address the problem was rule-utilitarianism, the idea being that what got your moral theory into trouble was testing the particular action for its utility upshots, rather than testing a rule by which the action is subsumed. (The *rule* "torture prisoners of war when there's money to be had, and execute them when they've become enough of a nuisance" would entail a different calculation: for instance, were such a rule in force, soldiers would be much more inclined to fight to the very end.) Act-utilitarians and rule-utilitarians argued for decades, among other things, over which view to attribute to Mill. That latter debate was, in my view, a mistake: both interpretations are unhelpful anachronisms.

    In Mill's scheme of things, whether a choice promotes utility depends on the preferences of the experienced. Now, as a matter of psychological fact, the objects of preference are sometimes more and sometimes less particular. Around election time, for example, voters develop preferences over particular candidates; they also often have much more general preferences, exhibited in choices of rules about how to vote (e.g., straight party ticket). Thus, the judgments derived from the preferences of the experienced will sometimes look more like act-utilitarian guidelines, and sometimes more like rule-utilitarian guidelines. (Mill is of course quite aware of the contrast between "acting on general rules" and "measuring the consequences of each act"; the phrases are quoted from a letter to George Grote [XV:762].)

Here's why the debate was *unhelpfully* anachronistic. The twentieth-century debate came to a close with Lyons, 1965, which argued that, as rules get more contoured, rule-utilitarianism collapses back into act-utilitarianism. That argument works because there are no limits to the complexity of a rule, and that presupposition was allowable because twentieth-century ethics had taken the same antipsychologistic turn as twentieth-century logic. Because Mill's experienced judges will not form preferences over arbitrarily complex rules, that collapse is preempted; that is, when you insist on framing your treatment of Mill in these anachronistic terms, you bypass the very material that allows Mill to do better than the parties to that debate did.

24. The first quote in this stretch of argument is from XXVIII:152; the others are from X:250f/U 5:25. Earlier versions of the considerations in play in the argument can be found in Bentham, 1950, pp. 54–59, 109–113, 115–119.

25. The phenomenon of a general-purpose means correctly coming to seem more important than any of the ends which it might be used to attain is pervasive. Another striking example is material objects, which Mill understood as 'Permanent Possibilities of Sensation.' Mill's phenomenalist analysis is very close to that of C. I. Lewis's more recently familiar view: a piece of paper's being on the table, for instance, is a matter of the sensations I would have if I went back into the room and looked—and many other counterfactual conditionals of the same ilk (IX:183, 197; compare Lewis, 1956, pp. 135f). Mill does not himself put the upshot as I am about to: that one can treat a material object, such as a piece of paper, as a tool for producing the sensations to be found in the consequents of the counterfactuals that constitute it. But that is what it amounts to, on the phenomenalist view, and because any material object is constituted by (for at least all practical purposes) infinitely many conditionals of this kind, "[t]hese various possibilities"—that is, the material objects—"are the important thing to me in the world. My present sensations are generally of little importance" (IX:179f). Material objects become associated with the variegated sensations they do and might produce; they normally end up mattering far more than the sensations; and rightly so, because, with the obvious exceptions, material objects are (like security, but unlike a fixed amount of money) not exhausted by the momentary pleasures they deliver.

CHAPTER 9

1. XVIII:261/OL 3:2; that latter phrase is Mill quoting von Humboldt, 1996.

2. In particular, a further family of arguments, turning on the thought that no one knows better than you what you want, and so that choices about how to get what you want are best left up to you, are again second nature to the inhabitants of contemporary democracies, and I will as before leave them to the textbooks. However, we should not simply assume that the arguments in this family *will* do the job, and that the alternative to them which we are about to engage is merely a backup. A few decades back, a fast-food franchise's market researchers discovered that when customers reported that they wanted more flavor, what in fact satisfied them was not more flavor, but more salt and more sugar. The notion that the person who has the desire is in the best position to know what would satisfy him is naive. As those in

the business of desire satisfaction know, expertise in these matters is the property of experts, not amateurs.

3. Although I am not taking up the arguments that turn on the ways that originality engenders and amounts to novelty here, see chapter 10, note 20, for a preview of the obstacles to working with these considerations.

4. Feuerzeig, 2005, could serve as a dramatic illustration of the distinction.

5. Here we are putting to one side an important aspect of the analytic mind that we have seen play an important role elsewhere: its tendency to disassemble complex ideas into their distinct components.

6. I:360; Mill continues, "and by all feelings which in any degree resembled them," but we will not need this part of the account for our argument.

7. I:357; poetry is the product of poetic minds, and we should register that Mill is likely to strike poetically inclined readers as describing precisely *bad* poetry; surely poetry produced this way would be emotionally uncompelling, and perhaps even unintelligible, to anyone but the poet himself. Mill allows that "poetry, which is the delineation of the deeper and more secret workings of human emotion, is interesting only to those to whom it recals what they have felt, or whose imagination it stirs up to conceive what they could feel, or what they might have been able to feel had their outward circumstances been different" (I:345f). But since the poet's pattern of feelings and associations will normally be idiosyncratic, the first of these effects will be rare; instead, the usual response to poetry, as Mill conceives of it, should be bemused curiosity, as one is given a guided tour of the inner workings of an excitable person's mind. Mill eventually noticed the problem himself (I:413f), and came to require of poetry that it "bring the materials which sense supplies, and fancy summons up, under the command of a central and controlling thought or feeling" (I:415). But we are not told what this means, over and above what we have already noted: that a strong feeling mediates transitions from idea to idea.

   Briefly, Mill's views on poetry are important for understanding his philosophical ideas, but he did not seem to have had a proper appreciation for it; this is perhaps a further reason that he was unable to articulate a satisfactory philosophical aesthetics.

8. He continues: "In England, rule has to a great degree substituted itself for nature. The greater part of life is carried on, not by following inclination … but by having no inclination but that of following a rule" (XXI:313/SW 3:14; cf. XVIII:264f/OL 3:6).

   We've already mentioned Gunn's novel (1961); its second part follows out what seem to be the utilitarian consequences of these observations; in doing so, it advances a subsidiary argument, that Millian improvements on Benthamism are an illusion rather than an option. It is, Gunn emphasizes, *hard* to be a Millian utilitarian: to opt for higher pleasures over lower ones, to maintain and balance the components of a flexible, nonfixated personality, to devote one's life to sympathy-driven altruism, to be an "experiment in living," and so on. Consequently, most of those who start out meaning to be Millian utilitarians will eventually give up, and lapse back into a life of lower pleasures. As the theory of cognitive dissonance reduction instructs us, people adopt views and systems of value that serve to justify the choices they've made. So most people who start out as Millian utilitarians will end up accepting Benthamite attitudes, and, eventually, reshaping the society in which they live along Benthamite lines. Now, it's not feasible to live as a Millian utilitarian in a determinedly Benthamite society. So Millian utilitarianism is a futile enterprise: a society that started out along Millian lines would end up a society of Benthamites, and the remaining Millian utilitarians would become persecuted outcasts. Once again, I do not think that Gunn's complaints have been addressed by contemporary utilitarians.

9. Mill discusses the intellectual's special case of this phenomenon:

> Who can compute what the world loses in the multitude of promising intellects combined with timid characters, who dare not follow out any bold, vigorous, independent train of thought, lest it should land them in something which would admit of being considered irreligious or immoral? ... No one can be a great thinker who does not recognize, that as a thinker it is his first duty to follow his intellect to whatever conclusions it may lead. (XVIII:242/OL 2:20)

> A person must have a very unusual taste for intellectual exercise in and for itself, who will put himself to the trouble of thought when it is to have no outward effect, or qualify himself for functions which he has no chance of being allowed to exercise. The only sufficient incitement to mental exertion, in any but a few minds in a generation, is the prospect of some practical use to be made of its results. (XIX:400/RG 3:2)

He makes related remarks elsewhere, for instance to the effect that

> the mind is called into far more vigorous action by being required to propose than by merely being called on to assent. (XXX:86)

Or again,

> a society which looks jealously and distrustfully on original people—which imposes its common level of opinion, feeling, and conduct, on all its individual members—may have the satisfaction of thinking itself very moral and respectable, but it must do without genius. (XXV:1131)

Finally for now, he approvingly quotes his law tutor, John Austin, to the effect that

> no man enters with heart and mind into any business committed to his care if nothing is left to his discretion. (XXIV:1065)

10. VII:218; as we saw in chapter 6, the *System of Logic* argues for the view that all inference, properly understood, is inductive. Thus "the opposition is not between the terms Deductive and Inductive, but between Deductive and Experimental" (VII:219).
11. Using his famous methods of agreement, difference, residues and concomitant variations (VII:388–406); these "four methods" are still taught today in informal logic classes.
12. VIII:900–906; elsewhere, endorsing a view he attributes to Thomas Carlyle, Mill tells us that "in the infinite complexities of human affairs, any general theorem which a wise man will form concerning them, must be regarded as a mere approximation to truth; an approximation obtained by striking an average of many cases, and consequently not exactly fitting any one case. No wise man, therefore, will stand upon his theorem only—neglecting to look into the specialties of the case in hand,

and see what features *that* may present which may take it out of any theorem, or bring it within the compass of more theorems than one" (XX:161). And Mill ascribed the success of his *Principles of Political Economy* in part to the way it "treated Political Economy not as a thing by itself, but as a fragment of a greater whole; a branch of Social Philosophy, so interlinked with all the other branches, that its conclusions, even in its own peculiar province, are only true conditionally, subject to interference and counteraction from causes not directly within its scope" (I:243/A 7:10).

13. VIII:890–893; compare VIII:946, on "the error ... of those who would deduce the line of conduct proper to particular cases, from supposed universal practical maxims." Again, in *Utilitarianism*, Mill replies to a complaint on the part of Herbert Spencer, Mill's correction being that "Bentham, certainly ... is least of all writers, chargeable with unwillingness to deduce the effect of actions on happiness from the laws of human nature and the universal conditions of human life. The common charge against him is of relying too exclusively upon such deductions, and declining altogether to be bound by the generalizations from specific experience which Mr Spencer thinks that utilitarians generally confine themselves to. My own opinion ... is, that in ethics, as in all other branches of scientific study, the consilience of the results of both these processes, each corroborating and verifying the other [that is, successful application of the Deductive Method], is requisite to give to any general proposition the kind and degree of evidence which constitutes scientific proof" (X:258n/U 5:35n).

14. X:93; or again: "He could, with close and accurate logic, hunt half-truths to their consequences and practical applications, on a scale both of greatness and minuteness not previously exemplified" (X:93).

The methodological correction may seem exotic, but it is of great political import. Mill launches his discussion of Coleridge with an explanation of the advantages of folding together the insights of opposing views; after rehearsing the motivating observations of the eighteenth-century political philosophers who prepared the ground for the French Revolution, he concludes: "One who attends to these things, and to these exclusively, will be apt to infer that savage life is preferable to civilized; that the work of civilization should as far as possible be undone; and from the premises of Rousseau, he will not improbably be led to the practical conclusions of Rousseau's disciple, Robespierre" (X:123). That is, the Terror was a result of a *methodological* mistake, that of attending to one set of considerations exclusively, when inferences in the social sciences go through, as we would now put it, only ceteris paribus. Or as Mill put it elsewhere, "general principles ... *are* dangerous things in the hands of men who use them ... without considering, when they run away with a principle, whether the reason of the principle accompanies them or not" (XXIV:1060).

15. The idea is brought to bear repeatedly: for instance, in considering what form the administration of India should take, Mill insists that whoever is running the government needs "advisers who will think for themselves; who by the collision of judgments will cause subjects to be examined in a variety of lights; who will correct his mistakes, complete what is imperfect in his information, and whose very errors will be useful by being of a different kind than his own" (XXX:211).

16. That process doesn't have to be indiscriminate: in his own case, while Mill went to great lengths to accommodate various of the insights of Coleridge, Carlyle, and others—to the extent, in fact, of being called a Romantic by one biographer (Capaldi,

2004)—he refused to give an inch to Kantian apriorists, or for that matter to the Church of England.

17. Perhaps not entirely unavailable; for a contemporary view of this sort, see Fehige, 2004.

18. Vogler, 2001, ch. 6.

19. XXIV:812, and even someone who is doctrinaire on a particular point can be helped out by the Deductive Method: "Anybody may have a fixed idea, on which he is inaccessible to reason, but it does not follow that he is never to add a second idea to it" (XXIV:931f).

As we saw, Mill's famous short works have often seemed to conflict with one another: in the example we've been treating, the Principle of Utility says that you have to do what will make most people most happy, but the Principle of Liberty says that you have to let someone do what he wants, no matter how unhappy others are made by it. John Ward (personal communication) has suggested a further way of resolving this standing puzzle in Mill scholarship: that in view of Mill's philosophy of science, we should see each of these short works as sketching a treatment on a par, formally, with the science of political economy. That is, each one handles a different aspect of a complicated domain, and each needs to be corrected and completed by the others. Whether or not this is correct as a reading of Mill, we can certainly imagine a reader of Mill taking this attitude toward the views he finds in Mill's writings.

20. Mill develops a related argument in the third chapter of *Utilitarianism*:

Society between equals can only exist on the understanding that the interests of all are to be regarded equally ... every one is obliged to live on these terms with somebody.... In this way people grow up unable to conceive as possible to them a state of total disregard of other people's interests.

So long as they are co-operating, their ends are identified with those of others; there is at least a temporary feeling that the interests of others are their own interests. [X:231/U 3:10]

21. Mill's argument for justice does not seem to be addressed directly to "moral unfreedom," but it's worth noting that justice does promote freedom of the will as Mill understood it. When we are considering justice, what is at stake is security in our expectations; it is plausible enough that if you are aware you might be assaulted, robbed, kidnapped, perhaps murdered, and so on, security will become a preoccupation, and one that is likely to trump any other combination of available concerns in your decision-making processes.

22. Carlisle, 1991, ch. 4, provides a Foucault-accented description of 'panopticism' in Mill's life.

23. I'm very grateful to Candace Vogler for conversation, and for many of the points in this section.

24. There are no doubt further desiderata, having to do with, among other things, stability and persistence of desire, and with the preferences of groups possessing discernible overall orientations, but we can leave those to other occasions. (For that second point, I'm grateful to Jessica Bucknell.)

25. Is that entirely fair? After all, in public political life, we opt for secret ballots; we don't implement Mill's schemes for plural voting; we permit money to be spent on political campaigns; the oddball design for parliamentary elections that he found in Thomas

Hare's *Treatise on the Election of Representatives* seems to me to be in practice an approximation to proportional representation, which is relatively unusual.

And Mill's requirements have to do not just with laws and administration, but social norms: for instance, organizing boycotts of public figures with unpopular opinions is a popular activity, but by the lights of *On Liberty*, it's not what anyone should be doing.

Because it's hard to see what a principled way of counting up the points of convergence and deviation would be, this is inevitably a judgment call. Nonetheless, it does seem to me that, on balance, the ways in which our institutions deviate from Mill's overall design are minor.

CHAPTER 10

1. Williams, 1973b, ch. 6, Čapek, 2008, Janáček, 1995; Williams's argument has somewhat more structure, and in case you'd like to drill down, here's the next layer of it. Reasons to live are 'categorical desires': desires that aren't contingent on your being alive, anyhow. (Recall that we introduced this concept back in chapter 1, note 11.) Now, if you live forever, either your activities will remain similar to what they are now, or they will vary. On the first branch of that fork, if you're seeing things correctly, then you'll respond to similarity in activities and states with boredom; Williams describes this as "a reaction almost perceptual in character to the poverty of one's relation to the environment." Extreme boredom will deprive you of your categorical desires, and so deprive you of your reasons to live. Thus, if your activities remain similar to what they are now, you'll eventually have no reason to live. On the second branch of that fork, there's a further fork: varied activities either affect you—that is, shape your character—or they don't. If your activities don't affect you, you must be, as Williams puts it, "detached and withdrawn." And in that case, you won't have many (or deep) categorical desires. So if your activities don't affect you, you will end up not having sufficient reason to live. On the other hand, if your activities *do* affect you, then the variation required to prevent eventual boredom will eventually change your character completely. In Williams's way of seeing things, one's character is made up largely of one's desires. And so, if your activities do affect you, the desires of your future self will be almost completely different from your present desires. It follows that none of that future person's reasons for living—his categorical desires—are reasons for you now. And what's more, your instrumental stake in near-future selves—that they will carry out your current plans and projects—is absent in this case: this far future self will no longer care about your plans and projects, and won't carry them out. So if your activities affect you, you have no reason to care if that future self lives or dies. Thus if your activities change, you have no reason to live forever, and summing up, we could have no reason for living eternally a human life.

   The argument is by no means airtight, but it exhibits very nicely what hinges on living by the instrumentalist idea built into Mill's official psychology, that your stake in both your activities and your own life has to be a matter of what it is that you at present want, like, and enjoy.

2. And he was regarded that way not just at home; from Germany, here is Lange, 1950, Book II, p. 235: "Since Hume England has produced no great philosopher, unless we concede this rank to the acute and energetic Mill."

3. For instance, and just as a reminder of how pervasive the consideration was, although Mill was generally careful not to advocate anything as controversial as actual divorce,

he wanted it to be feasible for couples to separate—that is, for them to undo their earlier decision to share a life (XXI:285/SW 2:1).

("Generally": under the heading of exceptions, you can find him saying, in a letter to the editor, that "I am one who thinks that not only divorce, but great changes in most matters are needed" (XXV:1181)—but the letter is signed only with the initial "C.")

4. And related matters, such as the distinction between believing and remembering, also fell between the cracks; we'll return to this point at 180ff; and recall also chapter 3, notes 10, 13, and 31.

5. What might this have looked like, if it had happened? One prominent twentieth-century philosopher was famous enough for this sort of ongoing reconstruction to have produced an entry in the *Philosophers' Lexicon*—under "Hilary Term"—gently ribbing him for it.

6. They are due, once again, to Bernard Williams (1973a, pp. 99f, 103f, 108–117); for a brief restatement of what is at stake in his argument, see Millgram, 2015, pp. 80f.

7. II–III: 199–214, 758–796, 975–987, 1006–1014. However, it's important not to conflate Mill's socialism with the retrospectively more familiar Marxist form of the doctrine; the theoretical machinery of dialectical materialism is of course missing (*Capital* did not appear in English until well after Mill's death), and Mill does not take himself to be promoting a revolution. Moreover, the versions of socialism that Mill found most attractive were local and voluntary organizations, rather than state-administered central planning: as the history of the kibbutz should remind us, the issues these raise for a Millian—Neeman, 2011, with its focus on character development in kibbutz youth, might serve as an entry point—are not the aspects of socialism and communism that the twentieth century found most pressing.

8. We do find a "principle of equality" mentioned in passing, along with a suggestion that it ought to allow for some individuals to be better off than others, "when [their] being so makes none of the others worse off than they otherwise would be" (III:980).

9. For evidence that Mill did perceive the tension, see II:209, III:978f (and especially the manuscript note on 978), or V:745f; Hayek, 1994, was an influential expression of the view that opting for equality means sacrificing liberty, and in his *Principles of Political Economy* (II:211) Mill anticipates one of the considerations that seemed decisive to the so-called Austrian economists, namely, that if the market does not match people to tasks, the assignment will require dictatorial powers. Mill *did* attempt to design political forms that would prevent the enfranchised working classes from simply ignoring the views of the better-off and better-educated (e.g., XIX:405, 446f/RG 3:12, 6:19–20, and ch. 7).

10. In a back and forth in the *Leader*, in 1850, Mill acknowledged the concern that "the organization of industry on the communistic principle" would make "the yoke of conformity … heavier instead of lighter; that people would be compelled to live as it pleased others … that their lives would be placed under rules, the same for all … and that there would be no escape, no independence of action left to any one, since all must be members of one or another community" (XXV:1179f).

11. One famous episode in this tradition, which is however largely unrecognized as an example of the preoccupation, is positioned as such by Fleischacker, 1999, pp. 153–160, 170.

12. There is a brief mention of the costs of foregoing competition—"To be protected against competition is to be protected in idleness, in mental dullness; to be saved the necessity of being as active and as intelligent as other people" (III:795)—as an objection to mainstream socialist platforms; and in various places Mill mentions the

positive effects on one's character of owning one's own farm, as opposed to being hired to work on someone else's, or being a "cottier" (e.g., XXIV:975f, 1004).

13. XXVIII:5–9; "almost everything else": the essays on religion (X:369–489) are about as half-hearted, perhaps for much the same reason: Taylor was sufficiently Victorian to feel religion to be a personally immediate issue, and to insist that it belonged on Mill's to-do list, whereas Mill's upbringing had left it too distant for him to care much about theological questions (I:41–45/A 2:2–4).

14. Hobsbawm, 1992, p. 74, calls this "retrospective nationalism."

15. XXI:288f, 293–295, 324–326, 329, 331–333/SW 2:4, 12, 4:4f, 10, 13f; we remarked (chapter 7, note 25) that the dimension along which characters were to be improved was by developing their freedom of will.

16. And political theorists do get called on such pronouncements. Compare the complaints, in Berkowitz, 1999, pp. 30f, that Judith Shklar's claims about the "salutary effect [of life in a liberal regime] on the characters of citizens" are backed up "with scarcely a shred of empirical evidence."

17. Not to be confused with the program of investigating animal behavior that wore that name during the twentieth century; cf. Tinbergen, 1976.

18. For the differing national characters of Frenchmen and Englishmen, see, e.g., I:59, 61/A 2:12, XXII:308f or XXIV:838f, 1051; for the contrasting characters of "an essentially *subjective* people like the Germans, and an essentially *objective* people like those of Northern and Central Italy," see X:105.

19. For some discussion, see Millgram, 2005a, pp. 71f.

20. Bain, 1861; Mill does say, in a letter to Bain, that "Ethology [is] a subject I have long wished to take up, … but have never yet felt myself sufficiently prepared" (XV:645; the letter is dated 1859).

Here is yet one more explanation for Mill's having never produced his projected sciences: that, for formal reasons, no science could have done everything Mill needed.

Sciences produce or consist of generalizations; a science of character would consist of or produce generalizations about types of character. These generalizations would be derived using associationist psychological theory, and they would in turn be applied to demonstrate the upshots for the utility or happiness of one or another policy or set of institutions. Ideally, they would show that liberty gives rise to characters of such and such types, and that, in a free society, people with those types of characters are going to be, as a former American vice president once put it, happy campers.

Mill's problem arises when we add in the thought that the type of character we are really after exhibits "originality" and "individual spontaneity" (XVIII:260f/OL 3:1–2). Now, the sense that Mill's word "originality" bears does not itself require novelty and surprisingness, but Mill took it that in fact originality, in his technical sense, often produces or amounts to originality in our more modern sense. But then, deeply original (and thus arbitrarily different) characters do not make up a type that could be the subject of scientific generalization. There is no such thing as the science of surprises, and consequently, the science of personality types will not turn out to include the science of surprising personalities. Consequently, neither ethology nor political ethology will provide the lemmas needed to construct one of the arguments that Mill was after, to the effect that a society containing surprising personalities will be happier than a society that does not, and that liberty is required to produce surprising personalities. (And for that reason, here I've focused on alternatives to that particular line of argumentation.)

1. However, keep in mind that poetic trains of thought aren't always about poetry: an artist I know prepares to design a space installation by visiting the location and looking for, as she puts it, clues; she is finding and following a train of thought, one that is sustained and largely visual.

2. And although not everyone is a philosopher, when what you follow is not the argument, your train of thought can still take you anywhere: the artist I mentioned in note 1 at one point found herself needing to read Walter Benjamin on the nineteenth-century French ancestor of the pedestrian mall.

   Woods, 1961, p. 66, puts Mill's wide-ranging interests down to "the lack of strictly drawn boundaries within [philosophy] and his own amateur status," and perhaps he is getting this much right: today professionalized philosophers face real institutional barriers to following out their trains of thought.

   But having noticed the problem, it is a good occasion to return to a puzzle I floated in chapter 1, note 37, as to why there's no survey of Mill's philosophical work that I feel comfortable recommending to a first-time reader. The obvious explanation has to do with what from our perspective looks like Mill's interdisciplinarity: as I suggested in section 9.6, the distinction between moral and political philosophy that we impose on his work is positively misleading, and over and above that, there are few philosophers today who would feel comfortable following Mill's train of thought across fields as disparate as philosophy of logic, moral philosophy, and philosophy of social science, not to mention empirical psychology, economics, French history—and the list goes on.

   And there is, it does seem to me, a further reason; after all, occasionally Mill's commentators *are* suitably interdisciplinary. As we now are aware, the keystone is missing. When you do move from one part of Mill's field of vision to another, very often you have to pass through a space that was either being held blank or occupied by a placeholder; those spots are waiting on the progress of ethology, which was supposed to hold it all together. Unsurprisingly, historians by and large respond by focusing on a particular subject matter in Mill's work that they find congenial, or instead treat Mill's many interests as comprising a mere list, rather than a unified intellectual enterprise.

3. Todhunter, 1876, vol. i, esp. ch. 15, and pp. 42f, 175, 227f; Whewell, 1853.

4. From time to time, philosophers try to say what this is like. Dewey, 1985, p. 186, for example, describes "intellectual thoroughness" as "*seeing a thing through*," and as "manifested in the firmness with which the full meaning of the purpose is developed [his emphasis]." When we are properly prepared, both intellectually and volitionally, we follow trains of thought in something like the way a tracking dog follows a scent trail, and as Vicki Hearne explains to us (1987, ch. 4 and esp. p. 96), training a tracking dog is in significant part a matter of getting it past the analogous distractions—in the case of her final exam, bacon grease and hormones in a bottle.

5. Murdoch, 1970, pp. 51ff, 64ff, 85ff.

6. I:126/A 4:20; and early on, we quoted Mill writing that

   When I had taken in any new idea, I could not rest till I had adjusted its relation to my old opinions, and ascertained exactly how far its effect ought to extend in modifying or superseding them. (I:163, 165/A 5:13)

   Recall also his remark that "as a thinker it is his first duty to follow his intellect to whatever conclusions it may lead" (XVIII:242/OL 2:20).

I am aware that the term "obligation" suggests enforcement, or an internal substitute for it, and my sense is that in Mill's case it did feel that way. But one might equally, as far as the argument requires, find following one's train of thought to be irresistably attractive. (I'm grateful to Mimi Himelman for pressing me on this point.)

7. Williams, 1981b, p. 18.

8. Williams, 1973b, esp. at pp. 173, 181, 204f; a more vivid picture of what tragedy so conceived amounts to can be found in Nussbaum, 1986, a follow-on treatment that explains Plato's solution to the problem posed by tragedy: systematically eliminating those conflicts, by reengineering human rationality, together with social and political life.

9. Auerbach, 2003.

10. Formally, the demand that one do so belongs among the imperfect duties, as Kant understood them: one inevitably exercises one's judgment in fulfilling these obligations, because they are open-ended, and you can live up to an open-ended requirement only by picking and choosing. For instance, if you take yourself to have a duty to dote on your child, you will find that there are always more ways to dote: you will have to settle on some, and let the others go. But someone can experience such an open-ended duty as something they cannot but do, as you will notice watching some doting parents—and the imperfect duties usually cited by Kantian moral philosophers (namely, helping others, and developing your skill set) can also press themselves on one in this way.

11. Williams, 1995, explores this way of spelling out the concept, and provides some but not all of the qualifications that seem to be needed.

12. Aeschylus, 1953, lines 217–221.

13. I have in mind the sort of thing that Anscombe, 1985, secs. 37f, called a "desirability characterization," but in a somewhat extended sense.

14. Mill's official but indirect investment in coherence was, we saw, unsurprising: if you are an instrumentalist, you investigate factual questions as a way of figuring out means to your ends, and the more pressing the apparent conflicts between your various subprojects, the more reason you have to look into surprising matters of fact that will allow you to negotiate those conflicts. Moreover, Mill shared the view philosophers standardly have, that if your views about matters of fact are inconsistent with one another, you must have made an error.

But remember from chapter 3 that Mill's response to the perceived coherence of the Benthamite vision underwrote what we were calling the superlative attribution to him of the life project; so the official story was not all there was to it. In another lap or two, we will be able to press a bit harder on the question of what drives coherence in life projects.

15. I want to put to one side two further shortcuts. In certain world views, your mortal life is a test of your fitness for a suitable afterlife, and in this manner God takes responsibility for the teleological integration—you yourself know not how—of your activities. There are of course religiously inflected forms that worries about the meaning of life can take: we still remember the complaint that generations come and generations go, and everything stays the same (*Eccles.* 1:5). Or again, the Joseph story, in *Genesis*, wrestles with the thought that, although your life is meaningful, in a world that is more or less God's chess board, you do not occupy a perspective that would allow you to know what its meaning is; for discussion, see Millgram, 2012, esp. pp. 201ff. Still, perhaps it is not a coincidence that such worries take the shape

we have been considering only once secular understandings of a person's place, or rather, lack of one, in the universe become current.

Next, apparent integration of the parts of a life is easy enough if you lower your standards for what counts as a tight enough connection. However, we are not interested in individuals who only *seem* to themselves to be leading lives that are meaningful, by the lights of the criterion we are investigating.

16. Briefly recapping that problem, as laid out in chapter 3, note 20: Any such explanation would be a stretch of practical reasoning, and any such reasoning would have to invoke pleasure and pain, construed as the only important practical considerations, as its starting point; so any such explanation would be viciously circular.

17. We have encountered what were no doubt some of their reasons in chapter 5; for a recap of the concerns about social propriety, see Himmelfarb, 1990, pp. 210–212.

18. E.g., ibid., pp. 187f, 190f.

19. Dickens, 1854/1981, pp. 15, 17, 186; Bentham, cited at Thomas, 1979, p. 17, seconded the view we are about to get, calling Harriet Mill "as good a creature as ever lived, but poor thing she has no mind in her body."

20. In this instance, what was important to the individual in question *was* closely connected with the other things that mattered in his life. Is it feasible to write out of your life something that matters to you, but is not connected in this way? Another first-person example: my cat mattered to me, but not because she helped out with my philosophizing, or because she accompanied me on hikes in the great outdoors, or gave a hand with the cooking; her place in my constellation of concerns violated the Wiggins-derived coherence condition. However, had I decided that she was not a part of my life, I would have been abandoning her: not just leaving her in the lurch, but overriding my own emotions and sense of commitment. That is to say that whether she was part of my life, in the sense that is now relevant, was not, after some point, up to me.

When views of the kind we have been engaging tell us to tie together all of the elements of a life, they take the scope or reach of a life for granted. We are not about to take on the philosophical problem of how it is to be demarcated just now, but it is important to realize that it needs to be on our collective agenda.

21. The two ensuing arguments are pulled out of XVIII:262f/OL 3:3–4.

22. Iris Murdoch's view was that in such cases what you saw and cared about would eventually outrun the expressive resources of a public language, and she accordingly took time out to attack Wittgenstein's private language argument, on which that would not be possible. For discussion, see Millgram, 2005a, ch. 5.

23. Might this be enough, after all? Richardson Lear, 2004, attributes to Aristotle the view that, when what you are after is unattainable, you can reasonably substitute a qualitatively very different approximation to it as your stop-gap ideal. However, the case she makes is historical: that Aristotle believed this, not that we should.

24. Recall that in Mill's own case, his appreciation for the coherence of his system of preferences, objectives and activities didn't function either as an additional goal or as an inference rule, but rather as the prompt to take full ownership of the Benthamite project he had inherited. And in retrospect we can now highlight a feature of that appreciation that is characteristic of aesthetic response, namely, that on reading Dumont, Mill had come to understand *for himself* how all the pieces of the Benthamite project fit together; that is, as Sibley, 1959, points out, aesthetic appreciation involves (what Mill called) originality.

While we are at it, let's register a tricky formal point (this one's for the practical reasoning aficionados). If we contrast inference to the most coherent plan or project with instrumental (means-end only) inference, it might seem straightforward to convert the former to the latter, by adding the goal of having more coherent projects or plans to an agent's list of goals. However, in an argument (famously involving a persimmon) in what has become somewhat of a philosophical classic, Thomas Nagel showed that these conversions shouldn't be assumed to go through smoothly (1978, sec. 6.5). The agent who is augmented with a goal that is supposed to substitute for a noninstrumental inference rule will take himself to have reasons to do different things than an agent who uses the inference rule natively.

In our own case, an agent whose interest in coherence is attributable to having coherence as a further *goal* will find himself trying to integrate his other goals with this one, whereas the coherentist reasoner proper will only be attempting to manage the integration of those other goals. The result can be expected to be substantively different courses of action, and the moral for the moment is this: when we are considering an independent interest in coherence as an ingredient in someone's mix of concerns, we have to decide whether what we have in mind is a goal, that is, something the agent wants, or responsiveness to what the agent takes to be a dictate of rationality, or—as in the aesthetic responsiveness we noticed in the young John Stuart Mill—neither of these.

25. Fisch and Benbaji, 2011, pp. 208–219, is an up-to-date attempt at a theory of problems. It is representative of current ways of thinking in treating problems as induced by goals: "We find the teleological dimension of problemhood inescapable, because we cannot think of anything we would be prepared to view as a problem other than in relation to the frustration or partial frustration of some desired objective" (p. 208). However, for the first of the alternatives I have just mentioned to that model, see Dewey, 2008; for the second and third, Millgram, 1997, chs. 5–6 and Millgram, 2005a, ch. 1.

In Fisch's and Benbaji's theory a further difficulty with such accounts comes to the fore. They hold that a theory of rationality ought to be responsible to the range of problems one faces (and I agree). But then one's conception of what a problem is should not, as theirs does, start out by taking for granted the correctness of a particular theory of rationality.

26. At various points, I've found it necessary to construct such arguments anyway; see Millgram, 1997, ch. 5, and Millgram, 2009a, sec. 4.5. And here is one further way you might convince yourself that you should be expecting surprises. We are boundedly rational agents, meaning that instead of solving problems the principled but very expensive way, we cut corners. That means using heuristics that work well on (weighted) average, but not stopping to check whether any particular case is one in which the heuristic will produce a correct answer; checking would mean losing the time-saving benefits of the heuristic. Thus, surprisingness is an expected effect of computational limitations in a highly complex system. By now we know that we're computationally limited, and that the world is highly complex.

Taking a different tack, we have the pieces of an argument that we are practically committed to the working assumption that surprising connections are in the offing. We know from experience that familiar, off-the-shelf inferences aren't enough to allow us to figure out how things stand, or what to do, on the basis of the truths, partial truths, and varied sorts of practical judgments that we have in play at any stage of our thinking. (See Millgram, 2005a, chs. 9–10.) We have to proceed on the assumption that we *will* be able to fold them together in ways that will allow us the sorts of conclusions we need. The connections it will take to do so are not just going to spring to mind. So we have to proceed on the assumption that following out trains of thought might take you surprising places—as we put it earlier, might take you just anywhere. That said, an argument that we have to treat something as a working assumption doesn't show that it is the case.

27. Interested readers can find a sketch of the problem in the appendix.

28. See chapter 3, notes 8, 10.

29. Recall that we took up this matter in section 3.6.

30. For pointers, see chapter 3, note 29.

31. One further, very suggestive piece of evidence: Vogler, 2001, ch. 5, documents that Mill worried a great deal about how the control of one's attention was possible. (You'll find the key passages at Mill, 1869, vol. ii, pp. 358f, 373n, 375–378.) She argues that his theory of mind could not make sense of it. We have seen repeatedly how Mill's theoretical concerns echoed his personal problems; if Mill was worried about the way he was reining in his own attention, it would not be surprising to find him attempting to produce such a theory.

32. Kant, 1785/1981, at Ak. 399.

33. The spirit of the objection is meant to be Anscombean; her followers have the view that instrumental rationality is a matter not of what goes on within your mind—how your desires and decisions fit together—but rather of how the actions you produce are structured. (For an overview, see Millgram, 2005b.) In this way of thinking, whether a lifelong pattern of activity is coherent in the Wiggins sense will be a matter of what actions explain what other actions; whether the associated desires clash with one another will be beside the point.

Bear in mind when considering this alternative that we were interested in the construction that Wiggins put on the notion of a meaningful life in part because it reflected the sensibilities of a camp in recent analytic moral philosophy. In that camp, the enterprise of articulating conceptions of the unified self has been understood as moral psychology, and unity, as a matter of how desires, maxims, intentions and so on fit and work together. (There are occasional exceptions: for instance, the argument of Korsgaard, 1996, ch. 13, makes the unity of agency out to be a matter of coordination of action; however, her later treatment of unified agency (2009) focuses once again on the internal deliberative procedures of the agent.) It would be hard to see a demand for coherence that bypassed motivations and the person's inner life to express the cluster of concerns that has driven this ongoing discussion.

CHAPTER 12

1. Wolf, 2010, pp. 58, 62.

2. For representative book-length manifestos, see Bechtel and Richardson, 1993, and Craver, 2007.

3. Arguments of this sort were advanced by the Austrian economists; see, e.g., von Mises, 1981, pp. 101, 103–105, 112f, 176, 181, 183, 186f, 407, 535 and esp. 477.

4. For a first round of those, see Millgram, 2002, secs. 1–2.

5. A further reservation, in passing: concepts, in the analytic tradition, are the correlates of properties possessed by objects (formally, they're functions that map individuals onto truth values). But not every component of our intellectual apparatus that we might want to analyze is a concept in this sense (see Millgram, 2015, chs. 5–6, 8,

for examples), and we should not assume that the cognitive function of calling a life meaningful is captured by treating the meaningfulness or lack of it as a property. (For discussion on this point, I'm grateful to Vladyslav Logvinov.)

6. I'm aware of the Chomskian point that early language learners do better than their quota of corrections will explain. However, as someone whose day job consists in part in correcting adults' failures to communicate successfully in their native language, in the interest of improving their performance, I stand by the illustration.

7. We are just starting to see empirical research by hedonic psychologists. See Sirgy, 2012, for a recent overview.

8. For a somewhat more complicated alternative hypothesis, on which views about the aprioricity of ethics do not amount to motivated self-deception, see Millgram, 2015, ch. 6.

   The Western and Greek record goes back somewhat over a couple of thousand years, but we should not overlook other traditions that are significantly older; for discussion of one of them, see Millgram, 2010.

9. Not that I'm about to recount the history of engineering here, but you can find an illustration or two at Millgram, 1997, p. 101n15.

10. Much earlier on, I laid out Mill's two-pronged attempt on a theory of free will, and it's finally time to disarm a response that specialists too frequently have to those reconstructions, namely, "*That's* not free will!"

    If you look back even over the twentieth-century history of that discussion, you will find that its stronger players have set their own agendas by giving new senses to (what is, if you think about it) the literally nonsensical phrase, "free will"—or, on occasion, tried making the case that doing so is a fool's errand (Albritton, 1985). When they did, they were creating new professional sandboxes, inside which different conversations could develop. So when someone insists, of an unfamiliar philosopher's different rendering, that *that's* not free will, what we are seeing is habituation to the confines of one such sandbox. What is needed instead is comparative assessment of the ways in which the inchoate notion is firmed up into one or another conception—along with, perhaps, further, novel alternative renditions.

Appendix

1. Here I'm helping myself to the very elegant reconstruction of the problem in Garrett, 1981.

2. Longuenesse, 1998, explains the way Hume's problems motivated Kant's Analytic.

Bibliography

Aeschylus, 1953. Agamemnon. In *Oresteia*, pages 33–90, University of Chicago Press, Chicago. Translated by Richmond Lattimore.

Albee, E., 1957. *A History of English Utilitarianism*. Macmillan, New York.

Albritton, R., 1985. Freedom of will and freedom of action. *Proceedings and Addresses of the American Philosophical Association, 59(2)*, 239–251.

Anderson, E., 1991. John Stuart Mill and experiments in living. *Ethics, 102*, 4–26.

Anderson, R. L., 2001. Synthesis, cognitive normativity, and the meaning of Kant's question, "How are synthetic cognitions a priori possible?" *European Journal of Philosophy, 9(3)*, 275–305.

Anderson, R. L., 2015. *The Poverty of Conceptual Truth*. Oxford University Press, Oxford.

Anderson, R. L. and Landy, J., 2001. Philosophy as self-fashioning: Alexander Nehamas's art of living. *Diacritics, 31(1)*, 25–54.

Anonymous, 1925. Bentham, Blackstone and the new law. *Times Literary Supplement, 24(1250)*, 901–902.

Anscombe, G. E. M., 1972. Contraception and chastity. *The Human World, 7*, 9–30.

Anscombe, G. E. M., 1985. *Intention*. Cornell University Press, Ithaca, N.Y., 2nd edition.

Auerbach, E., 2003. *Mimesis*. Princeton University Press, Princeton, N.J., 2nd edition. Translated by Willard R. Trask.

Austin, J. L., 1962. *Sense and Sensibilia*. Oxford University Press, Oxford. Edited by G. J. Warnock.

Bain, A., 1861. *On the Study of Character*. Parker, Son, and Bourn, London.

Bain, A., 1882. *John Stuart Mill: A Criticism with Personal Recollections*. Longman, Green, and Co., London.

Bain, A., 1966. *James Mill: A Biography*. Augustus Kelley, New York.

Bartlett, N., 1988. *Who Was That Man?* Serpent's Tail, London.

Bechtel, W. and Richardson, R., 1993. *Discovering Complexity*. Princeton University Press, Princeton, N.J.

Bentham, J., 1817/1983. *Chrestomathia*. Clarendon Press, Oxford. Edited by M. J. Smith and W. H. Burston.

Bentham, J., 1825. *A Treatise on Judicial Evidence*. J. W. Paget, London. Edited by Étienne Dumont.

Bentham, J., 1827. *Rationale of Judicial Evidence*. Hunt and Clarke, London. Edited by John Stuart Mill.

Bentham, J., 1830. *Traités de législation civile et pénale*. Rey et Gravier, Paris, 3rd edition. Edited by Étienne Dumont.

Bentham, J., 1838–1843. *Works*. William Tait, London. Edited by John Bowring.

Bentham, J., 1950. *The Theory of Legislation*. Routledge and Kegan Paul, London. Originally edited by Étienne Dumont from Bentham's manuscripts; translated into English by Richard Hildreth; edited by C. K. Ogden.

Bentham, J., 1984. *The Correspondence of Jeremy Bentham, vol. vi: January 1798 to December 1801*. Oxford University Press, Oxford. Edited by J. R. Dinwiddy.

Bentham, J., 1996. *An Introduction to the Principles of Morals and Legislation.* Oxford University Press, Oxford. Edited by J. H. Burns and H. L. A. Hart; Introduction by F. Rosen.

Bentham, J., 2002. *Bentham's Auto-Icon and Related Writings.* Thoemmes Press, Bristol. Edited by James Crimmins.

Bentham, J., 2006. *The Correspondence of Jeremy Bentham, vol. xii: July 1824 to June 1828.* Oxford University Press, Oxford. Edited by Luke O'Sullivan and Catherine Fuller.

Berkowitz, P., 1999. *Virtue and the Making of Modern Liberalism.* Princeton University Press, Princeton, N.J.

Blackburn, S., 1998. *Ruling Passions.* Oxford University Press, Oxford.

Bok, H., 1998. *Freedom and Responsibility.* Princeton University Press, Princeton, N.J.

Borchard, R., 1957. *John Stuart Mill: The Man.* C. A. Watts and Co., London.

Braithwaite, R. B., 1960. *Scientific Explanation.* Harper and Brothers, New York.

Bratman, M., 2007. *Structures of Agency.* Oxford University Press, Oxford.

Brooks, P., 1984. *Reading for the Plot.* Harvard University Press, Cambridge, Mass.

Brunner, J., 1968. *Stand on Zanzibar.* Ballantine, New York.

Calvert, K., 1992. *Children in the House.* Northeastern University Press, Boston.

Capaldi, N., 2004. *John Stuart Mill.* Cambridge University Press, Cambridge.

Čapek, K., 2008. The Makropulos case. In *Four Plays,* pages 165–259, Bloomsbury Methuen, London. Translated by Peter Majer and Cathy Porter.

Carlisle, J., 1991. *John Stuart Mill and the Writing of Character.* University of Georgia Press, Athens.

Carlyle, T. and Carlyle, J. W., 1977–1981. *Collected Letters.* Duke University Press, Durham, N.C.

Cartwright, N., 1989. *Nature's Capacities and their Measurement.* Oxford University Press, Oxford.

Connell, E., 1981. *Mr. Bridge.* North Point Press, San Francisco.

Connell, E., 2010. *Mrs. Bridge.* Counterpoint, Berkeley, Calif.

Cooter, R. and Rappoport, P., 1984. Were the ordinalists wrong about welfare economics? *Journal of Economic Literature, 22,* 507–530.

Cowan, R. S., 1983. *More Work for Mother.* Basic Books, New York.

Craver, C., 2007. *Explaining the Brain.* Oxford University Press, Oxford.

Dancy, J., 2004. *Ethics without Principles.* Oxford University Press, Oxford.

de Sousa, R., 1990. *The Rationality of Emotion.* MIT Press, Cambridge, Mass.

Dennett, D., 1984. *Elbow Room.* MIT Press, Cambridge, Mass.

Dewey, J., 1985. *Democracy and Education.* Southern Illinois University Press, Carbondale. Edited by Jo Ann Boydston, Patricia Baysinger, and Barbara Levine; Introduction by Sidney Hook.

Dewey, J., 2008. Theory of valuation. In Boydston, J. A. and Levine, B., editors, *John Dewey: The Later Works, 1925–1953, vol. 13,* pages 191–251, Southern Illinois University Press, Carbondale.

Dickens, C., 1854/1981. *Hard Times.* Bantam Books, New York. Introduction by Robert Spector.

Donner, W., 2011. Morality, virtue, and aesthetics in Mill's art of life. In Eggleston, B., Miller, D., and Weinstein, D., editors, *John Stuart Mill and the Art of Life,* pages 146–165, Oxford University Press, Oxford.

Dostoevsky, F., 2008. *Notes from the Underground* and *The Gambler.* Oxford University Press, Oxford. Translated by Jane Kentish, with an Introduction by Malcolm Jones.

Ellmann, R., 1988. *Oscar Wilde.* Vintage, New York.

Emerson, R. W., 1971–2013. *Collected Works of Ralph Waldo Emerson*. Harvard University Press, Cambridge, Mass.

Empson, W., 1828. *Rationale of Judicial Evidence, specially applied to English Practice, from the manuscripts of* JEREMY BENTHAM, Esq., Bencher of Lincoln's Inn. *Edinburgh Review, 48(96)*, 457–520.

Enoch, D., 2005. Why idealize? *Ethics, 115*, 759–787.

Fehige, C., 2004. *Soll ich?* Reclam, Stuttgart.

Feuerzeig, J. 2005. *The Devil and Daniel Johnston*. Sony Pictures.

Fisch, M., 1991. *William Whewell: Philosopher of Science*. Oxford University Press, Oxford.

Fisch, M. and Benbaji, Y., 2011. *The View from Within*. University of Notre Dame Press, Notre Dame, Ind.

Fleischacker, S., 1999. *A Third Concept of Liberty*. Princeton University Press, Princeton, N.J.

Florka, R., 2001. *Descartes's Metaphysical Reasoning*. Routledge, New York.

Foucault, M., 1984. What is an author? In Rabinow, P., editor, *The Foucault Reader*, pages 101–120, Pantheon Books, New York.

Frankfurt, H., 1988. *The Importance of What We Care About*. Cambridge University Press, Cambridge.

Frankfurt, H., 1999. *Necessity, Volition, and Love*. Cambridge University Press, Cambridge.

Garrett, D., 1981. Hume's self-doubts about personal identity. *Philosophical Review, 90(3)*, 337–358.

Gash, N., 1979. *Aristocracy and People: Britain 1815–1865*. Harvard University Press, Cambridge, Mass.

Gibbard, A., 1990. *Wise Choices, Apt Feelings: A Theory of Normative Judgment*. Harvard University Press, Cambridge, Mass.

Gibbard, A., 2003. *Thinking How to Live*. Harvard University Press, Cambridge, Mass.

Gilbert, D., 2005. *Stumbling on Happiness*. Random House, New York.

Guéhenno, J., 1967. *Jean-Jacques Rousseau*. Columbia University Press, New York. Translated by John and Doreen Weightman.

Gunn, J., 1961. *The Joy Makers*. Bantam, New York.

Halévy, E., 1972. *The Growth of Philosophic Radicalism*. Augustus M. Kelley, Clifton, N.J. Translated by Mary Morris, with a Preface by John Plamenatz.

Hare, R. M., 1961. *The Language of Morals*. Clarendon Press, Oxford.

Hare, R. M., 1972. "Nothing matters." In *Applications of Moral Philosophy*, pages 32–47, Macmillan, N.Y.

Hayek, F. A., 1951. *John Stuart Mill and Harriet Taylor: Their Friendship and Subsequent Marriage*. Augustus M. Kelley, New York.

Hayek, F. A., 1994. *The Road to Serfdom*. University of Chicago Press, Chicago.

Hearne, V., 1987. *Adam's Task: Calling Animals by Name*. Vintage/Random House, New York.

Hilton, B., 2006. *A Mad, Bad, and Dangerous People? England 1783–1846*. Oxford University Press, Oxford.

Himmelfarb, G., 1990. *On Liberty and Liberalism: The Case of John Stuart Mill*. Institute for Contemporary Studies Press, San Francisco.

Hobsbawm, E. J., 1992. *Nations and Nationalism since 1780*. Cambridge University Press, Cambridge, 2nd edition.

Hume, D., 1888/1978. *A Treatise of Human Nature*. Clarendon Press, Oxford, 2nd edition. Edited by L. A. Selby-Bigge and P. H. Nidditch.

Huxley, A., 1932/1998. *Brave New World*. HarperPerennial, New York.

Ishiguro, K., 1989. *The Remains of the Day*. Random House, New York.

Israel, J., 2001. *Radical Enlightenment*. Oxford University Press, Oxford.

James, W., 1956. The sentiment of rationality. In *The Will to Believe and Human Immortality*, pages 63–110, Dover, New York.

Janáček, L., 1995. *The Makropulos Case*. Kultur International Films, West Long Branch. Directed by Nikolaus Lehnhoff.

Kant, I., 1785/1981. *Grounding for the Metaphysics of Morals*. Hackett, Indianapolis, Ind. Translated by James Ellington.

Kinzer, B., 2007. *J. S. Mill Revisited*. Palgrave Macmillan, New York.

Korsgaard, C., 1996. *Creating the Kingdom of Ends*. Cambridge University Press, New York.

Korsgaard, C., 2008. *The Constitution of Agency*. Oxford University Press, Oxford.

Korsgaard, C., 2009. *Self-Constitution*. Oxford University Press, New York.

Kripke, S., 1980. *Naming and Necessity*. Harvard University Press, Cambridge, Mass.

Kubrick, S. 1971. *A Clockwork Orange*. Warner Studios. Adapted from the novel by Anthony Burgess.

Kubrick, S. 1980. *The Shining*. Warner Studios. Adapted from the novel by Stephen King.

Lange, F. A., 1950. *The History of Materialism*. Humanities Press, New York, 3rd edition. Originally published in 1865. Translated by Ernest Chester Thomas; introduction by Bertrand Russell.

LCD Soundsystem, 2007. *Sound of Silver*. Capitol Records, Hollywood.

Lewis, C. I., 1956. *Mind and the World Order*. Dover, New York.

Longuenesse, B., 1998. *Kant and the Capacity to Judge*. Princeton University Press, Princeton, N.J. Translated by Charles Wolfe.

Luce, R. D. and Raiffa, H., 1957. *Games and Decisions*. John Wiley and Sons, New York.

Lyons, D., 1965. *The Forms and Limits of Utilitarianism*. Clarendon Press, Oxford.

Mackie, J. L., 1983. *Ethics: Inventing Right and Wrong*. Penguin, New York.

Marmoy, C. F. A., 1958. The "auto-icon" of Jeremy Bentham at University College London. *Medical History*, 2, 77–86.

Mazlish, B., 1975. *James and John Stuart Mill: Father and Son in the Nineteenth Century*. Basic Books, New York.

McDowell, J., 1998. *Mind, Value, and Reality*. Harvard University Press, Cambridge, Mass.

McGinn, C., 1983. *The Subjective View*. Clarendon Press, Oxford.

Mill, H. T., 1998. *Complete Works*. Indiana University Press, Bloomington. Edited by Jo Ellen Jacobs and Paula Harms Payne.

Mill, J., 1858. *The History of British India*. Piper, Stephenson and Spence, London, 5th edition. Notes and Continuation by Horace Wilson.

Mill, J., 1869. *Analysis of the Phenomena of the Human Mind*. Longmans, London. Edited by John Stuart Mill; originally published in 1829.

Mill, J., 1992. Education. In Ball, T., editor, *Political Writings*, pages 137–194, Cambridge University Press, Cambridge.

Mill, J. S., 1967-1991. *Collected Works of John Stuart Mill*. University of Toronto Press/Routledge and Kegan Paul, Toronto/London.

Millgram, E., 1996. Williams' argument against external reasons. *Nous*, 30(2), 197–220.

Millgram, E., 1997. *Practical Induction*. Harvard University Press, Cambridge, Mass.

Millgram, E., 1999. Moral values and secondary qualities. *American Philosophical Quarterly*, 36(3), 253–255.

Millgram, E., 2002. How to make something of yourself. In Schmidtz, D., editor, *Robert Nozick*, pages 175–198, Cambridge University Press, Cambridge.

Millgram, E., 2005a. *Ethics Done Right: Practical Reasoning as a Foundation for Moral Theory*. Cambridge University Press, Cambridge.

Millgram, E., 2005b. Practical reason and the structure of actions. In Zalta, E. N., editor, *The Stanford Encyclopedia of Philosophy*, Metaphysics Research Lab, Stanford University.

Millgram, E., 2006. Candace Vogler, *Reasonably Vicious*. European Journal of Philosophy, *14(3)*, 430–434.

Millgram, E., 2007. Who was Nietzsche's genealogist? *Philosophy and Phenomenological Research*, *75(1)*, 92–110.

Millgram, E., 2008. Specificationism. In Adler, J. and Rips, L., editors, *Reasoning: Studies of Human Inference and its Foundations*, pages 731–747, Cambridge University Press, Cambridge.

Millgram, E., 2009a. *Hard Truths*. Wiley-Blackwell, Oxford.

Millgram, E., 2009b. John Stuart Mill, determinism, and the problem of induction. *Australasian Journal of Philosophy*, *87(2)*, 181–197.

Millgram, E., 2010. Review of Oscar Wilde, *The Picture of Dorian Gray*. Utilitas, *22(1)*, 93–96.

Millgram, E., 2014. Mill's and Whewell's competing visions of logic. In Loizides, A., editor, *John Stuart Mill's* System of Logic: *Critical Appraisals*, pages 101–121, Routledge, London.

Millgram, E., 2015. *The Great Endarkenment*. Oxford University Press, Oxford.

Millgram, H., 2010. *The Invention of Monotheist Ethics*. University Press of America, Lanham, Md.

Millgram, H., 2012. *The Joseph Paradox*. McFarland, Jefferson, N.C.

Murdoch, I., 1970. *The Sovereignty of Good*. Routledge Kegan Paul, London.

Nagel, T., 1978. *The Possibility of Altruism*. Princeton University Press, Princeton, N.J.

Nagel, T., 1979. The absurd. In *Mortal Questions*, pages 11–23, Cambridge University Press, Cambridge.

Nagel, T., 1986. *The View from Nowhere*. Oxford University Press, Oxford.

Neeman, Y., 2011. *Hayinu he-Atid*. Achuzat Bait, Tel Aviv.

Nehamas, A., 1985. *Nietzsche: Life as Literature*. Harvard University Press, Cambridge, Mass.

Nehamas, A., 1998. *The Art of Living*. University of California Press, Berkeley.

Nietzsche, F., 1886/1966. *Beyond Good and Evil*. Vintage Books, New York. Translated by Walter Kaufmann.

Nozick, R., 1981. *Philosophical Explanations*. Harvard University Press, Cambridge, Mass.

Nussbaum, M., 1986. *The Fragility of Goodness*. Cambridge University Press, Cambridge.

Nussbaum, M., 1990. Narrative emotions: Beckett's genealogy of love. In *Love's Knowledge*, pages 286–313, Oxford University Press, Oxford.

Packe, M., 1954. *The Life of John Stuart Mill*. Macmillan, New York.

Paolini, M. and Vacis, G., 2000. *The Story of Vajont*. Bordighera Press, Boca Raton, Fl. Edited and translated by Thomas Simpson.

Pappe, H. O., 1960. *John Stuart Mill and the Harriet Taylor Myth*. Melbourne University Press, Melbourne. Australian National University Social Science Monograph, no. 19.

Paul, L., 1998. The worm at the root of the passions: Poetry and sympathy in Mill's utilitarianism. *Utilitas*, *10(1)*, 83–104.

Peirce, C. S., 1992. Grounds of validity of the laws of logic. In Houser, N. and Kloesel, C., editors, *The Essential Peirce*, vol. I, pages 56–82, Indiana University Press, Bloomington.

Prescott, W., 2000. *History of the Conquest of Mexico and History of the Conquest of Peru*. Cooper Square Press, New York.

Putnam, H., 1981. *Reason, Truth and History*. Cambridge University Press, Cambridge.

Ravetz, J., 1979. *Scientific Knowledge and Its Social Problems*. Oxford University Press, New York.

Reeves, R., 2007. *John Stuart Mill: Victorian Firebrand*. Atlantic Books, London.

Reiner, R. 1985. *The Sure Thing*. Embassy Films.

Richardson Lear, G., 2004. *Happy Lives and the Highest Good*. Princeton University Press, Princeton, N.J.

Robson, J., 1989. Introduction. In *Autobiography of John Stuart Mill*, pages 1–23, Penguin, New York.

Rosati, C., 2013. The Makropulos case revisited. In Bradley, B., Feldman, F., and Johansson, J., editors, *Oxford Handbook of Philosophy of Death*, pages 355–390, Oxford University Press, Oxford.

Ruskin, J., 1906. *Modern Painters*. George Allen, London.

Sayre-McCord, G., 1996. Hume and the Bauhaus theory of ethics. *Midwest Studies in Philosophy, 20*, 280–298.

Scarre, G., 1989. *Logic and Reality in the Philosophy of John Stuart Mill*. Kluwer, Dordrecht.

Scarre, G., 2002. Was Mill really concerned with Hume's problem of induction? In Sánchez-Valencia, V., editor, *The General Philosophy of John Stuart Mill*, pages 31–48, Ashgate, Aldershot.

Semmel, B., 1969. *Democracy versus Empire: The Jamaica Riots of 1865 and the Governor Eyre Controversy*. Doubleday Anchor, Garden City, N.Y.

Shklar, J., 1969. *Men and Citizens*. Cambridge University Press, Cambridge.

Sibley, F., 1959. Aesthetic concepts. *Philosophical Review, 68(4)*, 421–450.

Singer, P., 2002. *Animal Liberation*. HarperCollins, New York, 3rd edition.

Sirgy, M. J., 2012. *The Psychology of Quality of Life*. Springer, Dordrecht, 2nd edition. Social Indicators Research Series 50.

Skorupski, J., 2006. *Why Read Mill Today?* Routledge, New York.

Stevenson, R. L., 1992. Ordered south. In *Essays and Poems*, pages 3–12, Charles E. Tuttle, Rutland.

Stokes, E., 1982. *The English Utilitarians and India*. Oxford University Press, Delhi.

Taylor, R., 1981. The meaning of life. In Klemke, E. D., editor, *The Meaning of Life*, pages 141–150, Oxford University Press, New York.

Thagard, P., 1989. Explanatory coherence. *Behavioral and Brain Sciences, 12*, 435–467.

Thagard, P., 2001. How to make decisions. In Millgram, E., editor, *Varieties of Practical Reasoning*, pages 355–371, MIT Press, Cambridge, Mass.

Thalberg, I., 1978. Hierarchical analyses of unfree action. *Canadian Journal of Philosophy, 8(2)*, 211–226.

Thomas, W., 1979. *The Philosophic Radicals: Nine Studies in Theory and Practice, 1817–1841*. Oxford University Press, Oxford.

Thompson, E. P., 1988. *The Making of the English Working Class*. Penguin, London.

Tinbergen, N., 1976. *The Study of Instinct*. Oxford University Press, Oxford.

Todhunter, I., 1876. *William Whewell, Master of Trinity College, Cambridge*. Cambridge University Press, Cambridge.

Velleman, J. D., 2009. *How We Get Along*. Cambridge University Press, Cambridge.

Velleman, J. D., 2015. *The Possibility of Practical Reason*. Maize Books, Ann Arbor, Mich., 2nd edition.

Verdi, J., 2010. *Fat Wednesday*. Paul Dry, Philadephia.

Vogler, C., 2001. *John Stuart Mill's Deliberative Landscape*. Garland Publishing, New York.

Vogler, C., 2002. *Reasonably Vicious*. Harvard University Press, Cambridge, Mass.

von Humboldt, W., 1996. *The Sphere and Duties of Government*. Thoemmes Press, Bristol. Translated by Joseph Coulthard.

von Mises, L., 1981. *Socialism*. Liberty Fund, Indianapolis, Ind. Translated by J. Kahane.

Watson, G., 2002. Volitional necessities. In Buss, S. and Overton, L., editors, *Contours of Agency*, pages 129–159, MIT Press, Cambridge, Mass.

Weinberg, J., Nichols, S., and Stich, S., 2001. Normativity and epistemic intuitions. *Philosophical Topics, 29(1 and 2)*, 429–460.

Weisstein, E. W., 1999. Lexicographic order. In *MathWorld*, Wolfram Web Resources. http://mathworld.wolfram.com/LexicographicOrder.html.

Wheatley, G. 1855? Letters written to my sister during a visit to Jeremy Bentham, in the beginning of the year 1830. Privately printed, by P. H. Youngman, Maldon, U.K.

Whewell, W., 1847. *The Philosophy of the Inductive Sciences*. John W. Parker, London, 2nd edition.

Whewell, W., 1853. *Of The Plurality of Worlds*. John W. Parker and Son, London.

Whewell, W., 1854. *The Elements of Morality, Including Polity*. John W. Parker, London, 3rd edition.

Whewell, W., 1862. *Lectures on the History of Moral Philosophy*. Deighton, Bell, and Co., Cambridge, 2nd edition.

Wiggins, D., 1991. *Needs, Values, Truth*. Blackwell, Oxford, 2nd edition.

Wilde, O., 2005. *The Picture of Dorian Gray: The 1890 and 1891 Texts*. Oxford University Press, Oxford. Edited by Joseph Bristow.

Williams, B., 1973a. A critique of utilitarianism. In Smart, J. J. C. and Williams, B., *Utilitarianism: For and Against*, pages 77–150, Cambridge University Press, Cambridge.

Williams, B., 1973b. *Problems of the Self*. Cambridge University Press, Cambridge.

Williams, B., 1981a. Moral luck. In *Moral Luck*, Cambridge University Press, Cambridge.

Williams, B., 1981b. Persons, character and morality. In *Moral Luck*, pages 1–19, Cambridge University Press, Cambridge.

Williams, B., 1995. Moral incapacity. In *Making Sense of Humanity*, pages 46–55, Cambridge University Press, Cambridge.

Williams, B., 2001. Internal and external reasons (with postscript). In Millgram, E., editor, *Varieties of Practical Reasoning*, MIT Press, Cambridge, Mass.

Wittgenstein, L., 1998. *Philosophical Investigations*. Blackwell, Oxford, 3rd edition. Translated by G. E. M. Anscombe.

Wolf, S. 1997. Meaningful lives in a meaningless world. *Quaestiones Infinitae XIX*. Public lecture given on her appointment as Belle van Zuylen Professor; published by Utrecht University.

Wolf, S., 2010. *Meaning in Life and Why It Matters*. Princeton University Press, Princeton, N.J. Includes commentary by John Koethe, Robert Adams, Nomy Arpaly, and Jonathan Haidt.

Woods, T., 1961. *Poetry and Philosophy: A Study in the Thought of John Stuart Mill*. Hutchinson, London.

Wordsworth, W., 1958. *Poetical Works*. Clarendon Press, Oxford. Edited by E. de Selincourt and Helen Darbishire.

Zastoupil, L., 1994. *John Stuart Mill and India*. Stanford University Press, Stanford, Calif.

Index

aesthetics, 15, 60
  considerations from, unavailable in
    project lives, 46–49, 73, 139, 148
  driven response, 37, 46–49, 60, 98, 169,
    222n7, 231–232n24, 230n14
  focused life, 6
  particularism characteristic of, 6
  of philosophical style, 61, 89
  of Utilitarian theory, 55–56, 60, 89, 98,
    105, 130, 135, 148
Agamemnon, 151–154
agency, 107
  boundedly rational, 232n26
  unified, 5, 151, 153, 157, 170–171,
    178–179
Allen, Woody, 136
analysis
  conceptual, 27, 173, 175, 178
  habit of, 64–67, 114, 205n7
analytic mind, 121, 132–133
analytic philosophy, 5, 17
  author's affiliation with, 13, 142
  content vs. presentation in, 61
  limitations of intellectual apparatus of,
    142, 167–168
  meaning of life as topic in, 1–2
  methods of, 27, 173, 175, 217–218n11
  position of aesthetics in, 37–38
  training in argumentation by, 22, 52
Anscombe, G. E. M., 187n4, 230n13, 233n33
aprioricity, 25–27, 42–43, 84, 86, 195n24,
    225n16
  of ethics, 176
argument, 147–148, 167
  ad hominem, 175
  by biography, 64, 175, 177–178,
    184n14
  circular, 82–83, 188n10, 194–
    195nn20–21, 231n16
  defeasible, 82, 155, 177
  Mill's competence with, 52, 75
  motivational elements in, 129

nonstandard function of, 110–111
  transcendental, 182
Aristotle, 64, 77, 176, 208n2, 231n23
association
  laws of, 46, 86, 97, 109, 121, 216n8
  natural vs. artificial, 64–65, 204n4
  strength of, 38–39
associationism, 9, 15, 38–42, 46, 60, 64,
    88–90, 112, 127, 144, 166, 180, 190n26
  action explained by, 39
  augmented by purposes, 95–96
  and instrumentalism, 205n5
attention, 233n31
Auerbach, Erich, 152
Austin, John, 102, 223n9
authority figures, 15, 63, 69–74, 77–78, 89,
    132, 139, 155

Bain, Alexander, 29, 31, 54, 138, 145,
    193n13, 208n1
behaviorism, 9, 40, 114
belief, 192n8, 194n17
  distinguished from memory and
    imagination, 169, 192–193n8, 227n4
  ephemeral when not contested, 108–111
  half-true, 108, 126–128, 130, 148,
    232–233n26
Benjamin, Walter, 229n2
Bentham, Jeremy, 9–10, 14, 20–23, 34, 37,
    42, 44, 52, 62, 66, 77, 143, 156, 231n19
  author of Rationale of Judicial Evidence, 9,
    53–56, 102, 145
  auto-icon, 20–21
  integrity of, 58
  Mill's assessment of, 57–58, 128, 145
  policy recommendations of, 20, 59–60, 86
Bentham, Samuel, 34
Berkeley, George, 40
Berrigan, Ted, 174
birth control, 24
boredom, 110–111, 136
botany, 170, 186n32

Braithwaite, Richard, 85
British Empiricism, 38, 40, 160, 169,
    180–181
bundle theory, 181–182

Cairnes, John, 31
Čapek, Karel, 136
Carlyle, Jane, 207n20
Carlyle, Thomas, 10, 67, 158, 197n1,
    207n20, 223n12, 224n16
character, 31, 57, 136, 141, 160, 202n29,
    226n1
  balanced, 103–104
  confirmed, 89, 96–98, 100
  formed by circumstances, 88–89, 97, 100,
    130, 227n7
  national, 143–144
  role in Mill's arguments, 143, 145
  science of (*see* ethology)
  unobservable, 89
  variety in types of, 119
childhood, 33–34, 50–51, 62, 203–204n2
coherence, 16, 31, 41–44, 73, 137, 154,
    230n14
  aesthetic, 6
  based inference, 31, 43, 232n24
  lack within life, 153, 174
  motivation for, 157
  unavailable consideration in project lives,
    14, 43–44, 48–49
  of values, 4–5, 149–150
Coleridge, Samuel Taylor, 189n18, 224n14,
    224n16
composition of causes, 126, 129
Comte, Auguste, 10, 31, 86, 149, 207n16,
    208n25
  Mill's debt to, 90, 210–211n17
conformism, 5, 30, 123, 133–134, 146,
    160–161, 163–164, 227n10
Connell, Evan, 5
constant conjunction, 180
contiguity, 180
Corn Laws, 28, 140, 150
Cortés, Hernando, 116
cost-benefit analysis, 19–20, 22, 24, 139–140
Crumb, Robert, 205n4

decided preference criterion, 42–43, 93, 101,
    111–112, 115, 196n33
Dennett, Daniel, 96–97

Descartes, René, 210n15
desire, 36, 41, 64, 95, 98, 183n11, 194n17
  arbitrary, 66, 69, 73, 93
  categorical, 184n11, 226n1
  definition of, 39, 96, 99
  evanescent, 109
  hardwired, 64–65, 204n4
  informed, 93
determinism. *See* Philosophical Necessity
Dewey, John, 229n4
Dickens, Charles, 50–51, 61, 158–159,
    187n5
division of labor, 161, 216n2
divorce, 226–227n3
Dostoyevsky, Fyodor, 211n19
Dumont, Étienne, 34, 37, 44, 53, 55–56,
    58–59, 78, 199n11
Durham, Lord. *See* Lambton, John
duty
  imperfect, 230n10
  military, 154

East India Company, 11, 29, 31, 100, 170
economics, 28, 70, 127–128, 144
Edinburgh Review, 51
education
  policy, 8, 10, 20, 66
  public, 24, 30, 198n6
  rote memorization, 51
Emerson, Ralph Waldo, 191n31
empirical law, 112, 127
end, 3, 7, 101–102, 109, 185n22, 232n25
  See also desire
equality, 140–141
  gender, 104, 134, 137, 214n25
ethology, 127–128, 137, 139, 144–145, 169
examples
  American Dream, 159–160, 162
  automobile advertisements, 39
  cat, 231n20
  dam, 19
  desert colors, 122–123, 132
  ditch digging, 4
  drawing ducks, 39–40
  driving, 109
  first philosophy class, 125
  five dollars, 113–114
  maritime career, 122
  medical career, 3

movie with simultaneous screenings, 180–181
parking meters, 102
Persian rug, 87
soccer-playing daughter, 165–166
soda machine, 39
speaking German, 176
straw hat, 65, 97, 132
sun rising, 81–82
temple, 3
experimental philosophy, 27, 111, 194n14

femininity, 103, 206n7
feminism, 8, 30, 134, 143, 159, 197n1, 216n2
Flaubert, Gustave, 152
Ford, Richard, 152
Foucault, Michel, 25, 184n16, 225n22
franchise, 20
Frankfurt, Harry, 97, 217n10
freedom
    of action. see liberty
    moral, 91–104, 121, 125, 129–130, 134–135, 161
    definition of, 92
    of religion, 8
    of speech and press, 8, 12, 108–111, 117, 125–126, 130, 134
    of the will, 15, 68, 80–104, 131, 137, 143, 168, 170, 178, 192n4, 234n10
French Decadence, 190n26
French Revolution, 224n14
Freud, Sigmund, 194n13
futility, 124

genius, 16, 29, 49, 78, 106, 119, 135, 139, 141–143, 163, 170, 184n14, 228n20, 231n24
    definition of, 120
    as higher pleasure, 120–124
    liberty required for, 29, 119–120, 124, 132–133
    required in project lives, 156
goal. See end
Goldwater, Barry, 97
Green, Thomas, 193n13
Gunn, James, 107, 222n8

habit, 95–96, 98, 128, 148, 212n11, 214n25
    See also analysis, habit of
Hamilton, William, 27, 211n19

happiness, 176
    differs from meaningfulness, 13, 29, 34
    as end, 67, 101
    identified with pleasure, 66, 146
    shaped by conditioning, 65
Hardy, Harriet. See Taylor, Harriet
Hare, Thomas, 225–226n25
harm principle, 124–125
Hartley, David, 51, 193n11, 193n13
Hearne, Vicki, 229n4
hedonic drift, 97–98, 100, 103, 137–138, 140, 142, 163
hedonic profile, 97–98, 100, 102
Himmelfarb, Gertrude, 208n22
Humboldt, Wilhelm von, 199n12
Hume, David, 22, 40, 77, 180–181, 198n4, 209n4, 211n17, 217n9, 226n2
Huxley, Aldous, 107, 188n10, 190n26

ideas
    blended, 196n28, 205n4, 205n7
    of infinity, 45–46
    marketplace of, 108
    theory of, 38, 129, 180, 193–194n13
    unconscious, 109, 194n13
imagination, 51, 57, 100, 175
incommensurability, 22–24
India, 30–31, 100, 214n21, 224n15
individuality, 30, 119, 129, 132
induction, problem of, 81–82, 84–85, 87, 90
instrumentalism, 3, 6–7, 33, 43, 46–47, 60, 64, 93, 150, 195n25, 230n14, 232n25, 233n33
intentional fallacy, 175
internalism, 4
intuition, 27, 31, 42–43, 111, 131, 173–175
Ireland, 10–11
Ishiguro, Kazuo, 12

Jamaica Affair, 11
James, William, 218n14
Janáček, Leoš, 136
Jordan's Theorem, 26
Joseph, 230n15
justice, 102, 108, 225n21
    as higher pleasure, 116–117

Kalanick, Travis, 205n4
Kant, Immanuel, 37, 77, 138, 171, 182, 195n24, 209n4, 230n10

Kant, Immanuel (*Cont.*)
  British reception of, 25–27, 193n13
  objection to hedonism of, 189n16
Kinks, 133
Kubrick, Stanley, 57, 190n26

Lambton, John (Earl of Durham), 11
Law of Universal Causation, 82
  inductive argument for, 84–85
legal reform, 20, 56, 102–103, 137, 202n29
Lewis, C. I., 221n25
Lewis, David, 90
lexicographic ranking, 93–95, 98, 116, 166,
    169
  psychological explanation of, 112–115
liberalism, 130, 134
  neutrality of modern, 103
liberty, 16, 97, 102, 104–131
  as higher pleasure, 111
  Principle of, 16, 106–107, 110, 125, 144,
    168, 215n25, 225n19
  and socialism, 141
life
  artwork, 4, 6
  conventional (*see* conformism)
  happy, 13, 34
  inclusion criteria for, 157
  templates for, 159–164
  project
    career as paradigm of, 2–3
    definition of, 7
    experienced as obligation, 151
    as meaning of a life, 2
    obscures reasons for, 49
    ownership of, 33–36
    spanning life stages, 9, 62
    workings of, 174, 177–178
literature, 117
Locke, John, 40, 51, 117
logic
  deductive, 81–85, 90, 149, 168
  as empirical science, 27, 31, 86
  positive, 87–88
logical positivism, 1
Luther, Martin, 97

Mach, Ernst, 210n14
Makropulos Case, 136
Malthus, Thomas, 24, 150
Martin, Judith, 163

McDowell, John, 97
meaning of life
  and meaningfulness, 2
  sense of, 1, 178–179, 186n36
means-end reason. *See* reason, instrumental
mechanism, 174, 177–178
memory, 181
  See also belief
Mental Crisis, 15–16, 29, 38, 54, 63–80, 91,
    103, 120, 130, 135, 137–139, 142, 148,
    152, 162–163, 171
  diagnoses of, 54–55, 61–69, 79, 97–100,
    104
mercantilism, 218–219n15
metaethics, 2
Method
  Deductive, 127–129
  Geometrical, 127–128
  Physical, 126–127
Mill, Harriet, 158
Mill, James, 9–10, 15, 23, 28, 30–31, 34,
    39–40, 53, 63, 73, 77, 158
  depicted by Dickens, 50–51
  editor of Bentham, 59
  educational practice of, 28, 40, 50–52, 72,
    89, 100, 106, 114, 198n2
  historian of India, 9, 51, 70, 89, 100,
    192n34
  Mill's assessment of, 70
  psychologist, 9–10, 40, 113, 180
Mill, John Stuart
  activism of, 8, 10–11
  commitment to Utilitarianism, 15, 35,
    137
  early education of, 9, 28, 40, 51–52, 89,
    100, 106, 114–115
  epiphanies of, 15, 35, 40–42, 53, 58, 115,
    201n22, 217n11
  hired by father, 31
  perversity in life of, 14, 29–32, 136,
    145–146, 153
  relations with family, 9
  research assistant, 51–52
  suicidal ideation of, 171
misers, 112–114
modus ponens, 209–210n8
money, 112–114, 161, 187–188n6
monitorial system, 10
Mormonism, 214n25
Murdoch, Iris, 149, 231n22

Nagel, Thomas, 232n24
narrative, 6
necessity, 27, 82, 190n22
  in argumentation, 38
  associations of, 88
  logical, 84, 87
  practical, 97, 151–152
Nehamas, Alexander, 6
Newton, Isaac, 46, 127
Nietzsche, Friedrich, 6, 184n13, 189n18
Nightingale, Florence, 80
noncognitivism, 2
novelty, 111, 120, 129, 132, 168, 228n20

obligation, 150, 152–154
occasionalism, 210n15
originality. See genius

pain. See pleasure
pain, higher, 114
Paradox of Hedonism, 67, 104
Paraparadox of Hedonism, 104
Parliament, 100
  Mill elected to, 12, 20, 138
  Mill in, 11
Paul, L. A., 213n14
Peirce, Charles Sanders, 44, 85, 182, 209n7
penal code, 35
personal identity, 27, 169, 180–181
phenomenalism, 169, 180–181, 221n25
phenomenological law. See empirical law
Philosophical Necessity, 68, 80–90, 95, 131, 134
Philosophic Radicals, 10, 12, 14, 22, 30, 86, 132, 150, 185n23
philosophy
  historiography of, 77–78, 107
  systematic, 90
Plato, 57, 77, 114, 152, 230n8
pleasure, 22–23, 43, 156
  belief-dependent, 110
  dissolved by analysis, 64–66, 68, 114
  higher, 45–46, 92–96, 144, 166, 188n10
    corrective function of, 94, 121, 123, 213n20
    definition of, 111–112, 115
    descriptive use of, 94
    difficulty of pursuing, 222n8
    as generic means, 112–117, 169, 214n25

plurality of, 96, 102
highest, 94–96, 98, 100–103
physical and organic, 64–66
role in implementation of desires, 23
traversing associations, 39–40, 65, 97
poetic mind, 121, 132–133, 148, 206n10
poetry, 68, 190n27
  semantic density of, 206n7
  tracks emotional associations, 99–100, 121–122, 148
Positivism. See Comte, Auguste
preference satisfaction, 23
Prescott, William, 116
problem, 148, 167
project
  ground, 184n11
  instrumentally structured, 3, 42, 164
  as open-ended, 3, 37, 42, 155, 197n36
  tightness of, 7, 164–166, 169
propositional attitude, 142
psychology, hedonic, 189n12
purpose, 98
  definition of, 95
Putnam, Hilary, 227n5

rationality. See reason
reason
  aesthetic, 6, 38, 60
  instrumental, 3, 7, 121, 155, 226n1, 232n24
    constitutive vs. causal, 194n19
  practical, 3, 5, 43–44, 232n24
  theoretical vs. practical, 3
reflective equilibrium, 27, 174
  objections to method of, 111, 178
regret, 153
religion, 9, 110, 164
  established, 108
  in Mill household, 100, 228n13
Ricardo, David, 51
rights, human, 217n11
Roebuck, John, 190n27
Rousseau, Jean-Jacques, 187n38, 224n14
Ruskin, John, 169, 196n29

science, 46
  Chemical, 196n28, 205n4, 206n7
  Deductive, 28, 126, 128–129
  social, 28, 127–128, 138, 143–145, 224n12
    methodology of, 28, 128

science *(Cont.)*
  three stages of, 86–87, 90
Scott, Sir Walter, 206n7
sensation, 22, 24, 38, 160, 188n10
Shelley, Percy Bysshe, 70
Shklar, Judith, 35, 228n16
Singer, Peter, 188n11
Skinner, B. F., 9, 40
Smith, Adam, 22, 198n4, 227n11
socialism, 139–142, 174–175
Socrates, 209n6
Spencer, Herbert, 211n17, 224n13
Stauffenberg, Claus von, 174
Stevenson, Robert Louis, 217n10
suffrage, 8, 11, 20, 104, 134, 198n1
superlative attribution, 36–37, 44–45, 49,
    123, 230n14
syllogism, 82–85, 149
  major premise of, 84
sympathy, 129–130, 213n14

Taylor, Harriet, 11–12, 15, 30–31, 63, 73, 89,
    138, 228n13
  collaboration with Mill, 12, 74–78, 119,
    132–133
  interest in socialism, 140
  marriage to Mill, 11, 158
  Mill's assessment of, 70–71
  tomb of, 70–71
Taylor, Helen, 15, 63, 77
  Mill's assessment of, 71–72
  secretarial assistance of, 72
Taylor, John, 75
Taylor, Richard, 2–3
tendency, 127, 187n2, 219n16
Thackeray, William Makepeace, 117
Thagard, Paul, 185n25
Tocqueville, Alexis de, 10, 207n16,
    208n25
tragedy, 6, 152–157, 169–171, 179
trains of thought, 147–151, 167–170

utilitarianism (moral theory), 8, 131, 140,
    216n4
  Government House, 197n35
  rule- vs act-, 220–221n23
Utilitarianism (movement), 8, 30, 131, 140,
    143, 218n11
  assessment of, 12, 134
  cost-benefit analysis in, 19, 22, 24, 42, 86
  panopticism in, 131–132

self-defeating program, 66
  See also Philosophic Radicals
Utilitarian Society, 10
utility, 22, 133
  as colligation, 195n24
  diminishing marginal, 188n6
  expected, 19, 187n2
  Principle of, 8, 15, 21, 24–25, 28, 31,
    34–35, 41–42, 73, 95, 106–107, 110,
    125, 141–142, 144, 161, 169, 225n19
  in Bentham, 101, 200–201n20
  formulation of, 18
  political or moral, 19, 218n11, 229n2
  Proof of, 22–23, 47–48, 101
  redefinition as basket, 23–24, 101–102,
    104, 134, 197n35
  as sensation, 22, 101, 188n10
  as usefulness, 22, 56, 198n4
  von Neumann-Morgenstern, 23, 214n22

values, 2, 4, 183n4, 183n5
  nihilism about, 12
  plenitude of, 47
Verification, 127, 224n13
vivacity, 39, 117, 121–122, 181, 210n14,
    216n8, 217n9
Vogler, Candace, 64, 66–67, 78–79, 129,
    205n7
Voltaire, 70, 200n20
voting
  plural, 30, 141, 225n25
  secret ballot, 31, 143, 225n25

Wellington, Duke of, 83
Westminster Review, 10, 28, 51
Whewell, William, 43, 149, 154
Wiggins, David, 2–4, 42, 47
  coherence condition, 6, 7, 12–13, 15–16,
    33, 47, 69, 73, 140, 148–151, 153–158,
    160–166, 171, 178–179, 233n33
  definition of, 4–5
Wilde, Oscar, 6, 107, 153, 207n17
will, weakness of, 149
Williams, Bernard, 4, 97, 136–137, 151, 153,
    171
Wittgenstein, Ludwig, 133, 152, 231n22
Wolf, Susan, 173, 177
women, nature of, 86, 207–208n12
Wordsworth, William, 68, 99–100, 208n1
  poetics of, 213n15

CPSIA information can be obtained
at www.ICGtesting.com
Printed in the USA
BVHW092340180123
656220BV00003B/10